Contents at a Glance

SAMS
Teach Yourself
obe® Premiere® 6.5
in 24 Hours

Jeff Sengstack

SAMS   201 West 103rd St., Indianapolis, Indiana 46290 USA

Sams Teach Yourself Adobe® Premiere® 6.5 in 24 Hours

Copyright © 2003 by Sams Publishing

International Standard Book Number: 0-672-32428-8

Library of Congress Catalog Card Number: 2002104074

Printed in the United States of America

First Printing: September 2002

05   04   03   02   4   3   2   1

Trademarks

All terms mentioned in this book that are known to be trademarks or service marks have been appropriately capitalized. Sams Publishing cannot attest to the accuracy of this information. Use of a term in this book should not be regarded as affecting the validity of any trademark or service mark.

Warning and Disclaimer

ACQUISITIONS EDITOR
Betsy Brown

DEVELOPMENT EDITOR
Jonathan Steever

MANAGING EDITOR
Charlotte Clapp

PROJECT EDITOR
Andy Beaster

COPY EDITOR
Bart Reed

INDEXER
Mandie Frank

PROOFREADER
Leslie Joseph

TECHNICAL EDITOR
Alan Hamill

TEAM COORDINATOR
Amy Patton

INTERIOR DESIGNER
Gary Adair

COVER DESIGNER
Aren Howell

PAGE LAYOUT
Michelle Mitchell

GRAPHICS
Tammy Graham
Oliver Jackson

Table of Contents

About the Author

Jeff Sengstack has worn many hats: TV news reporter/anchor, video producer, writer focusing on PC technology, high school math/science teacher, radio station disk jockey, and music publisher marketing director. As a news reporter he won a regional Emmy and two Society of Professional Journalists first-place awards. He's an ACE (an Adobe Certified Expert) on Premiere. He's written 300 articles and three books, co-authored two other books, and contributed to three more. These days his focus is creating family tree DVDs.

Acknowledgments

This book gave me the opportunity to reconnect with more than a dozen friends and colleagues in the TV news and video production business. They contributed the Expert Tips sidebars scattered throughout the book. They all are terrific folks, and I greatly appreciate their contributions.

A big thanks to Bruce Bowman, Adobe's "Dynamic Media Evangelist," who introduced me to Sams Publishing.

And to the editorial staff at Sams and the technical editor at Adobe, thanks for applying such a light touch to my words.

We Want to Hear from You!

As the reader of this book, *you* are our most important critic and commentator. We value your opinion and want to know what we're doing right, what we could do better, what areas you'd like to see us publish in, and any other words of wisdom you're willing to pass our way.

You can email or write me directly to let me know what you did or didn't like about this book—as well as what we can do to make our books stronger.

Please note that I cannot help you with technical problems related to the topic of this book, and that due to the high volume of mail I receive, I might not be able to reply to every message.

When you write, please be sure to include this book's title and author as well as your name and phone or email address. I will carefully review your comments and share them with the author and editors who worked on the book.

Email: graphics@samspublishing.com

Mail: Mark Taber
            Associate Publisher
            Sams Publishing
            201 West 103rd Street
            Indianapolis, IN 46290 USA

Reader Services

For more information about this book or others from Sams Publishing, visit our Web site at www.samspublishing.com. Type the ISBN (excluding hyphens) or the title of the book in the Search box to find the book you're looking for.

Introduction

Sams Teach Yourself Adobe Premiere 6.5 in 24 Hours is different from the rest of the dozen or so other Premiere how-to books. Those books tend to be highly detailed or greatly simplified reference manuals using impenetrable vernacular, or they tend to be collections of step-by-step instructions focusing solely on Premiere functions. Both types fail to create lasting impressions, and they don't teach you how to make videos.

What's missing is context. I think of those books as sort of like instructing budding artists how to use a paintbrush by telling them to swab the brush in paint and slather it on a canvas. Where's the art?

My goal with *Sams Teach Yourself Adobe Premiere 6.5 in 24 Hours* is to help you create high-quality, professional-looking videos. Rather than simply presenting a collection of disconnected tutorials, I will frequently remind you of the big picture and what you're trying to accomplish. That said, I haven't skimped on useful nuts-and-bolts instructions. I've tried simply to present them in a logical, easy-to-follow manner that reflects the way most Premiere users approach editing.

A Collaborative Effort

In a departure from traditional Premiere how-to books, I turned this into a collaborative project. I contacted several of my friends and former colleagues in the TV and video production business who provided dozens of expert tips to supplement this book's coverage of Premiere functionality. For instance, they provided advice about shooting high-quality video, writing effectively, and creating professional voiceovers.

The timing is right for this book, both on a personal level and in the marketplace. It fits my career path to a "T." I am an Adobe Certified Expert (ACE) in Premiere and have extensive television production credentials—TV anchor, reporter, photographer, and editor—plus I'm a recipient of a regional Emmy award and two Society of Professional Journalists first-place awards. I've written hundreds of articles, written or worked on eight books, and have been a high school science and math teacher. I tapped all that experience to create what I think is a logical, instructional flow using readily digestible chunks of information placed in a real-world context. *Sams Teach Yourself Adobe Premiere 6.5 in 24 Hours* will ensure you can track how each new task fits into your project goals.

The market is primed for Premiere 6.5. *Convergence* may be an overused word (third only to *paradigm* and *epiphany*), but it applies. Premiere continues to bring a reasonably priced, increasingly powerful video production tool to both Mac and Windows users (90 percent of Premiere users have Windows). High-quality digital video (DV) camcorders have dropped in price. Anyone with a laptop and a DV camcorder can operate as an independent video producer or TV news reporter. And capping that off, Premiere 6.5 now includes DVD authoring.

New Features in Premiere 6.5

The opportunity to create DVDs—from home movies to Hollywood productions—on PCs is a dramatic development, and Premiere 6.5 is at the forefront of this emerging technology. DVD authoring is a major industry shift. With the availability of high-speed PC processors, large and fast hard drives, reasonably priced DVD recorders and recording media, and increasingly powerful video-editing tools, DVD creation is now at your fingertips.

Other new features in Premiere 6.5 are real-time MPEG-2 video encoding, software real-time previews of transitions and effects, a professional text-creation tool, professional "audio sweetening" effects, several exciting video effects, and enhanced support for Windows Media, QuickTime, and RealMedia.

Book Organization

Sams Teach Yourself Adobe Premiere 6.5 in 24 Hours consists of 24 "lessons." Each should take about an hour—more or less—to complete. That's not to say that at the end of each lesson you'll have mastered its particular topic. To really become proficient in Premiere you'll need to reinforce what you've learned with practice. I'd suggest moving through a lesson, doing some additional work, and then taking a breather before tackling the next lesson.

I've tried to follow my own video production advice and keep it simple—and short—but I do know that some of you want higher-level Premiere and video production tips. So I've scattered such advice throughout all the chapters in the form of tips, notes, and cautions.

By buying Premiere you've joined the ranks of more than 750,000 video editors who recognize a high-quality video production product when they see one. Now, with the help of this book, you will soon be able to fully exploit all the powerful tools Premiere brings to bear. The ultimate goal is that you'll create videos that shine.

Premiere is a cross-platform, Windows/Mac product. Virtually all functions and commands are the same for both platforms, with a few exceptions (PC commands are on the left, Mac commands are on the right). We have made an effort to note all instances when commands or keyboard shortcuts differ. As a general rule of thumb

- Alt equals Option,
- Ctrl equals Command,
- Enter equals Return, and
- Backspace equals Delete.

Conventions Used in This Book

This book uses the following conventions:

Text that you type and text that you see onscreen appear in `monospace` type.

 A *note* presents interesting information related to the discussion.

 A *tip* offers advice or shows you an easier way to do something.

 A *caution* alerts you to a possible problem and gives you advice on how to avoid it.

PART I

Getting Started

Hour

HOUR 1

Camcorder and Shooting Tips

To make an excellent video production you need to start with high-quality raw material—the original footage. Most books on Premiere gloss over this subject, but no amount of clever, whiz-bang editing can turn mediocre raw video into a dazzling final product. The old computer-programming adage applies: garbage in, garbage out. Except in the TV world that adage has a slightly different twist: You *can't* fix it in post. That is, postproduction techniques will not resurrect reels of video junk.

I have 15 years experience in broadcast TV and video production. I've done my own shooting and have worked with some of the best photographers in the business. In this chapter I'll pass along some of their video-shooting tips that will start you on the right track to a finished product you can be proud of.

The highlights of this hour include the following:

- How to choose a camcorder that fits your productions
- Why digital video is the way to go
- Eighteen tips on shooting great video

Gearing Up: Choosing a Camcorder

First up is your gear—and topping the list is your camcorder. This is an exciting time. For years video pros have lugged around shoulder-numbing Sony Beta SP and Ikegami broadcast-quality cameras. Their rich colors and low-light capabilities used to put "prosumer" (a step up from consumer but still not broadcast quality) camcorders to shame.

Not any longer. Some may quibble and say today's top prosumer camcorders are not true "broadcast quality," but only the most highly trained eye can discern an appreciable difference between the $3,300 Canon XL1S or the $2,300 Sony DCR-VX2000 and anything a $15,000+ broadcast camera can crank out. See Figure 1.1 for some high-quality prosumer camcorder models.

FIGURE 1.1

Top-of-the-line pro-sumer DV camcorders. Canon XL1S (esti-mated street price $3,300), Sony DCR-VX2000 ($2,300), and Panasonic PV-DV952 ($1,400). You can't go wrong with any of these models.

Canon XL1S

Sony DCR-VX2000

Panasonic PV-DV952

Going Digital

Great video quality aside, the true *coup de grace* to the high-end video production world is that today's top prosumer camcorders are digital. This may be yesterday's news to some of you, but for those of you just getting your feet wet in the video production world, listen up. Digital video (DV) changes everything.

In the old days (a couple years ago) analog was it. DV was ridiculously expensive and definitely not a budget video production option.

An analog video signal is a continuous waveform. Small disruptions to that otherwise smooth, continuous signal lead to degradation in image and color quality. Simply dubbing (recording) an analog tape to another tape results in some quality loss. With each additional dub—each added "generation"—images look less defined, colors become increasingly washed out, and the pictures get grainy.

In tape-only editing systems, to make simple scene transitions such as dissolves or to add special effects such as showing videos in moving boxes means doing multiple edits or recording passes. Each pass adds more video "noise" to the tape. Editors using analog tape machines have to plan carefully to avoid creating projects with obvious shifts in video quality from one section to another.

DV makes generation quality loss a thing of the past. DV is a binary signal. A stream of ones and zeros. Unlike an analog signal, which has a wide range of data possibilities and many ways for electronic equipment to misinterpret it, a digital signal rarely loses quality during transmission and doesn't suffer from generation loss.

Home satellite systems that use those pizza-sized dishes are digital. To reach your home those digital TV signals travel from an earth-based transmitter to a satellite in geosynchronous orbit (22,000 miles into space) back to your parabolic pizza pie receiver—44,000 miles and the picture is crystal clear.

Although some noise may creep into the signal, electronic equipment easily can filter this out because all it's looking for are zeros and ones (see Figure 1.2). Little ragged edges on the signal rarely are large enough to lead to obvious signal quality loss.

FIGURE 1.2

Signal noise can dramatically affect analog signals but has virtually no impact on binary signals.

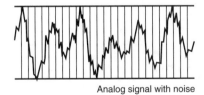

Analog signal with noise

Digital (binary) signal with noise

More importantly for our purposes, multiple DV edits or dubs do not lead to generational loss. The signal simply remains zeros and ones. You are no longer constrained to limiting your creative considerations to ensure low-noise video. No matter how many edits you perform, no matter how many layers of elements you pile up in a clip, there should be no discernible noise or degradation to fidelity.

Therefore, your first order of business is to buy, borrow, or rent a DV camcorder. A purchase will run you between $500 and $4,000 (see the upcoming sidebar review of a half dozen higher-priced prosumer products). Two things drive camcorder prices: features and chips. As you move up the price range you'll see an increasing number of competitive features—longer focal length lenses, larger LCD screen viewfinders, programmable settings, and fast shutter speeds. But the biggest differentiator is that top-end camcorders have three chips, versus a single chip for lower-priced products.

Camcorder Selection Tips

Camcorders use a charged coupled device (CCD) chip to convert brightness and color to a digital signal. Single-chip camcorder CCDs have to crunch a lot of data. Three-chip camcorders use a prism to divide incoming light into separate red, green, and blue (RGB) hues, thus letting each respective CCD gather more information within its designated segment of the color spectrum. Even though single-chip camcorders use special RGB filters to help their one CCD interpret color data, three-chip cameras have distinctly better color and low-light capabilities.

Your choice in camcorders then comes down to your audience. If your videos are only for home or Web page viewing, a single-chip camcorder will work fine. If you will be projecting your videos on large screens for sales presentations or shareholder meetings, you should give strong consideration to a three-chip camcorder. And if you want to move into the professional video-production business, a three-CCD camcorder is a must. Showing up at a client's office with a palm-sized, single-chip camcorder is a sure way to jinx a deal.

Prosumer Camcorder Reviews

Camcorder buying is one of those things that may simply come down to "feel." You pick up a camcorder and it fits well in your hands, the controls are logical and accessible, the menus make sense, and the images look right. Or not. When you start digging into the details—all those features—it becomes brain numbing.

So, here are the basics: Top-of-the-line gets you three CCDs and plenty of manual override options: focus, iris, shutter speed, and white balance. If you're serious about

1

shooting high-quality videos you'll want to have that level of control. For example, setting a higher shutter speed—the Panasonic PV DV952 I tested for this book has a superfast 1/8000th of a second shutter speed—means you can capture very crisp images of a very fast subject. Racecars and sprinters all look sharp at such shutter speeds. You do need plenty of light to make this work, though.

Other features of importance include the following:

- Substantial optical zoom—at least 10×, but 25× is better.
- Input and output capabilities. IEEE 1394 (the industry-standard means to transfer digital video) is a given, as is a means to record from and to a VCR or other camcorder (S-Video connectors are better than composite).
- An external mic plug is a necessity as well as a headphone plug.
- Optical image stabilizing using prisms or some other means (versus the less desirable electronic stabilization).

Superfluous features—and there are many—include the following:

- Digital zoom. All you get are chunky pixels. Use Premiere's Zoom features to handle this.
- Titler; Fade-in, Fade-out; and Digital Effects (picture in picture, wipes, multipicture mode, sepia, and so on). Premiere will handle all these without forcing you to fumble with awkward controls and menus.
- Wide-screen view, unless it's a true 16:9—few offer this. "Faux wide screen" simply adds black bars to the top and bottom of the screen covering parts of the image.
- Built-in lighting compensation modes, including back-lit, low-light, portrait, sports, and extremely bright settings (surf and snow). You'll use the manual features to more accurately handle these situations.

The prosumer industry de facto standard camcorder is the Canon XL1S, followed closely by the Sony DCR-VX2000 and the brand-new Panasonic PV-DV952.

Stepping down a notch but still prosumer-quality 3CCD camcorders are the Sony DCR-TRV950 and the Canon GL1.

Panasonic PV-DV952

Panasonic loaned me its latest high-end prosumer camcorder to use while writing this book. Although Sony and Canon grab plenty of prosumer mind share, the DV952 may just muscle its way into that vaunted group.

Outstanding standard features include 3CCD with 1.6 mega pixels (the Sony TRV is 1 mega pixel, or one million pixels), 25× optical zoom, 3.5" color LCD monitor, color viewfinder, easy-to-access manual controls, easy-to-use VCR controls, and a comfortable feel.

Other good features: The provided battery charges quickly and runs the camcorder for about two hours, the thumbwheel/pushbutton menu control is effective, audio quality is very good and minimizes sound from behind the camera, and the USB connection allows easy downloading of pictures and audio to your PC.

Some minor nitpicking: The DV952 tries to be the be-all, end-all prosumer/consumer camcorder. There are just too many superfluous features that probably jack up the price without giving much added benefit. The digital photo quality cannot match standard digital still cameras, the memory card audio recording feature is unnecessary (just use the DV tape and IEEE 1394 connector), the "zoom mic" appears only to increase the recorded audio volume without narrowing the focus of the sound, image stabilization had no obvious effect, and the low-light video quality is noisy.

The 952 and its older sibling, the 951, represent a significant leap forward for Panasonic. Their predecessor—the DV51D—was bulky and had a small monitor, a cheap "feel," and some awkward controls. The 952 has resolved all those flaws.

Legacy Analog Camcorders

You may own a legacy analog camcorder—VHS (dread the thought), S-VHS, or Hi-8—and aren't ready to shell out the cash for a DV camcorder. Your old clunker may get the job done, but the results will be several cuts below pure DV video. Image quality from most legacy camcorders falls below today's DV camcorders (Hi-8 still looks pretty good, and professional Beta SP is better than Prosumer DV). But no matter how good the original video looks, the final edited product will not look that great. That's largely because when loading the analog video into your PC (video capture), Premiere converts it to a digital video file (losing some quality in the process), and when you record it back to analog tape for viewing it will lose even more quality. Because Premiere stores video digitally, there will be no generation loss for converted-analog video (or DV) during editing.

One other minor fly in the ointment: You'll need to buy a video capture card (see Chapter 2, "Premiere Setup") with analog input connectors. A straightforward DV-only capture card will not work.

Video Shooting Tips

With your camcorder of choice in hand, it's time to venture off and shoot videos.

Here are my video-shooting axioms:

- Stripe your DV tapes.
- Adhere to the "rule of thirds."
- Get a closing shot.
- Get an establishing shot.

- Keep your shot steady—use a tripod.
- Let your camera follow the action.
- Use trucking shots to move with the action.
- Try out unusual angles.
- Lean into or away from subjects.
- Get wide and tight shots to add interest.
- Try to match action in multiple shots.
- Shoot sequences to help tell the story.
- Avoid fast pans and snap zooms—they're for MTV only.
- Remember to shoot cutaways to avoid jump cuts.
- Make sure you don't break the "plane."
- Get plenty of natural sound.
- Use lights to make your project brilliant.
- Plan your shoot.

I've jammed a lot into these 18 items. All will help make your video shine with a professional glow. I've discussed each in detail below.

Stripe Your DV Tapes

This is a tedious but ultimately timesaving step. Your DV camcorder lays down timecode as it records. Later, as you transfer DV to your computer, you'll likely use that timecode to create a video clip log. Once you've completed logging your tape or tapes, you'll tell Premiere to automatically retrieve the logged clips by automatically shuttling the tape to the timecodes noted in the log and then record them to your hard drive.

Most camcorders, when powered up, reset their timecode to zero seconds. If you do that more than once using the same videotape, you'll end up with several instances of the same timecode on one tape. As a result, Premiere probably will retrieve the wrong clip. Striping your tapes before doing any shooting resolves that. You stripe tapes by simply placing a fresh tape in your camcorder, capping your lens, pressing Record, and waiting for your camcorder to stripe the entire tape. Rewind the tape and you're ready to go. Now, as you use your camcorder, it'll record new video over the black video you taped but won't change the timecode.

Adhere to the "Rule of Thirds"

Composition is the most fundamental element of camerawork, and the "rule of thirds" is the textbook. When composing your shot, think of your viewfinder as being crisscrossed by two horizontal and two vertical lines. The center of interest should fall on one of the four intersections. See Figure 1.3 for a simple diagram. The standard amateur photographer mistake is to put the center of attention at the center of the image. The most common is portraits in which the eyes of the subject are dead center in the photo. One rule of thumb is to look around the viewfinder as you shoot, not just stare at its center. Check the edges to see whether you're filling the frame with interesting images.

FIGURE 1.3

The rule of thirds: Putting your image's most important element at one of these intersections will make it more pleasing to the eye.

Get a Closing Shot

This may seem like I'm taking things way out of order, but the one shot that should be uppermost in your mind is the closing shot (the opening shot or shots are important but have a much less lasting impact). Your closing images are what will stick in people's minds. They are what your audience will take away from your video production. If you start a shoot without knowing what your closing shot will be, you should be constantly on the lookout for that one shot or sequence that will best wrap up your story.

The importance of the closing shot came through loud and clear at a seminar I attended given by NBC-TV feature reporter Bob Dotson (see Chapter 6, "Story Creation, Writing, and Video Production Tips"). It could be as simple as someone closing a door, capping a pen, petting a dog, turning out the lights, or releasing a butterfly from their cupped hands. If you happen to see a Dotson feature story, consider its close. It's sure to be memorable.

1

Get an Establishing Shot

An establishing shot sets a scene. It doesn't have to be the opening shot. One of the greatest establishing shots of all time is in Robert Redford's *The Natural*. Those who have seen this marvelous film know what I'm talking about: the shot from the top row of the baseball stadium during a night game that takes in the entire field with blazing lights ringing the park. Anyone who has been to a major league ballpark gets goose bumps when that image appears onscreen. It tells a dramatic story in one image.

That should be your goal for your project's establishing shot or shots (you may need several if you're covering several topics in one video).

Although super-wide works sometimes—aerials make great establishing shots—it pays to think "outside the box." Don't fall back on the old stand-bys, such as the scoreboard, the corporate sign, or the medium shot of a hospital operating room. Try something different. A tight shot of a soccer ball with natural sound of children's voices, a low-angle image through a glass table of someone using your client's product, or a close-up of a scalpel with light glinting off its surface.

Each grabs the viewer's attention and helps tell your story.

Keep Your Shot Steady—Use A Tripod

We all know that photographers take the images we view on TV, and that someone uses a camera to create them. But as video producers we don't want to remind viewers of that. We want to give them the sense that they're looking through a window or, better yet, are there on location.

A shaky camera shatters that illusion.

Despite a recent trend away from the use of tripods—MTV started it and shows such as *48 Hours* have run with it—there's plenty to be said for smooth-looking video. If you're doing a sit-down interview or grabbing close-ups, put your camcorder on "sticks." When possible use a tripod with a fluid head. That'll let you make smooth pans or tilts. Good tripods are not cheap. Reasonably high-quality sticks start at about $150. See Figure 1.4 for a top-of-the-line example.

FIGURE 1.4
The Sachtler DA 75 L aluminum tripod weighs only 2 kg. It's DV 2 fluid head works well with lightweight camcorders.

If a tripod is too expensive, cumbersome, or inconvenient; if the action is too fast paced; or if you need to move the camera during the shot, then try to find some way to stabilize the shot. For still shots, lean against a wall, put your elbows on a table, or place the camcorder on a solid object. For moving shots, get the camcorder off your shoulder, hold it about waist high, and let your arms work as shock absorbers.

Let Your Camera Follow the Action

This may seem obvious, but keep your viewfinder on the ball (or puck, face, conveyor belt, and so on). Your viewers' eyes will want to follow the action, so give them what they want.

One nifty trick is to use directed movement as a pan motivator. That is, follow a leaf's progress as it moves down a stream and then continue your camera motion past the leaf—panning—and widen out to show something unexpected: a waterfall, a huge industrial complex, or a fisherman.

Use Trucking Shots to Move with the Action

This is an excellent way to follow action (so named because using a camera on a moving vehicle is one way to get this shot). Truck right along with some action. If you're shooting a golf ball rolling toward the cup, tag along right behind, in front of, or beside it. When walking through tall grass, dangle your camcorder at knee level and walk right through it, letting the grass blades smack into the lens. Ever wonder how they get those cool downhill snow-skiing shots? The cameraperson skis backwards with a heavy electronic news-gathering (ENG) camera on his shoulder or dangling from his hand at snow level (see the next section). I've watched my good friend Karl Petersen (see the upcoming sidebar) do that amazing maneuver several times.

Try Out Unusual Angles

Move your camcorder away from eye level. Shoulder shots have their place—they represent probably as much as 80 percent of all video—but getting the camcorder off your shoulder leads to more interesting and enjoyable shots. Ground-level "ferret-cam" shots are great for cavorting puppies or crawling babies. Climb a ladder or use a tall building to get a "crane" shot. Shoot through other objects or people while keeping the focus on your subject.

> You'll need "sticks" to create stop-action or time-lapse photography. Both methods require that the camera remain steady. The other requirement is that the focal length and aperture cannot change. So when you set your camcorder up to shoot the same scene for a long time, planning to compress time during editing, make sure your auto-focus, auto-white balance, and auto-iris are turned off.

Lean Into or Away from Subjects

Too many shooters rely too heavily on the zoom lens. A better way to move in close or away from a subject is simply to lean in or out. Lean way in and start your shot tight on someone's hands as he works on a wood carving; then lean way back (perhaps widening your zoom lens as well) to reveal that he is working in a sweatshop full of folks hunched over their handiwork. It's much more effective than a standard lens zoom and a lot easier to pull off.

Get Wide and Tight Shots to Add Interest

Most novice videographers create one boring medium shot after another. The reason: It fits our experience. Our eyes tend to take in things the same way. Instead, think wide and tight. Grab a wide shot and a tight shot of your subject. It's much more interesting.

When you grab your tight shots, try to avoid relying on your zoom lens. Instead, get as close as practical to your subject and then grab that tight shot. Unless you want your shot to look like you took it from a distance, it's much more interesting to change positions rather than simply toggle that zoom button.

Try to Match Action in Multiple Shots

Repetitive action—running assembly-line machinery, demonstrating a golf swing, or working in a barbershop—lends itself to matched action shots. A barber clips someone's hair and it falls to the floor. Get a shot of the scissors, the hair hitting the floor, a wide shot of the entire shop, and a close-up reflection of the scissors in the mirror or the barber's glasses. You'll later edit those separate shots into one smooth collection of matched action.

Shoot Sequences to Help Tell the Story

Shooting repetitive action in sequence is another way to build interest and even suspense. A bowler wipes his hands on a resin bag, dries them over a blower, wipes the ball with a towel, picks the ball up, fixes his gaze on the pins, steps forward, swings the ball back, releases it, slides to the foul line, watches the ball's trajectory, then reacts to the shot. Instead of simply capturing all this in one long shot, piecing these actions together in a sequence of edits is much more compelling. You easily can combine wide and tight shots, trucking moves, and matched action to turn repetitive action into attention-grabbing sequences.

Avoid Fast Pans and "Snap" Zooms

These moves fall into MTV and amateur video territory. Few circumstances call for such stomach-churning camerawork. In general it's best to minimize all pans and zooms. As with a shaky camera, they remind viewers that they're watching TV.

If you do zoom or pan, do it for a purpose: to reveal something, to follow someone's gaze from his or her eyes to the subject of interest, or to continue the flow of action (as in the floating leaf example earlier). A slow zoom in, with only a minimal change to the focal length, can add drama to a sound bite. Again, do it sparingly.

> Don't let this no-fast-moves admonition force you to stop rolling while you zoom or pan. If you see something that warrants a quick close-up shot or you need to suddenly pan to grab some possibly fleeting footage, keep rolling. You can always edit around that sudden movement later.
>
> If you stop recording to make the pan or zoom and adjust the focus, you may lose some or all of whatever it was you were trying so desperately to shoot. Plus you will miss any accompanying natural sound.

Remember to Shoot Cutaways to Avoid Jump Cuts

Cutaways literally let you cut away from the action or interview subject. One important use is to avoid jump cuts—two clips that when edited one after the other create a disconnect in the viewer's mind.

Consider the standard news or corporate interview. You might want to edit together two 10-second sound bites from the same person. Doing so would mean the interviewee would look like he suddenly moved. To avoid that jump cut—that sudden disconcerting shift—you make a cutaway of the interview. That could be a wide shot, a hand shot, or a reverse-angle shot of the interviewer over the interviewee's shoulder. You then edit in the cutaway over the juncture of the two sound bites to cover the jump cut.

The same holds true for a soccer game. It can be disconcerting simply to cut from one wide shot of players on the field to another. If you shoot some crowd reactions or the scoreboard, you can use those shots to cover up what would have been a jump cut.

Make Sure You Don't Break the "Plane"

This is another of those viewer disconnects you want to avoid. If you're shooting in one direction, you don't want your next shot to be looking back at your previous camera location. For instance, if you're shooting an interview with the camera peering over the left shoulder of the interviewer, you want to shoot your reverse cutaways behind the interviewee and over his right shoulder. That keeps the camera on the same side of the plane—an imaginary vertical flat surface running through the interviewer and interviewee. To shoot over your subject's left shoulder would break that plane, meaning the viewer would think the camera that took the previous shot should somehow be in view. Figure 1.5 shows an interview with correct and incorrect (broken plane) camera placements.

In general you want to keep all your camera positions on one side of that plane. This isn't true for all situations. Consider a TV show of a rock group performance. Camera crewmembers typically scramble all over the stage, grabbing shots from multiple angles, and frequently appear on camera themselves. That's much different from breaking the plane in a formal sit-down interview.

If you conduct formal, sit-down interviews with more than one person for the same piece, consider shooting each subject from a different side of the interviewer. That is, if you shoot one subject with the camera positioned over the left shoulder of the reporter, position the camera over the right shoulder of the reporter for the next interview. That avoids a subtle jump cut that happens when you edit two bites from two individuals who are both facing the same way.

FIGURE 1.5

The "plane" is an imaginary vertical wall running, in this case, through the reporter and interviewee. Breaking the plane— particularly when shooting a reverse cut- away—leads to camera shots that cause viewer disconnects.

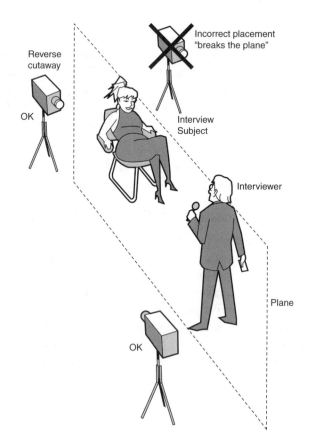

Shooting Tips
Karl Petersen—Chief Photographer, KGW-TV, Portland, OR

Karl Petersen is my favorite TV news photographer. We met in Boise, Idaho, where we worked at competing stations. We later worked together at KSL-TV in Salt Lake City. We formed a video production company in Oregon called Glint Video (we always tried to get a "glint" shot in all our news pieces). Then Karl moved on to KGW-TV in Portland, where he is now chief photographer.

Karl has seen and done it all. Absolutely nothing fazes him. He'll venture into the tensest situation and shoot with aplomb. When we went out on stories we had an unspoken understanding—I never had to tell Karl what kind of images and sound I needed. I knew he would always get exactly what would make the story "work." Karl's regular beat these days is chopper photog. "Sky 8," KGW's Bell 407, has two Flir cameras. One is infrared and can operate in *total* darkness.

Karl's advice is worth much more than the price of this book. Take it to heart:

- My first shooting advice is, don't do it. Pursue a career of doctor, lawyer, teamster, stevedore, whorehouse piano player, whatever.

- Having failed that, my first tip is always to shoot as an editor. Always think about how to get from one shot to the next. Try to get some kind of transition shot with either an entry or exit. Close-ups are especially helpful in editing to get from point A to point B.

- Get a good shot mix—wide, medium, close-up (extreme close-ups work well), and unusual angles. Get lots of shots. Variety is an editor's friend.

- Get an establishing shot that tells viewers where you are.

- Fundamentals: Make sure you have freshly charged batteries, always monitor audio by wearing an earpiece (if you don't you're guaranteed to get burned), and watch your color balance.

- For all indoor interviews, I recommend using at least two lights, three if you have time (I usually don't—TV news is hectic). If I'm to the reporter's right, I place a light with an umbrella reflector slightly to his left. That means the interviewee is looking toward the light. I place a Lowell Omni with "barn doors" (to keep it from shining into the lens) behind and over the left shoulder of the interview subject (that is, to my right). This adds nice highlights. If I have time, I place a third umbrella well behind the camera to add fill. See Figure 1.6.

- If I'm shooting in a room with sunlight coming in a window, I use blue gels—especially balanced for daylight—and then color balance for sunlight.

- For underwater photography I recommend using an Ewa-Marine plastic bag video camcorder housing (see `http://www.ewa-marine.de/English/e-start.htm`). They're good to a depth of about 30 feet, easy to use, and relatively inexpensive (about $350).

When shooting from "Sky 8" I sit in the warmth and comfort of the back seat and operate the cameras with a laptop and a joystick. Not many video producers have this luxury. For those who must shoot from a side window, here are some tips:

- Think safety first. Make sure nothing can fall off the camera—such as a lens shade—or out of the back seat and possibly hit the rotor. That makes the chopper spin like crazy so you get real dizzy before you die.

- Shooting with the door off is ideal (remove it *before* you take off).

- Try to keep the camera slightly inside the doorframe to keep it out of the wind.

- Have the pilot "crab" (fly sort of sideways) so you can shoot straight ahead. That's much more dramatic. It's a great way to fly along a river for instance.

- Have the pilot fly low. This allows cool "reveal" shots, such as flying over a ridge to reveal an expansive vista.

Finally, don't forget to grab that "glint" shot.

FIGURE 1.6

A Lowel Tota with an umbrella (right), and a Lowel Omni with barn doors (left). Images courtesy of Lowel-Light.

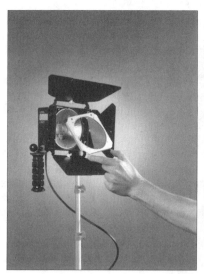

1

Get Plenty of Natural Sound

This is absolutely critical. We tend to take sound for granted. But, relying on your camcorder's built-in mic is not enough. Taking extra steps to improve the audio quality will dramatically improve the production value of your projects. I'll cover audio issues in depth in Chapter 7, "Adding Audio." For now, think in terms of using additional mics: *shotgun* mics to narrow the focus of your sound and avoid extraneous noise, *lavalieres* tucked out of sight for interviews, and *wireless* mics to get sound when your camera can't be close enough to get just what you need.

Use Lights to Make Your Project Brilliant

Lights add dazzle and depth to otherwise bland and flat scenes. An onboard camcorder fill light is a convenient way to brighten dull shots. And a full (but admittedly cumbersome) lighting kit with a few colored gels can liven up an otherwise dull research laboratory. If you don't have the time, money, patience, or personnel to deal with adding lights, do whatever you can to increase the available light. Open curtains, turn on all the lights, or bring a couple desk lamps into the room. One caveat: Low-light situations can be dramatic and flipping on a few desk lamps can destroy that mood in a moment.

No matter what kind of lighting situation you're in, you always need to watch your *white balance*. Different lights operate with different color temperatures. Your eyes automatically compensate for those color differences but your camcorder is not that proficient. These days most camcorders have auto-white balance, and many have manual white balance as well. Auto-white balance works in most situations. As you move from room to room or from inside to outside, the camera "assumes" everything in its field of view is gray and adjusts its color balance accordingly.

Problems arise when you shoot indoors and have a window in the scene. In that circumstance, whatever you see through the window probably will have a blue tint. The other tricky white balance situation is when you shoot a scene with a predominant color, such as doing product shots using a solid-color background. The auto-white balance will "think" that solid color is gray, and the image will look horrible. That's when you need to place a gray or white card in the scene, fill the viewfinder with that card under whatever lighting you plan to use for the product shots, and click the manual white balance button. For a fun practical lesson in the value of a manual white balance, roll tape throughout this procedure or when you walk from indoors to outdoors to watch the colors change.

Plan Your Shoot

When you consider a video project, plan what you need to shoot to tell the story. Videotaping your kid's soccer championship match, a corporate backgrounder, or a medical procedure each require planning to ensure success. Know what you want your final video project to say and think of what you need to videotape to tell that story.

Even the best-laid plans and most carefully scripted projects may need some adjusting once you start rolling and recording in the field. No matter how you envision the finished project, be willing to make changes as the situation warrants.

Summary

A high-quality video production must start with excellent video. Your gear is paramount—high-end camcorder (preferably DV or broadcast-quality analog), lights, mics, and sticks. When shooting your raw video, think outside the box. Don't settle for standard, boring shoulder shots. Get in close, get down low, look for that unusual angle. Natural sound is essential, and lighting adds sizzle.

Workshop

Review the following questions and answers to try to improve your field video-shooting skills. Also, take a few moments to tackle my short quiz.

Q&A

Q When I do quick interviews in the field using my handheld camera, people always stare in the camera and "act." Is there a way to fix that?

A You bet! *You* need to stop staring—at the viewfinder, that is. Try to frame up your "man on the street" (*MOS* in TV news parlance) in the viewfinder as casually as possible and then move your head away from the camera. Look your subjects in their eyes and instead of interviewing them, talk to them. They'll return the favor.

Q How am I supposed to keep my camera steady if I'm doing a trucking shot? What about videotaping something such as whitewater rafting? There's no way to keep it steady then.

A Correct! One powerful element of video is that it can transport viewers to someplace besides their living room or office. You keep your shots steady to avoid shattering that illusion. But if that "place" is full of action, then any camera movement simply mirrors what it would be like for the viewer to be there and to experience that excitement. Camera movement in moments of action, especially from a first-person perspective, is tremendously effective.

Quiz

1. If you're shooting a formal sit-down interview and the camera is positioned over the left shoulder of the interviewer, where should you place the camera for reverse cutaways?

2. What's the principal advantage of digital video over analog video?

3. Why should you "stripe" your tapes?

Quiz Answers

1. Place the camera behind the interview subject and shoot over his right shoulder. You can shoot a wide two-shot of the reporter and interviewee and a tight shot of the reporter to use as cutaways. If the reporter is not going to be part of the story (typically the case in corporate productions), then keep the camera in its original location and shoot tight hand shots and wider establishing shots.

2. Digital video is simply a collection of zeros and ones. There is no signal quality degradation during transmission or generation loss after multiple edits. Analog video suffers from both maladies.

3. "Striping" your tapes—that is, laying down continuous timecode from beginning to end before doing any videotaping—ensures that there will be no duplicate time-codes on the same tape. That means when Premiere later does an automated video transfer of selected clips, there will be no confusion about selecting between clips with the same timecode.

HOUR 2

Premiere Setup

Premiere's power is its flexibility and customizability. You have myriad means to accomplish your tasks, and you confront your first plethora of possibilities when you open Premiere for the first time: A/B or single-track editing, NTSC or PAL, DV or analog, QuickTime or Video for Windows? The options can be mind-boggling. In this chapter I'll clarify and simplify the startup process.

The highlights of this hour include the following:

- How to set up your hardware for video "capture"
- Taking a look at video capture card features
- What decisions you'll need to make when starting Premiere for the first time
- Why you should start with single-track editing instead of A/B editing
- Taking a brief, first look at your workspace

My Different Tack

This is where my book takes a different tack: moving to hands-on, step-by-step instruction. This book assumes you already own a printed Premiere manual and are at least somewhat computer literate.

I'm not going to point out every icon to click or present every shortcut. My goal is to help you create high-quality videos. So I'll focus my efforts more on explaining how to exploit Premiere's power. That said, I don't want to force you to jump back and forth between your manual and this book, so I'll try to include *all* the necessary steps for *some* critical functions and let you experiment and try other elements on your own.

Setting Up Your Hardware for Video Capture

Your first task is to set up your hardware to *capture* video—that is, to transfer video from your camcorder or VCR to your hard drive. (I'll get into the specifics of the capture process in Hour 3, "Video Capture and Scene Selection.") Your computer already may have a means to do that—a FireWire (Apple Computer), i.Link (Sony Corporation), or IEEE 1394 (everybody else) connection. Trademark issues have forced manufacturers into this acronym stew, but all the monikers mean the same thing—a high-speed technology to transfer data.

 It began way back in 1986 when researchers at Apple Computer developed what they called *FireWire*. Nine years later the Institute of Electrical and Electronics Engineers adopted FireWire as a high-speed serial bus standard and named it *IEEE 1394*. IEEE 1394 can swap data between PCs and printers, scanners, and hard drives as well as with digital cameras and camcorders.

The features that set IEEE 1394 apart from its SCSI, USB, and parallel interface counterparts are its high speed, small size, and hot "plugability" (you can plug in a device with your computer already turned on).

If you have an IEEE 1394 card, your capture card setup work may be done…maybe. It depends on the type of video you plan to transfer to and from your PC. If you'll be working only with DV, you're set. If you intend to connect analog equipment—VHS, S-VHS, Hi-8, or Beta SP—you'll need a video capture card with the appropriate analog adapters.

Going Over Video Capture Card Features

Analog camcorders output video in as many as three ways: composite, S-Video, and component (from lowest quality to highest). Each uses different cables and connectors, and each requires different technology to convert the analog signal to a digital stream for storage in your computer.

You'll need to select a video capture card with analog inputs that match your needs. The three primary capture card manufacturers are Canopus, Matrox, and Pinnacle (see Figure 2.1). All their capture cards have IEEE 1394 connectivity, and most have some number of analog input and output plugs. In addition, most support MPEG-2 compression and real-time effects rendering.

2

FIGURE 2.1

The three high-quality, mid-range video capture cards: Canopus DVStorm ($1,000 estimated street price), Matrox RT 2500 ($750), and Pinnacle Systems Pro-ONE ($850). The scope of your planned projects and whether you'll use analog video will dictate your card choice.

MPEG stands for Motion Pictures Expert Group, a standards-setting organization like IEEE. MPEG-2 has become the de facto means to "compress" DV (see the "Video Alphabet Soup" sidebar). It's the format used on DVD disks and for digital satellite systems.

Real-time effects rendering is a true plus for video professionals under tight time constraints. Both simple and complex special effects, ranging from standard dissolves to spinning 3D cubes, require substantial processor power to display as you create them. Even today's 2+ GHz processors are not fast enough to play back those transitions in real time. They first need to render them—perform millions of calculations and record these effects to the hard drive—before they can play them back as straight video clips. Rendering delays range from a few seconds to hours. Real-time video cards take on much of that number crunching and, depending on the number and nature of the effects, can play them back immediately.

If you are creating a home video, you may be willing to forgo the luxury of a real-time card. In addition, with Premiere 6.5 you now can preview slightly less-than-full-quality versions of those effects in real time. You'll need a high-end PC running Windows XP or a powerful Mac with OS X to exploit this feature.

On the other hand, professional video producers, with clients peering over their shoulders suggesting multiple edit changes, will consider a real-time card a necessity.

Video capture card prices start at about $500 and can range as high as $4,000 for a full-featured card with Beta SP *component* inputs (see the sidebar in Hour 3 for more on video capture cards).

One possible fly in the video capture card ointment: Most of these cards come bundled with Premiere. If you've already purchased Premiere separately, there's no way I know of to buy an "unbundled" capture card at a lower price. So, if you're thinking a bundled card deal works for you, you might find a way to return your hopefully still-shrink-wrapped copy of Premiere for a credit.

If you find opening your PC a bit nerve-wracking or resolving hardware conflicts daunting, your other option is to buy a system with a video capture card already installed.

I tested the Matrox RT 2500 on a Windows XP Pro PC from Mina Systems (www.minatv.com), an authorized Matrox Integrator. It ran smoothly, right out of the box.

Another company that consistently builds high-quality, reliable DV-oriented PCs is Alienware (www.alienware.com). Its top-of-the line DV system comes fully tricked out with dual Pentium processors and a Pinnacle Pro-ONE video capture card.

Neither company offers recordable DVD drives. One strength of Premiere 6.5 is its DVD Authoring module. To take advantage of that, you'll need a DVD recorder (see Hours 21–24 for more on DVD authoring) .

Connecting Your Camcorder and Monitor(s)

Now it's time to connect a monitor and a camcorder or VCR to your PC. An external TV monitor (as opposed to the monitor windows within Premiere's workspace and your computer's monitor) is not essential, but once you work with one you'll never want to do without. For projects slated for TV viewing, it gives you a truer feel for how your finished product will look, including colors and placement of titles. There's no need to buy a broadcast-quality monitor. You simply can use a small, portable color TV. Attach your camcorder or VCR to the monitor using the VTR Out jack. See Figure 2.2 for some possible configurations.

2

Then attach the IEEE 1394 or analog cable to the camcorder or VCR and to the IEEE 1394 or analog input on your computer.

 If you're using a camcorder, plug it into a wall outlet instead of using batteries. Most camcorders, when operating with batteries, drop into "sleep" mode after a period of nonuse. Because you not only want your camcorder to send DV to your computer but also want it to pass DV from your computer to the monitor (it acts as a real-time converter of the DV stream to an analog TV signal), you'll want to keep it turned on at all times. No need to keep a tape in record mode—or in the camcorder at all for that matter—while you're using it as a DV pass-through device.

Some higher-end video cards have analog video outputs as well as dual–computer monitor capabilities. In those cases you can connect your TV (external monitor) directly to the card, and you can spread out your Premiere editing workspace over two PC monitors. That's about as high-end a system as one can build with Premiere at its core.

I don't think I can remind you too frequently—Premiere opens up uncountable opportunities to you. Its options are limitless.

FIGURE 2.2

Using a separate monitor (an inexpensive portable TV works fine) lets you see exactly how your edits will look on TV. Here are three suggested configurations, from consumer level to professional.

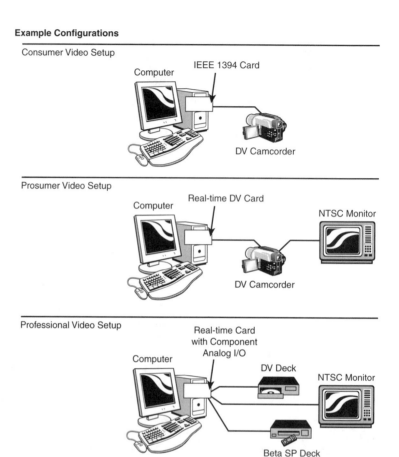

Starting Premiere for the First Time: To A/B or Not to A/B?

When you first fire up Premiere it immediately presents the first of many options, as shown in Figure 2.3. The standard take on this is that A/B editing is the most intuitive for first-time editors and single-track editing is best for experienced video producers.

I disagree. I think everyone should use single-track editing. I'll explain why in a moment. First, a bit of background.

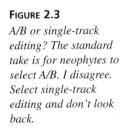

FIGURE 2.3

A/B or single-track editing? The standard take is for neophytes to select A/B. I disagree. Select single-track editing and don't look back.

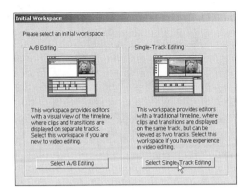

2

A/B editing is old-school, film-style editing. Film editors frequently use two reels of film—an A-roll and a B-roll, usually duplicates made from the same original. The two-reel approach permits nice, easy-on-the-eyes cross-dissolves, gradually fading down the images from one reel while fading up the other.

Still "Grabbing B-Roll" After All These Years

In the TV news business—back when everyone used film and didn't have time to make duplicate reels—the A-roll typically was the interview and the B-roll was everything else. They relied on two reels because the audio and images were not synced in the same place on the film. Older film projectors use a sound track that is 20–26 frames (about a second) ahead of the associated images because the sound pickup in the projector is not in the lens. If you've ever threaded a film projector you know how important it is to get just the right size loops to ensure the sound syncs to the images.

So in the old TV news film era, to get a sound bite to play audio at the right time, that clip had to play "behind" the B-roll for about a second to allow enough time for the sound to reach the audio pickup device. Only then would a director cut to the A-roll image to play the interview segment and then would cut back to the B-roll once the sound bite ended. Despite this now-outmoded means of editing or playing back news stories, news photographers still say they're going to go "grab some B-roll."

When stations began switching to ENG (electronic news gathering) video gear, there was no longer a need to use A/B-rolls. Audio and video are on the same place on videotape, but the only way to do those smooth cross dissolves was to make a copy of the original videotape (leading to some quality loss), run it on a second VCR, and make the cross-dissolve with an electronic "switcher." That was a time-consuming and cumbersome process fraught with timing problems. Older VCRs frequently were not "frame accurate" and you ended up with spasmodic-looking dissolves.

DV changes that. No more dubbing, no more generation loss, no more timing problems, and no more need to edit using ancient A/B-roll methods.

But that was film and this is video. So, when you open Premiere for the first time and note the choice between A/B editing and single-track editing, choose single-track.

 I'm guessing that this advice may be after the fact because you've probably already given Premiere a brief run-through. (It offers this option only once, skipping past it when you subsequently start Premiere.) If that's the case, I'll explain how to change your workspace into single-track editing in Hour 3.

The second reason to choose single-track will become apparent once you get past the next setup screen—Project Settings. If you choose single-track editing, Premiere's editing workspace defaults to two monitor windows versus an A/B Editing default setting of only one monitor. Two is better than one. I'll explain why in a few paragraphs.

Video Alphabet Soup

Deciphering digital video acronyms can put Premiere in perspective. I'll briefly go over video compression, DV formats, and NTSC.

Video Compression

Probably all the video you will edit using Premiere will be compressed. The reason is simple—uncompressed video requires massive data storage. One *second* of uncompressed NTSC video at its standard 720-by-486 pixel resolution consumes about 30MB of storage. A minute requires more than 1.5GB; an hour about 90GB.

All that data requires unbelievably massive calculations to perform even simple transitions and special effects—number crunching that is beyond the capabilities of even the highest-power PC or Mac—thus the need for video compression.

All video codec (compression/decompression) schemes reduce data while attempting to preserve video quality. Some codecs analyze video by looking for differences from frame to frame and storing only that relatively small amount of information. Others simply reduce frame size or frame rate to reduce data.

Each codec typically has some unique feature. Some are better at compressing video with lots of action, others offer smooth data flows rather than peaks that may cause stuttering during playback on Web pages, and some focus on preserving sound quality over image quality.

No matter how well a codec works, all are "lossy." All compressed video loses some quality when compressed.

MPEG-2 is the de facto standard codec for DV compression. It dramatically reduces the standard DV data rate from 3.6MBps down to 1MBps. DVD and digital satellite systems use MPEG-2, and the quality is excellent. But MPEG-2 is not geared to editing because it's one of the codecs that analyzes video frames for differences and stores only that information. Therefore, MPEG-2 frame-specific editing is impractical.

Digital Video (DV) Compression and Formats

I extolled the virtues of DV in Hour 1, "Camcorder and Shooting Tips." Now I want to clarify DV compression. DV comes in at least six flavors: DV25, DVCAM, DVPRO, DV50, DV100, and DigiBeta.

DV25 (Standard DV, MiniDV, or Digital8) is the consumer/prosumer variety. DVCAM and DVPRO offer slightly better quality, and DV50, DV100, and DigiBeta are geared for broadcast and professional video production.

Despite the high quality of each of these formats, they are all compressed. DV25, the format you will probably work with, needs *only* 13GB per hour (versus 90GB for uncompressed analog video).

Yet DV25 still looks great. The compression comes through reduced color sampling. All NTSC video use four pieces of information to illuminate one pixel on your TV screen: chrominance (red, green, blue) and luminance (light value from white through shades of gray to black). The human eye is much more sensitive to changes in luminance than chrominance. So reducing the chrominance data while retaining luminance information maintains most of the video quality.

DV25 removes color information from three of every four consecutive pixels—so-called 4:1:1 color sampling. The resulting compressed video requires 25 million bits per second (3.5MB, including uncompressed audio data), thus the name *DV25*.

One thing DV25 does not do well is *chroma-keying*—taping someone in front of a blue or green screen and electronically replacing that solid color with another image or video. TV weather people are "keyed" all the time (see Hour 14, "Compositing Part 1—Layering Images and Clips"). DV25 leaves slightly jagged edges through which the key color sometimes "bleeds." Higher-quality DV systems key cleanly.

DV50 (50Mbps) uses 4:2:2 color sampling (there are two samples of chrominance data for every four samples of luminance data), and DV100 is used for High-Definition TV. DigiBeta (Digital Betacam) is a high-end broadcast-quality digital video codec compatible with existing analog Beta SP tapes.

NTSC

What's with this crazy 29.97 frames per second? In the United States (as well as Japan and a few other places), alternating current runs at 60 cycles per second. In early black-and-white TV days engineers decided that half that rate would work well for TV (that is, 30 frames per second). That was a little faster than film at 24 fps, so the image looked smooth.

Then along came color TV. Instead of creating a new standard, the industry thought it best to ensure backward compatibility with B&W TVs, so they piggybacked chrominance data on top of the existing luminance signal. That increased the data in each frame by .1%, which led to the slightly slower 29.97 fps rate. This all played out more than 50 years ago, and we've been stuck with this oddity ever since.

To further clarify this: 29.97 fps means that instead of 108,000 frames every hour (the old 30 fps × 60 seconds × 60 minutes), color NTSC displays 107,892 frames every hour.

In other words, if you create a one-hour project using 30 fps non-dropped-frame time-code, your project will be 3.6 seconds (108 frames divided by 30 frames per second) longer than an hour.

That's why you need to select "dropped-frame timecode" if you work with NTSC and want to create an accurately timed project. Much ado about nothing?

Selecting Your Project Settings

The next window Premiere displays is Project Settings. A more descriptive name would be "Project Video and Audio Quality Settings." Your basic goal here is to ensure your production's final output quality is as high as its playback device allows.

If your playback "device" is a Web page using streaming video running in a tiny window, that requires much lower quality video and audio than DVD video playing on a High-Definition TV.

That said, my basic rule of thumb is to select settings that keep your source video as close to its original quality as possible. That would seem to be eminently logical but there is some history here that runs counter to that approach.

In pre–2GHz processor days, if video editors knew the final project output would be something like a QuickTime video running in a small window, they were inclined to reduce the quality of the original video before editing. That would speed up the editing process because there would be less data to crunch. Unless you're using an old clunker computer, I think that's yesterday's news.

These days my basic take is to aim high throughout the video-capturing and editing process. At the very least select settings that match your source video. That will ensure no degradation of video/audio quality from start to finish. You always can reduce video and audio quality later when you export your edited video production to whatever format suits your playback device. Figure 2.4 gives you a peek at Premiere's opening screen, where you make those choices.

As you create more projects, you may consider reducing the project video/audio quality to save hard drive space and processor cycles, but do that only if you're certain that later you won't need to ratchet up the quality to meet a higher-quality output format.

FIGURE 2.4

A rule of thumb: Whether you use DV or analog video, select project settings that match your source video.

Making the Easy DV Option Selections

DV users have the easiest ride through the Project Settings interface. The beauty of DV is that it should not suffer any quality degradation throughout the entire video-capturing and editing process. If you create a project in DV, you always can change the output settings to whatever you want, whenever you want. DV gives you flexibility and keeps things simple.

So if your "raw" video is DV, then your choices are easy. If you're in North America, Japan, or Korea you'll most likely use DV-NTSC. In Australia, China, South America, or most of Europe you'll probably use DV-PAL. And if you're in France, Africa, or the Middle East, SECAM is the TV standard.

NTSC, PAL, SECAM—what's with all the different standards? National Television Standard Committee (NTSC) is clearly the worst of these three TV standards. It has only 525 lines of resolution, versus the higher-definition 625 lines for Phase Alternate Line (PAL) and 819 lines for Sequential Couleur A'memorie (SECAM). Because of NTSC's tendency toward color variability, engineers jokingly refer to it as "Never The Same Color." There is a glimmer of hope: North America is grudgingly elbowing the higher-resolution PAL and SECAM folks aside with High-Definition TV (HDTV), which is set for full adoption in the United States by 2003.

You have only three other real options within the DV environment (other than NTSC, PAL, or SECAM): Real-time Preview, screen width, and audio.

Real-time Preview is new to Premiere 6.5. If you have a reasonably fast system, selecting a preset from this list means you can view video effects and transitions between clips in real time without rendering. Even if you don't opt for Real-time Preview now, you can easily select it later.

Screen width depends on the source: wide screen (16:9 aspect ratio) or the standard 4:3 ratio. Your most likely choice is "standard" because few camcorders have a true wide-screen setting.

> Many camcorders do offer a faux 16:9 option but accomplish that by merely cutting off the top and bottom of the image and interpolating information to stretch the remaining image. You end up with a wide-screen image with 20% less video data in it. Some higher-end camcorders do create true 16:9 views with larger CCDs or "anamorphic" lens adapters.

Your preset audio options are 32 KHz and 48 KHz (44 KHz is music CD quality audio). KHz is the audio "sampling" rate—in these cases, 32,000 or 48,000 samples per second. The higher the sampling rate, the closer the digital sound mirrors its original source. Rule of thumb: Because most DV camcorders record audio at 48 KHz, you should choose that figure.

Tackling the Trickier Analog Video Project Settings

Project settings become a bit less intuitive if you're capturing analog video or using video files from some other source, such as a CD-ROM.

When you capture analog video, Premiere will need to not only convert it to a digital format but "compress" it as well. Your choice of codecs is limited to QuickTime (usually used on Macs) and Video for Windows. Again, select a project setting that matches your source video, with the caveat that the codec should match your project's planned video output device. Here are some points to keep in mind:

- If you're working with D1 or other high-end professional analog video, select 720×480.

- If you plan to record your edited project back to an analog tape—VHS, Hi-8, Beta SP—either 720×480 or 640×480 should work fine.
- If you're going to play back your video from a CD-ROM, 640×480 works well.
- Your choice between Video for Windows and QuickTime may not be all that critical, but as a rule of thumb Mac users should stick to QuickTime.

> One workaround to dealing with analog video and all its associated unpredictability is to convert your legacy analog tapes to DV. Most DV camcorders have analog Video In inputs. You simply can dub your analog tape to DV by connecting the two camcorders and recording from the analog camcorder to the digital video camcorder. If your analog camcorder offers S-Video Out, use that instead of composite. Composite video uses an RCA jack (the same as the audio jacks), and S-Video uses a four-pin plug. In either case, don't forget to record audio as well as use the left and right (white and red) outlets/inputs.

You can tweak the heck out of the project settings by clicking the Custom button to open an interface with a drop-down list that lets you adjust general, video, audio, keyframe and rendering, or capture settings. See Figure 2.5 for an example. This is for projects with very specific source clips or output requirements.

FIGURE 2.5

Few editors will need to change the preset project settings, but for those with specific needs, selecting Custom in the Project Settings window brings up the New Project Settings dialog box.

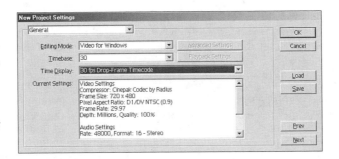

Checking Out General Settings

Before you venture past the Project Settings interface to the video-editing workspace, I recommend clicking the Custom button and briefly checking out the general settings. Use the drop-down menu to access that interface.

This presents one confusing aspect of Premiere and video editing in general: a collection of apparently impenetrable terms, including timebase, time display, time code, timeline, and frame rate.

If you select one of Premiere's presets, deciphering these terms is a nonissue. Premiere selects a standard editing scheme with all the appropriate "Time" issues to fit your project. Despite that easy fix, a little explanation is in order.

Timebase

Timebase refers to how Premiere divides its editing timeline into increments. It is *not* the frame rate but frequently is the same as a clip's frame rate. The timebase should match your source video standard: PAL and SECAM are 25 frames (or timeline increments) per second and NTSC is a confounding 29.97 fps (see earlier note). Film runs at 24 fps, and the default setting for Video for Windows and QuickTime is 30 increments per second.

Task: Explore How Timebase Settings Work

There's an easy way to see how timebase settings work:

1. Select the PAL, NTSC, or Analog preset and enter the editing workspace.

2. Highlight the timeline by clicking its title bar.

3. Press the hyphen (-) key (the key at the top of your keyboard, not the one on the numeric keypad) five times. This displays more time inside the Timeline window—in this case a full minute.

4. Now drag the triangular Edit Line button to the 59-second mark. Figure 2.6 shows that triangular button and the timecode. Use the time displayed in the Program window—the upper-right video screen—to see where you are in the timeline.

If you selected NTSC, you'll see that as you move past 59:29 (59 seconds, 29 frames) the time will jump to 1:00:02 (one minute, zero seconds, and two frames). It skips two frames every minute (with the exception of every tenth minute) to compensate for the convoluted NTSC 29.97 timebase and to accommodate that standard's *dropped* frames. No actual frames are lost, only frame numbers. The purpose of this "dropped-frame" scheme is to ensure time-accurate program lengths (see the "Video Alphabet Soup" sidebar).

If you select PAL, you'll see that each second is a constant 25 frames long, and if you chose a multimedia setting it'll be 30 fps. Much simpler.

FIGURE 2.6

Check how the time-base works by sliding the "edit line" button to the one-minute mark.

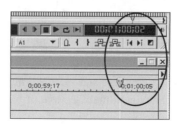

Frame Rate

The only time the frame rate won't equal the timebase is when you use Video for Windows or QuickTime. You'll notice this when you use existing Video for Windows or QuickTime files as source clips. Those clips may have been made at less than 30 fps to ensure they could run smoothly on slower systems.

Task: Working with the Timebase and Frame Rate

Here's one example of a video with a frame rate that's different from the timebase. The file sample.mov comes with the version of QuickTime bundled with your copy of Premiere. It runs at only 12 fps. Follow these steps to see the timebase and frame rate in action:

1. Select the default Multimedia QuickTime Project Settings.
2. Choose File, Import, File.
3. Locate sample.mov (in the QuickTime folder) and click Open. It appears in the Project window in the upper-left corner of your workspace.
4. Drag and drop sample.mov into the Monitor Source window.
5. Click the Play button below that monitor window and watch. Sample.mov appears to run relatively smoothly, but you may notice a slight stutter due to the reduced frame rate (12 fps is half the rate for motion picture film).
6. Click the Frame Forward button several times. See Figure 2.7 to locate that button.

You'll see that as you move through sample.mov, the time display will skip two or three frames for each Frame Forward button click you make: 12 frames per second spread out over 30 time increments per second (the timebase) amounts to about one frame of QuickTime video per three timeline increments.

It gets even weirder if you drag sample.mov to the timeline. You will need to click the Frame Forward button in the Program Monitor window two or three times before the image will change. The source side of the monitor plays the video in its original 12-frames-per-second mode. The program side plays it in the Project Setting's 30-increment-per-second mode.

Time Display

For all intents and purposes, time display is the same as timebase. The exception again is good-old North American NTSC. If you plan to play your edited NTSC video project on a TV set, stick with what's called Drop-Frame Timecode (see the "Video Alphabet Soup" sidebar). If you'll be playing back NTSC on your PC or the Web, Non-Drop-Frame Timecode works best. If you're using PAL or SECAM, stick to their 25 fps time displays. With film, you can use Feet+Frames.

FIGURE 2.7

Clicking the Frame Forward button moves you ahead one frame at a time. You need to move through two or three frames to see the actual next frame of this 12-frame/second QuickTime movie.

 As I mentioned in the "Video Alphabet Soup" sidebar earlier in this hour, Drop-Frame Timecode and Non-Drop-Frame Timecode are much ado about very little. If you manage to use the "wrong" one, it will probably have no discernible impact on your final product. Depending on your situation, your project will either run a few frames too long or too short. Practically, there's no difference between the two timecode schemes.

As a rule of thumb, the Project Settings interface's default presets should be more than adequate for most work. And again, if your source material is high-quality video (that is, DV or full-screen analog video), selecting projects settings to match means you'll have more output options later.

 Opening the Custom Settings interface presents numerous, sometimes bewildering options—for instance, Compression Settings (see "Video Alphabet Soup"). All video you'll work with in Premiere is compressed—even DV. That is, software has analyzed it and reduced its data rate while retaining as much of its original quality as possible. Premiere lets you choose from about 25 video compression algorithms or codecs.

If your source video is already a file—be it on a CD, your hard drive, or downloaded from the Web—it'll be a compressed file. Simply by looking at it, you can't tell what compression scheme was used. However, Premiere can tell you this even before you import the file into a project. Here's how:

1. Click through the Project Settings window to open the video-editing workspace.

2. Choose File, Get Properties For, File.

3. Locate and select the clip you want to analyze and click Open. Toward the bottom of that window, you'll see the compression scheme used. See Figure 2.8 for an example.

FIGURE 2.8

The Clip Properties dialog box. Of particular interest is the compression scheme or codec. In this case it's Sorenson Video, a compression algorithm used frequently when creating QuickTime videos.

A quick way to check whether your project settings are compatible with your clips and output settings is to open the Settings Viewer. Click Project, Settings Viewer. If you have multiple format source clips, selecting them in turn in the clip drop-down list will display any possible conflicts or incompatibilities in red. Figure 2.9 shows one glaring example. But conflicts do not necessarily mean real problems. There are too many combinations and permutations to offer any specific conflict-resolution advice. Each column's drop-down list gives you easy access to the respective project settings. Some trial and error may resolve most of those red warnings.

FIGURE 2.9

The Settings Viewer is a handy, big-picture view of your Capture, Project, Clip, and Export settings. The highlighted comments (Premiere displays them in red) indicate potential conflicts.

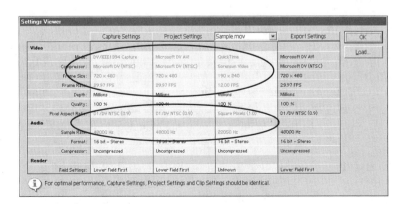

Taking a Quick Tour of Your Workspace

After making your Project Settings selection, Premiere opens its workspace. At first glance it may seem busy and counterintuitive, but after working with it for a while you'll come to appreciate its layout. For now, I'll limit my discussion to only two features:

Timeline—For those of you who started Premiere before cracking open this book, you already may have opted for the A/B Editing workspace. If so, your timeline—that collection of parallel, horizontal lines in the bottom left portion of your workspace—will say Video 1A and Video 1B with a transition line between them. You can switch that to single-track editing with a couple mouse clicks. I'll cover this in Hour 3. See Figure 2.10 for a view of both types of timelines.

FIGURE 2.10

If you opted for A/B editing, your timeline will look like the top window. The single-track editing workspace (bottom window) looks slightly different.

Monitors—This is the second reason why I think it's best to choose single-track editing instead of A/B. The default workspace setting for single-track has two monitors—two little TV windows (see Figure 2.11). One for your "source" video/images/graphics/audio and the other for the "program" (your edited project).

A/B editing defaults to a single monitor, which I think is counterintuitive and confusing. You *can* start Premiere by selecting A/B editing and then switch to two monitors (remember that Premiere is mind-numbingly configurable), but by opting for single-track editing you at least start with the right frame of reference.

I'll give you a more detailed workspace tour in the next chapter.

Figure 2.11

Selecting single-track editing means your default workspace opens with two monitors—a more intuitive work environment.

Summary

When visiting Premiere for the first time, you encounter a collection of sometimes confusing terms and setup options. In these first steps in editing videos on your computer, my advice is to keep it simple and use the default settings. My one slightly different tack is to recommend single-track editing instead of A/B editing, largely because single-track lends itself to computerized video editing. Using digital video (DV) will greatly simplify the entire Premiere process. If you do need to use analog video—either legacy from an older consumer camcorder or high-end professional Beta SP video—you will need a video capture card. You may find that using such cards is not all that intuitive.

Workshop

Review the questions and answers in this section to try to sharpen your Premiere setup skills. And take a few moments to tackle my short quiz.

Q&A

Q I use a DV camcorder but I'm going to record my project on a VHS tape. Should I select NTSC Video for Windows project settings?

A No. Because your original source video is DV, it's best to select DV-NTSC Standard 48 KHz. You want to select project settings that match the source material. Later when you "export" your project to tape or some other playback media, you can alter the output settings to match that medium.

Q I shot all my footage on DV but I want to include a couple Video for Windows (VfW) clips I downloaded from the Internet. Do I need to make any adjustments to my project settings.

A Probably not. But when you edit those VfW clips into your project, you may have to compensate for changes in aspect ratios and resolution (they probably will look distorted on a 4:3 aspect ration NTSC TV screen) and their quality will be notice-ably poor compared to your DV. You might consider putting them in a window or a box rather than display them in the final project as full-screen images (see Hour 16, "Tips, Tricks, and Techniques—Part 1").

Quiz

1. What can you gain by opening the Settings Viewer?

2. When will a clip's frame rate not equal the timebase?

3. What's the difference between the single-track editing timeline and the A/B editing timeline?

Quiz Answers

1. The Settings Viewer gives you an overall picture of your Capture, Project, Clip, and Export settings. If there are any conflicts, it allows easy access to the various settings menus for possibly quick fixes.

2. This happens only with multimedia clips made with Video for Windows or QuickTime. When you set export or output settings for VfW or QuickTime, you can lower the frame rate (and frame size) to allow smoother playback on the Internet, for example. But when you edit a reduced frame rate multimedia clip using the timeline, the frame rate usually will not equal the timebase—the number of increments per second on the timeline—which is usually 30.

3. Two things: The A/B timeline splits the Video 1 track into two tracks—A and B. Also, the single-track editing timeline does not display a transition bar, whereas the A/B editing timeline does.

HOUR 3

Video Capture and Scene Selection

Before you can make your first edit on your production you need to "capture" or transfer your video from your camcorder or VCR to your computer's hard drive. During this hour I'll cover capture techniques for both digital and analog video. The capture process also creates an opportunity to review your raw footage and to tour the Premiere nonlinear editing workspace.

The highlights of this hour include the following:

- The advantages of using a nonlinear editor
- The functions of each principal window in Premiere
- How to capture video
- How to critically select and organize your video clips

Capturing Video

"Capturing" or transferring video from your camcorder to your PC can be mindlessly easy or maddeningly difficult.

Digital video transfer falls on the easy end of the scale. Later in this hour I'll walk you through that relatively painless process.

On the other hand, analog video capture is fraught with potential snafus. For starters, you'll need a video capture card with analog video inputs. Installing and configuring such high-end cards can be frustrating. Understanding all their snazzy features—and idiosyncrasies—can take some real effort. And you have fewer capture options with analog. I'll relate my experience with one prosumer-level card, the Matrox RT 2500.

At some point in the capture process you'll need to critically view your raw footage—selecting "keeper" clips and sequences, reviewing interviews for the best sound bites, and listening for any natural sound that will enhance your production. I'll give you a few pointers on how best to approach that. I'll also suggest a means to organize your source material to ease the editing process.

Before we tackle all that, I want to introduce you to your editing workspace. No sense diving into video capture without first gaining some familiarity with the interface.

Premiere—A Nonlinear Editor

To begin, open Premiere to display your workspace.

Premiere is a *nonlinear editor* (NLE). It looks and feels a whole lot different from standard, linear videotape-editing systems. This may be patently obvious to you but bear with me a bit. Figure 3.1 is the default opening screen if you choose single-track editing.

On tape systems you need to lay down edits consecutively and contiguously. If you decide to expand a story already edited on tape by inserting a sound bite in the middle, you simply cannot slip that bite into the piece and slide everything after it further into the story. You need to edit in that sound bite *over* your existing edits and *reedit* everything after it. Alternatively, you can make a dub of the story after the new edit point and lay that down after adding the sound bite (causing generation quality loss in the process).

FIGURE 3.1

Here is one of hundreds of ways to configure your Premiere editing workspace. Two monitors are more intuitive than one, as is the single-track editing timeline.

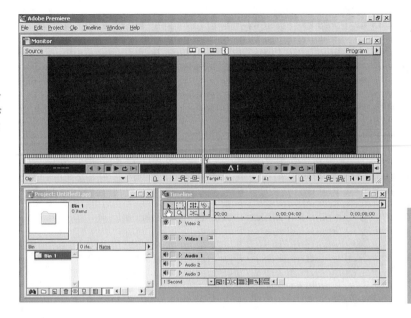

Makes me shudder to think of the news stories I produced, back in the days of videotape-only editing, that screamed for some minor mid-story fixes. But I knew those fixes would have taken too much time and caused too much reporter/editor grumbling to do. Such is life in deadline-driven TV news.

As newsrooms have moved to NLEs, reporter/editor tension (at least over silly little things such as adding a sound bite in the middle of a piece...ahhem) has dissipated.

Premiere (and other NLEs like it) has come to the rescue. Now you can make changes with a few mouse clicks. If you want to edit the all-important production close before editing anything else, that's fine. It's nonlinear. Feel free to do things nonsequentially.

The other overwhelming improvement over videotape-editing systems is immediate access to your video clips. No longer do you need to endlessly fast forward or rewind through miles of tape to find that one snippet of natural sound. With Premiere, and other NLEs, it's all a mouse click away.

Tour the Video-Editing Workspace

Before diving into nonlinear editing (Hour 4, "Using the Storyboard or Opting for Cuts-only Editing"), I want to give you a brief tour of the video-editing workspace.

Start at the lower-left side in the Timeline window.

The Timeline

This is where you'll do *most* of your actual editing (because this is Premiere, there are always multiple means to perform any one task). Figure 3.2 shows the standard Premiere timeline. Anyone who has edited with an NLE will feel comfortable using it. Anyone coming from the linear, videotape-editing world may find a timeline a bit daunting at first but soon will come to love it.

FIGURE 3.2

Premiere's NLE standard timeline approach is second nature to anyone who has worked with other computerized editing products.

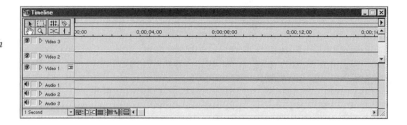

Basically the timeline is a collection of video and audio tracks with an option to display a transition track.

You can build transitions only between video clips on track one (1A and 1B in A/B editing mode). In addition, anything placed in a higher-numbered track covers up anything below it. You'll use those higher-numbered tracks to build special effects such as videos in small frames that slide over the screen, translucent images, or graphics with windows that let whatever video is below them show through.

Audio tracks follow different rules. One audio track does not cancel out another. All play back as an ensemble. Premiere's built-in audio mixer keeps multiple audio tracks from becoming a cacophony.

Premiere allows you to use as many as 99 video and 99 audio tracks. I can't imagine any project using that much real estate, though.

Configuring the Timeline

As I mentioned in Hour 2, "Premiere Setup," for those of you who fired up Premiere before cracking open this book, you already may have opted for the A/B editing work-space. Here's a quick means to switch to single-track editing.

The windows in Premiere have nifty fly-out menus accessible by clicking a handy little arrow in each window's top-right corner. I've highlighted it in Figure 3.3. In this case, click the arrow and then switch between A/B editing and single-track editing. You'll note that A/B editing fits the old film-editing model by displaying tracks 1A and 1B with a middle section labeled *Transitions*.

FIGURE 3.3

This handy fly-out menu lets you customize the timeline appearance and functionality.

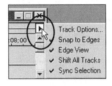

3

What supposedly makes A/B editing intuitive is that you can see how clips overlap so you can judge how long a transition will last.

If you switch back to single-track editing, you'll see that there is no "Transition" section. Not to fear—Premiere lets you create something like an A/B environment with the click of one other icon. See Figure 3.4 for that icon's location.

FIGURE 3.4

Click this tiny double-box icon and the single-track editing timeline will shift to something very much like an A/B editing timeline.

When you edit using a single-track timeline, you place a transition at the junction of two clips. Premiere automatically creates an overlap.

Here's the bottom line: Stick with single-track editing.

I'll explain more about transitions and how Premiere handles them in Hour 5, "Adding Transitions: From Dissolves to Zooms." For now, a little explanation may clarify things.

If you use A/B editing and want to make a dissolve, you place one clip on video track 1A and the next one on track 1B, such that its beginning overlaps the end of the previous clip. You drag a Transition icon to the Transition line between the two clips, and that transition will automatically last for however much time the two clips overlap.

In single-track editing, you place one clip on video track 1 and the next one on the same track, directly following and adjacent to the previous clip. There is no overlap. If you want to add a transition, Premiere automatically creates an overlap—the default is 30 frames or one second—by extending the first clip 15 frames beyond the end you previously selected and adding 15 frames to the beginning of the second clip.

Monitors

To reiterate, two monitors are better than one. The default workspace setting for single-track editing has two monitors, whereas A/B opens with only one monitor.

You can switch between one and two monitors by using the monitor window's nifty fly-out menu. Click the handy little arrow icon in the window's upper-right corner and then select Single View or Dual View (the third option, Trim View, is a means to edit two adjacent clips from within the Dual View window). A faster way to switch from one monitor to two is to click the little double-window icon above the monitor window. I've highlighted it in Figure 3.5.

FIGURE 3.5

It's easy to switch between one monitor and two. Click the little double-monitor icon.

Project Window

In the upper-left corner you'll find the Project window. This is where you store and access your original video clips—your raw footage—as well as audio files and graphics. It uses *bins* (Adobe's name for file folders) to organize your "assets." We'll take a closer look at this in the next hour.

Transitions, Video, Audio Palette

This window's tiny size belies its power. Neatly tucked away in its three file tabs are 178 special effects. Scene transitions, such as dissolves and wipes; video effects to alter the appearance of your clips; and audio effects to spice up your sound. I'll begin covering these powerful (but frequently overused) tools in Hour 5.

Task: Explore Premiere's Transitions

▼ TASK

For now, here's a quick and cool preview of coming attractions. Figure 3.6 shows how your Transitions window should look at the end of this little exercise:

1. Click the Transitions tab (if you don't see a Transitions window, click Window, Show Transitions).

2. Open the handy fly-out menu by clicking this window's little arrow in its upper-right corner.

3. Click Expand All Folders.

4. Click Animate.

5. Click anywhere inside the Transitions window.

▲ All the transition icons demonstrate how they work. Cool. This animate feature works only with transitions, not audio or video effect icons. You can drag the edges or corners of the Transitions palette to view more transition icons.

FIGURE 3.6

An easy way to see all your transitions in action.

3

Navigator, History, and Info

Here are two useful tools and one of only minor interest:

- Navigator gives you a visual representation of your entire project and allows you to move quickly to different locations. This comes in mighty handy if you are working on a long production.

- History tracks every step you take in your video production and lets you back up if you don't like your latest efforts. Its default display is the most recent 15 edits or changes, but you can change that to up to 99 steps. To do that, click Edit, Preferences, Autosave and Undo. Then type in a number in History/Undo Levels. When you back up to a previous condition, all steps that came after that point are cleared as well. You cannot extract a single misstep buried within the current list.

- The Info tab is of limited usefulness. It offers only a brief snapshot of whatever element—clip, transition, or effect—you've currently highlighted.

Organizing the Workspace

After you work with Premiere for a while, you'll want to organize the workspace to suit your needs. I like to see more of the timeline, so I minimize the Navigator and Transitions palettes and drag them to the bottom of the screen. Then I drag the right edge of the timeline all the way to the right. Figure 3.7 is my workspace at its normal 1024×768 resolution.

FIGURE 3.7

My personal workspace features a wider timeline and minimized Navigator and Transitions palettes.

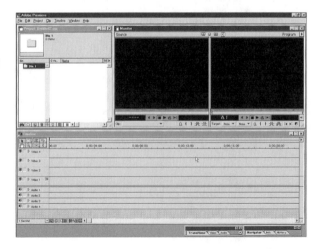

Because I'm the only one who uses my PC, I don't need to worry about some other editor messing with my Premiere workspace. If you share your computer with other editors who don't like your layout, you can save it by clicking Window, Workspace, Save Workspace. Then type in a name and press Return (Mac) or Enter (Windows). To open your custom workspace, click Window, Workspace and then select your named workspace.

Preparing for Video Capture

Before you transfer your first frame of raw video to your PC, you need to decide where to store your clips.

It all depends on your computer's hard drive configuration. Ideally you have more than one hard drive. One for your operating system (OS) and program files (including Premiere); the other for video, images, graphics, and sound—your so-called A/V (audio/visual) drive. The OS frequently accesses its hard drive even in the middle of an edit or video capture. Having separate OS and A/V drives ensures a smoother operation.

Your A/V drive should be able to sustain a throughput of 4MBps (more, if you're working with analog video). Most recent hard drive models can handle that easily. I have a 75GB IBM DeskStar and an 80GB Seagate Barracuda, and both sustain a transfer rate of 10MB or better.

If you have only one drive and it's reasonably fast, you should have no noticeable problems during video capture or later playback.

Task: Create a File Folder for Your Project

▼ TASK

Here's how you create a file folder for your project. It uses standard file-management techniques. If you're at all comfortable working with your computer, Figure 3.8 will look mighty familiar to you. Here are the steps to follow for this task:

1. Minimize Premiere by clicking the minimize button at the top-right corner of the screen.

2. Open My Computer (or however you access your hard drives).

3. Select the drive that you will use for A/V files.

4. To create a new folder in Windows, click File, New Folder. Name it something such as `Premiere A-V Files`.

▼

▼ 5. Double-click that file folder and create a subfolder in the same fashion. Name it something descriptive, such as `Soccer Championship Clips`.

▲ 6. Return to Premiere.

FIGURE 3.8

Using standard file-management tech-niques, you can add a file folder to your des-ignated A/V drive. I suggest naming it `Premiere A-V Files`.

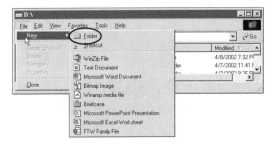

Now it's time to tell Premiere about that "video clips" file folder you just created and to make sure Premiere and your DV camcorder can communicate with each other. Once that's resolved, you can view, log, and transfer digital video to your computer (I'll cover analog video capture later) .

Task: Tell Premiere Where to Find Your Clips

You should be back in your Premiere editing workspace. First you'll tell Premiere where you want to store captured clips. In another bit of confounding, legacy nomenclature, Premiere calls these hard disk locations *scratch disks*. That's sort of a holdover to the days of massive, removable storage devices. Now, 75GB internal hard drives are com-mon, and removable storage is not that critical to computerized video editing. Here are the steps to follow for this task:

1. Click Edit, Preferences, Scratch Disks and Device Control to open the Preferences dialog box (see Figure 3.9).

2. Look inside the Scratch Disks section, click the drop-down menu arrow next to Captured Movies, and click Select Folder.

▲ 3. Locate your "video clips" file folder and click OK. Note that the file folder name appears below the Captured Movies drop-down window.

> You may go through the same process for Video Previews and Audio Previews, but leaving them in the default project file setting will work fine. The project file storage location defaults to your Premiere directory. Your project file does not actually hold your original clips, only data noting their location and any edits you've made to your project.

FIGURE 3.9

Use this menu to tell Premiere where your so-called "scratch disks" are.

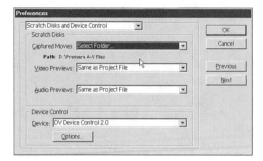

Task: Select Your DV Device

Keep the Preferences dialog box open. Here's where you select your DV device and set its control options. Figure 3.10 displays that interface. Follow these steps:

1. Make sure your camcorder or other DV device is hooked up to your computer, its power is on, and it's set to VTR/VCR (*not* Camera).

2. Look at the Device Control drop-down menu at the bottom of the Preferences menu. Probably, DV Device Control 2.0 already is selected. If not, click the drop-down arrow and select DV Device Control 2.0.

3. Click Options.

4. Click the Device Brand drop-down list and select your camcorder brand.

5. Previous versions of Premiere used to list model names in another drop-down list. Now all you need to do is make sure "Standard" shows up in the next window (it's not likely you'll have an "alternative" camcorder).

6. Check to see that "Drop-Frame" is in the next window.

7. Click Check Status. Here are the status types:

   - *Offline* means Premiere can't communicate with or control your DV device. Check to make sure you turned it on and it's in VTR or VCR mode (as opposed to Camera mode) .

   - *Detected* means Premiere can communicate with your camcorder but can't control it. Make sure you have inserted a tape in it.

   - *Online* means everything is in order.

FIGURE **3.10**

Accessing this window lets you check the status of your DV device. If all is copasetic, it displays "Online."

Logging and Transferring Your Clips

Premiere gives you the opportunity to complete two steps (more or less) at once: logging your raw footage and automatically transferring selected clips to your hard drive. But it uses a nomenclature that I find a bit confusing:

- *Movie Capture* basically means "manual video clip transfer." During movie capture you view your video, looking for clips you like, and then transfer them one at a time to your hard drive.

- *Batch Capture* basically means "logging your original footage and then automatically transferring video clips to your hard drive." In this case you use the Movie Capture window to view your video, create a list or log of segments you want to transfer, and then open the Batch Capture window to let Premiere transfer them all while you walk the dog.

There has to be a better way to name and perform these tasks, but this is how it works in Premiere.

In any event, the second task, the automated process, is the only way to go. But we'll start with the first task, the manual clip-at-a-time method, to give you a basic feel for how the video-transfer process works.

Task: Control Your DV Device with Your PC

▲ TASK

The fun is about to begin. If you haven't used a computer to remotely control a DV device, this task is guaranteed to elevate your heart rate:

1. Make sure your camcorder is on and set to VTR/VCR and that you've inserted your tape.

2. Open the Capture Movie window by clicking File and selecting Capture, Movie Capture. Figure 3.11 represents what you should have in front of you: a little TV set with standard video-editing-style VCR controls.

▼

▼   3. Click the play button. Is this not cool? There is your raw video playing on your computer.

4. Try out some of the other buttons: fast forward, rewind, and stop.

5. Now try some of the special buttons: Shuttle lets you move slowly or zip quickly, depending on how far you move the slider off center, forward or backward through your tape. You also have Frame Forward and Backward buttons, Forward and Reverse Slow Play, and a single-frame Jog control (the ruled line above all the

▲   other controls).

OK. Fun's over...for now.

FIGURE 3.11
The Movie Capture window. Using standard VCR and videotape-editing controls, you can easily find "keeper" video clips to transfer to your hard drive.

Task: Select Capture Settings

Next up: selecting capture settings. The default settings will likely work fine, but I'll run through this process just in case you want to tweak things a bit. Figure 3.12 shows the interface you will access next. Here are the steps to follow:

1. Look at the Movie Capture window. If you see only a TV display window and its controls, click that handy little arrow in the upper-right corner of the window and then click Expand Window. That'll open the Logging and Settings window on the right side of the TV screen.

2. Click that little arrow again to open a fly-out menu and select Capture Settings.

3. Confirm the capture format is DV/IEEE 1394 Capture. If it's not, click the drop-down list and select DV/IEEE 1394.

4. Click the Preroll Time field and type in **5**. This ensures that when you tell Premiere to grab a clip, it rolls the tape back five seconds to get your camcorder up to speed before it reaches the in-point. If you have a Matrox RT 2500 card, there is no need

▼

▼ for a preroll—it grabs clips "on the fly," which is a much faster and less machine-intensive process.

5. Leave the Report Dropped Frames box checked. It will display a message if any frames were lost during the transfer. The Abort on Dropped Frames box should remain unchecked.

6. I recommend unchecking the Capture Limit box. As long as you're going to specify the in- and out-points of all transferred clips, there's no need to have this feature keeping an eye on things for you.

7. Click the DV Settings button and note that all four boxes are checked. This means that as you preview your video, it will display and play audio on your computer (as opposed to watching it and listening to it only on your external monitor or camcorder viewfinder). You can uncheck these boxes if your processor can't handle the data load.

8. Click OK to return to the Project Settings dialog box.

▲ 9. Click OK to return to the Movie Capture window.

FIGURE 3.12

The default settings in the Project Settings dialog box should work fine. I recommend only that you uncheck the Capture Limit box.

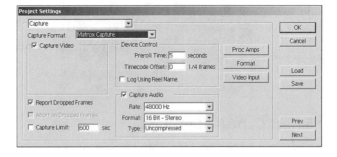

Before you "capture" your first clip, I want to clarify one point. *Capture* is another of those somewhat misleading terms used throughout the NLE world. On the digital video (DV) side of things, *transfer* would be a more descriptive term. Because DV already is digital, all Premiere does is tell your camcorder to transfer the selected digital clip data through the IEEE 1394 interface and onto your hard drive. Done. No "capturing" necessary.

In the analog world, "transfer, conversion, and compression" would more accurately describe the capture process. In that case your camcorder transfers the video and audio to an input on a video capture card. Then that card's built-in hardware converts the wave form signal to a digital form, compresses it using a codec, and stores it to your hard drive. It's a much less user-friendly process made even more tedious by the inability to remotely control your camcorder (in most cases). I'll explain that process later.

Task: Movie Capture—Manual Video Clip Transfer

Now, back to manual DV clip capture (or *transfer*). Figure 3.13 displays the Logging page you'll use to accomplish this task. Follow these steps:

1. In the Movie Capture window, click the Logging tab at the top right side of the screen.

2. Search through your videotape and find a scene you want to transfer to your computer.

3. Roll the tape back a couple seconds and then mark the in-point. You have two ways to do this:

   - Click the little "{" below the VCR control buttons.

   - Click the Set In button on the lower right side of the menu. Note that a time-code appears in the In window.

4. Now move your tape forward to the clip's end and let it roll for a couple more seconds to add a trailer.

5. Mark the out-point by clicking either the "}" or the Set Out button. Note, once again, that the timecode appears in the Out window, along with a calculated clip length.

6. Transfer that clip to your hard drive by clicking the Capture In/Out button below the In, Out, and Duration windows.

FIGURE 3.13

The Logging page extends from the Movie Capture window. Use it to set in- and out-points for individual clips.

Voila. Premiere takes control of your camcorder, rewinding it to the in-point, rolling it back five seconds (the preroll), playing the clip, transferring the data, and stopping the clip at the out-point. Pretty slick.

At this point Premiere asks you to name the clip. In general you'll want to use something descriptive so you can find the clip later (I'll cover naming conventions a bit later). Type in the clip's name, click OK, and Premiere stores your clip in the file folder you created at the beginning of this process.

I had you add a few extra seconds to the beginning and end of your clip for a reason. You'll need these extra bits of video during editing if you do long cross-dissolves or other transitions. And, even if you decide to use only a small portion of the clip you saved in your final project, you always can shorten anything you transfer. So a little extra is good.

In Premiere parlance you just did a "movie capture." In my view you just did a "manual video clip transfer." Manual labor is fine for a while. Automation is better.

Automating Your Video Transfers—Batch Capture

Here's one instance where DV really shines—the ability to automatically transfer selected video clips to your computer. In a few moments you're going to create a list of video clips, tell Premiere to transfer them, and then take the dog for a walk while Premiere handles the chores. Nice.

Before you grab the leash, I want to run through some scene-selection tips and naming conventions.

The basic rule of thumb in the video or film production world is that you will shoot a whole lot more raw footage than you'll put in your final production. Probably at least five times what you'll need. You've heard of film scenes "hitting the cutting room floor." Next time you watch a DVD movie, check to see if it has "deleted scenes." You'll be amazed at how many difficult-to-shoot, well-acted, and expensive scenes did not make it into the final cut.

Your task now is to critically review your tape(s) and weed out the chaff while retaining the grain.

You want to transfer only the best sound bites, the coolest scenes, and the highest-quality natural sound. If you did more than one take of a scene, find the one that works best. If you videotaped that soccer championship game, select all the goals, great plays, and enthusiastic crowd reactions, skipping most of the up-and-down-the-field ball handling.

Selecting Sound Bites

My view is that the video producer or writer can do a much better job telling the story than the folks you interview for the story. It's your job to distill factual information and create a coherent, cohesive story.

So it's best to use interview sound bites not to state facts but to present emotions, feelings, and opinions. You should be the one to say, "At the bottom of the ninth, the bases were loaded, with two outs." Let the batter, who is recalling this dramatic moment say, "My legs felt like jelly."

Even in a corporate backgrounder, employees should be the ones stating how enthusiastic they are about a new product. Your job is to say what that product does.

In general keep sound bites short. Let them be punctuation marks, not paragraphs.

> A caveat: None of these admonitions are carved in stone. Some characters you'll videotape are so compelling, quirky, or humorous that your best bet is to let them be the primary narrator. Then you'll want to consider what scenes you can use to illustrate their commentary. You don't want to fill your entire video with a "talking head."

Listening for Effective Natural Sound

As you review your raw footage, you should keep your ears tuned for brief instances of dramatic sound: a wire cutter clipping a piano wire (one of the most memorable for me—see the editing sidebar in Hour 5), the crack of a baseball bat, a gurgling brook, a hawk screeching.

You'll want to transfer these as separate clips even though you may also transfer a long clip of the soaring hawk with that sound somewhere in it. Why? Later, when you edit in that soaring hawk, you easily can find and edit in the screech "nat-sound" (which means *natural sound* in TV news parlance) to give the image more punch.

Logging Tapes and Using Consistent Naming Conventions

Now the winnowing down begins. Figure 3.14 shows the same Logging page you used to manually capture clips. Now you are going to log several video clips so Premiere can transfer them all at once later.

Task: Log Your Video Clips

To log your video clips, follow these steps:

1. Return to the Movie Capture window.

2. Click the Logging tab.

3. Highlight the Reel Name window and type in a descriptive name for your video-tape, such as Soccer Championship-1. You want to give each tape a unique name so that later, when you do automated transfer, Premiere will alert you to switch tapes.

4. Rewind your tape and then start moving through it.

5. As you find shots you want to transfer, mark the in- and out-points and then click Log In/Out. That pops up the File Name dialog box. You should enter a filename using the suggested video clip naming convention discussed next.

FIGURE 3.14
The now-familiar Logging page. This time you need to add a reel name.

Using Video Clip Naming Conventions

Think through how you're going to name your clips. You may end up with dozens of clips, and if you don't give them descriptive names, it'll slow down editing.

You might use a naming convention for sound bites such as Bite-1, Bite-2, etc. Adding a brief descriptive comment such as Bite 1 Laughs will help. With natural sound you could say Nat 1 Hawk screech.

> If your video clip naming convention uses numbers at the end of each clip name, Premiere will automatically add one to that number when you return to the Logging page. So if you name a clip Home Run-1, when you click Log In/Out, Premiere stores that clip in the Batch Capture window and then returns to the Logging page and automatically places Home Run-2 in the File Name window.
>
> Nice? Sort of. Turns out you don't necessarily have all the home runs back to back on your tape, so the next clip you log might be Crowd Reacts-3 and you'll have to type that over Home Run-2.

With all other scenes (that is, besides natural sound and sound bites), you can drop the prefixes and just give them consistent yet descriptive names: Goal-3, Crowd React-2 Applause, Hawk Soaring-4, and Interview cutaway-1 reverse.

> Later, just before you make your first edit, you'll organize your clips in file folders (Adobe calls them *bins*). My suggestion is to put each category of clip into a separate folder—natural sound, sound bites, and scenes. Depending on your project's size, you might want to use subcategories for scenes. Using a consistent naming convention will help in other areas. Because you can sort clips alphabetically, you can find all the nat-sound clips, select them all, and easily place them in the Nat-Sound file folder.

Completing the Batch Capture Process

When you enter a filename in the dialog box and click OK, it opens the Batch Capture window. As you move through your tape and select and name additional clips, Premiere adds each scene to that Batch Capture window.

You can log several tapes in this fashion, remembering to give each tape a unique, descriptive name. When you complete logging all your tapes, name and save the Batch Capture list:

1. Select the Batch Capture window by clicking somewhere in this window.
2. Click File, Save.
3. Type in a descriptive name (Soccer Champ-1, for instance) and click Save.

Task: Batch-Capture Your Clips

Now it's time to start the batch capture or automated transfer process:

1. Begin by clicking the little arrow on the upper-right corner of the Batch Capture window to open a fly-out menu and select Handles. Figure 3.15 shows you the simple Capture Handles dialog box.

2. When you did a manual "movie capture," you manually added a header and trailer to your clip. The automated batch capture process does that for you. Type in **90** (90 frames equals three seconds; Premiere will not let you type in more than 100) and click OK.

3. You return to the Batch Capture window. Just as in Figure 3.16, you'll note that all your clips have little diamonds in front of them. Premiere automatically selects all of them for automated transfer. To transfer only some clips, click the check mark in the upper-left corner to deselect all the clips; then click separately on each clip you want to transfer.

4. Click the red record button to start the automated transfer process. You can sit back and admire this slick technology in action or grab the leash and go.

5. When you return, Premiere will have stored the clips in your selected file folder and in the project window in your editing workspace.

FIGURE 3.15

The Capture Handles dialog box lets you specify the number of frames that should pre-cede and follow each transferred clip.

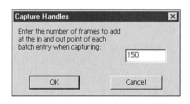

FIGURE 3.16

The Batch Capture window. Premiere will automatically transfer all clips with diamonds in front of them.

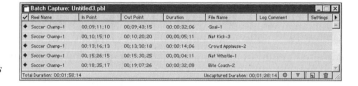

Tackling Manual Analog Movie Capture

If you are using an analog video capture card, the video transfer/capture process is slightly less user friendly.

You'll need to use your card's documentation to set up the capture criteria. Typically you do that when you first open Premiere and refine that later when you open the Project Settings, Capture dialog box.

The drop-down menus will display options with your card's manufacturer listed.

You'll then go through the movie-capture process in a much more hands-on fashion. For starters, the only way you can batch-capture is if your camcorder records industry-standard timecode on the tape and has device control. Most consumer analog camcorders do not do that. If you do have such a camcorder—it's probably a broadcast-quality Beta SP device—then follow the batch-capture process used for DV. If not, you'll manually transfer each clip, one by one.

Make sure your camcorder is turned on and set to VCR/VTR. Press play. If your video card installation and setup went smoothly (see the following sidebar for my setup woes), you should see the video in the Movie Capture window.

3

Using the controls on your camcorder, search for a scene you like, back the tape up a few seconds, press play, and then click the record button on the Movie Capture window. Your capture card converts that analog video signal into a digital format, compresses it, and sends it to the designated file folder on your hard drive. Some capture cards will split the signal into a video-only file and an audio-only file (you easily can sync them up during editing).

When you reach the end of that particular scene, press Esc or click the record button to stop the recording. Premiere will ask you to name the clip, just as it did during DV movie capture. Click OK to return to the Movie Capture window and continue selecting and transferring clips, one at a time.

When you're done, it's time to start editing.

Video Capture Cards Overview

Full-featured video capture cards serve two primary functions: analog video capture and real-time video effects.

The three main contenders on the PC side are Canopus, Matrox, and Pinnacle. Mac users have very few options. Matrox makes the RT Mac, and the only Adobe-approved Mac video capture card listed on the Adobe Web site (http://www.adobe.com/products/premiere/6cards.html) is the Aurora Video Systems Igniter (http://www.auroravideosys.com/).

You can spend several thousand dollars for a high-end, broadcast-quality card from these companies. But the more likely scenario is to buy a mid-priced but still very powerful and feature-rich card for $750 to $1,300. Keep in mind that most of these cards come bundled with full versions of Premiere, which has a street price of $550.

I won't attempt to dissect all the strengths and weaknesses of these cards. They all offer amazing functionality for the price.

Here are three PC cards that offer a similar range of features (with estimated street prices):

- Canopus DV Storm SE Plus, $1,200 (http://www.justedit.com/)
- Matrox RT 2500 Pro Pack, $800 (http://www.matrox.com)
- Pinnacle Pro-ONE, $800 (http://www.pinnaclesys.com)

Of these three market-leading, mid-priced video cards, the Matrox RT 2500 has received the most kudos from users and reviewers. Besides offering standard capture features such as IEEE 1394 as well as composite and S-Video inputs, it is fully integrated with Premiere, ships with its own set of snazzy special effects and transitions (see Figure 3.17), and does real-time rendering and MPEG-2 compression.

One unique strength is its ability to transfer multiple clips from a DV tape without stopping. Most cards stop at clip in-points, rewind to set up for a preroll, and then transfer the clip. The Matrox software grabs clips on-the-fly.

But the oft-repeated mantra for the Matrox RT 2500 is that it's a bear to install and configure. At the very least it requires several reboots simply to get up and running. Matrox graciously loaned me a card to test and use while preparing this book. I wanted to report that my experience with it belied those user-unfriendly configuration stories, but I too experienced the installation blues.

After three days of frustration and several technical support calls I finally gave up. Apparently, the RT 2500 needs so much "bandwidth" it precluded other peripherals from working smoothly on my 1.8 GHz P4. Even after removing all but two hardware cards, it still slowed my system to a crawl. Using Windows Me and a relatively new Intel motherboard apparently exacerbated the problems.

Matrox followed up on these problems by having one of their integrators send me a loaner system with the RT 2500 already installed.

The $2,295 Mina XS comes with a 1.7 GHz P4, XP Pro, two hard drives (100GB total) as well as the RT 2500 and a slew of software. It worked smoothly right out of the box.

It was a pleasure seeing the RT 2500 in action. Its uncountable transitions and effects options far surpass the standard Premiere set. Also, the slick and powerful editing interfaces worked smoothly and logically.

Several gee-whiz tools stood out: Particle effects explode, shatter, and blast apart images; real-time 3D distortions create animated shimmers, waves, bevels, and shower-door effects, and organic wipes use grayscale gradients to transition from one clip to another. The RT 2500 is a powerful tool with an impressive array of editing effects. One other caveat, though: Besides the tedious installation, it takes a dedicated editor willing to spend a lot of time to fully exploit the RT 2500's potential.

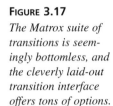

FIGURE 3.17

The Matrox suite of transitions is seemingly bottomless, and the cleverly laid-out transition interface offers tons of options.

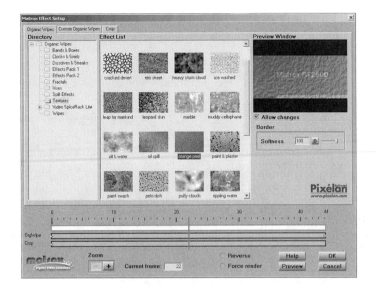

Summary

Premiere is a nonlinear editor (NLE). Adding new segments, rearranging edits, and editing your story out of order all work easily within Premiere. You can add multiple special effects, use numerous transitions, and layer several clips in one segment with no concerns about image quality degradation. Premiere's timeline interface follows industry standards, so experienced NLE users readily can make the shift to this powerful video-editing tool.

One of the great advantages of an NLE is instant access to all video clips. No need for endless fast-forwarding through reels of tape. It's all right there on your hard drive.

If you use DV equipment, getting that video into your computer is almost mindlessly simple. Analog tapes can be a bit more tedious and labor intensive, but the process is still a whole lot more user friendly and flexible than editing only with videotape.

Workshop

Review the questions and answers below to try to sharpen your Premiere video-transfer skills. And take a few moments to tackle my short quiz.

Q&A

Q I get a report that there were "dropped frames" during the batch capture. What's going on?

A If you experience dropped frames, you may have too many programs running in the background that are interfering with video capture. In Windows, press Ctrl+Alt+Del to see a list of software operating in the background. If it's more than three or four (Explorer and Systray are usually all you really need), you might disable some of them. Use care here. Your system may have some unique characteristics. If you're capturing analog video, you may be using an outdated codec or one with too high a data rate.

Q When I open the Movie Capture window I don't see an image in the video monitor and I can't control my DV camcorder.

A This could be one of several things: Your camcorder is not turned on (if you're using a battery, it might be in sleep mode), you have it in Camera mode instead of VCR/VTR, or you have not inserted your tape.

Quiz

1. In the movie-capture process, you have to manually add a header and trailer to each clip to ensure you have enough footage to do transitions. How do you automate that in batch capture?

2. If you'd rather use A/B editing (despite my sage advice), you may still work with two monitors— Source and Program. How do you change your A/B workspace from a single monitor to two monitors?

3. Why should you create a project video clip file folder on a drive other than the one your operating system is on?

Quiz Answers

1. Put some number of frames in the Capture Handles dialog box. Access that feature by opening the Batch Capture window, clicking the handy little arrow in the upper-right corner of that window to open a fly-out menu, and selecting Handles. Then type in the number of frames you want added before the in-point and after the out-point (30 frames equals one second).

2. The easy route: Click the little double-monitor icon above the monitor (the one on the left, not the one on the right; it's a special editing tool). Alternatively, click that handy little arrow in the monitor's upper-right corner to open a fly-out menu and then select Single View.

3. Your operating system regularly accesses its hard drive, even when your computer is otherwise idle. If that happens while you are viewing or transferring a clip, this may interrupt the flow. You also should install Premiere on a drive other than the one you're using for your video clips.

3

HOUR 4

Using the Storyboard and Timeline for Cuts-only Editing

Finally. Storytelling using your clips and Premiere. The easiest way to begin editing with Premiere is simply to lay down a series of video clips with no narration or music. That's the focus of this hour.

Premiere lets you either slip gradually into nonlinear editing or dive in head-first. I'll introduce you to both approaches. I'll show you how to use Premiere's storyboard to put your clips in a logical sequence. Its sequentially arranged thumbnail images of each segment of your video can simplify the editing process--for some projects. There you'll tighten your production by trimming your clips.

Then we'll move to the video editor's best friend--the timeline--a more practical and useful editing method. We'll focus on the standard news-story approach to editing--cuts-only. I'll toss in some useful and effective editing technique tips as well.

First, though, we'll do a little housework--putting your assets in their proper "bins."

The highlights of this hour include the following:

- Organizing your clips in bins
- Using the storyboard to build a "rough cut" of your video and trim individual clips
- Using the timeline to make a cuts-only project
- Trimming, rearranging, inserting, and removing clips from the timeline
- Adding a professional touch to your project with standard editing techniques such as matching edits, wide/tight shots, and cutaways

Managing Your Assets

Open Premiere to your workspace. If you just finished transferring clips to your "scratch disk," they should show up in your workspace's Project window.

But you may have shut down Premiere without saving your project and have just reopened it to find a Project window staring blankly at you--just as it's doing in Figure 4.1. Not to worry.

FIGURE 4.1

An empty Project window. Fill it up by right-clicking inside it and selecting Import, File.

The Project window is simply a means to help you organize and access your "assets"--video clips, audio cuts, and graphics. The Project folder is basically just a collection of links. Only the names of your assets will reside in the Project window. The files themselves--the video clips and so on--remain in their scratch disk file folder(s).

It's a good thing that the Project window contains only links and not actual asset files. It saves disk space by not copying assets to a new location. This means you can have multiple projects access the same assets without duplicating them. It also means you can delete a project file without mistakenly deleting your precious video clips.

Even when you trim a clip, the original clip remains untouched. Premiere doesn't lop off the unwanted sections, it merely records the data that *describes* how you trimmed the clip. Premiere is nondestructive.

I'll assume you need to gather your assets. As usual with Premiere you have several ways to do that. Here's the one I like. Right-click anywhere within the white area of the Project window (except for the little monitor in the upper-left corner). Figure 4.2 shows you how this action opens one of several right-click-accessible menus in Premiere.

FIGURE 4.2

Premiere's right-click menus provide a convenient way to perform many functions. Use the Project window's right-click menu to import your clips to a new project.

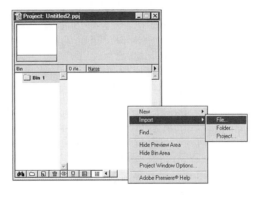

Right-click menus are accessible in at least three other currently open locations: the timeline, the monitor, and individual video clips. Give the timeline and monitor each a right-click trial run (if you have any clips in the Project window, right-click a clip icon). You'll see that the right-click menus nearly match the little fly-out menus accessible using those handy little arrows in the windows' upper-right corners.

Unfortunately, they aren't exact menu matches. For instance, the handy little arrow fly-out menu in the Project window inexplicably does not display that window's most important command--in this case, Import. And if you right-click in the gray area or within the little Project window monitor, you can access only a couple options.

Select Import, File and then locate your scratch disk. Once there, select whichever clips you want to use in this project. You can Ctrl-click (Windows) or Shift-click (Mac) file-names one-at-a-time to select more than one clip.

> You can import a plethora of file types. Just about any kind of video or graphics file format supported in Windows or on the Mac will work in Premiere.

Now that you've selected your files, you'd think you could just drag and drop them to your Project window, but Premiere won't let you do that. Instead you click the oddly named "Open" button, which *closes* the Import window, sends the selected filenames to the Project window in the editing workspace, and returns you there.

> Double-click in any empty area of the Project window to import files only (this won't let you import a folder full of clips).

Take a look at your assets. Figure 4.3 is representative of what you might see. The icons tell a story:

- A film strip icon indicates video with no sound.
- A film strip with a speaker icon indicates video with sound.
- A speaker icon indicates an audio clip.
- A page icon indicates a still image.

FIGURE 4.3

The Project window filled with clips. The icons visually charac-terize each clip's file type.

Play around with the Project window a bit. Just as I did in Figure 4.4, drag the window's right side to your workspace border. Turns out there's a lot of information associated with each listing. You can sort on each column's field by clicking that column header. Clicking Name alphabetizes your clips, and clicking Media Type groups them by, well, media type. Note that Video Info shows their resolution.

FIGURE 4.4

Expanding the Project window reveals more information about your clips.

Right-click a blank space within the Project window and select Project Window Options (if you right-click a clip you'll get a clip menu). Figure 4.5 shows a collection of check marks that indicate what columns will show up in the window you just stretched to the right.

The drop-down list lets you change the appearance of the clips in the Project window from the default List View to Thumbnail View or Icon View.

FIGURE 4.5

You access the Project Window Options dialog box by right-clicking within the Project window. This sets what will display in the expanded Project window.

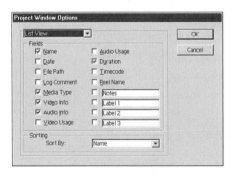

Thumbnail View displays the first image of a video or graphic along with its name and resolution. Icon does something similar but is more an unordered collection of thumbnails on a page than an ordered list.

> As with all things Premiere, surprise, there are other ways to switch among the various views. Check out the little icons at the bottom of the Project window. Let your cursor hover over each one. A tooltip will pop up telling you the button's function. The three toward the lower-right side will display Icon, Thumbnail, and List View, going left to right. You can scroll right-to-left through the clip list by dragging the scroll button in the lower-right corner.

I prefer the list approach. It has more readily available information and consumes less processor power than graphics-oriented listings.

Playing Your Clips

Now for a little fun. You easily can play any of your clips and view your graphics. Right-click a clip icon (if you right-click the clip filename, nothing will happen). This does two things: It places the clip's first frame in the little Project window monitor and opens a menu. As you can see in Figure 4.6, that menu offers a slew of choices. What you want to try out are Open in Clip Window and Open in Source Monitor.

FIGURE 4.6

The clip right-click menu gives you numerous options. For our purposes, try Open in Clip Window and Open in Source Monitor.

Open in Clip Window puts your clip in its own TV screen. The higher the resolution of your clip, the larger the screen. You can play it using the standard VCR buttons at the bottom of the screen.

Open in Source Monitor places the clip in the left monitor screen. Some editors call this the *preview screen*. As with the Clip window, you can use the VCR controls to view your clip.

In both the Clip window and the Source Monitor, you may notice some extra buttons in the lower-right corner that don't fit the standard VCR control style. I've highlighted them in Figure 4.7. These buttons are trimming and editing tools. I'll cover them in detail later.

FIGURE 4.7
The Clip window has standard VCR buttons as well as some editing tools.

4

You also can play a clip in the little monitor in the Project window. Clicking the little box in the lower-right corner replaces the menu thumbnail image (typically the first frame of video) with the selected frame (see Figure 4.8). One reason to select a new thumbnail is to make the video clip icon more representative of its contents--the first frame may be solid black, so the default thumbnail is black.

FIGURE 4.8
Use the little box in the Project Monitor to select a new thumbnail image.

Organizing Your Clips

If you want to place your clips in separate folders, now's the time. The purpose here is to avoid clutter and let you find clips faster. Typically creating three or four bins should be enough to accomplish that.

First, change the current default Bin 1 name to something more descriptive, such as Soccer. Right-click Bin 1 and select Rename Bin or click the bin name twice, slowly, and type in a new name.

Figure 4.9 shows you how to create a new bin—to store all your nat-sound clip names for instance. Right-click in the white area in the Project window and select New Bin (or click the little folder icon at the bottom of the Project window). Type in a name and click OK.

Now, click the Name heading at the top of the file column to alphabetize your clips. Select the clip names you want to place in the new folder. Ctrl-click (Windows) or Shift-click (Mac OS) one icon at a time to create a group of scattered filenames. Drag and drop the clip(s) to your new folder. Create as many new bins and relocate as many clip names as suits your project planning.

FIGURE 4.9

To create a new bin, use the Project window's right-click menu or the New Bin icon.

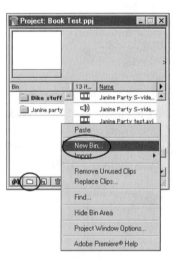

Creating Your First Project Using the Storyboard

Few video editors rely on the storyboard. It's more a bridge to editing than a true productivity tool. Like A/B editing, it got its start in film. It's still in heavy use today as a *pre*-production tool. Directors call on artists to sketch out scenes to help visualize story flow and camera angles. I've seen animated feature film storyboards (bulletin boards) that filled several conference rooms.

In Premiere its primary function is as a video *post*-production tool. You can display video clip thumbnails in the storyboard to help structure the flow of your production. It can come in handy by revealing gaps in your story--places that need fleshing out with more video or graphics. It's also a way to note redundancy. But for most folks it serves solely as a one-time introduction to nonlinear editing. Use it once and move on.

So here we go.

Click File, New, Storyboard. This opens a small empty, nondescript window like the one shown in Figure 4.10.

FIGURE 4.10

An empty Storyboard window.

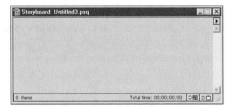

Select several clips from your bin(s) and drag and drop them to the Storyboard window. Voila--thumbnail images pop-up in an orderly fashion. Take a close look at your project or Figure 4.11. Premiere numbers the thumbnails sequentially, places arrows between them showing the story flow, places an × in a circle to indicate the final clip, labels each image with its filename and duration, and places the little descriptive icon in the graphic, noting the type of asset.

FIGURE 4.11

A storyboard filled with clip thumbnails and captions. The arrows signify story flow.

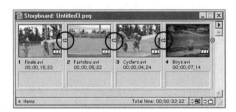

If you don't see all that caption information it's because your thumbnail icons are set too small. Right-click in the window or use that handy arrow in the upper-right corner of the window to access the Storyboard Window Options. As you can see in Figure 4.12, "options" is a misnomer. It's actually just one option: Icon Size. The larger the icon, the more information about the associated file will be displayed in the storyboard.

FIGURE 4.12

You have only one option in the Storyboard Window "Options" interface-- Icon Size.

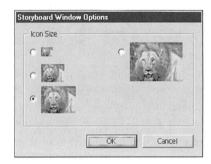

The thumbnail images default to the first frame of video for each file. As I mentioned earlier, you can set a new thumbnail image by playing the clip in the little Project window monitor and clicking the little box in the lower-right corner when you see a more representative image. If you change that image after you've placed the filename in the storyboard, Premiere will not change the thumbnail image in the storyboard. You can delete that file-name and drag it back in from its bin, and the new thumbnail will appear.

Now you can look over the storyboard and do two things: rearrange and delete clips. Remember, you're just deleting the filename from the storyboard. The file itself remains on your hard drive, and the filename remains in its Project window bin.

To rearrange clips, simply drag a clip to its new location. If you move the clip some-where earlier in the story--that is, to a lower sequential number--drag it to the clip you want it to precede. If you move a clip to later in the story--to a higher number--drag it to the clip you want it to follow.

To delete a clip, highlight it and press Delete. As with any file-management process, you also can Ctrl-click (Windows) and Shift-click (Mac OS) to select multiple clips, one at a time, and then delete them all at once.

As a further demonstration of the limited use of the storyboard, your only other option *within* the Storyboard window at this point is to change the speed of each individual clip--have a clip play in slow motion, for example. To do that, right-click a clip, select Speed, and change the percentage. A higher percentage speeds up the clip. 200 percent doubles the speed, thereby cutting the clip's time by half. 50 percent slows the clip down while doubling its length. It's a cool effect, but you don't need the storyboard to do it.

It would be nice if you could trim clips directly within the storyboard. You can't. What you can do is double-click a thumbnail and it'll pop up in the Source Monitor window. You *can* trim it there.

Double-click a clip you'd like to slim down. The Source Monitor window pops up over the storyboard with your clip's first frame on display (you also simply can drag your selected clip from the storyboard to the Source Monitor window).

This is where those extra icons in the Source window's lower-right corner come in handy. In Figure 4.13 I've circled two of them plus two others on the slider bar that you'll use to trim your clips.

FIGURE 4.13

You can trim your storyboard clips in the Source Monitor window using the two sets of in- and out-markers.

If you want to cut a little off the top, you can drag the little blue triangle--the Set Location slider--to an appropriate in-point. Then click the left bracket ({) to set the in-point. You can also drag the in-point bracket within the slider bar to an in-point as well. If you want to cut some off the tail, do the same either by moving the blue Set Location slider and clicking the out-point bracket (}) or by dragging the slider bar out-point } to your new out-point.

If you have the Storyboard window open, you may notice two things that I've highlighted in Figure 4.14: The clip duration in the storyboard thumbnail caption changes to reflect the newly trimmed time, and the total time for your piece (in the lower-right corner of the storyboard) changes.

Feel free to trim down as many of your clips as you like (you always can adjust those in- and out-points later in the timeline).

Once you're satisfied that your clips are in the right sequence, that you've weeded out the redundancies and trimmed the fat, it's time to save your storyboard and send your project to the timeline for additional editing.

FIGURE 4.14

*As you trim your clip
in the Source Monitor
window, your changed
clip time also shows
up in the storyboard
clip caption.*

You save your storyboard as a convenience. You may need to use all of it or segments of
it later. Follow these steps:

1. Simply click somewhere in the storyboard to select it.

2. Click File, Save. Premiere should default to your scratch disk file for a save location.

3. Type in a name and click Save.

Now you're going to move your storyboard clips to the timeline:

1. Click the Automate to Timeline button in the lower-right corner of the storyboard. I
   highlighted it in Figure 4.15 (the other icon lets you "export" the clips to video-
   tape--more on that in Hour 19, "Exporting Premiere Frames, Clips, and Projects:
   Part 1").

2. In the newly opened Automate to Timeline dialog box, shown in Figure 4.16, you
   face several options. Most of the default settings will work fine:

   Contents—You're sending the entire contents of the storyboard to the timeline as
   opposed to selected clips.

   Placement—You'll place your clips sequentially on the timeline as opposed to at
   unnumbered markers (something we haven't covered anyway).

   Insert At—You want your project to start at the beginning of the timeline as opposed
   to at an edit point.

Clip Overlap—Here's where I'd suggest you deviate from the defaults. Overlaps presume you are using A/B editing and that you will put a transition such as a cross-dissolve between each clip. Neither applies. I will mention, more than once, that transitions (and special effects) are overused and distracting, so fewer is better. Set Clip Overlap to zero.

Use Default Transition—Because you will opt for no transitions, uncheck this box.

3. Click OK and close the storyboard. This places your clips on the timeline.

FIGURE 4.15

The Automate to Timeline button will place your storyboard clips in sequential order on the timeline.

FIGURE 4.16

The Automate to Timeline default settings should work fine. Change only Clip Overlap to zero and uncheck Use Default Transition.

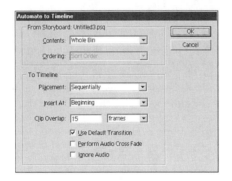

Taking a Timeline Tour

The timeline is the heart and soul of Premiere. Everything you do in Premiere relies on the timeline. Premiere records every editing decision you make here, and your output emanates from it.

The first thing you'll notice is your ordered clips residing on Video Track 1 with their audio (in this case, natural sound) on Audio Track 1. It should look a lot like Figure 4.17. The name of each clip appears right after each edit point.

Depending on the length of your project you probably see only a few of the clips. Expand the time displayed in the timeline by pressing the hyphen (-) key (the one at the top of your keyboard, not the key on the numeric keypad) as many times as you need to display all the clips in your project. Conversely, you reduce the time displayed by pressing the equal sign (=) key (the "+" is an uppercase "=" but you don't need to use the Shift key).

If you have a large project, this is also a good time to look at the Navigator palette. Simply click its tab to open that window. You can navigate to other parts of your project by moving the Navigator's large green rectangle.

FIGURE 4.17

The timeline, immediately after completing the Automate to Timeline process.

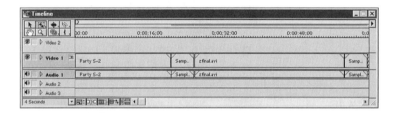

Take a look at your masterpiece in action. Press the spacebar and Premiere automatically jumps to the start of the timeline and plays whatever it finds there. It'll display your video in the program screen in the Monitor window. You can stop it by pressing the spacebar again. You also can use the VCR button controls in the Program Monitor.

You quickly can "scrub" through your project using the edit line and time ruler. I've highlighted them together in Figure 4.18. Click that time ruler and the edit line marker will jump to that point. Now drag the marker left and right and watch as you "scrub" through your piece.

FIGURE 4.18

The Timeline window's edit line marker. Click the time ruler to move it to that point and then "scrub" through your clips by dragging it left or right.

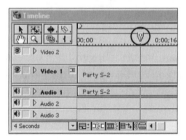

You gave the timeline a bit of a test drive in Hour 2, "Premiere Setup," when you switched from A/B to single-track editing. Now I'd like you take a closer look.

In a departure from standard Premiere how-to books, I think the best way to learn about using the timeline is to experiment with it a bit. When I first learned to use Premiere by reading how-to books, their narrow, specific, step-by-step explanations kept me from seeing the big picture. I think the way around that is for you to take Premiere's timeline for a test drive by doing a few straightforward edits.

And don't worry. There's really no way you can mess up your storyboard handiwork. Premiere is fairly forgiving. If you do something that looks wrong, you always can click Edit, Undo to fix it. Do several things "wrong" and you can use the History window to move back as many steps as you like. And if you totally botch things up, you always can reopen your saved storyboard (click File, Open Recent File and select your storyboard) and then automate it to the timeline again.

Manipulating Clips in the Timeline

One of the beauties of nonlinear editors is how easy it is to add clips anywhere in the project, move them around, remove them altogether, or change their lengths. Here's how you do all that.

4

Moving a Clip

Make sure your cursor icon is a little arrow (the Selection tool). If not, move your cursor to the upper-left corner of the timeline and click the arrow button (see Figure 4.19). You'll use this frequently enough such that you might as well learn the keyboard short-cut--press the V key to change your cursor to the Selection tool (note that the Timeline must be highlighted as the active window for this keyboard shortcut to work).

FIGURE 4.19
The ubiquitous and helpful Selection tool.

Now, grab a clip you want to move, drag it to a new location, either between two clips or at the beginning or end of your piece, and then drop it. The cursor turns to a hand and has to be over an edit point to make the move. You'll know that you can drop the clip at a specific location because you'll see the left part of the next clip turn blue. Releasing your mouse button will insert your clip at that edit point and shove the rest of the project to the right, increasing its overall length. That also leaves a gap where your clip used to be. We'll deal with that later.

Adding a Clip to Your Project

No matter how carefully you selected clips for your storyboard, you may choose to add a clip to your timeline later. Easy. Select a clip from one of your bins, drag it to an edit point, and drop it. It'll position itself in front of that edit point, and the rest of your project will slide to the right.

Removing a Clip

Select a clip by clicking it and pressing Delete. Gone. There's that gray gap again. We'll fix that later. If you want your clip back, select Edit, Undo.

As a reminder, you can undo *all* these edits. Clicking Edit, Undo will back up one step. Repeating that will take you back more steps. Clicking the History tab in the Navigator window will display a list of all recent edits. Scrolling up that list and selecting Automate to Timeline will take you back to the beginning of this project.

Changing a Clip's Length

Note that as you move your Selection tool across a clip, it changes shape to a left or right red square bracket--either "[" or "]". This little tool lets you change the length of a clip.

Move the bracket to the beginning of a clip, directly after the edit point. Notice that the bracket faces right. If you click and drag it to the right you will trim the beginning of that clip. You can look for an appropriate trim edit point by watching the Program Monitor screen. Release the mouse and your clip shrinks, leaving a gap where the trimmed footage used to be.

To trim the end of a clip, do the same thing except make sure the bracket faces left, into the clip. Then drag it to the left and release when you reach an appropriate edit point.

Premiere has a tremendously useful attribute called "Snap to Edges." It's a default setting, and in only a few instances will you want to deselect it. Snap to Edges means that as you drag a clip toward another clip, it'll jump to the edge of the clip to make a clean, unbroken edit. With Snap to Edges turned off you'd have to slide the new clip very carefully next to the other clip to ensure there is no gap.

It's also useful when making precise edits. Using the Selection tool to trim a clip is a bit inexact. You *can* make it frame specific. Locate the specific frame you want to edit to by scrubbing through your program to its approximate location and then use the Frame Forward buttons in the Program Monitor window to move to the specific frame. That places the edit line marker right at that frame on the clip in the timeline. Use the Selection tool and drag the edge of the clip toward the edit line marker. As it gets near it, it will "snap" to the marker, and you'll have made a frame-specific edit.

You can use this technique in all sorts of circumstances, including with the Ripple Edit tool.

Closing the Gaps

By now you may have left a few gray gaps in your production. Removing them and closing the gaps is a snap. Right-click a gap and select Ripple Delete (it's at the top of the pop-up menu because it's a very useful and frequently used tool). Ripple Delete fills the gap by sliding all the material after the gap to the left. Do this for all the gaps, and your production will play back smoothly.

Sometimes Premiere can be confounding. You'll drag a clip to an edit point and Premiere won't let you insert it. There may be a reason, but Premiere offers no explanation. It simply fails to cooperate. Sometimes you'll attempt to do a Ripple Delete and Premiere will "bing" and do nothing. Again, for no apparent reason. That is one reason why I like the idea of experimenting. If one means to accomplish a task does not work, try another route. If you can't use Ripple Delete, then use the Track Select tool (discussed later) to highlight all the clips to the right of the gray gap and drag them to the left to fill the hole.

4

Using the Ripple Edit Tool

One way to avoid creating some of those gray gaps is to use the Ripple Edit tool. It's one of the dozen or so editing tools in the toolbox in the upper-left corner of the timeline. I've highlighted the Ripple Edit tool in Figure 4.20. To access it, click the third icon from the left in the top row. That opens a little fly-out menu. If the Ripple Edit tool is not already highlighted, click it (it's the third icon in this group of five icons).

You use the Ripple Edit tool much like the Selection tool (its icon is sort of like a fat Selection tool bracket icon). Position it at the beginning or end of a clip you want to shorten and then slide it accordingly. Once you find the point where you want to make your edit, release the mouse button. The Ripple Edit tool shortens the clip and slides everything over to the left to close the gap.

FIGURE **4.20**

*The Ripple Edit tool.
Using it saves you the
extra step of doing
Ripple Deletes on gaps
in your timeline.*

Using the Other Editing Tools

Within the confines of those eight fly-out icon menus in the toolbox are several useful tools. These are noted in Table 4.1. I'll cover some in a moment, and the rest I'll save for other hours.

TABLE 4.1   Timeline Editing Tools

Tool Type	Icon	Tool Name	Function
		Selection tool	Multipurpose, all-around aide.
Select tools		Range Select tool	Discussed later.
		Block Select tool	Used to create a "virtual" clip. See Hour 16.
		Track Select tool	Discussed later.
		Multitrack Select tool	Discussed later.
Edit tools		Rolling Edit tool	See Hour 9.
		Ripple Edit tool	Already discussed.
	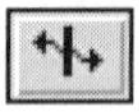	Rate Stretch tool	See Hour 9.
		Slip tool	See Hour 9.
		Slide tool	See Hour 9.
Cutting tools		Razor tool	Discussed later.
		Multiple Razor tool	Discussed later.

TABLE 4.1   Timeline Editing Tools

Tool Type	Icon	Tool Name	Function
		Fade Scissors tool	Discussed later.
		Hand tool	Discussed later.
		Zoom tool	Discussed later.
		Link/Unlink tool	See Hour 7.
In- & out-point		In-point tool	Discussed later.
		Out-point tool	Discussed later.

Select Tools

Not to be confused with the Selection tool, three of these tools let you select a group of clips. Once they're selected, you can slide them, delete them, cut/paste them, or copy/paste them.

- The Range Select tool lets you drag and drop a box over any number of clips on any adjacent tracks. The box selects any part of a clip inside it.
- The Track Select tool grabs clips on only one track. You can Shift-click to select other tracks.
- The Multitrack Select tool selects all tracks at once.

Block Select Tool

The Block Select tool has a completely different function than its three siblings. In Hour 16, " Tips, Tricks, and Techniques: Part 1," I'll show you how it creates "virtual clips."

Edit Tools

I've explained the Ripple Edit tool. I'll cover the other four in Hour 9. One you might experiment with now is the Rate Range tool. It lets you stretch or compress a clip and in the process slow it down or speed it up.

Cutting Tools

Razor and Multiple Razor slice a clip or clips in two. These tools have multiple uses, and I'll cover them in several chapters. The Fade Scissors tool has limited functionality (I

4

don't use it at all). It places two adjacent "handles" on audio and video "rubberbands." I'll introduce rubberbands in Hour 7, "Adding Audio."

Hand Tool

A limited-use tool, the Hand tool is used to move the entire timeline by grabbing a clip and sliding it to one side. It works the same as moving the scrollbar at the bottom of the Timeline window.

Zoom Tool

When you want to see a set of clips in greater detail, click and drag the Zoom tool around those clips. That decreases the time displayed in the timeline, thereby increasing the detail of the current view. Simply clicking the Zoom tool anywhere in the timeline is like pressing the =/+ key.

Link/Unlink Tool

This tool provides a means to link or unlink a video clip with an audio clip. By default, all your video clips have their nat-sound audio linked to them. There are times, however, when you'll want to unlink that audio to make certain kinds of edits. I'll explain more in Hour 7.

In- and Out-Point Tools

These are limited-use tools. Instead of dragging the edge of a clip to trim it, you can use these tools.

Adding a Professional Touch to Your Project

One reason for using the video shooting tips in Hour 1, "Camcorder and Shooting Tips," is to open more creative opportunities during editing. Right now you're doing fundamental, simplified editing, but trying out some standard professional editing techniques now will help as we move to more complex editing later.

Using Establishing Shots

Do you have establishing shots? You need them to let viewers know where they are. Try to place establishing shots near the beginning of any new setting or location.

Using Matching Shots

If you shot any repetitive action, look for matching shots. You might have a wide shot of someone typing at her computer and a tight shot of that person's hands on the keyboard. Edit them in order and make sure you avoid jump-cuts. The person in the wide shot may take her hands off the keyboard for a moment. If the tight shot is of her hands *on* the keyboard, make sure you trim the wide shot to the point where the person still has her hands on the keyboard.

Using Wide and Tight Shots

This adds interest. You might have a wide shot of a football game with the quarterback barking out signals. The next edit could be a tight shot of his face. You could have shot these two clips during two different plays, but by editing them back to back, it appears to be one play.

Sequences

This is a great way to build interest. The fish shops at Seattle's Pike Place Market provide a nonstop sideshow full of repetitive action. Most videographers would opt for a medium shot or two. Instead, put together a sequence of a tight shot of hands grabbing a fish from the display case, a medium shot from behind the shopkeeper as he tosses the fish to an employee, that employee catching the fish and placing it on a scale, and so on. Look for sequences like that in your raw video. Build your sequence well by using tight and wide shots and matching shots.

Cutaways

Avoid putting two very similar shots together. Two wide shots of the same soccer field for instance. Instead, between the two wide shots edit in a cutaway--a crowd shot, a parent shouting encouragement, or the scoreboard--to avoid creating a viewer disconnect. Same holds true for interviews. If you "butt together" two bites from the same interviewee, put a cutaway between them. A hand shot or a reverse cutaway of the interviewer.

> When using cutaways, usually you lay only video over the edited sound. But the techniques in this hour don't cover that. Using what you've learned here, if you insert a cutaway between two sound bites together, you'll have a silent gap where you want a continuous sound bite. Placing only video over two adjacent sound bites requires some specialized editing that I'll explain in Hour 7.

Finally, at any point in your production you can save your project. Select File, Save or Save As and select a location and filename. You always can save it under different names if you do any experimentation and want to try something else later.

Summary

Premiere lets you place your video clips in a storyboard, rearrange them into a logical order, and trim them to a manageable size. Then, with a click of a button you can transfer them to your timeline, the heart of Premiere's editing workspace. There you can trim some more, move them around, insert and remove clips, plus use some professional editing techniques to enhance your project.

Workshop

Review the questions and answers in this section to try to sharpen your Premiere timeline editing skills. Also, take a few moments to tackle my short quiz and the exercises.

Q&A

Q The storyboard is fine as an introduction to nonlinear editing, but I want to skip it and work directly on the timeline. How can I do this?

A This is the right approach. Instead of opening a new storyboard, just drag clips from your Project window and drop them on the timeline. Drop them all on the Video 1 track. You can select a number of clips at once and drag them all to the timeline. In that case, they'll appear in the same order they appeared in the Project bin.

Q I added some QuickTime multimedia files to my project. When I play them in the Source window they look fine, but when I add them to the timeline and play them in the Program window they look squashed. What's up?

A The QuickTime files you added have a different "aspect ratio." For instance, the Sample.mov file that comes with QuickTime has a 2.4:3 aspect ratio instead of the NTSC standard of 4:3. Sample.mov is tall and narrow instead of short and wide. But Premiere wants to display all clips in full screen, so it stretches and squashes your QuickTime clips to fit. There's a simple fix. For any clip with an aspect ratio other than 4:3 that you want to maintain, drag the clip to the timeline, right-click it, and select Video Options, Maintain Aspect Ratio.

Quiz

1. You set up the Project window to display thumbnails. But one thumbnail is black. Why? What can you do about it?

2. You've created a storyboard but several clips are obviously too long. How do you trim that excess baggage?

3. How do you trim a clip in the timeline without creating a gray gap?

Quiz Answers

1. It's black because the first frame of that clip is black. The thumbnail defaults to the first frame. To change the thumbnail image, select the clip, play it in the little Project Monitor window and when you see an image that represents the clip, click the little box in the lower-right corner. That sets a new thumbnail image. It should show up right away in the Project Bin window.

2. Double-click each extra-long clip to open it in the Source Monitor. Play it or drag the Set Location slider to where you want the edited clip to start. Click the left in-point bracket ({). Then do the same for the out-point. Notice that your clip's new time shows up in its storyboard thumbnail caption.

3. Use the Ripple Edit tool. You'll find it in the Timeline window's toolbox. It's the fat vertical line with arrows sticking out both sides. Move it to the end of the clip you want to shorten. Drag it to the new edit point and release. The clip will shrink and the rest of the project automatically will fill the gap.

Exercises

1. Take the right-click menu for a test drive (you've already used this technique to use Ripple Delete). Right-click a clip in the timeline and check out the various options. Video Option, Motion and Frame Hold are both excellent editing tools that I'll cover later--as are Duration and Speed. Try them out on some clips.

2. Shoot and edit a sequence. Grab your camcorder and head out looking not for a subject but rather for a sequence. For example, go to a public place such as a park and tape someone tossing a ball to his dog. Get wide and tight shots and various angles (oh, and get permission). Then transfer that video and build a sequence. This is a real test of editing skill because it involves editing techniques such as wide/tight and matching shots.

3. Open the Navigator window. Drag the rectangle around and see how it moves the timeline back and forth. Note the color scheme and how it matches the video and audio clips. I'll explain the meaning of those different colors in Hour 9. Click the little hill icons at the bottom to adjust the scale of the Navigator window.

4

HOUR 5

Adding Transitions: From Dissolves to Zooms

This is one of the principal reasons you bought Premiere. It does transitions. With a simple drag and drop, voila, you've turned a cut edit into a wipe—or a 3D spinning cube or a curtain opening to a new scene or a page peeling back—you name it.

Cuts-only edits can be abrupt. Transitions ease the change from one scene to the next. The most common is the dissolve—one scene fades as the next comes into view.

Premiere offers dozens of transitions. Most have very limited usefulness. They may look wildly entertaining but frequently can detract from your finished product rather than enhance it. First-time editors tend to go overboard when it comes to transitions—throwing in gratuitous tumbling boxes, swirling scenes, and sliding bars. I'll cover the best Premiere has to offer and explain when to use them.

The highlights of this hour include the following:

- A brief history of video editing
- When to use transitions
- Experimenting with transitions
- Testing transitions with multiple options
- Resolving transition technical issues
- Adding transitions to your project
- Editing tips from an expert

Editing: From Engineers to Artists

Premiere and other nonlinear editors like it have opened new opportunities. Anyone with a PC, even a laptop, now can do broadcast-quality video editing. What was once reserved for high-end video production studios and well-equipped TV stations, now has reached the mass market (at least those willing to spend $2,000 for software and a DV camcorder).

But just as buying a hammer does not make you an expert house builder, installing Premiere will not make you a stellar editor.

Moving beyond cuts-only editing to transitions means we are upping the ante—a lot. Before joining this higher-stakes game, a little history is in order.

Old-Fashioned Editing

In the early days of TV, engineers did the editing. They had to. They were trained to deal with unruly, bulky, and complex tape machines. They had to monitor things such as color framing, sync timing, and blanking.

Here's how John Crossman, a long-time editor friend of mine, puts it (see the "Expert Editing Tips" sidebar, later in the hour):

> The logic was that the same people who pushed the "record" and "playback" buttons in the tape room should be the ones to run the editing machines. Videotape editing then was considered a very technical job, not an artistic job.

Eventually, microprocessors resolved and automated many of those technical issues, and non-engineering people—folks with an eye for editing—started populating the editing bays.

However, prohibitive costs limited access to those machines. As recently as a few years ago, whenever I created a video that called for some special transitions, I worked "offline" (that is, I used copies of my original master tapes on a lower-priced editing system to create an Edit Decision List). Figure 5.1 shows a Premiere-created example. Then I took my original raw footage and that data file, with all the transition commands built in, to an expensive online facility that automatically (with some manual labor) cranked out a polished product. That process, while slightly more time-consuming than working online from start to finish, saved a ton of money.

FIGURE 5.1

An Edit Decision List created by Premiere.

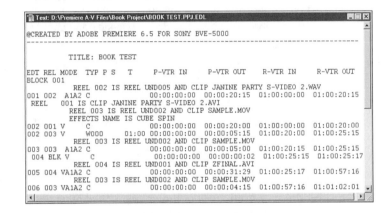

Today the pendulum has swung to the opposite extreme, and you are riding that pendulum. Anyone can work solely online (that is, use the original video footage from start to finish). No longer do video producers need to rely on high-priced production houses. Heck, now you can do it at home.

The purpose is to do it well, and that starts with the judicious use of transitions.

5

Using Transitions with Restraint

Watch some TV news stories. If you see any transitions other than simple straight cut edits, I'd be surprised.

Why? Time *is* a factor. But more and more stations these days have ready access to non-linear editors such as Premiere, and it takes almost no time to add a transition using an NLE.

The principal reason for the dearth of transitions is that they can be distracting. If a TV news editor uses one, it's for a purpose. Typically they take what would have been a jarring edit—such as a major jump cut—and make it more palatable.

An oft-heard newsroom phrase applies: "If you can't solve it, dissolve it."

On the other hand, consider the *Star Wars* movies. Remember all the highly stylized transitions? Obvious, slow wipes for example. George Lucas knows what he's doing. Each of those transitions has a purpose. In general they are reminiscent of old serialized movie and TV shows. Specifically they send a clear message to the audience: Pay attention. We're going to a new setting.

Transitions can add whimsy. Here are a few examples:

- Start on a tight hand shot of someone cutting a deck of cards and make a Swap Slide transition—one image slides to one side and another slides over it—to another card-related shot.
- Take a medium shot of a garage door and use a Wipe Up—one image moves off the top while another replaces it from below—to transition to the next shot of the garage interior.
- Start with a tight shot of a clock (analog, not digital) and use the aptly named Clock Wipe—a line centered on the screen sweeps around to reveal another image—to move to another setting and time.
- With some planning and experimentation, you can videotape someone pushing against a wall while walking in place and use a Push transition to have that person "slide" the old scene out off screen.
- Get that James Bond, through-the-bloody-eye effect using a QuickTime Explode transition.

Transitions can work with your video to add visual interest:

- Take a shot of a car driving through the frame and use a wipe, synced with the speed of the car, to move to the next scene.
- Transition from a shot of driving rain or a waterfall using the Slash Slide transition, in which streaks, like driving rain, slice through an image revealing another image below.
- Use the aptly named Venetian Blinds transition as a great way to move from an interior to an exterior.
- A Page Roll Away transition works well with a piece of parchment.

The possibilities are truly endless. During this hour I'll encourage you to experiment with all that Premiere has to offer.

Adding Some Straightforward Transitions to a Project

Once again, it's time to experiment.

Task: Review the Available Transitions

To review animated examples of Premiere's available transitions, do the following:

1. Open Premiere to your workspace.

2. Grab the Transitions palette and drag it to the upper-left corner of your workspace.

3. If the Transitions palette is not already open, open it by double-clicking its top bar.

4. Click the handy fly-out window arrow and select Expand All Folders.

5. Open that window again and select Animate.

6. Now expand the Transitions palette as much as you can by dragging the lower-right corner down and to the right. If you're working in a 1024×768 or higher resolution window, you'll see every transition Premiere has to offer. Figure 5.2 shows the screen at a lower resolution (1024×768 doesn't translate well to print), but it gives you an idea of what you should see.

7. Click somewhere inside the window and watch all the transition icons give you an idea of how they work.

▲

FIGURE 5.2

Dragging the Transitions palette to its full size is a good way to get an overview of all Premiere has to offer.

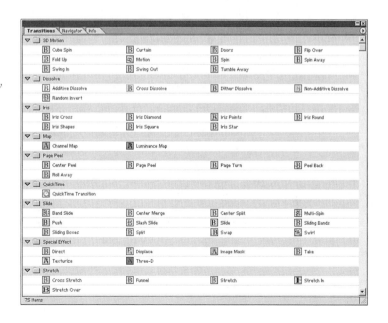

5

Where to begin? It's all a bit mind-boggling. To bring some order to this chaos, I'll show you a simple way to get a more precise idea how each transition works by starting with the most familiar and easiest-to-use transition—the cross-dissolve.

Find the Cross Dissolve icon in the Dissolve section of the Transitions palette and double-click it. As shown in Figure 5.3, this pops up the Cross Dissolve Settings dialog box. Every transition in Premiere has its own Settings dialog box, each with its own set of options. The cross-dissolve has only one option, and you may never use it (see the following note) .

FIGURE 5.3

The Cross Dissolve Settings dialog box for cross-dissolve transitions. This the most frequently used and easiest-to-use transition.

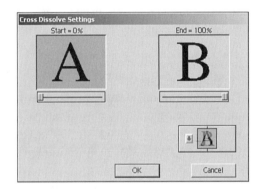

Every transition Settings dialog box in Premiere offers the option to swap the order of the clips within the edit. You do that by clicking the little arrow next to the animated window in the lower-right corner. I've highlighted it in Figure 5.4. The default setting has the arrow pointing down. Pointing to the right would be more intuitive, but the arrow's direction reflects old-school A/B transitions that went from track 1A (higher on the timeline) to track 1B (lower).

Pointing down means the transition will proceed sequentially, as you'd expect—clip A will transition into clip B. If you click the arrow, flipping it up, two things will happen: The animation in the small window will change (B will transition into A), and the A and B clips will swap places in the two larger windows at the top.

This is a useful tool if you place two transitions side by side while using the same clips. In that way, you can transition from one clip to another and then back to the original in one smooth, unbroken sequence.

FIGURE 5.4

The down (default) or up arrow sets the direction of the transition. Clip A to B (default) or B to A.

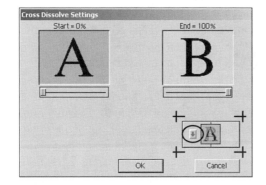

Drag the slider button beneath the A window and watch. That's a cross-dissolve. The A clip fades away while the B clip replaces it.

Taking Additional Transition Options for a Test Drive

I'll have you apply a dissolve to two clips in a few minutes. Before you do that, take a look at a few more transitions that offer some additional options.

Task: Test out the Page Peel Transition

To explore the Page Peel transition, do the following:

1. Cancel out of the Cross Dissolve Settings dialog box.

2. Double-click the Page Peel transition in the Page Peel section. Now, this looks cool. People used to spend big bucks and way too much time to add this to their videos. Now you can do it with a drag and a drop.

3. Drag the slider under window A again. That's how the transition will look.

4. Check out the little, constantly animating window in the lower-right corner. You'll note that a few features are added. Four miniscule triangles (one red and three white) and a tiny button labeled "F." I've highlighted them in Figure 5.5.

5. Click the F button and it changes to R. Note what that does. Instead of clip A peeling away to reveal clip B, clip B rolls over clip A. Although some may quibble with which transition is "forward" and which is "reverse," that's what those two letters stand for. Click the R to turn it back to F.

6. Now click one of the miniscule white triangles. In the "F=Forward" case, this changes the corner where the page curl begins. In the "R=Reverse" case, it's where the curl ends. Experiment with several possibilities.

TASK

5

FIGURE 5.5

Clicking one of the lit-tle triangles around the small window sets the direction of the transition animation. Clicking F or R alters the flow.

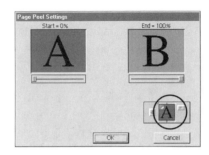

All but a handful of transitions let you switch between Forward and Reverse. Feel free to exit out of Page Peel Settings and take a look at two other transitions in the 3D Motion section at the top of the Transitions palette: Curtain and Fold Up (double-click one, try it out, and then cancel out of it; then double-click on the next one).

I've selected these because they are the only Premiere transitions that have just the Forward/Reverse option:

Curtain—The Forward setting has the A clip open like a curtain to reveal the B clip. The Reverse setting "closes" the curtain over A, revealing B.

Fold Up—The Forward setting has the A clip fold back, like a piece of paper being folded in half over and over, to reveal the B clip. The Reverse setting "unfolds" the paper on top of A, revealing B.

 Although double-clicking a transition icon gives you a quick visual representation of a transition's function, you can also access a written explanation. Merely select a transition in the Transitions palette and then click the Info tab in the Navigator palette. A one-sentence description pops up.

Task: Play with the Border Option

Next up, borders. Most of Premiere's 70+ transitions let you add a border to them. In most cases this helps viewers see that, yep, this is a transition. Premiere lets you adjust the width of the border and its color. Here's one standard example:

1. Cancel out of whatever transition you're working on and then double-click the Wipe transition in the Wipe section.

2. Move the slider under the A window to the right about half way.

3. Slide the Border triangle button to the right and watch as the line in the A window between clip A and clip B gets thicker. It should look like what's shown in Figure 5.6.

4. Click in the black Color box.

5. Click somewhere in the resulting rainbow-like window (the Color Picker) to select a color for the border. Note that you can type in specific color numbers to ensure an exact match with other borders if you want. Click OK.

6. Now you'll see that your border has more personality. Later when you place transitions between video clips you can select a color that matches or contrasts with the transition scenes.

FIGURE 5.6

Using the Border option is one way to make it clear to your audience that "this is a transition."

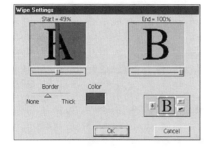

 If you click around the Color Picker long enough, you'll eventually select a color that prompts Premiere to pop up a little yield/exclamation mark sign stating, "Warning: Unsafe NTSC color" (see Figure 5.7). You've selected a color that will not display well on a standard TV set (it'll work fine on your PC's monitor, though). For instance, selecting a highly saturated color value of 250 or more for one color with a low number for one of the other two colors will cause the saturated color to smear on an NTSC monitor. You can fix that by typing in a lower number (249 or less should work) in the offending color's box or clicking around until you find a color Premiere likes.

5

FIGURE 5.7

Selecting a color value of 250 or more may lead to "smearing" on an NTSC monitor, thus leading to the little warning.

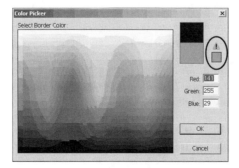

Every transition that offers a border option also has an anti-aliasing option. *Aliasing* is the jagged edge common along sharply defined diagonal lines in computer graphics and TV sets. If you look closely enough at a diagonal line, even in your PC monitor (which has a higher resolution than your TV set), you'll see stair steps. That's aliasing.

To get rid of aliasing, you select, ahem, *Anti*-Aliasing. Premiere's default setting is to disable anti-aliasing. I don't get this. Aliasing looks bad, so the default should be *anti-aliasing*. Nevertheless, on an effect such as a vertical or horizontal wipe, there should be no noticeable aliasing, whether you've opted for anti-aliasing or not. But if you click one of those little white triangles in the corners of the little monitor and switch to a diagonal wipe, you'll probably want to turn on anti-aliasing.

You do that by clicking the little stair-step icon that I've highlighted in Figure 5.8. One click puts anti-aliasing on simmer; two clicks and it's on high. One more click returns it to no anti-aliasing. You get some immediate feedback in the A or B monitor window. The border gets softer with anti-aliasing turned on.

FIGURE 5.8

Clicking the little Anti-Aliasing stair-step icon smoothes out the "jaggies" on diagonal transition lines.

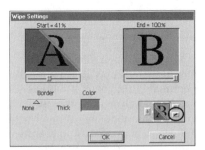

Testing Some Specialized Options

Hang in there for a few more minutes. We're almost ready to apply these transitions to your video clips. Before moving there I want to go over a few other sets of transition options.

A handful of transitions—seven at last count—let you select very specific locations for them to start or end. This can be very cool when you want to "pull" your next scene from a TV screen or a person's eye in the previous scene or "push" the first clip into a drain on the second. Let's look at an example.

Task: Grow a Transition from a Specified Point

To make a transition spawn from a specific point, follow these steps:

1. Double-click Iris Round.

2. Note the little white box in the center of the A window. I've highlighted it in Figure 5.9. That is the starting point for the transition.

3. Move your icon over the white box until it changes to a hand and move the box to some other spot in the window.

4. Move the slider under the A window and watch. The B clip will appear at that point and grow to full screen.

5. Later, when you make transitions using your original clips, you can display those clips in the A and B windows so you can precisely locate the start- or endpoint.

6. You can change the start point to the endpoint simply by changing the F (forward) button to R (reverse) .

FIGURE 5.9

Some transitions let you set the specific start- or endpoint for extra dramatic effect.

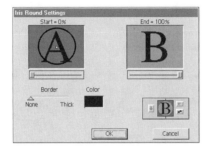

Other Transitions that allow a custom starting or ending point are 3D Motion Tumble Away, Iris Cross, Iris Diamond, Iris Square, Zoom, Zoom Cross, and Zoom Trails.

Task: Set Custom Transition Options

Some transitions offer custom options unique to those specific transitions. For example, the Venetian Blinds transition lets you select the number of blinds; for Random Blocks it's the number of blocks, and for Slash Slide it's the number of slices. Here's how this works:

1. Double-click Pinwheel in the Wipe section.

2. You'll notice it has a Custom button. I've highlighted it in Figure 5.10. Only about 15 transitions have this extra button.

3. Click the Custom button, select a number of wedges (the max is 32; each transition varies), and click OK.

4. Move the slider to see the effect. Note that you can add a color border plus choose Forward or Reverse.

FIGURE 5.10

About 15 Premiere transitions offer special custom settings unique to those individual transitions.

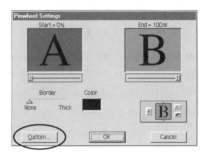

Before moving on I'd suggest trying out some other transitions with special custom options such as Iris Shapes, Band Slide, and Swirl (Slide).

Give the 3D Motion Flip Over transition a test drive. It takes the A clip and spins it like a flat board horizontally or vertically and then reveals the B clip on the "board's" other side. That flipping motion briefly leaves an empty space behind the board. You can change the color of that space and split the "board" into as many as eight slats by opening the Custom dialog box.

I have touched on most of the primary types of transitions but have purposely skipped several. They are specialized transitions that require a little more editing experience to tackle, so I'm saving them for Hour 9, "Advanced Editing Techniques and Workspace Tools," which is a catchall for other editing techniques. There, I'll go over the Image Mask, Gradient Mask, and QuickTime transitions. The latter rivals Premiere's entire set of 70+ transitions, all within one little icon. As an exercise later I'll suggest you do a little experimenting with the QuickTime transition just to get a taste for its depth.

I'll also explain why and how you can string together several transitions.

Resolving Transition Technical Issues

Finally, it's time to use transitions on real video clips. First, however, I want to use the sample clips provided with your copy of Premiere to show you a "gotcha."

Add the sample files to your Project window:

1. Right-click a white area in the Project window to open a menu and select Import, File (or use the double-click shortcut to open the Import window directly).

2. Go to the Premiere file folder. Its default location is C:/Program Files/Adobe/Premiere/Sample Folder.

3. Select the five AVI files and click Open.

4. Drag two of those clips (it doesn't matter which two) one at a time to the Video 1 track on the timeline.

You may notice something about their appearance. They have little gray triangles in their upper-right and upper-left corners. I've highlighted those triangles in Figure 5.11. They mean that the entire original clip is on the timeline. No extra tail or head frames are available in the original clip file to create an overlap for a transition.

FIGURE 5.11

The triangles in the upper corners of the clips indicate there is no extra head or tail material to create a properly overlapped transition.

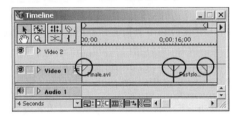

You need overlapping video to make a transition—extra tail material in the A clip and extra head material in the B clip to allow one scene to move into another.

You have at least two ways to remedy this. The first involves the standard means to add a transition to your project—dragging and dropping a transition from the Transition window to the edit point on the timeline. You will do this time and time again. This will be your first crack at it.

Task: Use Freeze Frames to Generate Head and Tail Material for a Transition

▼ TASK

5

To use the freeze-frame technique to create head and tail material for a transition, follow these steps:

1. Open the Transitions palette.

2. Locate the Cross Dissolve transition (actually just about any transition will do).

3. Drag it to the edit point of the two sample clips, make sure it changes color to show it's in the proper position, and then drop it there.

   A dialog box like the one shown in Figure 5.12 pops up, telling you that there are not enough tail and head frames to make a transition. In this case there are none.

4. You have only one option in this case—Repeat Last and First Frames. This option creates a "freeze frame" from the last frame of the A clip and another freeze frame from the first frame of the B clip. Premiere then uses those freeze frames as overlap material. Select OK to accept the default values.

▼

FIGURE 5.12

This dialog box pops up when you place a transition at an edit point and the two clips do not have enough frames to make a smooth overlapping transition.

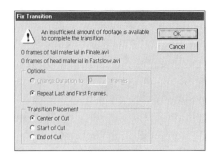

To see how this transition looks using the actual video, follow these steps:

1. Double-click the light-purple transition segment on the timeline (if the segment is not wide enough to locate with the Selection tool, press the =/+ key to expand the scale).

   Up pops the now familiar Cross Dissolve Settings dialog box. This time, as noted in Figure 5.13, it has a new check box: Show Actual Sources.

2. Check that box, and your two clips show up in the two windows.

3. Drag the slider under the A clip box and watch your dissolve in action.

FIGURE 5.13

When you drag a transition to an edit point between two clips on the timeline, a new check box appears—Show Actual Sources.

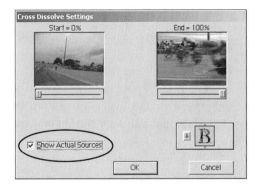

Dragging a slider is not the most elegant means to view your dissolve. At this point, it's sort of a stopgap approach. If you go to the timeline and drag the edit line to the Cross Dissolve transition segment and press the spacebar to play that segment, you will not see the dissolve but rather only a straight cut edit. Premiere needs to "render" that dissolve before it can play back in real time. We'll take care of that later.

On the other hand, if you have a high-end video card such as the Matrox RT 2500, a simple dissolve will play back in real time from the timeline without rendering. Also, if you have a high-end PC with Windows XP or a Mac with OS X, you can use Premiere 6.5's new Software Real-Time Preview.

The second means to resolve clips with no extra tail or head frames is to use the old-fashioned A/B editing style.

Although I don't recommend switching from single-track to A/B editing in the middle of a project, in this case it's a good alternate way to resolve this non-overlap issue.

Task: Use A/B Editing to Create an Overlap for a Transition

To create an overlap for a transition by using A/B editing, follow these steps:

1. Use the fly-out arrow to open the Timeline window's menu.

2. Select A/B Editing. Your timeline should look like the one in Figure 5.14. Note the gray areas I've highlighted. Those are the freeze frames Premiere automatically built to create something like faux overlap frames.

3. Delete the two clips and the Cross Dissolve transition by selecting them one at a time and pressing Delete (or right-clicking them and selecting Cut).

4. Drag and drop one of the sample AVI clips to the Video 1A track.

5. Drag and drop another sample AVI clip to the Video 1B track. You'll notice that you can drag either clip anywhere on those bars—even if they overlap. If they overlap and you move the edit line to them to view them, only the clip in the Video 1A track will display. As with single-track editing, the highest clip in the timeline covers everything below it.

6. Drag the clip in Video 1B so most of it is to the right of the clip in Video 1A. Leave some overlap (a second or so; use the timeline as a reference) as I did in Figure 5.15.

7. Drag the Cross Dissolve transition icon to the Timeline transition line and drop it between the two clips at the overlap point. It automatically sets a length that equals the overlap amount. I added that in Figure 5.15 as well.

8. Double-click the purple Cross Dissolve transition segment to open the Cross Dissolve Settings dialog box.

9. Select Show Actual Sources and drag the slider under the A clip window. This time you will see no freeze frames. The dissolve will look much nicer.

10. Complete this task by closing the Cross Dissolve Settings dialog box and switching back to single-track editing (use the fly-out menu).

▼ TASK

▲

5

FIGURE 5.14

Switching to A/B editing shows how Premiere handles transitions for which there are not enough head or tail frames. The highlighted gray boxes are sets of "freeze" frames.

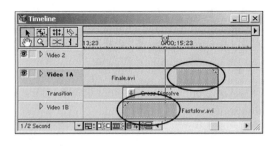

FIGURE 5.15

Starting fresh in A/B mode shows how you can overlap clips to add a transition without forcing Premiere to resort to using "freeze" frames.

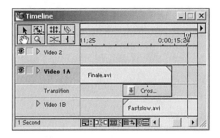

The resulting edit is sort of difficult to decipher in the single-track view. To get a better picture, click the little two-box icon next to the Video 1 track label. It will split the track so you can see the edit in more detail. Unfortunately, this is for display purposes only. You can't make adjustments to this kind of overlap edit in single-track mode, whether in this expanded view or not.

While in the expanded single-track editing view, if you delete the transition by selecting it and pressing Delete, the two clips will jump back to a non-overlapping-style straight cut edit. You may note, as highlighted in Figure 5.16, that those little gray triangles are no longer in the corners of the two clips at the edit point. The reason: When you created the original edit in A/B mode you overlapped the tail and header of each clip. When you removed the transition, that sliced off the overlapping frames, leaving enough tail and header frames available in the original clips to make a transition. If you switch back to the unexpanded single-track mode and drag a transition to the edit point, no warning box will appear. There are enough tail and header frames available to make the transition.

FIGURE 5.16

Using the expanded single-track editing view and deleting the transition made in A/B mode cuts off the over-lapping footage.

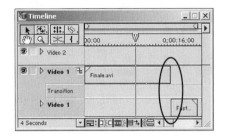

Adding Transitions to Your Own Project

Okay, this time for sure. It really is time to add transitions to *your* project. If you saved your project, simply click File, Open Recent Project and select your project name.

If instead you simply want to experiment on a few clips, add them to the Project window and drag them in succession to the Timeline Video 1 track.

Now all you have to do is drag and drop transitions to your heart's content to edit points on your project. Try out a whole bunch of transitions. You easily can replace one transition with another by simply dragging the new one on top of the old one. It'll automatically replace the rejected transition.

If you want to lengthen or shorten a transition, simply right-click the purple transition segment, select Duration, and type in a new time. One second is the default transition time.

Task: Preview Your Transitions

▲ TASK

Instead of using the Transition Settings slider to preview your transitions, you can use the Program Monitor screen. If your computer has the horsepower, you can preview the transitions in real time. If not, you can scrub through them manually.

Here are the steps to use Real-Time Preview:

1. To check whether you selected Real-Time Preview during startup (or to select that mode now), select Project, Project Settings, Keyframe and Rendering from the main menu. Make sure you've placed a check mark in the Real-Time Preview box.

2. Click OK.

3. Place your edit line in front of the transition you want to preview and press Enter/Return. You should see that transition playing in the Program Monitor screen.

If your computer processor cannot perform a real-time preview smoothly, you can do it
▼ manually by using a scrub preview. Here are the steps:

5

1. Drag the timeline's edit line to just before your transition.

         2. Release the mouse button.

         3. Press Alt (Windows) or Option (Mac), click and hold the edit line, and drag it
            across the transition. The transition will display in the Program Monitor screen.

      This is not true real-time preview, but if you drag the edit line smoothly, it'll be close
 enough.

Task: Render to View a Transition in Real Time

Once you've created a transition to your satisfaction, you may want to have Premiere
"render" it. This process converts the transition from a series of mathematical calculations to a straight video clip, making it easier for Premiere to play it. You'll eventually
have to render all such transitions and other effects before you record your project to
videotape or to your hard drive later. Therefore, taking care of some individual transitions now will save you time later. Also, these transitions will be displayed smoothly
from this point on without the need to use Real-Time Preview or a scrub preview. Here's
how you render a transition:

         1. Double-click the yellow bar above the timeline. That shortens the "work area" to
            only the current active window.

         2. Grab the handles at the ends of the bar (one at a time) and drag them to the edges
            of the transition you want to render. I've highlighted those handles in Figure 5.17.
            If Snap To Edges is enabled, the handles will "snap" to the edges of the transition.
            This tells Premiere to render only that transition.

         3. Press Enter, which starts the rendering process and pops up a progress indicator
            like the one in Figure 5.18. Once the process is completed, Premiere automatically
 plays the rendered transition in real time so you can check out your handiwork.

FIGURE 5.17

*Setting the work area
to only your transition
makes the rendering
brief and gets you to
real-time playback
more quickly.*

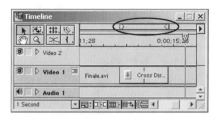

FIGURE 5.18

*While Premiere
"builds" your preview
(renders your transi-
tion), a little progress
indicator pops up.*

If you don't like what you see—it's too short, too long, the border is the wrong color or is too thick—simply double-click the transition segment and make some adjustments in the Settings dialog box. To see your fixes in real time, you'll need to do that rendering thing again.

No matter—this is the time to experiment. Look for clips that lend themselves to specific transitions. Try out a variety. Then after you've had some fun, be sure to use transitions judiciously. Restraint is a good thing when it comes to transitions.

To give you an overview of virtually all the transitions Premiere has to offer, see Table 5.1.

TABLE 5.1   Premiere Transitions

Transition Type	Name	Image	Border/ Anti-Aliasing	Forward/ Reverse	Custom
3D Motion	Cube Spin		**	**	
	Curtain			**	
	Doors		**	**	
	Flip Over			**	Number of bands/color
	Fold Up			**	
	Motion			**	12 motion files
	Spin		**	**	
	Spin Away		**	**	
	Swing In		**	**	
	Swing Out		**	**	
	Tumble Away		**	**	Change disappear point

5

TABLE 5.1 Continued

Transition Type	Name	Image	Border/ Anti- Aliasing	Forward/ Reverse	Custom
Dissolves	Additive Dissolve				
	Cross Dissolve				
	Dither Dissolve		**		
	Non- Additive				
	Random Invert				Invert A or B; change box sizes
Iris	Iris Cross		**	**	Start location
	Iris Diamond		**	**	Start location
	Iris Points		**	**	
	Iris Round		**	**	Start location
	Iris Shapes		**	**	Number of shapes; three shape types
	Iris Square		**	**	Start location
	Iris Star		**	**	Start location
Page Peels	Center Peel			**	
	Page Peel			**	Start corner
	Page Turn				Start corner
	Peel Back			**	

TABLE 5.1 Continued

Transition Type	Name	Image	Border/ Anti-Aliasing	Forward/ Reverse	Custom
Slide	Band Slide		**	**	Number of bands; movement direction
	Center Merge		**	**	
	Center Split		**	**	
	Multi-Spin		**	**	Number of boxes
	Push		**	**	Movement direction
	Slash Slide		**	**	Number of slices; movement direction
	Slide		**	**	Movement direction
	Sliding Bands		**	**	Movement direction
	Sliding Boxes		**	**	Movement direction
	Split		**	**	Movement direction
	Swap		**	**	Movement direction
	Swirl		**	**	Number of boxes; percent of movement completed at end
Special	Displace				Various settings
	Image Mask		**		Can use any mask
	Texturize				

5

TABLE 5.1 Continued

Transition Type	Name	Image	Border/ Anti-Aliasing	Forward/ Reverse	Custom
	Three-D				
Stretch	Cross		**	**	Movement direction
	Funnel		**	**	Movement direction
	Stretch		**		Movement direction
	Stretch In				Movement direction
	Stretch Over		**	**	Movement direction
Wipe	Band		**	**	Movement direction
	Barn Doors		**	**	Movement direction
	Checker Wipe		**	**	Movement direction
	Checker- board		**	**	Movement direction
	Clock Wipe		**	**	Movement direction
	Gradient Wipe			**	Movement direction; graphic selection
	Inset		**	**	Movement direction
	Paint Splatter		**	**	Movement direction
	Pinwheel		**	**	Movement direction; number of wedges
	Radial Wipe		**	**	Movement direction

TABLE 5.1 Continued

Transition Type	Name	Image	Border/ Anti- Aliasing	Forward/ Reverse	Custom
	Random Blocks		**	**	Movement direction; number of blocks
	Random Wipe		**	**	Movement direction
	Spiral Boxes		**	**	Movement direction; width of spiral
	Venetian Blinds		**	**	Movement direction; number of bands
	Wedge Wipe		**	**	Movement direction
	Wipe		**	**	Movement direction
	Zig-Zag Blocks		**	**	Movement direction
Zoom	Cross				Specific movement direction (begin and end)
	Zoom		**	**	Specific opening location
	Zoom Boxes		**	**	Number of shapes
	Zoom Trails				Specific opening location; number of trails

5

Expert Editing Tips

Forever seared in my brain is one edit. It was in my first "magazine" piece for KSL-TV in Salt Lake City. This was back in the mid 1980s. The national Radio and Television News Directors Association had just named KSL the TV news station of the year. An honor KSL would win an unprecedented two years in a row. KSL had the highest rated (by percentage of viewers) news shows in the country. It was a TV news powerhouse. I had just

moved there from a medium-sized market and was in awe of the professionalism, the scope of the news operation, and the array of high-tech goodies.

John Crossman, Crossman Post Productions.

Buried deep in the editing bays was something akin to the command center of the Starship Enterprise. At its helm was John Crossman, KSL's chief editor. For me, having come from a station with *no* editors (the photographers did all the editing), this was a tad overwhelming. One of my first assignments was a long, feature story on a local piano manufacturer. I had never done a magazine-style piece and handed John a straightforward news-style voiceover. He barely batted an eye.

A couple hours later he called me into his realm wanting to show me how the piece was coming together. It sang. It danced. It had rhythm. I was confounded. The segment ended with a Billy Joel piano crescendo followed by a loud "clip" of a wire cutter snipping a piano string. I looked at John and at all his whiz-bang electronics and said one of the dumbest comments I've ever muttered in my TV career: "This equipment is amazing!" Fortunately he forgave me my egregious error and we got on famously after that.

John spent eight years at KSL and now runs Crossman Post Production (www.xmanpost.com) just outside of Salt Lake City. He provides video editing, graphics, and computer-generated animation for a lengthy list of corporate, educational, and broadcast clients. He's won five regional Emmys, 26 national Tellys, and a slew of other awards.

John is a wonderfully talented guy who has a true passion for the art of editing. Here are his editing tips.

To begin, good editors need certain basic talents:

Rhythm—Life has a rhythm, so does editing. If you can't "feel it," it's very hard to learn.

Visualization—Good editors can see the completed project before they start. The actual editing is just the detail work. The images are already completely edited in their minds.

Patience—Even when you can see it in your mind's eye you will have to make compromises on every project. The true test of an editor is if he can make compromises work well. The best editors make it look like every single choice was the best choice.

Positive attitude—Your attitude will go a long, long way toward determining your success. You will spend numberless hours editing in a small dark space, usually on a deadline, and always with budget pressure, client pressure, spouse pressure...you name it. And the better the attitude, the better the job will go.

Team player—You are part of a team. Try not to criticize the other members. Remember, you didn't have your eye in the viewfinder when the bomb went off. Thinking you could have had that shot when you are looking at the tape hours and miles away is easy but not productive. Let the producer say, "I wish he had gotten closer." You say, "Well let's do it this way and it will still work." That's where the editor earns his money, his reputation, and his loyalty.

To edit well you need to do the following:

Use motivation and logic. This is the most important concept in editing. Your editing should be motivated. You should have a reason for the shots you select and the order in which you select them. There should be a purpose to why you dissolve, why you use a wipe, as well as why you cut. Your goal is to communicate clearly what has happened. Your shot selection and the time spent on each shot should reinforce the narration while conveying information.

Plan as you digitize. As you digitize the video you should see in your mind's eye how the pictures are going to line up to get you to where you want to be at the end. Is the shot a great scene setter (beginning), is it incredibly beautiful (possible ending shot), is it self-explanatory or incomprehensible (possible "cutting-room floor" material)?

Build new skills. If you are in the professional ranks, or want to be, you must budget a considerable amount of time and money on keeping current. At the very least you're going to need to learn about how to incorporate graphics, animation, compositing, and special effects into your editing to serve the demands of your clients.

In the world of broadcast television you are surrounded by people who know how to create good stories. In corporate production you may be working with someone who has no clue. At this point you become 90% teacher and 10% editor. Your attitude will win you a loyal client or lose you a lifetime customer.

Like music in a movie, good editing helps communicate your message and shouldn't really stand out to the viewer. The editing is not the message, but the editing can make the message work, not work, or work better than it should.

5

Summary

Adding transitions to your project ratchets it up several notches. It also can distract viewers. Judicious use of transitions is the best use. Premiere offers more than 70 transitions that you easily can add to your project by simply dragging them to edit points. If there aren't enough tail or head frames for a sufficiently long overlap to make a smooth transition, Premiere will turn those last and first frames of video into a collection of freeze frames. Most Premiere transitions have several customization features, including adding a border to better mark the transition line(s) between clip A and clip B, multiple motion options, and setting the number of objects—spinning boxes, expanding diamonds, Venetian blinds—within the transition.

Workshop

Review the questions and answers in this section to try to sharpen your Premiere transition-editing skills. Also, take a few moments to tackle my short quiz and exercises.

Q&A

Q I go to the Transitions palette and open a transition to preview it, but all I see are those A and B clips in the windows. I want to see my clips, and there is no check box labeled Show Actual Sources.

A You need to drag the transition to the edit point on the timeline. Unless you tell Premiere what source clips you're using, it can't display them. Despite this, double-clicking a transition is the fastest way to preview it.

Q Finding transitions by name is cumbersome. I remember seeing some with descriptive names, but searching through all the Transition palette sections is tedious. Is there a better way?

A You bet. Use the Find tool. Click the little binoculars icon at the bottom of the Transitions palette and then type in part or all of the transition name, as you remember it. Just like using the Find feature in a word processor, it'll take you to each instance of that word, one after the other.

Quiz

1. What's the difference between offline and online editing?
2. How do you add a thick, colored border to a Wipe transition?
3. How do you view your transitions in real time?

Quiz Answers

1. Offline editing adds an extra step to the production process. Typically offline editing takes place on lower-priced editing systems using less than the full-quality of the original video to save storage space and speed up editing. Editors use that process to create Edit Decision Lists (EDLs), which they then plug in to higher-priced online editors to create the finished product. That process is still common for high-end projects such those that use Beta SP analog video, but DV and products such as Premiere are making it more economical to do everything online.

2. Open the Transition Settings dialog box, move the Border slider to the right, click the Color box, and select a color. Preview the border size and color by clicking Show Actual Sources and moving the preview window's slider to the right.

3. If your computer has enough processor power, you can preview your transitions in real time by checking the Project Settings, Keyframe and Rendering, Real Time box and then placing the edit line ahead of the transition and pressing Return/Enter. You can manually preview your transitions either in each individual transition's Project Settings dialog box or by Alt/Option-clicking the edit line marker and dragging it through the transition.

Exercises

1. Take the QuickTime transition for a test drive. You'll be amazed at the voluminous amount of material tucked behind that one little icon in the Transitions palette. It does not offer those A and B clip windows, so if you want to see previews of your transitions you'll need to drag the QuickTime transition icon to an edit point between two clips. I'll cover this powerful tool in some depth in Hour 9.

2. Fade up from black and fade to black. This is the standard way to start and end a production. Here's how you do it. Right-click the file side of the Project window (or click the New Item icon at the bottom of that window). Select Black Video. Drag it to the timeline either in front of your first clip or at the end of your production (it's default length is 5 seconds). Drag a cross-dissolve to that edit point. Done.

3. The Transitions palette has some customization features. In particular it allows you to create a personalized collection of favorites. Do that by creating a new folder and then dragging and dropping your favorite transitions into it. You can go so far as to create subfolders. Also, you can hide transitions you don't plan to use to minimize the clutter.

5

PART II
Enhancing Your Video

Hour

HOUR 6

Story Creation, Writing, and Video Production Tips

Premiere is a powerful video production tool. By choosing Premiere, you've made a commitment to take your video production quality up several notches. To do that requires more than learning new editing techniques. You also need to hone your story-creation skills, writing style, and even business acumen. By moving to Premiere you're showing the kind of interest in video production that frequently leads to a profession within that industry.

This hour will take a break from step-by-step Premiere techniques and address those issues. I've turned to some colleagues and friends in the TV news, film, and video production industry and asked them to offer expert tips within their specialty.

The highlights of this hour include the following:

- NBC-TV correspondent Bob Dotson's story-creation tips
- Writing in the "active voice"

- The Good Writer's Dazzlin' Dozen from noted writing consultant, Mackie Morris
- Scriptwriting tips from the respected Hollywood writing team of Stephen Black and Henry Stern
- Expert advice on shooting film from noted German cinematographer Charly Steinberger
- Practical suggestions on how best to start a video production company from industry veteran Sam Prigg
- Tips on doing on-location, multicamera videotaping from multiple-award winner Joe Walsh

Getting the Story Right

I worked in the TV news business as a reporter and anchorman as well as shooter and editor. In my 11 years working on-camera and off, I constantly critiqued my work and asked others to do the same. Some offered their advice in writing and I hung on those words of wisdom:

- An NBC producer who ran the affiliate "feed"—a daily collection of stories made available to local network stations for their use—once wrote about a prison counseling piece I submitted to him. He said that my "story *talked* about" the subject "but *showed* nothing" about it. My tape "cried out for some natural sound of a session in progress."
- A Seattle TV news director wrote that my stories had a sameness—a voice track, a sound bite, more voiceover, another sound bite, and a standup close. "Mix 'em up," he suggested.
- And a consultant took me aside to tell me to "break up my on-camera pacing with pauses."

I took all those tips to the bank. The NBC producer ended up buying about a story a week from me. The news director helped me get a job in a much larger market. And the consultant's advice helped me land an anchor job at that station.

I'm a believer in heeding expert advice.

In putting together this book, I've had the enjoyable opportunity to contact many of the people who have given me advice or from whom I have gained a lot of practical knowledge. Each agreed to provide expert tips focusing on their specialty. You've already met photographer Karl Petersen in Hour 1, "Camcorder and Shooting Tips," and editor John Crossman in Hour 5, "Adding Transitions: From Dissolves to Zooms."

I compiled six such expert columns for this hour. I lumped them together because I think they all speak to enhancing your skills beyond the fundamentals of camerawork, editing, and simply learning how to use Premiere's toolset. Further, you may want to take what you do with Premiere and move into a career in video production. These experts speak to that.

Up first, Bob Dotson.

Story-Creation Tips

NBC-TV *Today Show* correspondent Bob Dotson is, I think, the best human-interest feature-story TV reporter. Dotson has received more than 50 awards. The National Press Photographers Association award committee wrote, "Bob Dotson's reports help us understand ourselves a bit better. They show that all our lives are important and really matter. After all, this country was built not by great heroes or great politicians, but by ordinary people—by thousands whose names we don't know, may never know, but without whose influence America wouldn't exist."

Bob Dotson, NBC-TV reporter.

Although you probably are not a TV newsperson, you probably will create human-interest stories. Dotson's forte. If there's a storyteller out there you should emulate, I think he's the one. During my TV reporting days I tried to watch all his stories, and when a station I worked for offered me the chance to attend one of his seminars, I jumped at it.

I've reproduced my notes, with his approval, here. I took many things away from his class. Three points stand out:

- Give viewers a reason to remember the story.
- When interviewing people, try not to ask questions. Merely make observations. That loosens people up, letting them reveal their emotional, human side to you.
- Make sure you get a closing shot. Most video producers look for dramatic opening shots or sequences (and that's still a good thing), but your viewers are more likely to remember the closing shot.

6

Bob Dotson's Story Checklist

Dotson's "Storyteller's Checklist" inspired his book *Make It Memorable* (Bonus Books) and a companion videotape of all the stories in the book. He prepared his list (and book) with TV news reporters in mind, but his tips apply to professional, corporate, and home video producers as well:

- Always remember that the reporter is not the story.

- Make sure the *commitment* is present. Commitment is the story stated in one sentence—what you want the audience to take away from the report. The commitment should be stated as a complete sentence with subject, verb, and object. "Outside money is altering the city's architecture," "This cow has never taken an order in her life," "You can't murder a pumpkin," and so on. You formulate the commitment to yourself to help guide the story creation. Then you use your images to prove the commitment visually. Very seldom will you state the commitment verbally in any story.

- Write your pictures first. Give them a strong lead, preferably visual, that instantly telegraphs the story to come.

- The main body of the story should usually be no more than three to five main points, which you prove visually once you have identified them.

- Create a strong close that you can't top, something you build toward throughout the story. Ideally, the ending is also visual.

- Write loose. Be hard on yourself as a writer. Say nothing in the script your viewers would already know or that the visuals say more eloquently.

- Throughout the story, build your report around sequences—two or three shots of a guy buying basketball tickets; two or three shots of a husband and wife drinking coffee at a kitchen table, and so on. Sequences demand matched action.

- Allow for moments of silence. Stop writing occasionally and let two or three seconds or more of compelling action occur without voiceover. For a writer, nothing is more difficult to write than silence. For viewers, sometimes nothing is more eloquent.

- Use strong natural sound to heighten realism, authenticity, believability and to heighten the viewer's sense of vicarious participation in the events you're showing. Some reports merely let you watch what happened. The best reports let you experience what happened.

- Tell your story through people. People sell your story. Try to find strong central characters engaged in compelling action that is visual or picturesque.

- Build in surprises to sustain viewer involvement. Surprises help viewers feel something about the story; surprises lure uninterested viewers to the screen. Surprises can be visual, wild sounds, short bites, or poetic script. Always, surprises are little moments of drama.

- Short sound bites prove the story you are showing. Don't use sound bites as substitutes for more effective storytelling.

- Address the larger issue. "A trailer home burned down." Such a story fails to meet the "so what?" test. "The trailer home burned down because the walls are full of flammable insulation" describes the larger issue and meets the "so what?" test.

- Finally, make your story memorable. Can your viewers feel something about the story and its subjects? If feeling is present, the story will be memorable. It will stick in the viewer's minds.

Keep It Simple...and Short

As a coda to Dotson's advice, I'll add that you need to remember, this is only TV. You need some mighty compelling or entertaining material to keep viewers glued to the tube for more than a few minutes. Think about whatever message you're trying to get across in your video project and consider what images, sound, and graphics will convey that message in the briefest, most effective manner. Then shoot with brevity in mind.

That's not to say that you don't grab unplanned video that looks great. Or that you cut interviews short even if you haven't heard some compelling sound bites. Videotape is expendable. Feel free to shoot plenty. Although it's true that you may have to wade through a lot to find the best shots, the advantage of DV is that once these shots are located, you can simply capture them to your hard drive and they become immediately accessible.

Writing in the "Active Voice"

6

It's a rare classroom experience that can cause a tidal change. One of those for me was a seminar with Mackie Morris (see the upcoming section). Morris makes his message clear. "Write in the active voice." For example, instead of writing

A bill was passed by the Senate.

write this instead:

The Senate passed a bill.

Put the receiver of the verb's action after the verb. Instead of the passively voiced "John Doe was arrested by police" (Doe is the receiver of the action and is ahead of the verb), change that to "Police arrested John Doe."

Morris emphasizes that passive voice deadens, complicates, and lengthens writing. It's not ungrammatical but it's more suitable for print than television copy. You use passive voice sparingly in everyday conversation, and you should use it sparingly in video productions. You are asking people to listen to your words, not read them. Make it easy. Make it active.

It takes some effort to make the shift from passive voice to active. Simply recognizing passive voice takes extra attentiveness. The biggest giveaway is some form of the "to be" verb in a verb phrase. The following sentences are all in the passive voice:

The students were praised by the teacher.

The unruly customer was told to leave by the maitre 'd.

The forest was destroyed by fire.

Make them active by moving the receiver of the action to after the verb:

The teacher praised the students.

The maitre 'd told the unruly customer to leave.

Fire destroyed the forest.

That one fundamental technique makes your sentences simpler and shorter.

Morris calls it "straight-line meaning." The listener understands the copy better because it flows in a straight line. You know that when you read a newspaper you frequently go back and reread some sentences because something didn't add up. Video viewers don't have that luxury.

Besides simply switching the sentence around ("relocating the actor," as Morris puts it), you can fix passive sentences in three other ways:

- **Identify the missing actor and insert it into the sentence.** Change "The airplane was landed during the storm" to "A passenger landed the airplane during the storm."

- **Change the verb.** Instead of writing "The bell was sounded at noon" write "The bell rang at noon." (Or tolled, pealed, chimed—using active voice fosters the use of more descriptive words.)

- **Drop the "to be" verb.** Change "The spotlight was focused on downtown" to "The spotlight focused on downtown."

Not all "to be" verb phrases are passive. "The man was driving south" contains a verb phrase and a "to be" helper. But the man was performing the action, not receiving it. Therefore the sentence is active. A sentence is passive only if the receiver of the verb's action precedes the verb.

Writing in the active voice forces you to get out of your writing rut. Instead of saying the same old things in the same old "to be" passive way, you will select new active verbs and constructions. You'll write more conversationally and with a fresher and more interesting style.

That's not to say that you'll write exclusively in the active voice. You should write, "He was born in 1984," or "She was injured in the accident" because that's what people say.

Focusing on active voice will make your copy more interesting and easier to understand.

Mackie Morris' Writing Tips

Few if any media consultants match Mackie Morris' 25-year record as a journalism and communications seminar leader, teacher, coach, and practitioner. Founder and president of Mackie Morris Communications, he works with a wide range of corporate and public service clients to enhance their communication skills.

Mackie Morris.

6

Previously Morris served as chairman of the Broadcast News Department at the University of Missouri School of Journalism. He later worked as a vice president and lead consultant for Frank N. Magid Associates, a major media consulting firm, where he implemented a series of instructional workshops for broadcast professionals. It was at one of those seminars that I became a devotee of Morris's "active voice." Morris continues to be one of the most sought-after broadcast writing seminarians ever.

The Good Writer's Dazzlin' Dozen

At his seminars Morris relentlessly hammers home his active voice message. But peppered throughout his presentation he interjects other useful writing tips. He calls them "The Good Writer's Dazzlin' Dozen":

- **Write factually and accurately.** The best technique and the finest form mean nothing if your copy's wrong.

- **Write in the active voice.** This technique will make your copy tighter, complete, easier to listen to, and more interesting. Do whatever you must to avoid the passive voice.

- **Write in the present or present perfect tenses.** They make your copy more immediate, and immediacy is more interesting. Avoid the word *today*. If you use past tense, make sure you give a time reference to avoid confusion.

- **Keep your writing simple.** Choose positive forms over negative forms. Write one thought to a sentence. Don't search for synonyms, because repetition is not a sin. Don't search for complicated, "intellectual" language. Give the audience the best possible chance to understand the story.

- **Be complete and clear.** In your quest for brevity and conciseness, don't omit necessary information.

- **Be creative.** Stick to the rules but develop your own style. Try to say the same old thing in a different, new way. Make use of writing devices that make copy easier to listen to and more interesting, such as using the "rule of threes" (that is, grouping items by threes, such as red, white, and blue; left, right, and center; over, under, and through). Saying things in groups of three always sounds better. Pausing before saying the third item is even more effective.

- **Write to be heard.** Maintain a sense of rhythm in your writing. All life has rhythm, and rhythmic writing is easier to hear. Avoid potentially confusing homonyms. Always, always test your copy by reading it aloud.

- **Avoid interruptives.** Don't force the listener to make difficult mental connections. Put modifiers next to what they modify. Don't split verb phrases (split infinitives).

Incorrect: Will eventually decide.

Correct: Eventually will decide.

Incorrect: Doctors only gave him six months to live.

Correct: Doctors gave him only six months to live.

- **Avoid commas.** A comma demands a hitch in reading and the resulting jerkiness frustrates the listener. Avoiding commas also will eliminate subordinate clauses. Such clauses kill the impact of copy, especially if they come at the top of a story or sentence.

- **Avoid numbers.** The listener has trouble remembering them.

- **Avoid pronouns.** If you must use a pronoun, make sure the pronoun agrees with its antecedent and appears close to the antecedent. For example, "John Doe hit Bob Smith on the head and paramedics took him to the hospital." In this case, instead of "him" use "Smith."

- **Write to the pictures but not too closely to the pictures.** Remember that more specific video requires more general writing, and vice versa. Utilize the touch-and-go method, wherein you write directly to the video at the beginning of a sequence and then allow the writing to become more general with background information and other facts as the video continues.

Storytelling with Video

That's what you do. You're a storyteller. In most cases you may go out on a shoot with only a basic idea of what you're going to tape and how you're going to piece it together. That kind of approach will get you only so far.

As you up the ante in your work there will be times when you'll want to work from a script. It may be as straightforward as a corporate safety production with employees doing the acting, or you may have aspirations to create a dramatic feature.

In either case, some fundamental scriptwriting skills will help you raise the bar of your production. I've tapped two of Hollywood's top writers to do the honors.

6

Stephen Black and Henry Stern's Scriptwriting Tips

I count myself fortunate to have Stephen Black and Henry Stern as neighbors and friends. Their TV scriptwriting and producing credits would fill this page. They forged new directions in episodic dramas with their work on *Dynasty*, *Falcon Crest*, *Flamingo Road*, *Matlock*, and *Knot's Landing*. Their work as head writers on *As the World Turns* and consultants for *One Life to Live* stirred things up and added sizzle to both of these long-running daytime staples. They've had a hand in a half-dozen TV movies, including the only TV film starring Audrey Hepburn, *Love Among Thieves*.

Stephen Black (left) and Henry Stern (right), TV scriptwriters and producers.

They got their start as a writing team doing comedies in the mid 1970s. Stern had been one of Broadway's youngest producers, and Black had written a couple plays. Despite failing to sell their first comedy script to the *Mary Tyler Moore Show*, they were given free access to the set where they watched rehearsals and show tapings, all the while taking copious notes. That led to a brief stint writing for a new show called *The Love Boat* ("It paid the bills and got us in the Writers Guild") and finally landed them a job with Norman Lear Productions, the company behind *All in the Family*.

These days they're working on their second novel and a movie script. Here's their advice to aspiring scriptwriters:

- The most important thing is that we like to tell stories.
- And the most important thing in stories is the characters. The best kind of character is one with the ability to surprise you. The audience is not dumb. You've got to come up with something unpredictable. You don't want a white hat or black hat. You want people wearing gray hats. People you can't read. You want to be interested in what happens to them.
- It's *not* a good idea to start your script writing with a plot. It's better to start with a theme. Know what you want to say, how you want to say it, and where you want to be at the end. The theme of our current film script is, How does the death of someone affect his three closest friends?

- With the theme in hand we next create the characters. What is their arc and how will that change throughout the story? We invent detailed character bios. Where did they go to school? What were their parents like? What was their childhood like? We don't have to use all that in the script, but it's good for us to know to help craft the story.

- Next we sit down with a yellow legal pad and make 30 to 40 story points, such as guy robs bank, hides in mother's house, falls in love with neighbor, and so on.

- Then we write an extensive narrative outline—30 pages or more. We include texture—the tone and detail. We take time to describe settings and characters. Instead of merely using physical descriptions of characters, such as Bob is 6'2" with the torso of a long distance runner, we're more likely to write, "as John was driving up Canyon Avenue, he looked out his rain spattered window and caught sight of Bob, one more time, running in the rain." That says a lot. We love doing that. It makes it easier to do the script.

- It's really crucial that you learn how to structure a piece so your story will make sense. Know where your story is going and how plot elements and character elements will build on each other so they peak at certain points. An excellent film example of structure is *Two for the Road*, with Audrey Hepburn and Albert Finney. Even though they use multiple flashbacks, you know that from beginning to end this is a story of a marriage on the skids.

- Tell as much of the story as you can without dialogue. Tell it cinematically. Don't give camera directions such as wide, tight medium. That's the director's job and disrupts the story flow. But it's okay to script camera *angles*. We wrote a scene where a woman was about to tell her husband their son was killed in combat. The husband ran a steak house and happened to be in the walk-in freezer when his wife arrived. We directed the camera to look through the window and, without any dialogue, watch the woman tell the husband and see the reaction.

- You can't write if you're not an observer. We're constantly eavesdropping in restaurants. We're acutely aware of dialogue going on around us. Our characters have to speak in the vernacular of the time.

- Dialogue is more than just writing down what two people say to each other. Good dialogue is succinct, crisp, entertaining, and rich. It's a level above conversation.

- Bury the "pipe." The pipe is the exposition, the conduit of information, the stuff the audience needs to know to make sense of the story. Say the character's been divorced three times, has six kids with six different women, and runs a grocery. You don't come out and say that. You impart it to the audience in an interesting way.

6

- Scriptwriting is collaborative. Everyone has a hand in it. A screenplay will go through 10 to 15 drafts before shooting begins.

- Writing is hard work. To sit there in front of a blank, empty computer screen knowing that you have to come up with compelling characters and stimulating plots, week after week after week can be daunting. Back in 1970 we were working with Leon Uris on a musical production of his novel *Exodus*. After several tiring meetings with potential backers Stephen asked him if he had any advice for aspiring playwrights. He said, "Put your ass in a chair in front of a typewriter." This was the most succinct, valuable information we were ever given.

Unblocking Creativity

Writer's block strikes us all. As Black and Stern noted, it's darned hard to sit down in front of a blank computer screen and start putting words in the computer.

Here are some ways to get the creative juices flowing:

- Bounce ideas off others. Simply talking about your project typically will give you a whole new perspective. Listening to questions posed to you about your work will help you focus your writing.

- Change your work environment. I have the luxury of going outside and sitting on a rocking chair overlooking a lovely valley. That moment in the fresh air helps bust loose a few cobwebs.

- Turn away from your computer and grab a yellow legal pad and a felt-tip pen. Scribble down some ideas. Connect the thoughts on paper.

- Take a break. Listen to a great tune. Take a jog. Then get back to work—you're on deadline!

Stepping Up to Film

I count myself fortunate to have one of Germany's top cinematographers, Charly Steinberger, as a friend. He's served as director of photography on scores of movies and TV shows. His films have won numerous prestigious awards, including German Film Award – Best Cinematographer, Venice Film Festival – Best Film, and the New York Critics Award – Best Film.

Charly Steinberger, cinematographer.

Steinberger has worked with some of Europe's most famous actors: David Niven, Roger Moore, Kim Novak, Gina Lollobrigida, Sophia Loren and, topping his personal list, Marlene Dietrich. Few readers of this book will have the opportunity to work at this top end of the film production scale, but I think everyone can take Steinberger's advice to the bank.

Charly Steinberger's Tips For Prospective Filmmakers

Steinberger's guidance comes from the perspective of a filmmaker who has seen absolutely everything. He has a pragmatic view. Here are his filmmaking tips:

- The most important component of a film is a good script. Unfortunately that happens only rarely.
- Next in importance is a solid budget.
- A good production team can make or break a film. Topping the list is the director and the cinematographer, followed by the set designer, costume designer, makeup artist, lighting specialist, grip, and editor. Overseeing it all should be a producer with a reputation for spending money wisely. Too many producers try to cut corners and save money by hiring less experienced (that is, *cheaper*) crewmembers.
- The photographer's primary responsibility is to use the camera to tell the story well. Too many cinematographers get lost attempting to create brilliant and grand images.
- A point that often gets neglected is the critical search for and selection of locations—be they cafes, apartments, or offices—to help give characters their correct motivation. The right settings bring life and depth to your characters.
- In the post-production world there is no longer any difference between film and video. Both now use nonlinear digital editors.
- I still work with film instead of video because film has higher resolution, truer colors, more accurate reproduction, more brilliance, and solid contrasts. That said, it won't be long before video will equal film in quality.

6

The Business of Video Production

I've been here. In the early 1990s, photographer Karl Petersen and I started Glint Video back in Portland, Oregon. We had two good-sized clients and occasionally picked up smaller gigs along the way.

We sought advice from our mutual friend, news photographer Sam Prigg, who had turned some weekend freelance assignments into a growing video production business—with an office and his own gear and even employees! When we saw all that he had done to get where he was, it gave both Karl and me the jitters.

So we stuck to what amounted to a freelance, on-call arrangement. Soon there were dry spells and too many wannabe competitors with Video Toasters and low-ball bids. Karl got an offer to be chief photographer at the local NBC-TV affiliate, and one of our clients asked me to write a book. So we parted ways.

It's tough to get into any business, especially into a high-tech, creative field such as video production, where client expectations shift as quickly as the technology.

Despite that, Sam Prigg is still at it. While other production firms in Utah have folded their tents, Prigg has adjusted to the shifting landscape and grabbed greater market share. Here's his advice.

Sam Prigg's Tips on Starting a Video Production Company

Sam Prigg, the "Head Wabbit" at White Rabbit Productions in Salt Lake City (http://www.xmission.com/~whiterab/index.html) has never taken himself too seriously. That hasn't stopped him from creating one of Utah's most successful video production houses. His client list and "statues," as he puts it, make that clear. He's worked for all the major networks, plus Disney, Apple, Intel, and many other "big name" clients. During the Winter Olympics he had eight crews working full-time for folks such as Jay Leno, David Letterman, and MTV. His "statues" include Emmys, ADDYs, Tellys, DuPonts, and "Most Improved" in bowling.

Sam Prigg, "Head Wabbit," White Rabbit Productions.

Sam Prigg is one of the good guys. I thoroughly enjoyed working with him in the mid 1980s during my four-year stint at KSL-TV in Salt Lake City. He has a degree in broadcast journalism and a minor in cinematography. For the first half of his 27-year TV and film career he thought he was going to live and die working for a TV station. But then the business changed and so did he. Local news operations cut staff while adding news shows (news is relatively inexpensive programming), and TV networks found it was cheaper to make layoffs and hire local freelance crews instead. Sam began shooting on the side and soon started making more money working on weekends and vacations than he was in his day job. Since he also was becoming disenchanted with that TV news job he knew it was time to leave. How hard could it be, he thought, to do freelance full time and make a killing? He soon found out, and along the way, acquired a few tips that others might use to *not* make the same mistakes. Here's what he has to say:

- **Learning about business is essential to survival.** I have a degree in Communications and lots of worldly experiences, but the business world is a whole different animal. You will need to learn about insurance, taxes, bonding, business plans, advertising, equipment purchases or leases, office space, phones, faxes, furniture, marketing, pricing, invoicing, bad debts, good demo reels, production schedules, contracts, the IRS, accounting, hiring freelance workers, firing freelance workers, security, and credit. It's no surprise that most small startups fail after a few years.

- **Working with a partner…or not.** I started our company with a partner, thinking our skills complemented each other. Turns out there was a lot about him I didn't know. There was conflict and I ended up buying him out. Dissolving a partnership can be like getting a divorce. Partner up if you must but be aware of the ramifications. Put your expectations in writing. Spell out the rolls each partner will take, where the money will go, and be prepared to review the contract frequently.

6

- **Don't put all your eggs in one basket.** When I started my business I had one client that accounted for most of my work. It was great. I traveled around the United States, shot all kinds of neat stuff, edited to my heart's content, and enjoyed life in the freelance world. Two years later the client's company got sold and everything stopped. I forgot to broaden my base and to do that marketing thing. I had to scramble to find some new clients. It took a couple of years until I felt comfortable again, but I learned a few things. One is that eggs-in-one-basket rule, and the other is that the time to do your marketing is when you are busy with the project you currently are working on.

- **Figure out what kind of video production company you are.** When I started out I was going to offer to do anything at the highest possible level. I planned to shoot, write, and edit commercials, news, documentaries, corporate videos, sports, accident re-creations, school plays, weddings…well, no weddings, but just about anything else. My market was the world. And I could do it on film or video—I thought. It took a long time to discover who I was, but now I can say our mission statement in one sentence: We shoot high-end video for television networks, news magazine shows, and corporations, and we specialize in making people look good. Once we figured that out, it was easier to focus our marketing and purchase the right equipment.

- **Create a demo reel.** Your demo reel represents who and what you are. It is your most valuable marketing tool. There are plenty of views about what makes a good reel. My take is that you may only have 30 seconds to make a favorable impression. Why? I know of TV news directors who view aspiring reporters' demo reels—chock full of stories, on-camera stand-ups, and clever on-set repartee—for all of 30 seconds. That's all the time they need to make such important decisions. Make sure you gear your reel for your target audience and have it quickly demonstrate your core values. Our reel has a fast-paced introduction with several shots of well-lit people, well-composed shots of a variety of subjects, and lively music. It includes a few graphics-laden segments and ends with contact information. It runs about seven and a half minutes. I like to watch it. And it has helped us get lots of jobs.

- **Educate your clients.** When I meet a new client for the first time I usually have to educate them about the steps involved with producing an effective video. It starts with identifying the audience—their age, education, and preconceived attitude about the subject. I then outline the dozen or so steps involved with most productions—concept, writing, storyboarding, casting, location scouting, crew, equipment, production shoot, narration, editing, graphics, and music.

- **Don't burn a client.** If you make a mistake with some clients—bad lighting, poor composition, arriving late, faulty equipment, dead batteries—they may forgive you once. TV networks are less forgiving. One mistake and they will not come back.

- **Adapt to change, because things will change.** I try to stay up on the newest trends in equipment and technology, such as new recording formats and delivery systems. It's important to understand why they have been developed and how they change the way we do business. Many clients now ask about having their video streamed or converted to DVDs or CD-ROMs. As a means to stay current, subscribe to technology magazines and join an industry organization such as the International Television Association for its conferences and seminars. View the work of others to see what kind of competition you might be facing and what kind of markets you might be missing.

- **Deciding what to charge.** For the high end of the video production market, it's easier to determine what to charge because TV networks, union contracts, and a universal fee schedule set the parameters for what the market will pay. In the television news, news magazine, and corporate worlds, using broadcast Betacam SP cameras, professional audio equipment, extensive lighting, and grip equipment and being backed by 15 to 20 years of experience, a two-person crew, consisting of a camera person and audio tech, can get between $1,200 to $1,500 for a 10-hour day. You can charge additional fees for the use of a wide-angle lens, matte box with filters, HMI or daylight-balanced lighting, and other production tools. Beginning photographers can usually charge $200 to $350 a day plus $150 to $200 for a mini-DV camera, a small lighting package, and a selection of microphones.

- **Consider working for someone else.** It is easier and much less expensive to work for the kind of company you would like to become. Get your experience with another production company that has its own equipment and clients. Perfect your techniques and broaden your knowledge by working for someone else. Then, as you understand the market and maybe find your niche, you can branch off on your own with a better understanding of the business and where your market might be. Our company is always looking for a photographer with a good eye as well as audio techs, gaffers, grips, teleprompter operators, writers, producers, and just about anyone else who can help make us look good.

Doing the Video Production Thing

White Rabbit's specialty is making interviewees look great. Painting them with the right lights, placing them in visually appealing settings, and creating a film-like look using videotape, normally a harsh and all-too-realistic-looking medium.

Other production houses move to other specialties. One focus for Cinemagic Studios in Portland is on-location, multicamera videotaping. Corporate roundtable discussions, live musical performances, and sporting events all fall into this realm. It takes a team of pros who have worked together for years to pull off something this fraught with complexities and possible snafus.

Joe Walsh's Event Shooting Tips

Joe Walsh and his team at Cinemagic Studios were my "go-to" guys when I worked as an independent video producer in Portland. I knew I could count on Cinemagic Studios to tackle whatever I threw at them. Walsh founded Cinemagic in 1980. His truly dedicated team, several of whom have worked for him for many years, has gained the confidence of a broad range of clients by meeting their unique needs and solving their communication problems.

Joe Walsh, Cinemagic Studios, CEO.

Cinemagic offers a full range of film, video, animation, and multimedia services for commercials, documentation, promotion, training, instruction, seminars, business meetings, and corporate backgrounders. Their work has garnered 26 Telly Awards (www. cinemagicstudios.com).

One of Cinemagic's fortes is shooting events using multiple cameras and switching them live. Here's Walsh's checklist:

- **Make sure you have a clear understanding of your client's expectations and budget.** Crew prices vary depending on the market. In Cinemagic's case, we charge $1,500 per day for a standard DVCAM or Beta SP camera package with a cameraman and an audio person.

- **Do a site check and rehearsal to determine the best camera locations.** For two-camera remotes it is best to have a back and front position. Place the cameras on risers so you can shoot over people's heads. Position the cameras so you don't "cross the plane" and shoot toward each other. Use the rehearsal to iron out details with the people in charge of the location.

- **Use multiple cameras and switch the event live to minimize editing afterward.** Later, if the budget allows, you can improve the product by tossing in some post-production editing and graphics. Cinemagic's remote multicamera setup includes a digital switcher, intercom system, audio mixer, studio recorder, and monitors for each camera crew, plus preview and program feed monitors. Budding producers take note: To buy the equivalent gear for your own two-camera remote setup would cost about $75,000.

- **Always have the cameras record separate tapes.** Even though we switch events live, if the technical director makes a bad switch or a cameraman makes an awkward move, we *can* fix it in post.

- **"Jam sync" all recorders before starting to record.** Setting the timecode to zero makes it much easier to find footage that you need if you have to fix something in editing.

- **Have a pre-production meeting with your crew to discuss the project and assign their responsibilities.** Onsite setup usually takes one hour for a single camera and two hours for multiple cameras. Make sure that all the cables are tucked away or taped down. After the setup, do a test record and playback check. During the event we always monitor the audio and video signals.

- **Ensure your location is well lit.** For a lot of our events the house handles the lighting, which makes our job a lot easier. If not, we typically turn to our basic light kit: a Lowel light system with two broad throw Tota lights and one wide-focus-range Omni to use as a key- or backlight (see Figure 6.1).

FIGURE 6.1

Lowel Tota light (top) and Lowel Omni light. (Images courtesy Lowel-Light Manufacturing, Inc.)

6

- **Audio is crucial.** When events handle their own audio, we take a line feed from their soundboard and use shotgun mics for backup and ambient audio. Otherwise, we rely on our standard mic kit: camera mic, shotgun, lavaliere, handheld, and PZM (pressure zone microphone, useful for a conference table with several speakers).

- **When using wireless mics, select UHF instead of VHF to avoid frequency conflicts.** All sorts of fun stuff can go wrong with wireless mics. Your receiver can pick up other sources on your channel, such as radio stations (I always get country music), pizza delivery guys, or other wireless mics from local commercial TV stations. The UHF wireless mics have multiple channels at the higher MHz frequency range, so there is less chance of interference. Always keep fresh batteries on hand. As the batteries grow weak, reception problems occur.

  Our favorite wireless mic story happened when we were taking an audio line feed from the house. The house audio man placed a wireless mic on the presenter. Just moments before he was to go on, the presenter went to the bathroom. Not only did *we* pick up the very graphic audio, so did the 500 people in the auditorium.

Summary

Premiere is not like a word processor. You didn't buy it just to do some writing and not worry about all those other hard-to-decipher bells and whistles. You bought it because it offers so much more power than, well, those lower-priced also-rans.

The likelihood then is that you want to do something other than create vacation movies to show your (ungrateful) relatives. To up that production ante means improving your story creation, writing, and video production business acumen. The advice given here comes from folks who've been in the trenches for years. They know from where they're speaking.

Workshop

We'll dispense with the usual Q&A for this hour. However, some exercises may be in order.

Exercises

1. Scriptwriter Stephen Black's dad fostered his writing from very early on. One exercise he asked his son to do while they were working on a novel together was to sit

down during a large family gathering and invent characters for the novel using the characteristics of the gathered guests as his inspiration. It worked for Black. It's also a great way for you to avoid the usual idle family chitchat.

2. Take a local newspaper story about an event or breaking news. Read it aloud with an ear for passive-voice phrases, such as "She was hit by a speeding car," "The house was destroyed by the blaze," and "The budget was presented by the Governor." Rewrite the story in active voice.

3. Contact a local TV station or production company and get permission to tag along during a remote, multicamera taping. They might let you help set up (it's called "gaffer's tape" not "duct tape") and sit in the control room. That will be an eye-opening and educational experience.

6

HOUR 7

Adding Audio

Audio is crucial. The best images will lose their impact if their audio is mediocre. Premiere offers plenty of ways to give your project a sonic boost.

You'll need to acquire some of that audio during on-location taping. Relying solely on your onboard camcorder mic may lead to disappointing results. Choosing and using additional mics will sweeten your sound. Once you're back in your studio—be it at home or work—you will likely add a narration. No need to rent an expensive audio studio—your camcorder and a simple makeshift audio "recording area" will do the trick. Some professional narration techniques will help as well.

The highlights of this hour include the following:

- Selecting mics that suit your video-production needs
- Expert sidebar—audio tips from a senior engineer with the world-leading microphone manufacture Shure, Inc.
- Building a voice recording area and creating effective voiceovers
- Basic Premiere audio editing
- News-style audio editing
- Using the Audio Mixer

Selecting the Right Mic for the Job

First order of business: Get a headset. Plug it into your camcorder. As you record, listen. Is that how you want your video production to sound?

So-called *onboard mics* take the middle ground. They pick up sound from everywhere, including camera noise and wind. If you zoom in on a subject, onboard mics don't zoom with you. They still pick up noise from all around you. Crowd noise, sound reflecting off walls, the hum from the air conditioner, the zoom lens itself as well as noise you create while handling the camcorder.

What you need are some external mics. Specialized mics that serve narrow but useful functions. I've illustrated them in Figure 7.1. Here are the five basic types:

- Handheld
- Lavaliere
- Shotgun
- Surface mount
- Wireless

And, if purchasing some number of these mics has not totally overwhelmed your budget, add a wireless mic setup.

FIGURE 7.1

Five standard-issue mics: Handheld, shotgun, wireless handheld, boundary, and lavaliere. (Products provided by Shure, Inc.)

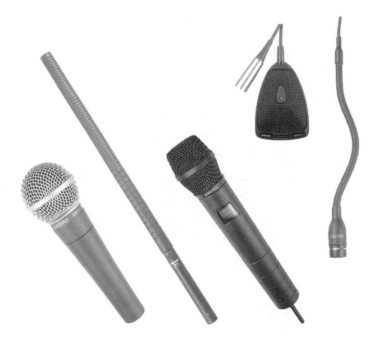

Handheld Mic

If you own only one external mic, make it a handheld. They're the rugged workhorses of the audio industry. Built with internal shock mounts to reduce handling noise, you'll use these mics for interviews, place them on podiums to record speeches, and use them to create narrations.

Many handheld mics are "omnidirectional," meaning they pick up sound from all directions. So they'll pick up ambient room noise as well as close-up audio. To minimize that unwanted noise, keep the mic as close to your subject as practical—about a foot from the speaker's mouth works well.

A top-of-the-line, rugged, durable handheld will cost from $150 to $250. Shure, Inc., the world's leading mic manufacturer, loaned me a handheld—as well as a lavaliere and a shotgun mic—to test while writing this book. (A senior engineer with Shure provided the expert sidebar later in this hour.) The Shure handheld SM63 performed flawlessly within a wide frequency range, accurately capturing low and high voices. It retails for $225.

Most handheld mics use what's called a *dynamic transducer*. As Figure 7.2 illustrates, the transducer is a thin diaphragm attached to a tiny coil. As sound waves vibrate the diaphragm, the wire moves over a magnet, which converts that physical energy into an electrical signal. Dynamic transducer mics do not require any electrical power to operate.

The other type of mic—the condenser transducer, also shown in Figure 7.2—needs so-called "phantom" power provided by a mixer or batteries. It uses a thin, flat plastic or metal diaphragm layered over another piece of metal or metal-coated ceramic. It is typically very small and has an extremely weak signal that requires preamplification before sending it to your camcorder or a mixer.

FIGURE 7.2

Cutaway views of a dynamic transducer mic (left) and a condenser transducer mic (right). (Illustration courtesy of Shure Inc., 2002.)

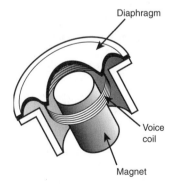
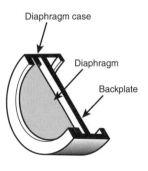

7

Lavaliere Mic

Most lavalieres use condenser transducer technology. They're perfect for formal, sit-down interviews. Their tiny size means you can conceal them to minimize that "Oh, we're watching TV" disconnect. The downside is that most require batteries. As you know, batteries invariably can fail at critical moments, so always use fresh, high-quality mic batteries. It *is* possible to power lavalieres directly from some mixers, but few budding video producers will use mixers.

I tested Shure's WL50B. The clear and crisp sound was a cut above the handheld and is reflected in its higher price: $316.

Shotgun Mic

So-named because it resembles a shotgun barrel, the shotgun mic's "unidirectional" barrel (called an *interference tube*) narrows the focus of the audio field to about 30 degrees.

A shotgun mic can handle a number of tasks. I picked up one idea from top freelance photojournalist John Alpert. He's a "one-man band" who ventures into uncomfortable and frequently dangerous situations and uses his affable demeanor to get some amazingly revealing sound bites. Instead of shoving a handheld mic into his subjects' faces—which frequently leads to "mic-stare" and other nervous reactions—he uses a shotgun mic tucked under his armpit. He leans his head away from the camera viewfinder and simply chats with his subjects in his unique, "gee-whiz" kind of way. It works like magic.

One thing shotgun mics don't do is zoom. As Chris Lyons, the Shure engineer who wrote the audio expert sidebar says, "They're more like looking through a long tube at someone." They narrow your "view" of the sound.

 The telephoto lens equivalent in the microphone world is a parabolic dish. You've seen networks use them along the sidelines of NFL games to get those great "crunching" hits.

Good shotgun mics will set you back about $1,000. I tried out Shure's superb SM89 ($1,180). This is a condenser mic and needs phantom power that a standard prosumer camcorder cannot provide. A $100 PB 224 portable phantom power adapter from the Rolls Corporation (www.rolls.com) will take care of that.

Boundary or Surface Mount Mics

You'll use these very specialized mics to pick up several speakers at a conference table or on a theatre stage. They are built to be placed on a flat surface and will pick up sound waves in both the air and from the hard surface. A good omnidirectional boundary mic costs about $160.

Wireless Systems

A wireless system is a major purchase that may set you back about as much as a medium-quality DV camcorder. But it can make your life a whole lot simpler and give you some incredible audio.

Wireless mics open a whole new spectrum of possibilities—a presenter at a tradeshow, the priest at a wedding, or a football coach working the sidelines. Wireless mics enable you to grab sound from a distance. Once you use one, you'll wonder how you got along without it. They are a luxury, and good ones are priced to match. My Shure UP4 test unit, including receiver and small body-pack transmitter, retails for $1,638 (see Figure 7.3) .

FIGURE 7.3
The Shure UP4 wire-less setup.

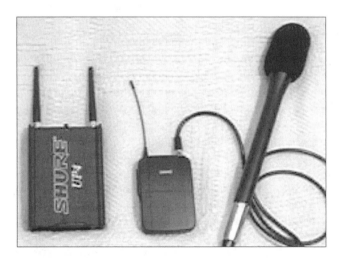

Connecting Mics to Your Camcorder

Surprisingly, this is the place where most mic problems arise. Most consumer and pro-sumer camcorders do not have decent mic input connections. They typically do not have enough amplification to "hear" low-impedance mics like standard handheld mics. What's more, they use mini-plugs, whereas most professional mics use rugged, reliable XLR jacks. What you may need is a transformer with an XLR to mini-plug cable to increase

7

the impedance and allow you to connect your mic to your camcorder. Such transformers are passive, meaning they do not require electricity. Shure has just such a transformer—the A96F—for $54. If you use a powered mic such as a lavaliere, you may need only the XLR to mini-plug converter cable.

Getting the Most from Your Mics—Expert Audio Tips

When I considered whom I'd tap for audio expertise, only one name came to mind: Shure, Inc. Throughout my TV news and video production career, Shure mics have been the staple in our audio kits.

This 77-year old company is a world leader in microphone technology, playing a roll in audio history from the Japanese surrender ending World War II and President John F. Kennedy's inaugural address to Woodstock and the 2002 Winter Olympics, where Shure's wireless systems captured all the opening ceremonies' audio moments.

Shure's "Elvis mic," the Unidyne, kicked things off when the company first introduced it in 1939. Frank Sinatra and the Rolling Stones field-tested the SM58—the world's best-selling, all-purpose vocal mic, introduced in 1966. And now groups such as 'N Snyc and D'Angelo rely on Shure's Beta Series.

Shure put me in touch with Chris Lyons, a Senior Engineer in Shure's Applications Group. In his 12 years with Shure he has served as Technical Liaison for Shure's broadcast customers and as Product Line Manager for Wired Microphones. Chris has presented hundreds of audio training seminars to broadcasters, educators, government agencies, and audio/visual production specialists. He has written and edited numerous articles and technical papers, including the booklet *Guide to Better Audio for Video Production*, available for free download at http://www.shure.com/booklets/techpubs.html.

Chris offers this expert advice:

- **Always place the microphone as close as is practical to the sound source.** Every time the source-to-mic distance increases by a factor of two, the sound pressure level (SPL) reaching the mic decreases by a factor of four, making clear sound pickup progressively more difficult. This is called the *inverse-square rule*, and it applies whether the distance increases from 6 inches to 12 inches or from 6 feet to 12 feet. This means that the talker-to-mic distance must be cut in half to cause a significant improvement in sound quality.

- **Use the fewest number of microphones necessary for the situation.** People sometimes have a tendency to "over-mic" a shot, using three or four microphones when one or two would be sufficient. Using excess mics means more background noise pickup, greater chance of feedback or "tin can" sound, and more levels for the operator to keep track of. If additional mics don't make things sound better, they probably will make things sound worse.

- **Advice for using a handheld mic:** Whether held in the hand or mounted on a stand, place this mic about 6–12 inches from the talker's mouth, pointing up at about a 45-degree angle (see Figure 7.4). With some types of microphones, holding the microphone very close (3–6 inches) will cause additional emphasis of the lower frequencies (known as *proximity effect*), resulting in a "warmer," bass-heavy sound.

- **Advice for using a lavaliere mic:** For best results, clip a lavaliere mic on the outside of clothing, about six to eight inches below the chin. You can clip the mic to the collar of a shirt or blouse, but sound quality in this position tends to be somewhat muffled because some high frequencies (which contain consonants) do not fully wrap around to the area under the chin.

- **Advice for concealing a lavaliere mic:** Concealing the mic gives your production an extra level of quality. Make sure you keep both the microphone and the first few inches of cable from rubbing against either the body or clothing, which will cause noise. Try taping the "lav" under the shirt collar near the opening in front. The cable can be routed around to the back of the neck, over the collar and under the shirt. Alternatively, tape it to the interviewee's eyeglasses on the inside by the temple. Route the wire over the ear and down the back.

- **Advice for using a surface mount mic:** These are great for panel discussions and work best when positioned on a smooth, flat surface, such as a table or desk. A thin piece of soft foam rubber or a computer mouse pad underneath the mic helps minimize problems created by surface vibrations. Small surfaces—less than three feet square—reduce the pickup of low frequencies and may improve the clarity of deep voices by reducing "boominess."

- **Advice for using a shotgun mic:** Avoid aiming shotgun mics at hard surfaces such as tile floors, brick walls, and flat ceilings. These surfaces reflect background noise into the microphone or cause the sound to be slightly hollow. Place a heavy blanket on a reflective surface to provide some sound absorption. Shotgun mics are more sensitive to wind noise than standard microphones, so use a foam windscreen and don't move them too rapidly. A rubber-isolated shock mount will help control handling noise.

- **Use only low-impedance microphones.** Low-impedance or "Low-Z" mics (less than 600 ohms) allow you to use very long runs of cable (more than 1,000 feet) with negligible loss of sound quality. "High-Z" mics (greater than 10,000 ohms) lose high frequencies and begin to sound muffled with 20-foot cables. The impedance of a microphone should *not* match the impedance of the input to which it is connected. Matching the impedance causes significant signal level loss. Always connect low-impedance microphones to higher-impedance inputs—preferably 5 to 10 times greater. Inputs on professional mixers typically have an impedance of 1,000 ohms or more.

- **Tips on using wireless systems:** Try to keep the distance from the transmitter to the receiver as short as possible. Always do a "walkaround" with the mic before the event. If dropouts occur, try moving the receiver a few feet and repeat the walkaround. Dual-antenna "diversity receivers" minimize dropout because it is unlikely that the signal to both antennas will be interrupted at the same instant. If possible, do your sound check at the same time of day as the event to discover whether there are any nearby users of your wireless frequencies. When using belt-pack-type transmitters, make sure the antenna cable is hanging straight. Coiling it up in the wearer's pocket significantly reduces transmission distance. With handheld transmitters that have an external antenna, discourage users from holding their hands over the antenna to avoid reducing transmission range and increasing dropout.

7

- **Use "balanced" cables and connectors.** Their metal shielding keeps the audio signal free of interference from things such as florescent lights, dimmer switches, and other audio or electrical cables. Use cables with braided or mesh shielding. They are more resistant than metal foil shielding to cracks or tears, which cause electrical shorts.

- **Plan ahead.** This is the most important thing you can do to improve the audio quality of your productions. When you set up your equipment, look for things that might cause a problem with your audio—air conditioning ducts, noisy doors, fluorescent lights, and so on. Check for things that you can use to your advantage—sound-absorbent carpeting or a built-in PA system. Experiment with different mic placements but don't gamble an important project on a method you've never tried. Monitor your audio and listen carefully for anything that sounds unnatural. As the saying goes, "If you notice the sound, there's something wrong with it."

FIGURE 7.4

Proper placement for a handheld mic.

Building a Simple and Inexpensive Voice-Recording Area

To create your voiceover narration you'll need a quiet, sound-absorbing location. I touched base with the industry leader in sound absorption material, Auralex Acoustics.

They suggest the easiest solution is to build a temporary recording area simply by hanging some thick blankets or fiberglass insulation on two joining corner walls. Egg cartons, carpeting, and foam rubber do not work well. That is an old "audio myth." If you can create something like a four-sided cubicle, so much the better.

If you drape the blankets only in one corner, point the mic toward that corner, place yourself between the mic and the corner, and speak *away* from the blankets. It seems counterintuitive but the mic is sort of like a camera. It "sees" what's in front of it (even if it is omnidirectional). In this case it "sees" your face and the hanging, sound-absorbing blankets.

If you want to take your voice-recording area quality up several notches, consider purchasing Auralex's studio foam sheets or a portable recording area kit. These kits range in price from $159 to $999. Figure 7.5 illustrates two of these "acoustic environments," as Auralex calls them. The company emphasizes that these kits are not true "isolation" booths. Those are intended to keep sound out and require some "serious construction." Visit http://www.auralex.com/ for product and dealer info, plus a contact phone number. They are very customer-service oriented and will help you find a solution.

FIGURE 7.5
"Acoustic environments" from Auralex. Left: MAX-Wall 420. Right: MAX-Wall 1141VB. (Photos courtesy Auralex Acoustics.)

Voicing Solid Narrations

Creating narrations is as easy as turning on your camcorder. If you have a handheld mic (or some other external mic), plug it into your camcorder. Otherwise, you can use the built-in, onboard camcorder mic.

Before you record your voiceover go over this checklist to make sure you're ready:

- **Read your copy out loud.** Listen to your words. They should sound comfortable, conversational, even informal.
- **Avoid technical jargon.** That demands extra effort from your listeners, and you may lose them.

7

- **Short sentences work best.** If you find yourself stumbling over certain phrases, rewrite them.

- **Stress important words and phrases.** As you review your copy, underline important words. When you record your voiceover you'll want to give those words extra emphasis—more volume and punch.

- **Mark pauses.** Go through your copy and mark logical breaks with short parallel lines. They'll remind you to pause at those points. Avoid overly smooth and constant pacing. That's characteristic of a scripted delivery and, once again, you don't want to remind viewers that this is TV. It's real life. It's conversational.

- **Break up your copy into shorter sentences.** Always be on the lookout for convoluted, wandering sentences. Too many modifiers can be unwieldy. Break long sentences into several shorter ones. Shorter sentences tend to have only one key point. It's easier to emphasize one key point in one sentence versus multiple points in a rambling speech.

- **Punch up your voice.** When reading copy it's too easy to slip into a dull, monotone voice. Instead, add some zest and enthusiasm to your narration. As one consultant told me, "Pump up your projection." You want people to pay attention. You do that by speaking as if the subject truly interests you. On the other hand, you are not trying to be a professional announcer. No need to put on airs or use a *basso profundo* voice.

- **Practice.** Record a couple narrations and listen. Have others listen. Most first-time narrators mumble or "swallow" words. Have you made yourself clear?

- **Use a windscreen.** Although you need to record close to the mic for best effect—12 inches away or so—getting too close can lead to "popping P's." As you say "P" words, you project a small blast of wind at the mic. Using a windscreen minimizes that, as will not speaking directly into the mic.

- **Wear earphones.** In this case the purpose is not to make sure you're actually getting audio, rather it's to hear yourself. That may seem a bit odd. You can hear yourself just fine without a headset. But you need the headset to see how the mic "hears" you. You'll also discover if you're popping any P's or speaking with too much sibilance—an overemphasis on the "S" sound.

Editing Audio Using Premiere

Before you add your scintillating sound to your project, I want to show you a few audio fundamentals.

Task: Experiment with an Audio File Waveform

To experiment an audio file waveform, follow these steps:

1. Open Premiere to your workspace. No need to open your project just yet. First you'll take a look at an audio file waveform in the Clip window.

2. Double-click your Project window and import the sample audio file included with Premiere: `Music.aif`. If you have some other audio file you'd like to use, that should work fine. Premiere can handle most standard audio types, including AIF, WAV, MP3, AVI, MOV, and Windows Media Audio (WMA). (I'll cover music CD audio a bit later.) You should find `Music.aif` in the `Premiere/Sample Folder` directory.

3. Right-click the clip icon and select Open in Clip Window. This is the audio clip's waveform. It should look like Figure 7.6.

FIGURE 7.6

Use the Clip window to view an audio clip's waveform.

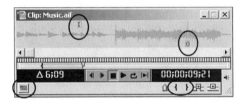

4. Experiment with this waveform for a while. Drag the edit line to the beginning and play. The amplitude of the waveform reflects the volume of the original clip. The fatter the line, the louder the sound. `Music.aif` has some extreme dynamics that show up as huge changes on the waveform.

5. I've highlighted a few icons in Figure 7.6. The waveform in the lower-left corner lets you increase the time displayed, just like clicking the "minus sign" in the Timeline window. Click four times to go through all the views and return to the default setting.

6. You can set in- and out-points the same way you did in the Video Clip window by using the "{" brackets or the edit points in the Slider/Jog bar. Note the extra visual aides on the waveform when you do create new in- or out-points—a green *I* for in-point and a red *O* for out-point.

7. Drag the `Music.aif` clip (or whatever audio file you decided to use for this exercise) from the Clip window to the Audio 1 track. You also can close the Clip window and drag the original, untrimmed clip from the Project window to the timeline.

7

▼   8. Press the =/+ key a couple times to expand the view of the audio clip on the time-
         line until it fills the screen width. This will ensure you see the waveform when you
         open it in the next step.

      9. Click the little triangle to the left of the words "Audio 1." I've highlighted it in
▲   Figure 7.7. This pops open an expanded view of the audio track.

FIGURE 7.7

*Use this little triangle
to expand the audio
track on the timeline.*

This view differs from the Clip window. Here you have four viewing options, highlighted
in Figure 7.7: waveform, a "keyframe" icon, a red volume-control "rubberband" icon,
and a blue audio pan "rubberband" icon. I'll introduce keyframes in Hour 11, "Creating
Video Effects." You use the red rubberband to adjust volume and the blue rubberband to
pan audio left and right. Click the little red icon in the lower-left part of the Audio 1
track box to switch to the red volume-control rubberband. I highlighted this icon in
Figure 7.8.

FIGURE 7.8

*The red icon displays
the "volume" rubber-
band on the audio
waveform.*

To view the audio waveform in the timeline's audio track, click the
Waveform button to the left of the red volume-control rubberband. The
narrow waveform display on the Timeline window doesn't take up much
real estate, which can make it difficult to note where you may want to grab
or make "handles" on the red rubberband. To expand the height of the
audio track, right-click in the timeline, select Timeline Window Options,
select the largest icon, and then click OK.

When you edit your project, you may want to drop or increase the volume of an entire clip—or several clips. For example, you may want to bring the natural sound down by half while you narrate. To do that you use one of the toolbox audio tools—the Fade Adjustment tool. I've highlighted it in Figure 7.9.

Place it on the rubberband and drag the red line higher or lower to decrease or increase the volume for the entire clip. Later, when you add "handles" to the rubberband, you can use the Fade Adjustment tool to change the volume between any two handles.

FIGURE 7.9

Use the Fade Adjustment tool on the red rubberband to change the volume.

 Whatever changes you make to the rubberband won't change the original clip's volume. It changes only how it plays back in your project. The default setting for the rubberband line is 100%. That is, it plays source audio clips at their original volume unless you tell it to do otherwise.

Task: Fade Up Audio

Frequently you'll want to fade up the audio at the start of your production. Here's how:

1. You'll note that there are little red boxes (known as *handles*) marking the beginning and end of the rubberband. Move the Selection tool over the left box at the start of the clip.

 As the Selection tool approaches the rubberband, it turns into a pointing finger. When that finger moves over a handle, it turns gray, indicating you can grab that handle.

2. Click and drag the left red rubberband handle all the way down. I've highlighted that handle (it's the one with the hand pointing at it) in Figure 7.10. That sets the opening audio level to zero (silence). If you do nothing else, when you play the clip, its volume gradually will increase until it reaches 100% at the end of the clip. But that's not what you want to do here.

7

3. You want to set a volume control point or handle a second or so into the clip where the volume will reach 100%. Click the red line a little way into the clip. That places a red handle on the rubberband. As I've highlighted in Figure 7.10, drag that handle back up to the center of the waveform to approximately the original 100% volume level.

FIGURE 7.10

By dragging the first rubberband handle down all the way, you set the opening volume to zero. Placing a handle a short way into the clip fades up the volume to 100%.

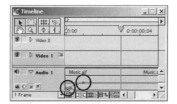

To return the audio volume-control rubberband exactly to the original 100% volume level (or any other level from 0 to 200%), hold down the Shift key, select that newly created handle, and then move it up or down. As illustrated in Figure 7.11, Premiere will display the exact volume level percentage. When holding down the Shift key, you can drag the red line far above or below its audio waveform track to set the exact percentage.

FIGURE 7.11

Holding down the Shift key while dragging the red rubberband changes the volume in one-percent increments.

Task: Fade Out Audio

▼ **TASK**

Just as you'll frequently fade up audio to start a project, you'll likely fade it out at the end. Basically it's the same procedure as fading up, except this time I'll show you how to save a step:

1. Click the red rubberband at a point about a second from the end of your clip. That places another handle there and does not change the volume level.

2. Move your Selection tool over the red box at the end of the clip. When it turns into a gray pointing finger, grab the box and drag it down as far as you can. This drops the volume to zero at the end and uses the newly created marker as the starting point for the fade.

If you want to delete an audio rubberband handle, grab it *without* holding down the Shift key, drag it outside the waveform track, and then release the mouse button. Goodbye handle.

Editing Two Audio Clips

Just as you created transitions between video clips, you can make a smooth transition between audio clips. It's called a *cross-fade* and works just like a video cross-dissolve in that the audio in the first clip fades down as the audio in the next clip increases in volume.

It adds a real nice touch to your project. I recommend using it virtually every time you make some kind of smooth video transition.

You'd think that Premiere video transitions would offer a button to make an audio cross-fade at the same time. But that's not the case. There may be a good reason for this, but I don't know what it is.

Instead you have to do some manual labor. And if you are cross-fading two audio clips that are linked to video, it becomes even more labor intensive.

First, try a cross-fade with two audio-only clips.

Task: Cross-fade Between Two Audio-Only Clips

In a departure from the standard single-track editing model, Premiere forces you to work in something like an A/B editing mode. Again, I don't understand why. That's just the way it is. Regardless, here are the steps to follow:

1. Delete the clip(s) from the timeline and drag `Music.aif` back to the Audio 1 track.

2. Drag another instance of `Music.aif` to the Audio 2 track.

3. Open the waveform track for both by clicking the small triangles next to each audio track name so you can see how this works.

4. Slide the Audio 2 `Music.aif` clip to the right so its beginning overlaps slightly with the end of the Audio 1 `Music.aif`. Your timeline should look like the one shown in Figure 7.12.

5. Make the cross-fade by clicking the Cross-fade tool. I've highlighted it in Figure 7.13. It's the first icon in the audio portion of the toolbox. Then click the `Music.aif` clips on Track 1 and Track 2, in order. Both tracks will flash to indicate that the cross-fade took.

7

FIGURE 7.12
How your timeline should look before you make your audio cross-fade.

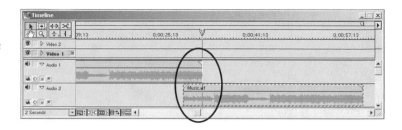

FIGURE 7.13
The Audio Cross-fade tool.

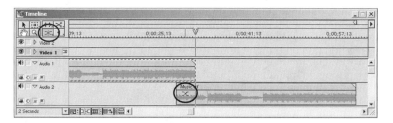

As highlighted in Figure 7.14, the volume-level rubberbands now each have handles at the start of the edit. The Audio 1 rubberband will drop to zero, and the Audio 2 rubberband will climb to 100% by the end of the edit.

FIGURE 7.14
The volume-level rubber bands now have handles.

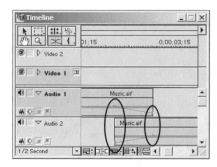

Once you create a handle, you can drag and drop it left or right along the waveform rubberband line as far as the next handle in either direction. Handles are merely a convenience. They're not stuck at any one location.

Cross-fading Audio Clips That Are Linked to Video

Now for some real hands-on work.

Task: Start with a Video-Only Transition

Delete the audio tracks in the timeline. Double-click the Project window, navigate to `Premiere/Sample Folder` and import `zfinal.avi`. If you want to use your own clip(s), that's fine. Just make sure it's a video clip with audio—a so-called *linked clip*. Here are the steps to follow:

1. Drag `zfinal.avi` to the Video 1 track. Notice two things:

    - Its audio portion jumps automatically to Audio 1.
    - Both clips are green. The green color code means the audio and video are linked and synced. They belong together.

    If you use the Selection tool to drag a video segment endpoint to shorten the clip, the audio portion will drag right along with it.

2. Drag another instance of `zfinal.avi` to Video 1, following the first instance.
3. Shorten that clip by dragging its beginning to the right a couple seconds.
4. Shorten the first clip by dragging its end to the left a couple seconds.
5. Slide the second clip to the left (or do a *ripple delete* by right-clicking the gray space and select Ripple Delete) adjacent to the first clip.
6. Drag and drop a *video* (not audio) cross-dissolve transition to the edit point on the Video 1 track. It should look like Figure 7.15.

You just created a video-only transition. The audio portion will not transition smoothly between the two clips. Play it to see. The loud `zfinal.avi` fuzz-tone guitar music cuts abruptly to the acoustic guitar opening of the next clip.

FIGURE 7.15

How your timeline should look after making a video cross-dissolve.

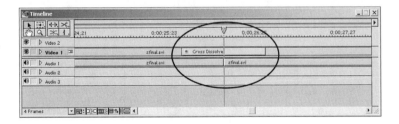

7

> Take the "pan" rubberband for a trial run. It lets you slide monaural and stereo audio clips to the left or right channel. Adobe makes a point of saying you can pan a monaural signal but can only adjust the balance of a stereo signal. Whatever. It sounds more or less the same in both cases. The pan rubberband is the blue icon next to the red volume-control rubberband icon.
>
> If you have a video clip with a car driving through the frame, use the pan rubberband to move the audio with the video. If you have someone talking in your shot and that person is off to one side of the screen, pan the audio to match.

Task: Finish the Cross-Fade

Here's how you make that transition sound as smooth as it looks. To do this you need to unlink the audio and video of the two clips:

1. To unlink one clip at a time, select the Link/Unlink tool. It's the third audio tool in that part of the toolbox. I've highlighted it in Figure 7.16.

2. Click the video track for the first zfinal.avi, then click its associated audio track. They'll flash and then the video portion will turn yellow and the audio portion will turn blue, showing they are now unlinked.

3. Do the same for the second zfinal.avi clip.

4. Move the second zfinal.avi audio track to the Audio 2 track.

5. Now create an overlap between the two clips, just as you'd do if you were creating a video transition in A/B editing mode. Use the Selection tool (keyboard shortcut V) to drag the endpoint of the Audio 1 clip farther into the timeline and to extend the start of the Audio 2 clip toward the start of the timeline (don't drag the entire clip—only the end or beginning to lengthen it). Take a look at Figure 7.17 to see what I mean. You have created overlapping audio clips.

6. Now create the cross-fade the same way you did before by selecting the Cross-fade tool from the audio section of the toolbox and clicking the audio clips on Audio 1 and Audio 2 in succession.

7. Now listen to your edit (remember, you can't see the video dissolve unless you render it first). Depending on where you positioned the overlapping clips, it may work like a charm. The hard-rock guitar will fade out and the acoustic guitar will gradually fade in.

FIGURE 7.16

The Link/Unlink tool.

FIGURE 7.17

How your timeline should look after you've unlinked and overlapped the two audio clips.

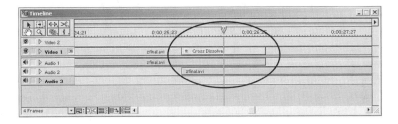

If the edits do not fit just right, you can play with them by linking the audio and video again, sliding things around, unlinking them, changing the size of the overlap, and sliding the rubberband handles left and right and/or up and down.

You can unlink all linked clips in an entire project with one mouse click. Locate the Toggle Sync Mode icon at the bottom of the timeline. I've highlighted it in Figure 7.18. Note that it has what looks like a number 8 on the left side. That's two chain links. Click that icon and the links go away. Now all audio and video clips are unlinked.

FIGURE 7.18

The Toggle Sync Mode icon. Use it to link/unlink all clips in a project.

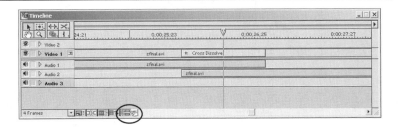

News-Style Editing: Using Cutaways with Sound Bites

The task here is to place a cutaway over the edit point of two adjacent sound bites. This is a practical and frequently used technique that requires even a bit more manual labor.

Now it's time to use *your* video clips. What would work best are two sound bites from the same person that you want to place back to back. If you don't have two such clips, you can use any two clips (plus a cutaway) just to get a feel for how this works. For instance, two soccer goals plus a crowd shot cutaway will work well. Make sure all three clips have video *and* audio. Here are the steps to follow:

1. Import the sound bites (or whatever clips you're using) plus the cutaway to the Project window.

2. Delete all the clips in the Timeline window.

3. Drag the sound bites to the Video 1 track on the timeline, one after the other. Now play the clips. If this is an interview, there probably will be a slight image jump between clip 1 and clip 2 because the interviewee moved a bit or you moved the camera.

The object here is to cover that jump-cut. You'll do that by removing part of the end of the video portion of clip 1 and replacing it with a video-only segment of the cutaway clip. This is a very labor-intensive process that will become second nature once you do it a few times. Figure 7.19 shows the process after completing nine steps so you can see where this is going:

FIGURE 7.19

How your cutaway edit will look after following the first nine steps.

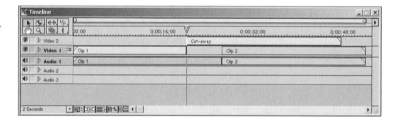

1. Unlink clip 1 from its associated audio using the Link/Unlink tool from the audio section of the toolbox.

2. Find a logical place to insert a cutaway at the end of clip 1 by moving the edit line back from the end of the clip. A good amount of time for a cutaway is two to three seconds, so look around there for a logical point to lay in the cutaway (note that as you drag the edit line, the unlinked audio portion does not change). There is no hard-and-fast rule here—simply setting the edit point at three seconds before the junction of the two sound bites will work fine. As you get better at this you'll try to match an interviewee's head movements to the cutaway.

3. Find and select the Razor tool in the upper-right corner of the toolbox. I've highlighted it in Figure 7.20. Use this to slice the clip 1 sound bite in two by placing it over the edit line and clicking.

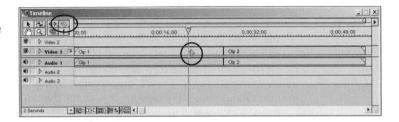

FIGURE 7.20

The Razor tool lets you slice a clip in two.

4. Use the Selection tool (keyboard shortcut V) to select the portion of the clip you don't need and delete it, leaving a gap in the video at the end of clip 1.

5. Locate the cutaway clip in the Project window and drag it to the Video 2 track (*not* Video 1). The linked audio portion should drop automatically into Audio 2.

6. Unlink the audio from the video using the Link/Unlink tool.

7. Delete that unlinked audio portion of the cutaway clip. You don't want the audio portion from the cutaway playing while the interview is playing.

8. Use the Selection tool to trim the beginning of the video portion of the cutaway clip until you reach a logical spot to begin the cutaway. Typically that's when your interviewer is calmly looking at the interviewee or when the hand shot cutaway matches the hands in clip 1.

9. Drag the newly trimmed cutaway clip so its beginning lines up with the spot you cut out of clip 1. If this sounds a bit confusing, take a look back at Figure 7.19.

10. Use the Selection tool to trim the end of the cutaway (or use the Razor tool) so it lines up with the start of clip 2. Because you're using the default "Snap to Edges," all these trims and razor slices should work smoothly. You now have created a cutaway that will fit exactly into the gap you created in clip 1.

11. Finally, drag the cutaway into the gap. Done. Whew!

Take a look at your edits to see whether the cutaway plays smoothly and eases the transition between the two clips.

You may notice that using this technique means the cutaway ends exactly as the next sound bite begins. That's a method I like because usually the second sound bite is a new thought and it "feels" more natural to see the interviewee as he or she starts a new comment. That's not always the case, and you may want to move the cutaway farther into clip 2 or even start it right at the beginning of clip 2.

7

If you slide unlinked audio or video clips along the timeline (as opposed to shortening them by trimming their in- or out-points), you will take them out of sync with their formerly linked partner. Those unsynced clips will have little red triangles at the start of both the audio and video segments to show they are out of sync. If you click and hold that triangle, Premiere tells you how far out of sync the clips are. If you click that triangle and drag the mouse a little ways into the clip and then release, the clip will resync itself with its associated audio or video clip. This applies whether you unlinked clips globally using the Toggle Sync Mode button or individually using the Link/Unlink tool.

News-Style Editing: Using J-Cuts and L-Cuts

Frequently you'll want to start a clip by having its sound play "under" the previous video clip and then transition to its associated video. This is a great way to let your audience know that someone is about to say something or that a transition is coming. It's kind of like foreshadowing. This is called a *J-cut*.

Conversely, another slick editing technique is to let the audio tail off under the next video clip. This is an *L-cut*.

Because you know how to use the Link/Unlink tool, the Selection tool to trim clips, and the Cross-fade audio tool, I won't go over all the detailed steps. Figure 7.21 shows a J-cut.

Here's the basic approach to making J- and L-cuts:

1. Place two clips adjacent in the Video 1 track. Make sure you have enough spare frames available to extend the audio to create the sound-under.

2. Unlink the clip you want to extend.

3. Drag the audio for the clip you want to extend down to a different audio track (usually Audio 2, but it can be any audio track other than Audio 1 in this case).

4. Drag the end of that audio clip either under the end of the previous clip (J-cut) or under the beginning of the next clip (L-cut). Remember, don't *slide* the audio clip. That will unsync it. Rather you are extending the duration of that audio clip by using the Selection tool to drag its end.

5. Place a cross-fade from the first clip to the second. Done.

FIGURE 7.21

A J-cut. Used to lay audio under a preceding video clip and gradually increase its volume to the point where its associated video pops onscreen.

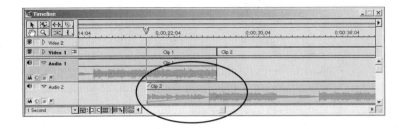

Now play your edited selection to see how that sound-under style works. If you want to adjust volume levels, it's a simple matter to open the audio waveform portion of the audio track and drag the red rubberband handles around.

> When editing clips in the Source window, holding down the Alt (Windows) or Option (Mac) key and dragging the in- and/or out-points will split them into separate video and audio in/out-points, allowing for an L- or J-cut before the clips are even in the timeline. While the modifier key is held down, the in- and out-points for audio and video are edited separately. Once released, they will move together with the newly created offset.
>
> This tip is provided by Adobe Systems Premiere evangelist Daniel Brown. See Hour 16, "Tips, Tricks, and Techniques: Part 1," for seven more of his expert tips.

Using the Audio Mixer

The Audio Mixer is a mixed blessing. It can automate volume changes on multiple tracks, but making individual track adjustments can be tedious and error prone. Many times it's easier to use the red rubberband volume control.

I won't go into too many details because the Adobe manual explains things well. However, I do suggest experimenting with the Audio Mixer:

1. Leave the J-cut or L-cut you just made open on your Timeline window.

2. Go to Window, Audio Mixer and up pops the Audio Mixer. Note that it displays as many audio tracks as you have in your timeline. You can add audio tracks by using the Timeline fly-out menu and selecting Add Audio Tracks.

3. Each audio track in the Mixer has three icons at the top: Automation Read, Automation Write, and Automation Off. Select the first, Automation Read, for each track (probably only tracks 1 and 2). I've highlighted that icon in Figure 7.22.

7

4. Drag your edit line in front of the J- or L-cut you made and play your piece. Watch the sliders on the Audio Mixer move as the volumes change in your edit. Nifty.

5. Play that segment again and grab the slider controls and move them up and down. Note that they change the audio playback levels, but there is a little disconcerting delay. That is one of the minor drawbacks to the Mixer.

6. Stop playing your clips and return the edit line to somewhere ahead of the edit. Click the Automation Write icons—the middle "pencil" tools—and start playing your piece.

The sliders will once again move to follow the cross-fade you created, but you can override that by moving the associated track slider. You'll notice that if you release the slider it returns automatically to the volume level you originally set.

FIGURE 7.22

*Audio Mixer controls.
From left to right:
Automation Read,
Automation Write, and
Automation Off.*

Stop playing and take a look at the red rubberband. It should be chock full of red handles, signifying each volume adjustment you made using the slider.

> The default setting for Automation Write on the Audio Mixer is called "Touch." The Mixer will record new volume levels only if you're dragging and *holding* the volume slider. Release it and the volume returns to whatever was on the track to begin with. You can change that setting to one of several other options by right-clicking or Option-clicking in the Mixer window, selecting Audio Mixer Options, and selecting a new Automation Write option.

In most cases these new handles are serious overkill. Rarely does anyone need all those minute adjustments. You could have accomplished the same effect by simply creating a new handle on the rubberband and dragging it to a new volume level.

Where the Mixer shines is "gang" volume control—that is, controlling more than one track at once, in unison. This is helpful if you have natural sound plus a music track and you want to drop their volume when the narration starts. Instead of dropping each separately, you can adjust them en masse with the Mixer.

To "gang" tracks, simply right-click a slider and assign it a gang number. Do the same for other audio tracks, assigning them the same gang number. Click the Automation Write icons for each track. Now when you move the slider, it sets new volume levels for all ganged tracks.

If you don't like how you did the volume change, go back by using the History palette or Edit, Undo.

When you use the red audio volume rubberband, make sure the Audio Mixer is closed. When it's open, it overrides changes you make on the rubberband.

Audio Special Effects and Music

Premiere comes with several audio "sweetening" tools, including a new set of three highly customizable plug-ins. I'll cover them in Hour 11. I'll also show you how to "rip" tunes off music CDs to use in Premiere and create your own high-quality, royalty-free tunes in Hour 9, "Advanced Editing Techniques and Workspace Tools." They'll sound terrific. Really.

Summary

Audio is critical to a high-quality video production. Most important is the original footage. Take some extra measures to ensure high-quality audio. Select the right mics for the job, turn to wireless audio if the budget allows, and use professional voiceover techniques.

Some standard, news-style audio-editing styles will take your audio one step higher. Use cross-fades, L- and J-cuts, and cutaways to give your piece a quality "feel." Use the Audio Mixer to adjust the levels of more than one track at once to bring sound under a narration and then bring it back up during narrative breaks.

7

Workshop

Review the questions and answers in this section to try to sharpen your audio-acquisition and Premiere audio-editing skills. Also, take a few moments to tackle my short quiz and the exercises.

Q&A

Q **When I videotape indoors, my audio has a "tin can" quality. What's going on?**

A This happens for one of two reasons. The simplest reason is that the mic is too far from your subject and you're in a room with reflective surfaces such as flat walls and an uncarpeted floor. Move the mic closer. The other is more complicated and involves what audio engineers call the "3-to-1 rule." If you use more than one mic for several speakers, as in a panel discussion, you need to place the mics three times as far apart as they are to the speakers. That is, if a mic is two feet from a panelist, the next mic should be at least six feet away from the first mic. Otherwise, they pick up audio at about the same time, cancel each other out, and create that "tin can" sound.

Q **I bought professional-quality mics but I can barely hear them in my headset and later when I listen to my tape. Why?**

A Unlike with professional camcorders, there are no mic standards for consumer and prosumer camcorders. If you read your camcorder's spec sheet, you probably won't see anything about the mic input, whether it's stereo or mono, and whether it needs external amplification. If you're using a low-impedance mic, such as a professional handheld mic with a cable longer than 20 feet, you probably will need a transformer for most camcorders. That should resolve your low-volume problem. If you're using an unpowered condenser mic, such as a shotgun, you will need "phantom power," either from a mixer or a portable phantom-power adapter.

Quiz

1. Your audio and video clips have little red triangles in the upper-left corners. How did that happen? What can you do about it?

2. Why use an L-cut or a J-cut? What are the basic editing steps?

3. Why should you use external mics?

Quiz Answers

1. The red triangles mean what were once linked and synced video and audio clips are now out of sync. They got that way because you unlinked them and then slid either the audio clip or video clip (or both) along the track. To resync the clips, click and drag a red triangle a short distance into one of the clips and release the mouse button. That clip will jump back to a synced position.

2. In both instances, you are creating smooth transitions to either ease a cut with specific sound into your project or let it fade out. An *L-cut* starts audio under the preceding video cut (which also has associated audio) and then fades up as you transition or cut to the video portion. A *J-cut* fades audio under the next clip as a way to ease out of that audio clip. You create both edits by unlinking the audio from the clip you're going to extend under an adjacent clip, moving that audio to a different audio track, extending the audio in the appropriate direction, and then adding a cross-fade (or you can do it manually).

3. Your camcorder's onboard mic is a jack-of-all-trades and a master of none. It picks up sound all around you, including noise you make when handling the camcorder. External mics capture sound at the source. Using external mics is invariably better and greatly improves the quality of your production.

Exercises

1. J-cuts, L-cuts, and cutaways should be a part of every production. The only way that's going to happen is if you get comfortable doing them. Make a few of each.

2. When using a narration, typically you'll lay down some of that voiceover, put in a clip with some nice natural sound, and then add more narration and more natural sound throughout your story. Give that process a try by cutting your narration with the Razor tool and inserting nat-sound clips at those breaks. Use J- and L-cuts liberally.

3. I'll cover audio special effects in Hour 9. But you can preview that process by adding an audio clip to the timeline. The best is a narration, because you know what it should sound like and any changes you add will be more obvious. Open the Audio tab in the Transitions palette, open the Reverb & Delay submenu, and drag and drop Reverb on your audio clip. That opens a small effects control window. Click Setup, which opens the Reverb Settings window. Click Preview Sound and then start sliding the four sliders to your heart's content. When done you can erase your efforts by opening the History tab and clicking the item above "add filter."

7

HOUR 8

Tackling Text: Using the Title Designer

Onscreen text helps tell your story. Using a location "super" (superimposed text) sets the scene and saves the narration for other relevant points. Displaying an interviewee's name and title at the bottom of the screen reminds viewers who this person is. Using onscreen bulleted points reinforces the message you're trying to get across.

Premiere 6.5's new *Title Designer* is such a full-featured product, you may never fully tap its potential. With it you can create simple text, rolling credits, and colorful shapes. Your text can be any color (or multiple colors), any degree of transparency, darned near any shape—you have 90 fonts to choose from—and can move in any direction.

The highlights of this hour include the following:

- Using supers to tell your story
- Taking a tour of Adobe's new Title Designer
- Creating straightforward text using color, gradients, opacity/transparency, and drop shadows

- Adding motion to your text
- Using text-based graphics

Using Supers to Help Tell Your Story

Consider this opening sequence. A telephoto shot of scorched desert sand with rippling heat distorting the scene. Dry, desiccated, lifeless sagebrush. A lizard slowly seeking shade beneath a small stone. And a small plume of dust in the distance. Attention-getting stuff.

Now a narrator intones, "The summer heat beats down on the Bonneville Salt Flats." Effective. But what might work better is a *super* (onscreen text). Something such as "Bonneville Salt Flats." Then, as the plume of dust moves toward the camera, add another super: "Speed Trials—Summer 2002." Then a rocket-shaped vehicle screams through the scene.

Rather than interrupt the building suspense with a dulcet-toned narrator, save him for later. Instead, simply slap on a couple supers to set up your story.

Here are a couple other sample instances where text can be an effective alternative to voiceovers:

- Instead of using a voiceover to say "John Jones, president of the XYZ Association for the Preservation of Salient Sayings." Put that information in a super at the bottom of the screen.
- Instead of simply saying a collection of statistics, such as 12 drummers drumming, 11 pipers piping, 10 lords a-leaping, and so on, use a collection of bulleted points that you pop onscreen with each new numbered item. If you have small graphic images of each element, you can add them along with the text.

Text strengthens your project.

Taking a Tour of Adobe's New Title Designer

Open Premiere to your workspace. Locate the Title Designer. It's not where you might expect—under the Windows drop-down menu along with Audio Mixer, Navigator, History, and the like. Instead, it's in the File menu.

Select File, New, Title. That pops up the Title Designer. As you can see in Figure 8.1, at an 800×600 screen resolution, the Title Designer consumes your entire screen and then some.

FIGURE 8.1

Premiere 6.5's new Title Designer.

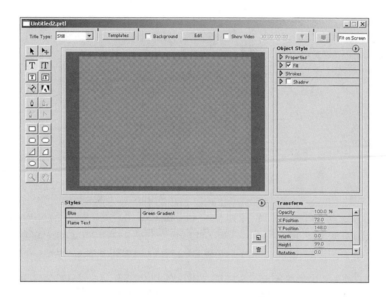

Before you type your first letter, note that when you open the Title Designer interface, Premiere adds a Title drop-down menu to the main interface.

Briefly check that out. Note the overwhelming number of fonts. One way to get a grip on them is to click Browse. Scroll down in the Browse window to Wingdings and select that typeface by clicking it.

> Check out some other items on that drop-down menu. Most are standard typeface elements: Font Size, Alignment (left, center, right), Orientation (horizontal or vertical), and Word Wrap (while typing, when you reach the end of the line, Premiere automatically moves the cursor to the next line).

Now for a little experimentation.

Click inside the large gray box. That places a cursor at that location. Start typing. Because you selected Wingdings, you should get some wild looking text—something like what's shown in Figure 8.2.

Note what happens as your text approaches the edge of the window. The cursor jumps to the next line because the Word Wrap default value is "On."

FIGURE 8.2

Taking the Title Designer for a test drive with Wingdings.

Try dragging and dropping your Wingdings text. As with similar text boxes in word processors, you can move your cursor into the box, wait for it to turn into a four-arrow diamond, and then drag the Wingdings text box around anywhere on the screen. If you grab a handle at a corner or edge, you can expand or contract the box.

Take a look at what happens when you do that. The text stretches or compresses as you move the box handles. This is the default Point Text setting.

Creating Text

Premiere offers three means to build text. I've highlighted them in Figure 8.3. From top to bottom they are Point, Area, and Path. The three text types in the left column orient text horizontally. The top two in the right column orient text vertically.

FIGURE 8.3

Three text types from top to bottom: Point, Area, and Path.

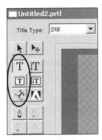

Here's an explanation of each type:

Point Text—This style builds a text "bounding" box as you type. Once you stop typing, if you change the shape and size of the box, that action correspondingly changes the shape and size of the text. Stretching the box stretches the text.

Area Text—In this case you set the size and shape of your text box before entering text. After selecting this tool, you need to define your text boundary by dragging and

8

dropping a box in the text window. Changing the box size later displays more or less text. It does *not* change the shape or size of the text.

Path Text —You can build a path for your text to follow by clicking and moving your cursor around the text window. This is not an animation tool. It merely creates a line—albeit as contorted as you want—for the text to set on. You can use Path text also to create something simple, such as a rainbow-shape curve of text. Give these text-creation styles a test drive.

Task: Test the Point Text Style

To experiment with the Point Text style, follow these steps:

1. Return to Point Text by clicking the large "T" in the upper-left corner of the Title Designer window.

2. Click anywhere in the gray text box, and a cursor appears.

3. Type several letters and spaces, making sure you let Word Wrap take you down a couple lines.

4. Move your cursor to the corners of the newly formed text bounding box. As you approach each corner, the cursor turns into a double arrow, indicating you can stretch the box. But if you move the cursor a bit farther out of the box, it changes into a looped arrow like the one in Figure 8.4. Use that to spin the box to any angle you choose.

5. As you spin the box, look at the Transform section in the lower-right corner of the Title Designer window. I've highlighted it in Figure 8.5. Note how the values for Rotation change.

6. Move the box around the text window and watch the X-position and Y-position change.

▲   7. Finally, change the box shape and watch Width and Height values change.

FIGURE 8.4

Placing your cursor right outside the corner of the bounding box pops up the loop arrow, which allows you to rotate a Point Text box on its axis.

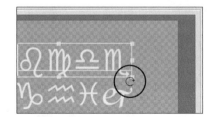

Figure 8.5

The Transform section tracks or directs your text location.

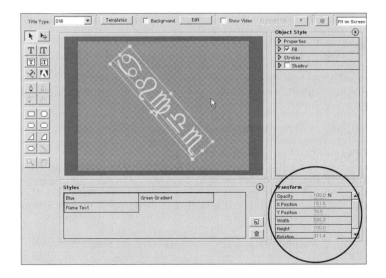

If you need to place your text in a very precise location, the Transform window gives you that option. For the most part, manually dragging and dropping your text will work fine.

> To see how the Transform options work, click the Transform Opacity number, fill in something less than 100%, and press Enter (Windows) or Return (Mac). Note how your text becomes transparent. Change the setting back to 100%.

Delete all your text by placing the cursor over the text area, dragging it over the text to highlight it, and pressing Delete or Backspace to remove all the text. Alternatively, you can drag your cursor over all the text to highlight it and then press Delete.

> You can delete the entire contents of a text bounding box as well as the box itself. Highlight a box by clicking a letter that belongs to that box. Move the cursor in the box until it turns into that diamond-shaped four-arrow box-moving cursor. Click. That highlights the box instead of placing a text cursor in the box. Now press Delete.

Task: Test the Area Text Style

To experiment with the Area Text style, follow these steps:

1. Try Area Text by selecting its tool—the "T" in a white box. In this case, before you can start typing text, you need to create the text bounding box. Position your cursor in the text window, click to set an upper-left corner to your bounding box, and then drag your cursor down and to the right to create the bottom-right corner.

2. Fill the box with text. You'll notice the first difference between Area Text and Point Text. Instead of expanding to accommodate more text, as the Point Text box did, the Area Type box has your type disappears off the bottom of the screen. Figure 8.6 demonstrates that.

3. If you expand the box, the text doesn't change shape or size, but the altered box reveals the text that ran outside the box's original confines.

FIGURE 8.6

The Area Text bounding box does not expand laterally to accommodate more text. Rather, your text runs down the screen.

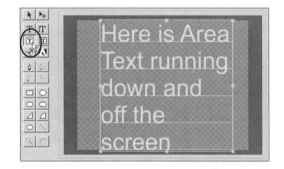

While you're doing your text testing, try the two vertically oriented text types. They're the two large T's with arrows pointing down. There really is hardly any difference between these two and their horizontal partners. True, as you type, the letters run from the top of the bounding box to the bottom, but they still display side by side, not standing on top of each other. The only difference is in the rotation. Instead of rotating on an axis at the center of the box, as do the horizontally oriented text tools, the vertical text boxes rotate on a point outside and "above" the boxes. Give that little feature a try.

The Path Text tool is both elegant and tricky. It allows you to build simple or complex, straight and/or curved paths for your text to follow.

If you've worked with the Pen tool in Adobe Photoshop, you know how to use the Path Text tool. You create the path(s) by clicking somewhere in the text window, clicking somewhere else, and so on. Each click redefines the text bounding box. If you click out-side the box, it expands to accommodate. If you click inside this box, another point is added on your lengthening path. If you click and drag away from the previous point, you create a curve. As Figure 8.7 demonstrates, it's all too easy to create a convoluted route.

FIGURE 8.7
The Path Text tool can create a twisting text display.

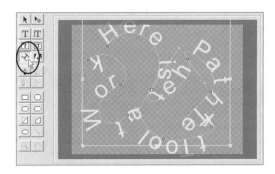

It takes practice to perfect this technique, but if you give it a few tries you'll get a basic idea how it works. Once you complete your path, type in a message and watch as it wends its way along your path, twisting and turning—and even inverting.

Working with Object Style

If the Transform window, with all its finely detailed text location and orientation data, seemed like overkill, the Object Style data will completely overwhelm you.

Adobe refers to your text as "objects." The Object Style section of the Title Designer interface is in the window's upper-right corner. It contains four drop-down menus: Properties, Fill, Strokes, and Shadow. I've highlighted them in Figure 8.8.

FIGURE 8.8
The Object Style sec-tion defines your text's characteristics.

Configuring Properties

Click the little triangle next to Properties to open its drop-down menu. In some ways this is similar to the Title drop-down menu in Premiere's workspace menu bar. Its primary purpose is to define the size and spacing of your text.

8

I'd suggest you enter some text in the text window and then change some of the following Properties values to see their effect:

Typeface—Use the drop-down menu to choose from 90 fonts and from each font's available style (bold, italic, and so on).

Font Size—The default is a very large 100. Change it to something more manageable.

Aspect—How fat or thin each letter is.

Leading—How much space there is between text lines.

Kerning—Spacing between letters on a line.

Tracking—Spacing between letters within the entire bounding box.

Slant—Tilts letters either to the right or left, depending on whether you use a positive or negative number. This is great if you want to give text that "speedy" look.

All Caps and Underline—Just like in a word processor.

Adding Fill to Text

Use the Fill fly-out menu (you may need to scroll down the Object Style window to see it) to fill in your text with color. The variability of the options, once again, is mind-boggling.

Because the selection of the fill color(s) for your text may be largely dependent on any video running beneath the text, now is a good time to place an image from a video clip in the Title Designer's text window.

Task: Place a Video Clip Image in the Title Designer's Text Window

To place an image from a video clip in the Title Designer's text window, follow these steps:

1. Shrink down the Title Designer by clicking the little dash in the upper-right corner.

2. Find a video clip to put under the text you're about to create. Because this is just an exercise, any clip will do.

3. Place the clip on the timeline and move the edit line over an image.

4. Open the Title Designer by clicking its "double box" icon or double-clicking its title bar.

5. Put a check mark in the Show Video box. I've highlighted that box in Figure 8.9. Your clip should appear inside the Title Designer's text window. If you now add text, as I've done in Figure 8.9, the video frame will display behind it.

FIGURE 8.9

The Show Video box displays whatever frame is under the timeline's edit line. You can type in a specific frame by clicking the "parking meter" icon.

From within the Title Designer window you can select a specific frame of video based on its timeline location. Click the little icon that looks like a parking meter at the top of the Title Designer window. I've highlighted it in Figure 8.9. That displays the current timeline location of the current image displayed in the text window. Simply type in a new time, using the format hours:minutes:seconds:frames, and see what pops up.

Task: Use Your Video Image to Select Fill Colors

Here's one way to use your video image to help select fill colors:

1. Make sure the Fill box is checked. Open the Fill menu by clicking the triangle next to the Fill check box.

2. Click the Fill Type drop-down menu and select Solid.

3. Use one of two ways to choose a color: Either click the little box to open one of those rainbow-style color-selection interfaces or use the Color Fill tool. In this case, select the Color Fill eyedropper.

4. Move the Color Fill eyedropper, highlighted in Figure 8.10, over your clip image in the text window. You will get immediate feedback. As you hover the eyedropper over an object, the text matches the object's color. When you find the color you want, click to select it.

This serves two purposes: First, it lets you select a text color that is not "jarring" to the viewer—not distinctly different from the color scheme on screen at that moment. Second, it's an excellent way to ensure that any text you place over a screen image will be legible. Without testing a color over an image, you could select a color that causes the text to blend in.

FIGURE **8.10**

The Color Fill eye-dropper lets you select a font or graphic color from your clip.

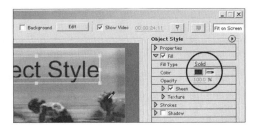

8

Using Gradients

The Fill Type drop-down menu offers six other options. I'll cover the three that make up the gradient options. The other three—Bevel, Eliminate, Ghost—fall into the category of extra credit. As I've mentioned before, Premiere is deep. There is more to discover in Premiere than most video producers have time or energy to learn.

Task: Create Type with a Linear Gradient Fill

This task applies two colors to each letter—from top to bottom. Figure 8.11 shows how the fill looks after you've applied it to text. Here are the steps to follow:

1. Make sure you have some text in the text window.

2. Select Linear Gradient from the Fill Type drop-down menu. That opens a thin, horizontal color bar. Two little boxes, capped by triangles, appear below it. I've highlighted all three items in Figure 8.11.

3. Double-click one of the little boxes. This opens a color-selection spectrum window. Select a color. You'll note that it appears in the corresponding half of the horizontal color bar.

4. Do the same for the other box using a different color. Your text should now be two-colored, with the colors blending from top to bottom.

5. Drag one of the little boxes along the color bar. Note that the relative amount of the color in the text increases or decreases as you move the box, proving once again that Premiere is eminently configurable.

FIGURE **8.11**

Text colored by the Linear Gradient fill type.

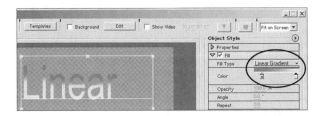

Radial Gradient

The fun doesn't end with something as mundane as a *Linear* Gradient. Take the *Radial* Gradient for a test drive. It applies one color to the middle of each letter (if that letter is an *O*, you may not see that center color) and places the other color on the edges of each letter. I created an example in Figure 8.12. Here are some points to note:

- The left color in the horizontal color bar is the center color.
- The right color goes around the edges.
- You can adjust the relative amount of each color by moving the little boxes, just as you did with the Linear Gradient.
- The closer the two boxes are together, the less of a gradient there is between the colors in the text. When they're side by side, there is no gradient. When they're far apart, there is a very gradual change from one color to the next.

FIGURE 8.12

Text colored using the Radial Gradient tool.

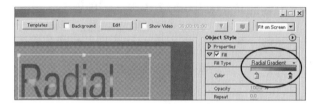

4 Color Gradient

This is the Linear Gradient times two. Open it and you have four little boxes to play with. It appears Peter Max posters (visit www.petermax.com for an example) were the inspiration for this font style. I created a 4 Color Gradient text example in Figure 8.13.

FIGURE 8.13

4 Color Gradient text.

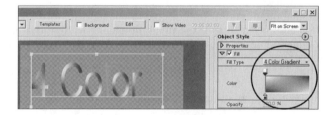

For a fun little exercise, expand your text by dragging the corner of the text-bounding box—if you selected Point Text. Otherwise, go to the top of the Object Style window and change the font size to 200 or so. This will make this effect you're about to create easier to see.

Go back down the menu and select either your Linear Gradient or Radial Gradient text. Within the Fill section, locate Repeat. Type in a low number (5 will do) and press Enter. Look at your text now. Bull's eye. My example is shown in Figure 8.14. Drag the color sliders to adjust the effect.

FIGURE 8.14

A bull's eye created with a Radial Gradient and a Repeat value of 5.

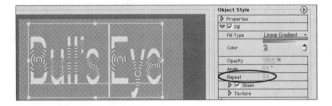

Changing Opacity/Transparency

Sometimes it's nice to be able to see through your onscreen text. The default setting for any text is 100% opacity—in other words, opaque.

Task: Change the Opacity of Solid-Color Text

Changing the opacity percentage for a solid color is simple:

1. The best way to view the effect of a change in opacity is over a video still shot. Therefore, make sure your video clip displays in the text window by checking the Show Video box.

2. Make sure you have some text onscreen.

3. Select the Solid Fill type.

4. Change the opacity percentage to something less than 100%. In Figure 8.15, I've highlighted the Opacity option in the Fill section. About 50% is a good number to get a feel for how this works.

FIGURE 8.15

Changing the opacity creates transparent text.

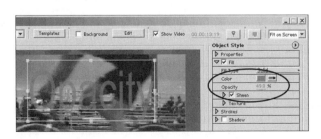

Task: Change the Opacity of Gradient Text

Changing the opacity of gradient text is more interesting and offers more options:

1. Select one of the Gradient Fill types.

2. Make sure you have some text onscreen. You may have to double-click one of the Gradient color boxes and click OK when the color spectrum selection box opens to get the onscreen text style to change to the gradient.

3. Change the opacity. Notice that it changes only the color you just selected. The other color remains opaque—at an opacity of 100%.

4. Change the opacity of the other color(s) if you want. This, too, is a super-creative little tool that lets you toy around with fonts to your heart's content.

If you created those bull's eyes by following the previous tip, then use them (or re-create them) to demonstrate one cool opacity effect. You can select one of those bull's eye text's colors and reduce its opacity while keeping the other color at full capacity. You'll get a collection of truly bizarre-looking text. See my example in Figure 8.16.

FIGURE 8.16

The bull's eye with reduced opacity for one of its colors.

Creating Shadows

Going several steps beyond most word processors that simply offer a shadow feature, Premiere lets you define your shadows' characteristics to the *n*th degree.

The Shadow tools are in the bottom drop-down menu within the Object Style window. I've highlighted them in Figure 8.17. Here they are, in order:

FIGURE 8.17

The Shadow tools.

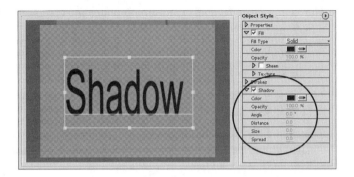

8

Opacity—Usually shadows are less opaque (more transparent) than the text "throwing" the shadows.

Color—Intuitively shadows are black or dark gray, but in real life shadows falling on grass have a green hue. You can mimic that by the selection of the shadow's color.

Angle—The shadow's direction is relative to the text in degrees. You'd think that 0 (or 360) degrees would throw the shadow above the text, and 90 degrees would mean the shadow would fall perpendicularly to the right. But Premiere takes a different view. Not only do the angles move counterclockwise but 0 degrees is to the right (at what most of us would consider 90 degrees—east of the text), 90 degrees is up (go figure), 180 is left (west), and 270 is down (south).

Distance—This is how far the shadow falls from the text. A setting of 10 is a good starting point.

Size—Self-explanatory. A setting of 0 equals the size of the original text. Each unit of 10 about doubles the width of the shadow.

Spread—This helps you replicate soft lighting. Sharply focused light sources create clearly defined shadows. Soft lighting throws less distinct shadows. Increasing the spread softens the shadow by diffusing it. It also gives the illusion that it's falling a bit farther back from the text.

Task: Experiment with the Shadow Effect

Start by turning off the Show Video button. This makes it easier to see the shadows. By step 7, your text should look like Figure 8.18. Here are the steps for this task:

1. Either change your currently selected text into a solid color or create some solid-color text.

2. Turn the Shadow effect on by checking its box. Note that all the default values are 0 (except Opacity) so no shadow should appear under your text just yet.

▼ TASK

▼

3. The first order of business is to set a distance for your shadow; otherwise, it will remain out of sight "behind" your text. A setting of 10 is a good starting point.

4. Set an angle. A "comfortable" angle is 315 degrees (falling down and to the right).

5. Set the size at something greater than 0 but not too large. A setting of 5 is a good starting point. It's just a little larger than the text.

6. Set the opacity at something less than 100% (50% looks "realistic").

7. Change the Spread setting. A value of 20 takes the hard edge off your shadow. Changing the opacity has a similar effect but does not give your shadow that realistic soft edge achieved when using Spread.

FIGURE 8.18

Text with full shadow effects.

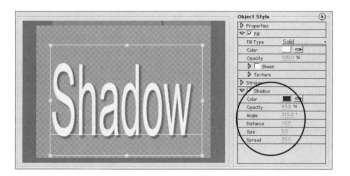

Adding Strokes to Text and Objects

Strokes is Adobe's term for outlines. The Title Designer lets you create two kinds of strokes—outer and inner. An outer stroke expands the size of your text or objects by adding an outside edge. An inner stroke keeps your objects the same size but puts a colored edge around the inside of the objects' perimeters. As with Fill, you can adjust the color, fill type, opacity, and other characteristics of your strokes.

Task: Create a Stroke for an Object

TASK

When I wrote this book, Strokes was not functioning. As we went to final copy edit, Adobe had just added most elements of that feature, so I did not have time to fully test it. This, then, is a barebones rundown on how to add Strokes to your text or objects. In Figure 8.19 I've illustrated how this process should look by the time you've reached step 4. Follow these steps:

1. Select the object to which you want to add a stroke.

2. In the Object Style section of the Title Designer, click the arrow next to Strokes to open it.

3. Click the word *Add* next to Inner or Outer and then click the triangle to expand your selection. Outer is more intuitive, so I'd suggest starting with it. I used both in Figure 8.19.

> Every time you click Add, it adds another Stroke drop-down options list that you can apply to another text or object.

4. You'll see a check box next to Outer Stroke. If you add multiple strokes, more than one Outer Stroke check box will be visible. It would be more intuitive to label these boxes Outer Stroke 1, Outer Stroke 2, and so on. Click its triangle to access the following options:

Type—Depth gives a 3D feel, Edge surrounds the entire object, and Drop Face was nonfunctional when I wrote this section.

Size—This is the stroke width in pixels.

Angle—Works with Depth to create a drop shadow–like effect.

Fill Type—Has the same features as Fill Type under the Fill Object style.

Sheen—Adds a "glint" to the text or object.

Texture—Adds a bitmap image to your object. Clicking the empty box beneath Texture opens a file menu asking you to select an image.

FIGURE 8.19
Use Strokes to add outer and inner edges to text and objects.

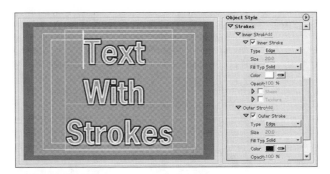

Creating and Saving Your Text

At this point in the hour, I think you have the tools to create basic text to suit your project. Once you've finished creating your text, select File, Save As and then select a location—your "scratch disk" is a logical choice. Give it a descriptive name and then click Save.

Once your text is saved, you can always reedit it. If you create a unique text and graphic style that you think will help viewers recognize your productions or give them some consistency, you can simply change the wording in saved text files while retaining the style. This comes in very handy if you've created a standard way to "super" locations or interviewees' names.

Any newly created and saved text shows up automatically in your Project window with a page icon indicating it's a graphic. Drag it to a video track above your project. You can Alt/Option-scrub through the piece to preview it or use Premiere's new real-time preview feature by pressing Shift+Enter.

If you're creating a video project for viewing on an NTSC TV set, you want to make sure your text falls within the so-called NTSC "safe zone." Most TV sets are guilty of overscan—they cover the edges of the original full-screen video images. So you want to make sure your titles fall within the safe zone. To check that when using the Title Designer, use your workspace's main menu bar and select Title, View, Safe Title Margin. If you want to see the safe zones on your Source and Program Monitors, click the Monitor fly-out menu and select Safe Zones (see Figure 8.20) .

FIGURE 8.20

The Program Monitor with Safe Zones turned on.

Adding Motion to Your Text—Rolling and Crawling

You've seen opening and closing movie and TV show credits hundreds of times. In Premiere, that's *rolling text*.

Also, you've seen news bulletins that slide along the bottom or top edges of the page. In the TV news business, we used to call them *Chyron Crawls* after the once de-facto industry-standard, text-creation tool (Chyron Corp. is still a major player in the graphics and TV production world). In Premiere, they're *crawling text*.

In either case, they take only a couple additional text-creation steps to make.

Task: Set Up Rolling Text

To set up rolling text, follow these steps:

1. Go back to the Title Designer interface. Select Roll under Title Type in the upper-left corner. I've highlighted this in Figure 8.21.

2. Type in your rolling text. If you don't press Enter or Return and Word Wrap is on, you'll continue typing down the page. At the end of each line of text you can press Enter or Return to start a new line or let Word Wrap take care of that for you.

   As you fill the page you'll notice something new. A scrollbar appears on the right of the text window. This lets you see what you've written off the page that will scroll up as you animate this rolling text.

3. Once this is done, select Title, Roll/Crawl Options from the workspace's main menu bar. Figure 8.22 shows the options you can tap to describe the timing of the credits:

   Start Off Screen—Do the credits start completely off the screen and roll on?

   End Off Screen—Do you let the credits roll completely off the screen?

   Pre-Roll—The number of frames before the first words appear onscreen.

   Post-Roll—The number of frames after the final credit before the next edit (could be simply a fade to black) .

   Ease-In—Indicates the number of frames to get up to full speed when the first words appear.

   Ease-Out—Slows the credits down at the end.

4. Once you've made your selections, click File, Save As in the workspace's main menu and select a location and a name. When you go to your project, this new text will be in your `Project` folder with a filmstrip icon showing that its animated.

5. Drag it to your timeline and then drag it to fill whatever length you want. Then either Alt/Option-scrub it or render it to see how it'll look.

FIGURE 8.21

Title Type with Roll selected.

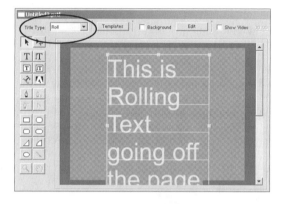

FIGURE 8.22

The Roll/Crawl Options dialog box lets you control the timing of moving text.

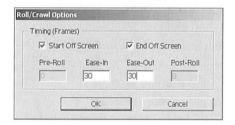

Creating Crawling Text

You create crawling text the same way as rolling text, only you start by selecting Crawl in the Title Type window. As you type, your text will roll off the right side of the text window. In this case, the scrollbar appears at the bottom of the text window, allowing you to see all your text.

Using the Title Designer to Make Simple Graphics

If you've created shapes in software such as MS Paint, you know how to create graphics in Premiere.

Select from the various shapes to the left of the text window, drag and draw the outline, and release the mouse. The Line tool creates line segments only. Click to set a starting point and then drag and click to set the endpoint. Each segment has its own bounding

8

box. Unlike with Path Text, you cannot add curves or create more vertexes. You can use Fill to color the line and Strokes to create a color border or interior. In Figure 8.23 I drew a few shapes and added some gradients and various opacity levels to demonstrate what you can do.

FIGURE 8.23

Some graphic objects created with gradients and various opacity levels.

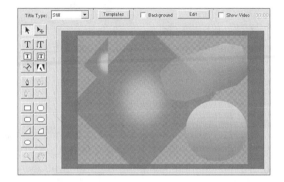

When you draw objects, they will appear as solid gray with no borders. You can add a border by changing the Line value in the Object Style/Properties window. You can change the graphic's appearance just as you did with text by adjusting Fill Color, Opacity, and Shadows.

> If you want to create a square, circle, right triangle, or a "square" clipped rectangle (as opposed to a rectangle, oval, non-right triangle, or stretched clipped rectangle), then hold down the Shift key when dragging the shape's border. If you want to maintain the aspect ratio for a shape you've already made, hold the Shift key before resizing that shape.

It's fairly easy to build layers of graphic objects and add text as well. You can send an object backward or forward by highlighting it, selecting Title, Arrange and then choosing from Bring to Front (that is, on top of all other objects), Bring Forward (on top of the next highest object), Send to Back (that is, make it the bottom/deepest object), or Send Backward (behind the next lower object). In Figure 8.24 I created a three-layer frame with text as an example.

Using transparent layers as backgrounds for supers is an excellent way to create a production studio or product line identity. Once you have a "look" you like, save it. Then double-click it in the Project window to reopen it within the Title Designer and make only textual changes while retaining the layered graphic look.

FIGURE **8.24**

Layered graphics create a nice background for your "supers."

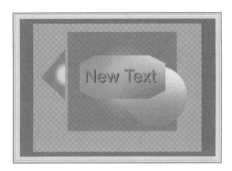

Summary

Adding text or "supers" to your video project gives it another element and adds depth. Text sometimes can send a message much more succinctly and clearly than a narration. It can reinforce narrated information or remind viewers about the people in your piece and the message you're trying to convey.

The text tools in Premiere are similar to those in standard graphics/text programs, with several extra features tossed in. The infinite customizability of your text's appearance means you can create a "look" unique to your productions.

Workshop

Review the questions and answers in this section to try to sharpen your Premiere text-editing skills. Also, take a few moments to tackle my short quiz and exercises.

Q&A

Q When I resize my text "bounding box," the text changes shape and size. How do I change the box without changing the contents?

A You're using Point Text, Premiere's default text style. Instead, select the "T" in the white box (Area Text), drag and drop a text bounding box, and start typing. If you need to increase the size of the box, the text will remain the same shape and size.

Q I want to make a circle in a square, but all I get are ovals in rectangles.

A You need to hold down the Shift key before you define the size of the quadrilateral or round figure. Doing that keeps all sides equal and forces your oval to be a circle.

Quiz

1. How do you keep text from running outside the viewable area on a typical NTSC TV set?

2. Premiere ships with 90 typefaces! How can you wade through all that and quickly find one that works for you?

3. How do you create a rectangle with a gradient inside it and a two-color border?

Quiz Answers

1. Use the Title Safe Zone option, accessible in the Title menu or in the Monitor menu for viewing in the Source and Program Monitors.

2. Browse. Go to Title, Font, Browse and scroll all the font samples.

3. Open the Title Designer. Create a rectangle by selecting the Rectangle tool and clicking and dragging within the text window to define a rectangle. Select Fill, Fill Type, Linear Gradient and select two colors in turn. Select Strokes, Inner and Outer Stroke, in turn, and give each inner and outer border a color and other characteristics to suit you.

Exercises

1. Create rolling credits with different font sizes and text alignments. Main headings could be aligned left and individuals' names centered.

2. Make a rainbow using the Line tool. Click one side of the text window and then click the other, making a straight line. Then drag the center handle to make a curve. Repeat this three or four more times and color each line to create a rainbow feel. Now add text along another arc over the rainbow. Do you feel a song coming on?

3. Create a three-layer collection of rectangles with varying transparencies and drop shadow values. Create the three rectangles by dragging and dropping them in separate locations. Make the large one opaque (100% opacity) with a drop shadow of 50% opacity, the middle one 40% opacity with a drop shadow of 20% opacity, and the small one 25% opacity with a drop shadow of 30% opacity. Then select colors and gradients that give a contrast so you can see one through the other. One other suggestion: Give one or two of the rectangles a Repeat value to create parallel lines to make them stand out even more. Also, pick a drop shadow that is similar in color to the object on which the shadow falls.

4. Create a standard interviewee super with one font, two text sizes (larger for the name, smaller for the title), a colored line running between the two text lines, and three overlapping and transparent boxes on the left, acting as a unique production studio identifier. Make sure you save this. You actually may want to use it.

HOUR 9

Advanced Editing Techniques and Workspace Tools

I believe that only after you learn the fundamentals should you start specializing. If all a basketball player practices is a spinning, reverse, wrong-handed flip shot, he'll make no more than a bucket a game. Not many opportunities for that shot arise.

By now, given enough practice, you may have mastered straightforward Premiere techniques, such as cuts-only editing (including matching edits, wide/tight shots, and avoiding jump cuts) as well as standard transitions, with all their options, and straight-up audio editing and text creation.

That being the case, this hour will ramp up those fundamental techniques a bit. I'll show you some other ways to manipulate clips, go over some standard professional editing techniques, explain some higher-end transitions, present an automated means to add music, and show you how to make a quick music video.

The highlights of this hour include the following:

- Playing clips backward, adjusting their speed, and creating still frames
- Rolling, slip, and slide edits
- Using special transitions, including masks and QuickTime, and stringing together multiple transitions
- Adding music to your projects
- Setting timeline markers and making an automated music video

Playing Clips Backward, Changing Speed, and Freezing Frames

By the time you finish this section you'll know how to create a video sequence that incorporates all three of these concepts.

Playing Clips Backwards

First, a fun and simple technique—playing a clip backwards. Consider the possibilities. Kids diving "out" of a pond, a pitcher "retrieving" his fastball, and a reverse replay of an explosive building demolition.

Task: Play a Clip Backwards

To play a clip backwards, follow these steps:

1. Select any clip, either on the timeline or in the Project window.

2. Right-click (Windows) or Option-click (Mac) to open the clip menu. Select Speed and change the New Rate percentage to –100 (negative 100) in the Clip Speed dialog box (see Figure 9.1). Click OK.

3. Play the clip either by dragging it from the Project window to the Source Monitor screen or by playing it from the timeline.

If you have audio associated with the clip, it'll play backward too. You can unlink that audio and change it back to +100 or unlink it before making the reversal.

Notice a couple things. If you changed the clip in the timeline, it'll have an altered *slug*—the name listed on the timeline—with x-100% at the end. I've highlighted that "tag" in Figure 9.2. If you changed the clip in the Project window, it does not display that extra bit of information in its slug, and there's no way to know whether the clip will run backward unless you play it or drag it to the timeline and note the x-100% tag.

FIGURE 9.1

The Clip Speed dialog box, where a setting of -100% plays the video backward and 200% doubles the speed and cuts the clip time in half.

FIGURE 9.2

Giving a clip a new speed adds an x-% tag to its timeline "slug."

It's easy to change clip names or copy clips and give them new names within the Project window. To give a clip a new name—such as Kids Dive - reverse 100—slowly double-click the clip name and type in a new one. A better solution is to create a whole new clip. To do that, right/Option-click the clip you want to duplicate and select Copy. Then right/Option-click in the white area in the lower-right side of the Project window and select Paste. There is your duplicate clip. You can change its speed/direction and rename it to reflect that. Those changes will not affect the original clip on your scratch disk.

Changing Speed

Using the same right/Option-click Speed menu, you can speed up or slow down a clip. Simply change the percentage: 200% will double the speed while cutting the clip time in half, and 50% will slow things down by half and double the clip time. If there's a top percentage limit to speeding up clips, I haven't found it. Try a setting of 1,000% just to see how that looks. The bottom limit is 1%. Try that and notice that your clip is now 100 times longer! View it and you'll see that it's just a collection of still frames that change every few seconds.

Once again, your clip timeline slug will reflect whatever speed change you make by adding an x-% tag at the end.

Task: Play a Clip at Different Speeds

It's a simple matter to take a clip at regular speed and change its speed midway. Here's how:

1. Select a clip and drag it to the timeline. Use the edit line to find a place within the clip where you want to shift speed.

2. Select the Razor tool from the toolbox. As a reminder, I've highlighted it in Figure 9.3.

3. Move it to the edit line and click to slice your clip in two.

4. Press the V hotkey to switch the cursor to the Selection tool (or click its icon in the toolbox) and then right/Option-click the clip segment whose speed you want to change.

5. Select Speed and change the percentage. Note the new x-% tag on that segment.

 6. Play those two segments back to back to see how this works.

> If you change the speed of the clip such that it plays slower (that is, in slow motion), you can improve the quality of the motion by turning on Clip, VideoOptions, FrameHold, FrameBlending. This feature will smooth out the motion.

FIGURE 9.3

The Razor tool. Use it to slice clips in two.

Adding Freeze Frames

If you want to create a sequence that starts with a regular-speed clip, slows down, stops, shifts to a slow reverse, and finishes at full-speed reverse, then you need to create a freeze frame.

You also can use a freeze frame as an effective way to close a segment or an entire production. Freeze the final frame and then fade to black.

To do either you first need to create a freeze frame. If you want to create a sequence, drag a clip to the timeline with the frame in it that you want to freeze. Otherwise, any clip will do, just so you can see how this works.

Task: Create a Freeze Frame

To create a freeze frame, follow these steps:

1. Use the Selection tool to drag the end of the clip to the frame you want to freeze. For instance, if the clip is of kids diving into a pond, you may want that point to be just as their bodies are about halfway into the water.

2. Right/Option-click on your clip and select Copy. Click the timeline after that clip and then right/Option-click and select Paste. You have now added a duplicate of the clip to the timeline. You will turn this duplicate clip into the freeze frame clip.

3. Right/Option-click and select Video Options, Frame Hold. The Frame Hold Options dialog box appears.

4. The Frame Hold Options dialog box contains several options. In this case, as I've highlighted in Figure 9.4, you want to check the Hold On box and select one of its three options: In Point, Marker 0, or Out Point. In this case, choose Out Point (I'll cover markers later in this hour).

5. This creates a clip that consists of only one frame that holds for the length of the original clip. You can play it or drag the edit line through it to confirm this. Note that the timeline slug does not change to reflect this clip's new freeze frame status.

6. Give it a new name by right/Option-clicking, selecting Set Clip Name Alias, and typing in something descriptive, such as Freeze - Kids Dive.

FIGURE 9.4

The Frame Hold Options dialog box. Use it to create a freeze frame.

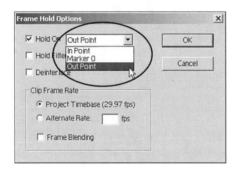

I had you give this clip an "alias" because of an unpredictable characteristic of Premiere. I'm not sure whether it's a bug or a feature, but when you create a freeze frame and then add a transition to it, the freeze frame sometimes changes to another frame within the original video clip. Apparently, a way to avoid that is to give the freeze frame a new name.

You now can use that clip in a sequence: forward regular speed, slow motion, freeze frame, reverse slow, and reverse regular speed. I suggest doing that in the exercise segment at the end of the hour.

Task: Add a Freeze Frame and Fade to Black to End a Piece

To add a freeze frame and fade to black at the end of a piece, follow these steps:

1. Create "black video" by right/Option-clicking in the white area of the Project window below your clips and selecting New, Black Video. Alternatively, you can click the little icon highlighted in Figure 9.5 to open the Create window and select Black Video from the drop-down list. Either method adds a black video clip to the Project window.

2. Drag the black video clip to the end of your piece after the freeze frame.

3. Open the Transitions palette and drag and drop the cross-dissolve at the edit point between the freeze frame clip and the black video.

4. To view the dissolve, use Alt-scrub (Windows) or Option-scrub (Mac), use the Real-time Preview feature, or render the dissolve.

FIGURE 9.5

The Create Item icon in the Project window lets you place a black video clip in the Project window.

Using the Create Item window or Project window's right/Option-click menu and then selecting New lets you add other types of clips to your Project window:

- Universal Counting Leader is that black-and-white spinning countdown you used to see in movies.

- Bars and Tone lets engineers adjust their playback devices to the right audio and video levels for their projects (not as important a feature as it was before automated systems).

- Color Matte lets you create a full-screen, solid-color clip for use as a background.

This is another way to access the Title Designer and to create an "offline file" (see the next note).

An *offline file* is sort of a placeholder for a video clip you intend to transfer to your hard drive later. You can edit that placeholder clip on your timeline, and when you finally do capture the clip to your hard drive, you can replace the offline clip with the actual clip. To do that, highlight the offline clip, select Project, Replace Clips, locate the newly captured clip, and click OK.

9

Rolling, Slide, and Slip Edits

You'll tap this set of editing tools when you want to preserve the overall length of your program. They come in handy for precisely timed projects such as 30-second advertisements.

In many cases it may simply be easier to make individual edits and forgo these special tools, but it's good for any professional editor to know how to do slips, slides, and rolling edits.

Table 9.1 provides a basic overview of these three specialized edits:

TABLE 9.1 Rolling, Slide, and Slip Edits

Edit	Effect	Clip Length(s)	Clip(s) In/Out
Rolling edit	Changes the duration and in/out-points of two adjacent clips.	Changes	Changes
Slide edit	The selected clip remains unchanged, but in/out-points and lengths of both adjacent clips are changed.	Unchanged	Unchanged
Slip edit	Changes only the selected clip's in/out-points.	Unchanged	Changes

Making a Rolling Edit

This is the easiest of the three. It lets you change the in/out-points of adjacent clips. Remember, all three of these special edit types will preserve the length of your piece.

Task: Make a Rolling Edit

▼ TASK

To begin, place three clips side by side on the timeline's Video 1 track. Make sure all of them have plenty of head and tail frames to allow for the edits. The easiest way is to shorten each clip by dragging in the beginning and end (the in- and out-points). Here are the steps to follow:

▼ 1. Select the Rolling Edit tool from the Edit Tool pop-up menu on the timeline's tool-box. I've highlighted it in Figure 9.6.

2. Position the edit line at or slightly ahead of the edit point.

3. What makes this edit different from any you've done to this point is that you'll use the monitor screens to make the edit. Click the Trim Mode button (perhaps Adobe should have called it the Rolling Edit Mode button) above the monitors. I've high-lighted it in Figure 9.7. That automatically moves the edit line to the next edit or keeps it on the current edit (that's why I asked you to place the edit line a little in front of the edit point).

4. Place your cursor between the Source and Program Monitors, and it turns into the Rolling Edit tool. Nifty. Now drag it right or left. Note three things: The edit line in the timeline moves, the in- and out-points in the monitor screens shift, and the
▲ video clips shift accordingly.

Dragging the cursor left shortens the A clip and lengthens the B clip. Dragging it right lengthens the A clip and shortens the B clip. In both cases, the story length remains unchanged.

FIGURE 9.6
The Rolling Edit tool.

FIGURE 9.7
Click the Trim Mode button in the Monitor window to switch to Rolling Edit (or Trim) mode.

Using the Slide Edit Tool

The Slide Edit tool lets you slide a clip forward or backward between two other clips without changing the selected clip. Rather, you shift the in- and out-points of the adja-cent clips to accommodate your clip's new position in the project. Once again, the over-all length of your production does not change.

Task: Slide a Clip Between Two Other Clips

To slide a clip forward or backward between two other clips without changing the selected clip, follow these steps:

1. Select the Slide Edit tool. I've highlighted it in Figure 9.8.

2. Place it over the clip you want to move; then click and hold down the mouse button. As I've illustrated in Figure 9.9, four screens appear in the Monitor window.

3. Move the Slide Edit tool left or right and notice that the clip on the timeline slides left or right and the two outside monitor screens change. The left screen is the out-point of the previous clip. The right screen is the in-point of the next clip. The two middle screens are unchanging reference frames. They are the in- and out-points for the clip you're sliding back and forth.

4. Use the changing screen images to select a new edit point and then release the mouse.

FIGURE 9.8

The Slide Edit tool.

FIGURE 9.9

Using the Slide Edit tool pops up four screens in the Monitor window. Use them to find the best in- and out-points for the two outside clips.

Making a Slip Edit

The Slip Edit affects only one clip. Think of this as slipping a clip right or left under the clips on either side. By slipping it right or left you change the in- and out-points of the selected clip while retaining that clip's length and not changing the two adjacent clips.

Task: Make a Slip Edit

To make a slip edit, follow these steps:

1. Select the Slip Edit tool from the toolbox. I've highlighted it in Figure 9.10.

2. Position it over the clip you want to edit. Note that you are *not* positioning it over an edit point. The Slip Edit tool changes the in- and out-points of only the selected clip.

3. Click and hold down the mouse button. Notice that just as with the Slide Edit tool, four screens pop up in the Monitor window. The left and right screens are reference points and won't change during this edit. The left screen is the end of the previous clip and the right screen is the beginning of the next clip. The two middle screens are the in- and out-points of the clip you're going to change.

4. Move the Slip Edit tool left and right and watch as the clip's in- and out-points change. Use the left and right screens to help find edit points that work best; then release the mouse button.

FIGURE **9.10**

The Slip Edit tool.

Although the Slip Edit tool is intended to adjust the in- and out-points of a clip between two other clips, you can use it on the first or last clip of your piece. Give that a try to see how it works.

The Rolling, Slide, and Slip Edit tools work with both cuts-only edits and transitions. However, I recommend you remove any transitions before using these tools and then reapply those transitions to make sure they work the way you expected. One example: You may have created a transition with a move that starts at a specific point in clip A and moves to point in clip B. Those start- and endpoints will likely shift as you make adjustments using a rolling, slide, or slip edit.

Creating Special Transitions

Back in Hour 5, "Adding Transitions: From Dissolves to Zooms," I skipped a few of the more-involved transitions. I'll run some by you here.

Creating Image Mask Transitions

This is more like a special effect than a transition. Basically you use any image—black and white, grayscale, or full color—as a means to display part(s) of clip A and part(s) of clip B at the same time.

Clip A shows through the black area of your image (or any part of it that is 50% or more gray), and clip B shows through the white area (or any part that is less than 50% gray). To reiterate, in this case Premiere sees things only as black or white. Even if you use a mask with color, Premiere will make the transition by converting the color image to grayscale.

To do this, you'll need a mask. To get some hand's-on experience, I'd suggest you make a rudimentary mask using a tool such as MS Paint. Create your mask and save it on your Premiere scratch disk.

Figure 9.11 shows how a mask might look. Basically it's a stark black-and-white graphic. Remember the black area will let that part of clip A show through, and the white area displays that section of clip B.

FIGURE 9.11

A rudimentary mask created in MS Paint for use with the Image Mask transition.

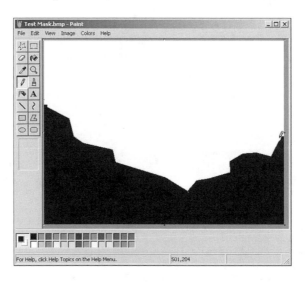

Task: Create an Image Mask Transition

 TASK

To create an Image Mask transition, follow these steps:

1. Open Premiere to your workspace.

2. To make it clear how the Image Mask transition works, I'd like you to make two color mattes. Right/Option-click in the Project window (or click on the New Item icon—it's the little folded up page in the bottom of the Project window) and select New, Color Matte. Select a color and give your matte a descriptive name. Do that again for a distinctly different color.

3. Drag each matte to the timeline Video 1 track.

4. Locate the Image Mask transition in the `Special Effect` folder in the Transitions palette and drag it to the edit point between the two mattes. This pops up a small Image Mask Settings dialog box, as illustrated in Figure 9.12. This is a tad confusing because you'd expect to see a standard Transitions Settings dialog box with a Custom button instead (we'll get to that dialog box in a moment).

5. Click Select Image, locate your mask, and double-click it. When this brings you back to the Image Mask Settings dialog box, click OK.

6. Now open the regular Image Mask Settings dialog box by double-clicking the transition on the timeline. Ah-ha. This looks more familiar (see Figure 9.13). Check Show Actual Sources, give your mask transition a border (with a nice complementary color), and then admire your work.

▲

FIGURE 9.12

The preliminary Image Mask Settings dialog box.

FIGURE 9.13

The actual Image Mask Settings dialog box.

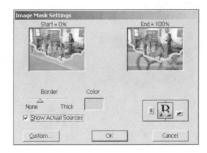

As with most transitions, if you click the little down arrow, you'll switch how Premiere performs this transition. Instead of letting clip A show through the black portion of your mask, clip A now shows through the white and clip B shows through the black.

Creating Gradient Wipe Transitions

This is more like what you'd expect to see in a transition. It works like the Image Mask transition in that it lets parts of clip A and clip B display together using a custom mask, but the Gradient Wipe transition actually moves from one scene to the next using a smooth animation.

In a reversal of the Image Mask transition, clip A shows through the white area whereas clip B shows through the black. Also, in this case, Premiere does see things as gray—gradually. As the transition progresses, the gray areas "darken" and more of clip B shows through until at the end of the transition only clip B is onscreen.

As with the previous task (the Image Mask transition), I'd suggest you create a grayscale gradient mask. Figure 9.14 shows a very rudimentary example using black, two grayscale areas, and white.

FIGURE 9.14

A rudimentary grayscale mask created in MS Paint for use with the Gradient Wipe transition.

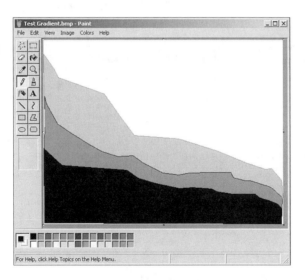

Task: Create a Gradient Wipe Transition

To create a Gradient Wipe transition, follow these steps:

1. Return to your timeline and replace the Image Mask transition with the Gradient Wipe transition (it's in the Wipe folder).

2. This, too, pops up a little preliminary Gradient Wipe Settings dialog box, as shown in Figure 9.15. Click Select Image, locate your gradient graphic, and double-click it.

3. This returns you to the preliminary Gradient Wipe Transition dialog box. Select a Softness setting (this smoothes sharp edges in your gradient graphic). Click OK.

4. As with the Image Mask transition, open the real Gradient Wipe Settings dialog box by double-clicking the transition on the timeline.

5. Check the Show Actual Sources box and preview your transition by dragging the slider under the first window.

FIGURE 9.15

The preliminary Gradient Wipe settings dialog box.

Similar to the Image Mask transition, you can change how this transition works by clicking, in this case, the R button. This starts the transition from the top instead of the bottom.

Creating QuickTime Transitions

I don't know why the QuickTime transitions get such minimal coverage in the Premiere manual or other how-to books because they are almost as varied and customizable as all the standard Premiere transitions.

Using the same two color mattes (or two video clips of your choosing), find the QuickTime transition (in the QuickTime folder) and drag and drop it over the edit point. It'll replace the Gradient Wipe transition.

This automatically opens the Select Effect dialog box shown in Figure 9.16. If you scroll down the transition menu you'll see a lot of familiar names—Cross Fade (same as Cross Dissolve), Push, Radial, Slide, Wipe, and Zoom. There is some redundancy here, but the customizing tools are different and in some ways are an improvement over Premiere.

Just to see how the QuickTime transition process compares to Premiere's, select the now familiar Gradient Wipe transition. I've highlighted it in Figure 9.16.

FIGURE 9.16

The QuickTime transition interface with the Gradient Wipe transition customization interface.

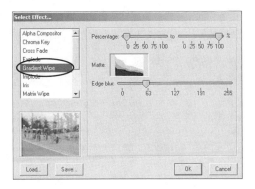

Note that QuickTime transitions automatically display a real-time preview. Nice. Adjust the Edge Blur setting to see how that changes things.

If you double-click the Matte window, you can select your gradient graphic and see how that'll work.

The Percentage sliders work much like the sliders in Premiere's Transition Settings dialog box—they indicate where the transition will start and end. If you make the first slider 100% and the second 0%, that is like changing the direction of the arrow in the Premiere Transitions Setting dialog box.

Select the Iris transition and open the Wipe Type drop-down menu. Here is the QuickTime transition's real power. Check out all those types of irises. Try a diamond; then change the Horizontal and Vertical repeat numbers to something like 2 and 3. Add a border (4 pixels works well), select a color, and soften the edges. It should look like Figure 9.17.

FIGURE 9.17

QuickTime's Iris transition offers infinite customizability.

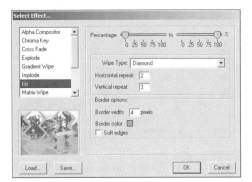

Try the Implode transition. This is the perfect means to let one image slide down a drain to reveal a sink. Using an X/Y axis you can select the specific endpoint.

Finally, explore the Wipe transitions—all 36 of them!

You may notice that the QuickTime color-selection tool is different from Premiere's. This, too, is an improvement. To see how it works, open any QuickTime transition with a border—Iris, Matrix Wipe, Radial, and Wipe—and click the small Border Color selection box. If you click somewhere in the color spectrum window and click OK, your border color will *not* change. As I've highlighted in Figure 9.18, you need to click in the spectrum window (note that it displays the color from dark to light in a vertical column to the right), use the slider to select just the right color, click the Add to Custom Colors box, and then click OK.

FIGURE 9.18
QuickTime's border color selector interface gives you additional options over Premiere's standard color picker.

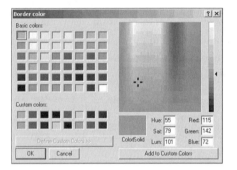

As you've worked with the timeline, you may have noticed that the clip and time bar colors change.

Here's the basic color scheme:

- A video-only clip is yellow.
- An audio-only clip is blue.
- A linked video/audio clip is green.
- A graphic is purple.
- A matte is reddish orange.
- The yellow bar near top of timeline indicates the work area.
- Red bar(s) near top of timeline indicate segments needing rendering before the project is completed.

Task: Stringing Together Multiple Transitions

▼ TASK

This is an instance where you'll want to shift the regular direction of a transition from clip A to clip B, to clip B to clip A. Backwards.

It's best to use the A/B editing mode because you need to have a large overlap. After eight steps your timeline should look like Figure 9.19:

1. Switch to A/B editing. As a reminder, use the fly-out menu in the timeline's upper-right corner and select A/B Editing.

2. Place a clip on Video 1A and another directly below it on Video 1B. Neither should be too long—30 seconds or so will work fine.

3. Select a Transition—I suggest Venetian Blinds—and place it between the two clips on the transition line. It automatically takes up the entire overlap.

4. Shorten the transition by right/Option-clicking it, selecting Duration, and changing the duration to about one-fourth its original amount. If you try to shorten the transition by dragging its right end to the left, you will shorten clip A as well.

5. Add the same transition to the transition line at about the middle of the clip. This time it will automatically have the default duration of 30 frames.

6. Add one more transition to the end of the overlap.

7. Slice out the portion of clip A that is above and between the first two transitions to let clip B play through. Remember, the highest clip in the timeline covers all clips below it.

8. Change the little arrow in the second transition so it will operate "backwards"—that is, transition from clip B to clip A. Your timeline should look like Figure 9.19.

9. Alt/option-scrub through your project to see how this works. You can switch back to single-track editing and everything should work fine.

▲

You can use multiple transitions to give a brief glimpse of a clip before going back to it.

FIGURE 9.19

Multiple transitions let you shift from clip A to clip B then back to clip A.

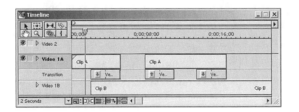

Adding Music from CDs or SmartSound Quicktracks

Ripping music from a CD is a snap. For Mac users, Premiere has a built-in ripping function. Select File, Open. Navigate to your music CD, select a track, specify a location, and click OK. You can change some options such as the audio quality, but the default is your best bet.

PC users must use a third-party CD ripper. The most accessible is the Windows Media Player. Start it and select Copy from CD. I've highlighted that process in Figure 9.20. You can select multiple tracks and rip them at once. Very simple. Now they are available for use in your project as WMA files. To use them, simply double-click in your Project window, locate and select the file(s), and click Open.

FIGURE 9.20

Windows Media Player lets you "rip" cuts from non-copy-protected music CDs.

This all comes with the usual admonition that these are copyrighted tunes. There are all sorts of takes on the so-called "Fair Use Law" regarding copyrighted items and who can use them and how. I won't weigh in on that. That's your choice.

Using Quicktracks

To avoid any possible copyright conflicts, you can turn to SmartSound Quicktracks—a very slick tool that ships with Premiere. It's an optional install, so you may not have installed it yet. Do that now. Install all the audio files (600+ MB) so you don't have to access the CD each time you use SmartSound.

Task: Add Quicktracks to Your Piece

Once you've completed the install, a "plug-in" is added within Premiere that lets you create various styles of music with very specific lengths. Here's how it works:

1. Select File, New, SmartSound (installing SmartSound added this option to the File, New menu).

2. The SmartSound Quicktracks menu opens (see Figure 9.21). Select Start Maestro.

3. Now for some fun. It's experimentation time. Select a style or browse the music files alphabetically. Click Next until you get the option to play your selected piece. Not too bad. You were probably expecting some cheesy MIDI music. Not so. This stuff sounds great!

4. Click past the preview section and give your selection a time. If you know your piece will run a certain length (hours:minutes:seconds:frames), choose that or select an approximate time. You always can change it later.

5. Click Finish and choose a save location. Your scratch disk is best. Click Save to save it at the specified location and load it in your Project window.

FIGURE 9.21

The SmartSound Quicktracks Maestro menu. Use it to create professional accompaniments that fit your project's exact length.

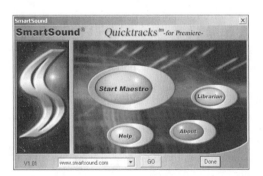

You have created a tune that you can import to your Project window. This tune has a special built-in time-adjustment feature. Here's how you can see it in action: Drag the clip to an audio track. If you decide that it's not the right length for your project, double-click it. Voila, up pops the Maestro interface, letting you change the length to suit your current needs (you may need to click the Back button in Maestro to find the song's Duration/Time window).

No matter what length you give your selection, Maestro creates a smooth finish—not just a fade out. Very slick.

Setting Timeline Markers and Making an Automated Music Video

I saved the fun task for last. Here, you're going to place a music clip on your timeline, add *markers* to match the beat (or wherever you want to place them), and then automatically add video clips, one for each marker. Voila—a music video. Well, it's not exactly MTV, but you'll see how this works.

Task: Set the Timeline Markers

▼ TASK

Follow these steps to set the timeline markers:

1. Clear your timeline by selecting everything (use the Select tool in the toolbox—it's the dashed box) and pressing Delete. Drag one of your music tracks to the Audio 1 track.

2. Now play that audio clip. Listen for places where you'd like to make an edit to lay in a new clip and for each instance press the asterisk (*) key on the numeric keypad (*not* Shift+8). If you're using a laptop and don't have a numeric keypad, you can use Alt+Shift+=.

3. Each time you press the * key, you're adding a marker to the timeline. They'll appear when you stop the music. Do that as many times as you like, keeping in mind you'll need one clip for each marker. Because you *can* slice clips into smaller, discrete segments before making this "automatic" music video, feel free to go overboard. You also can use the clips more than once if you do not have a clip for each marker.

4. At the end of the song, or when you think you've made more than enough markers, stop the music. As shown in Figure 9.22, a whole slew of little gray tab stops appear on the timeline.

▲

FIGURE 9.22

The timeline loaded with markers, ready and waiting to make a music video.

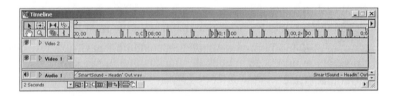

Check out the markers. As you roll your cursor over each one, the cursor changes to an icon reminiscent of the Rolling Edit tool. It signifies you can move a marker to a new location. If you right/Option-click the timeline, various marker options appear. For instance, if you want to start all over, right/Option-click and select Clear Timeline Marker, Clear All Markers.

Task: Fill in the Video Clips

We're going to use the good old storyboard to do the heavy lifting in this task. Here are the steps to follow:

1. Select File, New, Storyboard.

2. Start filling it with video clips. If you don't have enough to match the number of markers, add some clips more than once.

3. If you have duplicate clips, you can slice them up now or after you've "automated" them to the timeline. I'd recommend slicing them now to create a more "finished" look immediately after you use the Automate to Timeline command.

As a reminder, the way to edit a clip in the timeline is to double-click it. It opens in the Source Monitor, where you can slide the in- and out-points or click those brackets—"{" and "}"—to make in- and out-points. As you fix each clip, simply close the Monitor window to return to the storyboard.

4. Once you have your clips arranged, sliced, and trimmed, click the Automate to Timeline icon. To remind you, I've highlighted it in Figure 9.23.

FIGURE 9.23
The Automate to Timeline icon.

5. That pops up the Automate to Timeline dialog box. Figure 9.24 shows the interface properly filled in for this music video. In this case you want to change Placement to At Unnumbered Markers, change Insufficient Material to Fit to Fill (this automatically creates slow motion for clips that are too short to fill a gap), and check the Ignore Audio box, because you may not want natural sound stepping on the music, and you certainly don't want slow-motion sounds.

FIGURE 9.24

The Automate to Timeline dialog box, filled out to make a music video.

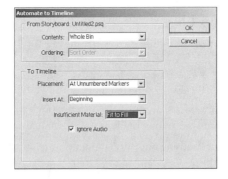

 If you want to include the nat-sound audio on your clips in this music video, you'll need to place the music clip on Audio 3. When you use the Automate to Timeline command with Ignore Audio unchecked, it automatically places the audio on Audio 1 and Audio 2, alternating each clip.

6. When you've made all the selections, click OK. Your timeline should fill up with clips. Move the edit line to the beginning and play. Slick.

Note any slow-motion clips. Just to see how Premiere fills a gap by adjusting the clip speed, right-click a slow-motion clip and select Speed. If you want to edit any of the clips, you know the drill.

Summary

In this hour we've gone beyond straight cuts-only, news-style editing. Adjusting clip speed and direction plus adding freeze frames expands your editing possibilities. Rolling, slide, and slip edits take that cuts-only style ever further. Opening the one, easy-to-overlook QuickTime icon vastly expands your transition options. The two "mask" transitions let you use custom images to display two clips at once. Multiple transitions applied to the same clips let you glance at a clip and return to the previous clip. And adding music and creating "instant" music videos is straightforward and, well, fun.

Workshop

Review the questions and answers in this section to try to sharpen your Premiere editing skills. Also, take a few moments to tackle my short quiz and exercises.

Q&A

Q **When I use the Rolling, Slide, and Slip Edit tools, the clip frames shift in the monitor screens, showing the new edit points, but after a while they stop and won't let me move the edit point any farther. What's up?**

A You've reached the end of the line—the beginning or end of the original clip. There are no additional head or tail frames to allow you to move the edit any farther.

Q **When I use the storyboard to make an "instant" music video, it inserts all the clips ahead of the music track. Why?**

A You did not check the Ignore Audio box. By leaving that unchecked, Premiere automatically includes all the natural sound in your project and puts the audio portions on the Audio 1 and Audio 2 tracks. I'm not sure why this happens—it may be a bug—because your video clips all go on the same track and the audio clips should all go on track 1. If you want to include nat-sound audio in your music video, place the music clip on the Audio 3 track.

Quiz

1. You've completed a project that is exactly one minute long and needs to stay that length. You like one clip but want to shift its position slightly between two other clips. What edit tool do you use? Why?

2. What are the principal differences between the Image Mask and Gradient Mask transitions?

3. You created music to exactly fit your project's length using SmartSound Quicktracks, but your project ended up going a bit longer. How do you make the music fit the new project length?

Quiz Answers

1. The Slide Edit tool. It lets you slide a clip between two others, changing their in- and out-points while keeping the selected clip intact.

2. The Image Mask transition sees everything in black or white. No gray area for that guy. The Gradient Mask transition has a built-in transition motion, revealing the next clip either from the bottom of the screen going up, or starting at the top and going down.

3. Place your edit line at the end (or use the hotkey, End) to see the exact length of your project. Double-click the audio clip to automatically open Quicktracks. Click the Back button to go the Time window. Change the time to fit your new project length. Click Finish. If you edited any of your clips to fit the beat of the music, I'm afraid you'll have to go back and make some adjustments.

Exercises

1. Create a sequence using regular forward motion, slow motion, stop action, reverse slow motion, and reverse full-speed motion.

2. Two QuickTime transitions that differ from anything you'll find in the standard Premiere transition set are Implode and Explode. Apply those to a project and adjust the X/Y coordinates to set the start- or endpoint to match something in your video clip.

3. Create multiple edits on two clips and have the first edit move from a specific location on the first clip and then have the second edit move from a specific spot on the second clip.

HOUR 10

Adding Audio Effects

Until now you've concentrated on editing techniques—piecing your project together. In this hour I'll introduce you to several ways you can change the characteristics of individual clips by adding special effects.

Premiere's audio effects "sweeten" your sound. Premiere lets you change the shape and size of a video clip and put it in motion. And its video effects can do dozens of tasks—from simply adding some contrast to a clip to animating clips with swirls, waves, and streaks.

Because there are so many possibilities over such a wide range of effects styles, I'll focus only on audio effects in this hour and use three additional hours to take you through video motion and effects.

The highlights of this hour include the following:

- Getting a grip on the Effect Controls palette
- Adjusting sound—an overview of Premiere's standard audio effects
- Sweetening sound with some higher-end—and fun—audio effects
- Trying out Premiere 6.5's brand-new and exciting TC|Essentials audio production tools

Managing Effects

Every time you add a clip to the timeline, Premiere prepares a little, heretofore hidden, interface called the Effect Controls palette. If each clip had its own palette, things could get mighty cluttered on your workspace, so there is only one palette that changes what it displays, depending on the clip you've selected.

To see how this works, open Premiere to your workspace and drag a few clips—at least one audio-only, one video-only, and a linked audio/video clip—to your timeline.

Open the Effect Controls palette by selecting Window, Show Effect Controls. Up pops a little interface, illustrated in Figure 10.1, with a scale and style much like the Navigator/Info/History palette. Drag the top of the Effect Controls palette so there's enough room to display a few effects.

This would be a good time to add the Effect Controls Palette to your personalized workspace. I discussed saving your workspace back in Hour 3, "Video Capture and Scene Selection." I like minimizing the Effect Controls palette (along with Navigator and Transitions) and placing it below my timeline. Once you've added Effect Controls to your workspace, you can save or resave your workspace by selecting Window, Workspace, Save Workspace. Then type in a name and press Enter (Windows) or Return (Mac). To open your custom workspace, click Window, Workspace and then select your named workspace.

With the Effect Controls palette open, select a video clip. Note what happens in the Effect Controls palette. As illustrated back in Figure 10.1, that clip's name appears with the words *Motion* and *Setup*. This shows you that for every video clip, Premiere assumes you may want to give it some motion (and size and shape) characteristics. The check box next to Motion is unchecked to show that you have not chosen to add motion yet.

When you select a clip, its name shows up in the Effect Controls palette along with one of two messages, depending on the location of the edit line. If it's within your selected clip, the Effect Controls palette will note its time on the project timeline. Otherwise, it'll state "Edit line is outside of clip."

Just to get a taste of what's to come, click the Motion check box. Up pops the Motion Settings dialog box, as highlighted in Figure 10.2. Now this looks cool. I'll cover it in detail in the following hour, but feel free to experiment.

FIGURE 10.2

The Motion Settings dialog box: a taste of things to come in Hour 11, "Creating Video Effects."

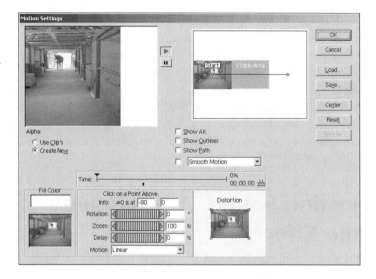

10

 Task: Add a Command to the Effect Controls Palette

Take a look at the other tab in the Effect Controls palette: Commands. This lists all the preset function key shortcuts. For instance, you can switch from the single-track editing workspace to A/B editing by pressing Shift+F10. These are all customizable. (What element in Premiere isn't?) To add a command, follow these steps:

1. Click the Commands tab.

2. Open the fly-out menu.

3. Turn off Button Mode by selecting it.

4. Choose Add Command in the fly-out menu, opening the Command Options dialog box shown in Figure 10.3.

5. Type in your new command name.

▼   6. Select the function from the main menu.

     7. Select a function key (or combination) from those still available in the drop-down
        list.

▲   8. Click OK.

FIGURE 10.3

The Command Options dialog box, where you can add your own hotkey function commands.

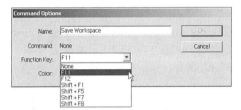

Close out of the Motion Settings dialog box and select an audio clip. Note that the display in the Effect Controls palette changes to show the audio clip name only. You can't apply motion to audio, so that option does not appear in the palette. If you select a linked video/audio clip, the Effect Controls palette displays the palette for whichever part of the clip you've selected—audio or video. Even though that clip is linked, Premiere knows you can apply only audio effects to the audio portion and video and motion effects to the video portion.

Adjusting Sound: An Overview of Premiere Audio Effects

Premiere's audio landscape improved with the release of version 6.5. Included in it is *TC|Essentials*, a suite of three professional audio-sweetening tools from TC|Works, a German company.

Those tools effectively replace 11 of Premiere 6.0's 20 audio effects, although Adobe still included them in Premiere 6.5.

I'll take you through the TC|Works products in a few minutes. First, though, a few fundamentals:

1. Open the Transitions/Effects palette.

2. Select the Audio tab.

3. Expand all folders by opening the fly-out menu and selecting that option.

4. As I did in Figure 10.4, drag a corner of the palette to open it wide enough to see all 24 audio effects icons.

FIGURE 10.4

Premiere's full set of audio effects.

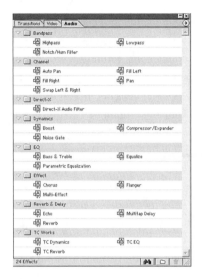

There are seven categories (eight if you count DirectX, but it merely opens the TC|Works tab). If you're not an audio engineer, some of the terms—Bandpass, Channel, and EQ—may be a bit obtuse.

Here's a quick take on the categories:

Bandpass—These three effects remove specific audio frequencies. However, there's no reason I can think of to use them because the TC|Works TC EQ tool handles the features of all three Bandpass effects. Highpass removes low frequencies (it "passes" high frequencies through), Lowpass removes high frequencies, and the Notch/Hum Filter removes a specific, user-selected frequency. You can use Lowpass, for example, to create sound geared for a subwoofer or use Notch/Hum Filter to remove power-line noise (a narrow 60 Hz tone in the United States).

Channel—Five effects handle one very basic function—adjusting where you hear the signal (left, right, or somewhere in between). Auto Pan lets you automate sound going back and forth from the right channel to the left. You can use the timeline's audio track blue "pan" rubberband to do most of the channel functions as well.

> To access that blue audio pan rubberband, click the small triangle next to Audio 1 to expand the audio track (just as you did when you used the red "volume" rubberband in Hour 7, "Adding Audio"). Click the blue icon to open the blue audio pan rubberband. Dragging the blue line up moves the audio to the left channel, sliding the line down, moves the audio to the right channel. You can add "handles" by clicking the blue line and dragging those handles up or down.

10

DirectX—Simply accesses the TC|Works effects.

Dynamics—Boost, Compressor, and Noise Gate all adjust volume characteristics. The TC|Works Dynamics filter replicates and refines these functions.

EQ—Equalization. TC|Works also tackles this section's three functions: Bass & Treble, Equalize, and Parametric Equalization. If you have an ounce of audiophile in you, you probably have an equalizer on some stereo equipment. Basically it lets you selectively change the volume for specific frequency ranges.

Effect—This may be Premiere's most enjoyable set of audio effects. I'll have you put them through their paces in a few minutes. Chorus adds one or more voices to a single voice (or instrument) by replicating the original sound at a slightly different frequency ("detuning" it). Do that a couple times and you have, well, a chorus. But it can sound kind of "warbly." Flanger creates a similar effect using a different technique. It inverts the phase of the audio signal at its center frequency. And Multi-Effect takes something close to the Chorus effect and constantly shifts the pitch of the added voice.

Reverb & Delay—The TC|Works Reverb tool smoothly handles most of the functions of these three effects. Echo is what you'd expect—a direct repetition of your audio set for a specific delay. Reverb is like Echo but muffles the repeated and delayed sound to simulate an acoustic environment, such as a large room. TC|Works handles both functions better. Multitap Delay is the only Premiere audio effect in this section that TC|Works does *not* replicate. It lets you turn on up to four delayed audio "taps." I'll go over this in detail later. As an exercise, I'll suggest you experiment with this fun effect.

TC|Works—This set of three tools—Dynamics, EQ, and Reverb—takes on virtually all the functions of the Premiere Dynamics, EQ, and Reverb & Delay audio effect sections. At first its interface, illustrated in Figure 10.5, is a bit daunting, but you'll come to enjoy its responsiveness and customizability.

FIGURE 10.5

The TC|Works EQ interface. One of three TC|Works tools that at first may appear complicated but will end up improving your project's audio quality.

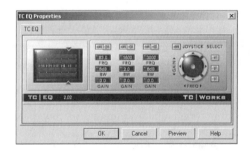

Task: Add an Audio Effect to a Clip

I'll save TC|Works for last and first go through the basics of how you add, preview, and layer multiple audio effects. Follow these steps to add an audio effect to a clip:

1. Add a video/audio or audio-only clip to the timeline.

2. Drag and drop the Lowpass effect (from the `Bandpass Audio Effects` folder) on your audio clip.

3. Open the Effect Controls palette. The Effect Controls palette has two controls and two check boxes. The little *f* I've highlighted in Figure 10.6 indicates the effect is enabled (or *functioning*). The bottom of the screen tells you one effect is enabled. Click the *f* and that number changes to 0.

4. Click the other, empty check box. The little stopwatch I've highlighted in Figure 10.6 indicates that keyframing is enabled. I'll cover keyframing in Hour 11 (see the following note). Uncheck Keyframing.

5. You can change the two Lowpass controls from within the Effect Controls palette, but clicking Setup opens the Lowpass Filter Settings dialog box, which lets you preview the audio as you make changes. So, click Setup.

6. Click the Preview Sound check box and then experiment with the Lowpass Filter settings. This filter cuts out higher frequencies but lets you mix the original full-frequency clip with the altered lower-frequency version. Under the Mix setting, Dry means you'll hear only the original clip, and Effect means you'll hear only the Lowpass version. Any frequency above the cutoff frequency will not play in the "Effect" portion of this clip.

7. Find settings that work for you and click OK. Note that the new setting values show up in the Effect Controls palette.

10

FIGURE 10.6

The Lowpass Filter with the enabling "f" and keyframing stop-watch highlighted.

Keyframing is similar to adding handles to the red "volume" rubberband. To get a brief idea of what's to come, leave the keyframing stopwatch "on" in the Effect Controls palette and expand the audio track with the selected

audio clip. As I've highlighted in Figure 10.7, to the left of the red rubberband icon you'll see a gray/white diamond. Click it and a blue/white line
replaces the red rubberband line. You'll use this line to change an audio or
video effect's value within the clip. Not all effects offer keyframing. Now,
uncheck the stopwatch icon to disable keyframing.

Task: Add Multiple Audio Effects to a Clip

You can add multiple audio (and video) effects to the same clip. Here's how:

1. Keep Lowpass enabled and drag Auto Pan to the same audio clip or to that clip's
    Effect Controls palette. As shown in Figure 10.8, this adds Auto Pan below
    Lowpass in the palette.

2. Click Setup. That opens the Auto Pan Settings dialog box.

3. Click the Preview Sound check box and listen. Your Lowpass-adjusted clip will
    now zip back and forth between your right and left speakers. Experiment with the
    settings. Depth adjusts how "wide" the pans will be, and Rate specifies how
    quickly the pans will take place. If the idea of motion sickness appeals to you, set
    the Rate relatively high. Whew.

4. Click OK to close the Auto Pan Settings dialog box. Note that your new settings
    appear in the Effect Controls palette.

FIGURE 10.8

*Each additional effect
that you add to a clip
shows up in the Effect
Controls palette.*

For a little fun, add both a Highpass and Lowpass filter to a clip. Set each to full Effect Mix, meaning don't play any of the original full-frequency clip, and set high and low cutoff frequencies to the same value in the middle of the audio spectrum—5,000 Hz or so. The result should be silence.

The palette works on a first-come, first-served basis. If you click Setup in the Palette's *top* effect (in this case, Lowpass) and select Preview Sound, you will hear only the Lowpass effect. If you select Setup for the effect *below* Lowpass in the Effect Controls palette (in this case, Auto Pan), you'll hear the combined result of the two effects—and so on down the line. Each subsequent effect adds itself to those above it.

To isolate just the Auto Pan effect, disable Lowpass by clicking (turning off) its little *f* icon. Now if you preview Auto Pan, you'll hear only that specific effect.

To remove an effect from the palette, select it by clicking its name. Then click the waste-basket icon at the bottom of the palette (pressing the Delete key also will remove the clips from the timeline).

If you want to change the order of the effects in the Effect Controls palette, just drag an effect up or down until a horizontal line appears. Then drop that effect in the new location.

Generally there is no need to render audio effects on the timeline to hear them (see the following caution). Simply place your edit line on your clip and press the spacebar or the play button in the Program Monitor window to listen to your audio effect in real-time.

Depending on your computer's processor power and overall system performance, you may hear pops and clicks while playing back audio with more than one effect or from more than one track. In this case, you will need to render or use Premiere's new Real-time Preview feature to hear the combined audio effects.

If you hear those pops and clicks, you should change the audio rendering settings to more accurately reflect your system's power. Select Project, Project Settings, Audio. Then reduce the number of audio tracks and audio effects so Premiere won't try to play back too many audio tracks and effects on the fly. I've highlighted those numbers in Figure 10.9.

10

FIGURE 10.9

Use the Audio Project Settings dialog box to reduce the number of audio tracks and effects (filters) to mini-mize audio popping and clicking when lis-tening to multiple audio effects.

Experimenting with Fun Audio Effects

You may have noticed that the Bandpass and Channel Audio effects have very narrow functions—and they're not all that much fun.

You'll find the fun stuff in the `Effect` folder along with Multitap Delay in the `Reverb & Delay` folder.

Give Chorus and Flanger test drives. Their purpose is to give breadth—"depth and char-acter" as the Premiere Help section puts it—to solo voices or instruments. If you have CDs that fit this bill, now's the time to rip a couple tracks. But, it's also fun to use your own singing voice—on pitch or not. Here's how:

1. In either case, drag a solo instrument/voice audio track to the timeline.

2. Select it and drag the Chorus Audio effect (it's in the `Effect` folder) to that clip or to the Effect Controls palette.

3. Click Setup. That pops up the Chorus Settings dialog box, as in Figure 10.10.

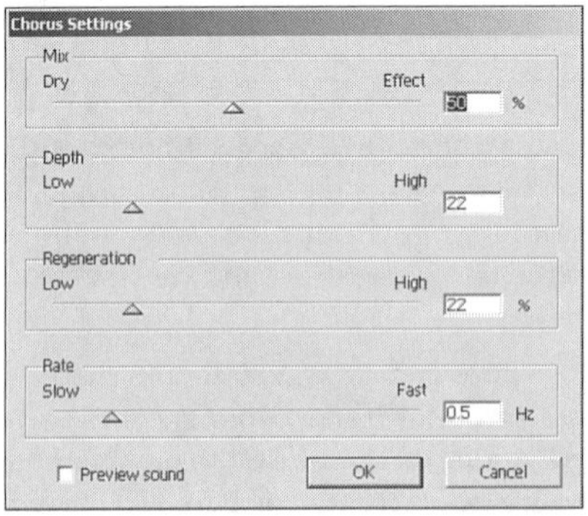

FIGURE 10.10

The Chorus Settings dialog box.

In the Chorus Settings dialog box, you'll encounter yet another example of Premiere's arcane and sometimes confusing taxonomy. There's the now familiar Mix with its Dry (original audio) and Effect (altered audio) settings. But what's Depth? It's actually *Delay*. And then there's Regeneration? That's another word for *Echo*. At least, Rate is self-explanatory. Here's the skinny:

Chorus—Lets you create another "voice" that's of a slightly different pitch than the original voice. Try different settings and see how it helps your music—or *if* it helps. It's frequently not an improvement.

Flanger—Remove Chorus from the Effect Controls palette and replace it with Flanger. This alters the phase of the audio at its center frequency and sounds like the Chorus effect but can be a bit "wavy." It has three of Chorus's four controls. It does not have Regeneration (Echo).

Multi-Effect—This is an enhanced Chorus effect. As highlighted in Figure 10.11, it allows you to create a second, delayed voice and to modulate (change) its pitch using either a smooth, regularly changing sine wave or a random pattern. Once again, confounding terminology makes deciphering this more difficult than it should be. In this case, Feedback (how much of the delayed audio is added back to the original audio) is very similar to Mix, and Delay Time is self-explanatory (same as *Depth* in the Chorus effect).

10

FIGURE 10.11

Multi-Effect works like an enhanced Chorus effect.

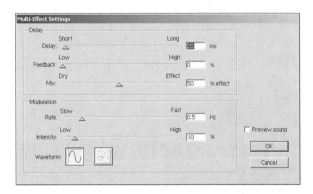

Multitap Delay—This is a fun way to alter music that has a persistent beat—especially electronic dance music. You can switch on up to four, delayed audio "taps." Each tap offers Delay, Highpass/Lowpass, Feedback, Channel controls (Left, Right, Both) and Cross (bounces echoes between channels). Its Musical Time Calculator, highlighted in Figure 10.12, lets you synchronize the effects to the beat.

FIGURE 10.12
FIGURE 10.12

Multitap Delay is the most complex of Premiere's standard set of audio effects.

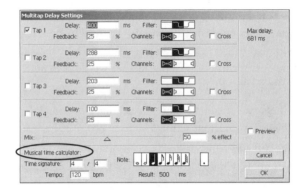

Task: Experiment with Multitap Delay

This is the trickiest effect from the standard Premiere palette. Here are a few steps you can follow to see how it works:

1. Apply Multitap Delay to a music clip (if you have one; otherwise, any audio clip will do).

2. Select each of the four taps, one at a time, and give each one a delay (up to 681 milliseconds).

3. Click a filter icon to create a Lowpass or Highpass effect.

4. Adjust the feedback to set how much delayed audio you add to the original audio.

5. Choose the channel(s) to receive the delayed effect.

6. Use Cross to bounce echoes between channels.

7. Use Mix to set the relative amount of the original clip with the output of all the taps.

Creating Professional Audio Enhancements with TC|Works

TC|Works creates audio software for multiple platforms. Its parent company, TC Electronic, is a well-respected manufacturer of professional audio hardware for studios and live performances.

The three TC|Works audio tools included with Premiere 6.5, collectively called *TC|Native Essentials*, are DirectX-compatible plug-ins.

Each one has an interface that resembles the front panel of typical TC Electronic hardware. Two of the three audio tools—EQ and Dynamics—use SoftSat, an algorithm that

TC|Works claims gives its audio that "lovely warm sound often associated with analog tube equipment." I'm inclined to agree.

Whereas the standard Premiere audio effects sometimes sound a bit artificial, the TC|Works effects are smooth and more realistic. When you select "Huge Cathedral" from the TC Reverb presets, it sounds like a huge cathedral.

For more details about these TC|Works products, access the TC Essentials PDF file in the TCWorks/TCNativeEssentials202 file folder on the same hard drive as your Premiere 6.5 folder. Figure 10.13 shows its cover page.

FIGURE 10.13
The TC|Native Essentials manual.

10

Exploring TC Reverb

I'm going to take you through all three TC|Works tools. To start, clear the Effect Controls palette and then drag the third TC|Works audio effect, TC Reverb, to the palette or to your audio clip on the timeline. This pops up an intuitive interface, as shown in Figure 10.14, intended to resemble audio electronics hardware.

FIGURE 10.14
The TC Reverb interface has the "feel" of professional audio hardware.

TC Reverb replaces the functions of Premiere's Reverb & Echo, plus some attributes of Multitap Delay. I'll take you through its interface:

Preview—Switch this on to hear a repeated segment of your audio clip. Unlike Premiere's Preview Sound option, which does not react immediately to changes you make, the TC|Works plug-ins are very responsive.

ROM, Decay, and Mix—To change any TC Reverb settings, click one of the buttons—ROM (TC|Works presets), Decay, or Mix—then click the control knob and drag your mouse up or down. Alternatively, you can place your mouse over any of the illuminated displays and right-click to increase its value one step at a time or left-click to decrease its value. Do that for the ROM setting and see how the different simulated "rooms" sound.

The right/left-click "value change" technique plus the following three functions all work similarly for all three TC|Works plug-ins. Give each of the following a test drive:

- Click the TC Works logo bar to display a drop-down list of presets.
- Right/Option-click the VU meter to turn it on or off, display a line showing your audio clip's peak volume, or convert a monaural clip into a stereo signal.
- Manipulate the VU meter sliders—they let you manually set the volume levels for input and output.

> Experiment with TC Reverb. *Decay* means how long it takes for your echo to fade away. *Mix* is the relative amount of the original and the echo in the combined version. Set Mix to 100% and ROM to Large Cathedral. It'll sound like you're standing at a cathedral's entrance in the back.

Exploring TC Dynamics

This TC|Works plug-in replaces most of the functions of two of Premiere's Dynamics audio effects—Boost and Compressor/Expander—plus some functions of Noise Gate. Its purpose is to shrink the dynamic range of a clip—the difference between the loudest and quietest sounds.

Typically you'll use this when you have very quiet passages. In those cases, if you simply increase the gain (the volume) the moderately loud audio will be too loud. Therefore, you use a compressor to bring up quiet passages while holding down loud sounds. This can help your audio levels sound more even and consistent throughout the length of the audio clip. Remove TC Reverb from the Effect Controls palette and replace it by dragging in TC Dynamics. As illustrated in Figure 10.15, its interface is a little busier than TC Reverb's. I've highlighted its four control knobs:

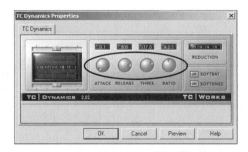

FIGURE 10.15

TC Dynamics with its four control knobs highlighted.

Attack—This is the amount of time in milliseconds it takes for the compressor to kick in. A small number works well with sudden sounds such as drums, keeping them from suddenly overwhelming a quieter passage. A larger number works well with strings, easing up their volume.

Release—This is the time taken for the compression to return to normal. A long release time causes a sound's attribute to fade away slowly, whereas a short release time causes it to drop out quickly.

Threshold—This is the volume level, in decibels, at which the compressor starts working—from –60 to 0 dB. Settings close to -60 effectively amplify the quietest sounds. Settings close to zero minimize the compression effect.

Ratio—This sets how far the compressor will pull the top volume down when its signal is above the threshold level. A setting of 5 (5:1 ratio) means that if the signal is 10 dB above the threshold, the compressor will cut that to 2 dB above the threshold. Compressors pull down peak volumes.

> The Compressor lowers the level of the input signal when it is above the threshold. The amount that is lowered is determined by the ratio and the input level. As a general rule, use high ratios with relatively high thresholds and low ratios with low thresholds.

Task: Listen to the Attributes in Action

To hear all the TC Dynamics attributes in action, follow these steps:

1. Within the TC Dynamics interface, select Preview.

2. Now make some adjustments to those four knobs. Depending on your audio clip, you may notice some dramatic changes.

3. Turn on SoftSat. I've highlighted it and two other options—SoftKnee and Automatic Make-Up Gain —in Figure 10.16. With SoftSat selected, the sound should take on a "warmer" characteristic. Turn off SoftSat.

▼   4. Turn on SoftKnee. This smoothes the transition into compression. If you've
        selected extreme compression settings—very low thresholds or very high ratios—
        this may produce better results. Turn off SoftKnee.

     5. Right/Option-click the VU meter. Select Automatic Make-Up Gain. The volume
        level should increase dramatically. You may need to leave this on if you plan to do
▲   a lot of signal compression.

FIGURE 10.16
*TC Dynamics and its
three extra features.*

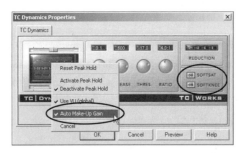

I don't want to understate the value of Automatic Make-Up Gain. This para-
meter has a *huge* impact on the overall behavior of the TC Dynamics plug-in.

With Auto Make-Up Gain set to Off, the average audio signal is compressed,
without a compensating overall increase in gain. This is the behavior of a
standard compressor. With Auto Make-Up Gain set to On, the average audio
signal is compressed and then raised to meet the levels of the highest gain.
This ensures your project has a consistent audio output level.

Set the TC Dynamics VU meter to Activate Peak Hold. Right/Option-click the
VU meter to make that menu selection. Note the peak volume level in dB
(it's hard to read the numeric values—blue/green are negative values, yellow
is positive, and red means "hot"). Then select your threshold level at slightly
less than the peak volume.

Exploring TC EQ

Remove the TC Dynamics plug-in from your audio clip and replace it with TC EQ, as
shown in Figure 10.17. I'm not sure why it's simply called "TC EQ" because this tool
replaces and improves upon six Premiere audio effects: the three EQ audio effects (Bass
& Treble, Equalize, and Parametric Equalization) and the three Bandpass effects
(Lowpass, Highpass, and Notch Filter).

FIGURE 10.17

The TC EQ interface does not resemble the consumer-style equalizer most of us are used to. This one is digital and gives you more precise control.

An equalizer lets you make precise volume adjustments to selected frequencies or frequency ranges. You may have a so-called *graphic equalizer* on your car or home stereo. It has a series of sliders (faders), each for different preset frequency ranges—from deep bass to high treble. Guys who like thumping bass in their cars crank up the sliders on the low end of the frequency scale.

10

The term *graphic equalizer* comes from the curved shape the sliders/faders create on the frequency response line. Most audiophiles like to boost the bass and treble, making a wide curving "smile" graphic equalizer shape.

Parametric equalizers boost specific, narrow frequency ranges. You can convert a thin vocal into a full-bodied powerhouse by rolling off the high frequencies and boosting the bass.

Finally, TC EQ has several undocumented features: Notch Filter, Low Shelf, and High Shelf. I'll explain each in a couple minutes.

The TC EQ logo bar menu has some presets that warrant experimentation (see Figure 10.18). Selecting one, such as Lowshelf/Parametric/Highshelf (the default setting), automatically selects those features across the three bands and inputs preset values. With Preview on, change the Gain or other settings to see how the presets work.

Note also that SoftSat (the "warm" sound algorithm) is on by default. Selecting Only Parametric without SoftSat turns off that feature.

FIGURE 10.18

The TC EQ menu, accessible by clicking the logo bar, offers several presets for the three EQ "bands."

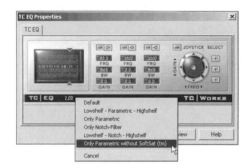

The interface takes some getting used to. I've highlighted a few elements in Figure 10.19. Each of the three columns has three options:

- FRQ is frequency—the audio pitch in cycles per second or hertz (Hz). The audible portion of the frequency spectrum runs from about 20 Hz to 22,000 Hz (22 KHz) or about 10 octaves.

- BW is bandwidth—the frequency range in octaves centered on the selected frequency that you will increase or decrease in volume.

- Gain is how much extra or reduced volume you want to apply to a frequency range.

You can set numeric amounts for these features in one of three ways:

- Click the illuminated number to pop up a slider.

- Double-click to type in a specific number.

- Use the joystick to adjust the gain and/or frequency. You need to turn the joystick on and select which column/band you want to control.

FIGURE 10.19

The TC EQ bands and their numeric settings.

The joystick—I've highlighted the on/off and settings buttons in Figure 10.20—is not immediately intuitive. To use it, turn it on by clicking the On button; then click one or more of the band numbers to its right. Use your mouse to increase or decrease the gain by dragging the joystick up or down. Decrease or increase the frequency by dragging the joystick left or right.

Depending on your presets, you may notice that the joystick does not allow you to adjust the gain and frequency through their full range. This is intended to give you more accuracy. To change those presets, right-click any of the three numbered buttons to the right. I've highlighted one of the drop-down menus in Figure 10.20. "Gain Absolute" means you can use the joystick to adjust the full 36 dB range, "Gain Relative" cuts that range in half. Selecting something other than "Frequency Absolute" narrows the range to two or four octaves.

FIGURE 10.20

The TC EQ joystick takes some getting used to.

You can turn on/off a band by clicking its associated On button above its respective column. The little button next to the On button represents the column's current function. Here's a rundown of that button's features:

 Low Shelf—This is an undocumented feature. Use it to boost or reduce the entire low end of the frequency spectrum *prior to* the selected frequency. It's sort of like using the bass control on your stereo. The "Shelf" numeric values are a bit confusing. As I've highlighted in Figure 10.21, instead of inputting a bandwidth amount in the BW window, you input a dB (decibel) level (+/-) to increase or decrease gain for that low-end range (this works for High Shelf as well). Gain multiplies that dB level, so a 12 dB setting coupled with a –3 Gain setting means the Low Shelf frequency section will be 36 dB quieter than its normal volume.

 High Shelf—This is the opposite of Low Shelf. In this case, you boost or reduce the entire high end of the frequency spectrum *starting at* the selected frequency. This more or less replicates the treble control on your stereo.

 Parametric EQ—You use this to boost or reduce a specific frequency or frequency range. Use BW to set the bandwidth centered on that frequency.

Notch Filter—Another undocumented feature. This silences anything from a single frequency—such as the 60 Hz power-line hum—to a wider frequency range. Note that when selected it automatically sets the Gain to "-inf" (that is, silence).

FIGURE 10.21

With Low or High Shelf selected, the BW (bandwidth) window (highlighted) is where you input the dB (decibel) change for the shelf.

Now's the time to experiment with this powerful audio production tool. There's so much it can do to enhance your sound. And remember, you can use any of the TC|Works tools multiple times on the same audio clip. So if you want to create a true graphic equalizer with 15 bands, for instance, you can use TC EQ five times, defining three narrow "parametric" bands in each instance.

Summary

Adding effects to clips on the Premiere timeline can bring a project to life. The Effect Controls palette tracks each clip's effects, lets you arrange them in a logical order, lets you temporarily turn them off to further clarify how they're working, and lets you remove them from the clip.

The Audio Effects palette offers the 20 audio effects from Premiere 6.0. However, three new audio-sweetening products from TC|Works—TC Dynamics, TC EQ, and TC Reverb—replicate and improve on 11 of those. These powerful tools offer remarkable control and customizability while adding a "warm" and smooth sound to your project.

Workshop

Review the questions and answers in this section to try to sharpen your Premiere audio production effects skills. Also, take a few moments to tackle my short quiz and the exercises.

Q&A

Q **I applied three audio effects to a clip. When I play it back on the timeline, it sounds horrible—full of clicks and static.**

A You've exceeded your computer's processing capabilities. You need to first render this segment of your project and then change the Audio Project Setting to reduce the number of tracks and effects Premiere will try to play back without rendering.

Q **Besides giving "oomph" to a thin vocal, what else can I use the TC EQ for?**

A If you have isolated recordings of instruments in a band, you can add presence to each one by boosting portions of their frequency range. Giving them a little more treble increases their "attack." If you have trouble with audio hum or "popped P's," then reducing the low frequencies may help. You can use TC EQ to "carve out" a vocalist's range within an instrumental, giving that singer more "visibility."

Quiz

1. You need to boost treble and bass. What's the easiest way to do that?

2. There are at least two ways to make audio move from the right channel to the left and back. What are they?

3. You recorded a speech but the presenter is too quiet and the waiter's clattering trays are too jarring. How can you fix this?

Quiz Answers

1. You can use Premiere's standard Bass & Treble effect in the EQ folder. But for a warmer sound use TC EQ and select High Shelf and Low Shelf. The easiest way to do this is to use the default TC EQ settings, turn off the middle band (it's set to Parametric), change the High Shelf frequency (the right band) to about 10,000, and increase the gain on both the left (Low Shelf) and right bands to suit your tastes.

2. First, you can use the blue audio pan rubberband. Expand the audio track by clicking the triangle next to Audio 1. Click the blue icon and then drag the blue line all the way down (right channel), click it midway through the clip to make a handle, and drag it all the way up (left). Then click the end handle to drag it back down (right). Second, use Auto Pan. Set Depth to Wide (full right to left pan) and set Rate to suit your clip. This takes some experimentation, but a rate of 0.1 Hz moves the audio from right to left and back in about 10 seconds.

3. You want to minimize the clattering trays by reducing the high end of the volume when that clattering happens. Also, you want to increase the low-volume portions to better hear the speaker. Use TC Dynamics (or Compressor/Expander) to do both.

Turn on Preview to watch the VU meter volume levels. Set the threshold a few dBs below the peak value (set the VU meter to Activate Peak Hold to mark that peak value) and adjust the ratio to suit the situation. The ratio is how far you cut the loudest sound.

Exercises

1. Experiment with the Multitap Delay audio effect (in the `Reverb & Delay` folder). Use it on a solo instrument, a solo voice (record you own, perhaps), and music with a hard beat. Try out its Musical Time Calculator to synchronize the delay effects with the music. This is a slick and exciting toy.

2. Create a "chorus" using your voice. Use your camcorder to record yourself (or a "volunteer") singing a song. Capture it and drag it to your timeline. Then use the Chorus or Flanger audio effect on it several times, altering the settings for each instance.

3. Create a full-featured graphics equalizer by layering three TC EQ plug-ins on the same clip (any more and you'll probably need to render the clip). Once you've set a full-bandwidth of "faders" and applied them to your audio, open the Effect Controls palette and turn one or more of them off (click the *f* check box). Then listen to the difference.

HOUR 11

Creating Video Effects

Premiere's video effects give you more ways than you can imagine to jazz up your video and dazzle viewers. You can put clips in motion, distort them, shrink them, fly them across other clips, and change their color, style, and overall appearance.

You can apply these effects—video *and* audio—gradually over time or immediately. You can combine effects. For instance, you can "posterize" a clip, flip it around, and fly it off screen. It's a cliché, but it applies—the only limit is your imagination.

The highlights of this hour include the following:

- A brief introduction to video effects
- Using keyframes to change audio and video effects over time
- Applying motion and changing clip shapes

Introducing Premiere's Video Effects

This hour marks the beginning of a three-hour "video effects" section. Premiere 6.5 ships with 79 effects, and dozens more are available from third-party providers.

Take a quick look at the Video Effects palette. I've illustrated part of that palette in Figure 11.1. (The screen resolution would have to be set to 1280×960 to display all the effects.)

FIGURE 11.1

The Video Effects palette.

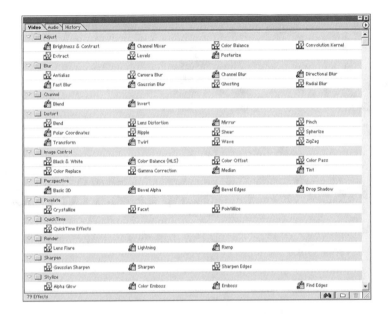

As a convenience Adobe created 14 categories to organize these video effects, but you'll find that one category can sometimes seem a lot like another, and video effects in different categories can be very similar.

You'll notice there are two Video Effects icons: the one with the *V* is a standard Premiere *Video* Effect, and the one with the number 4 is an Adobe After Effects–created effect. We'll look at the AE effects—they tend to be a little wilder and more involved—as well as the After Effects software in Hour 13, "Wrapping Up Effects with After Effects."

You apply video effects much like audio effects, by simply dragging and dropping them to a video clip or the Effect Controls palette for a selected video clip. As with audio effects, you can add multiple video effects to a single clip. But unlike multiple audio effects, adding more than one video effect to a clip sometimes has surprising and unpredictable results.

I'm going to have you briefly try out a few video effects just to get an idea of their variety and value. Then I'll ask you to put them aside while you tackle keyframes and motion/shape settings.

Task: Convert a Clip to Grayscale

I'll begin with Premiere's simplest video effect—Black & White. It converts any clip to grayscale (shades of gray). Follow these steps:

1. Add a brief video or linked video/audio clip to your timeline. Select the video portion of that clip by clicking it with the Selection tool.

2. Open the Effect Controls palette.

3. Open the Video Effects palette by double-clicking its tab in the Transitions/Effects palette.

4. Open the `Image Control` file folder and drag and drop Black & White on the clip on the timeline or to the Effect Controls palette. As with audio effects, this action adds the video effect name to the Effect Controls palette. I've illustrated this in Figure 11.2.

FIGURE 11.2

After the Black & White video effect is applied to a clip, it appears in the Effect Controls palette.

11

The Black & White video effect happens immediately. The video image in the Program Monitor screen shifts instantly to a grayscale image.

You may note that the Black & White video effect has no options. It's either on or off. In this case, because the little *f* is visible next to its name, it's on.

Alt/Option-scrub through your clip to see the Black & White effect "in action."

If you want to see video effects in real time, you have two options:

- Use the time-honored Alt/Option-scrub method.
- Try Premiere 6.5's new real-time preview. Shift+Enter will play back your clip with the video effect applied. It may be a bit jumpy, depending on your system power.

Note that if Preview to Screen is on in the Project Keyframe and Rendering settings, then Shift+Enter will build a preview file. In that case, simply using Enter runs the real-time preview.

You may recall from Hour 7, "Adding Audio," that if you don't have too many audio effects, you don't have to render (or preview) the clip to hear it. That's not the case with video effects. You need to preview or Alt/Option-scrub to see them.

Task: Try the Camera Blur Video Effect

 TASK

Black & White is as basic as Premiere's video effects get. To move things up a notch, try the Camera Blur video effect:

1. Remove Black & White from the Effect Controls palette.

2. Open the Blur file folder and drag and drop Camera Blur onto the timeline or the Effect Controls palette.

3. This effect has one control: Percent Blur.

4. Click Setup to view the Camera Blur Settings dialog box.

5. Move the percentage slider to see its effect in the Preview window (see Figure 11.3).

FIGURE 11.3

Camera Blur has only one option—Percent Blur.

> When you preview an effect in its Settings window, the image displayed is always the first frame of the video clip. You can have Premiere display a different frame. Move the edit line to that frame, right-click (Windows) or Option-click (Mac), select Set Clip Marker, and then select 0 Poster Frame.

As with most video effects (and audio effects), Camera Blur has a keyframe option—the little grayed-out box next to the *f*. I'll explain keyframes in a few minutes.

Experiment with the following simple video effects:

Facet—Found in the `Pixelate` file folder, this effect is reminiscent of Gauguin paintings. It creates a smooth oil painting–like effect by clumping together pixels of similar color values. As with Black & White, there are no options.

Crystallize—Found in the `Pixelate` file folder, this effect creates a distorted mosaic by placing adjacent pixels into solid-colored polygons. Choose a value from 3 to 300 pixels per polygon. A setting of 5 works nicely.

Pointillize—Found in the `Pixelate` file folder, this effect is reminiscent of a Seurat painting. But even at the lowest setting (3), the chunky points don't match his fine style. Pointillize does work well with landscapes.

Replicate—Found in the `Stylize` file folder, this effect divides the screen into tiles and displays the whole clip in each tile—from a 2×2 grid to 16×16.

Solarize—This effect is found in the `Stylize` file folder. By blending between a negative and a positive image, Solarize makes your clip look like film briefly exposed to light during developing. A setting of 0% leaves your clip unchanged, whereas 100% turns it into a negative image.

Before moving to keyframes, I want to take you through a few more basic-but-useful effects.

Task: Apply the Spherize Video Effect

The Spherize effect distorts your image, making it look like someone's pushing a basketball against it. Here are the steps:

1. Remove Camera Blur from the Effect Controls palette.

2. Open the `Distort` file folder and drag and drop Spherize into the Effect Controls palette.

3. As shown in Figure 11.4, this video effect has one numeric value and an additional control: Mode. Adjust these as desired. Here are some points to keep in mind:

▼ • Adjusting the Amount setting from –100 to +100 either "pushes" or "pulls" the clip
     into a spherical shape.

   • Under Mode, you face three options: Normal, Horizontal Only, and Vertical Only.
     Normal looks like a ball, whereas Horizontal Only and Vertical Only expand out
     and squeeze in along their respective axes.

   • The little buttons (+ and -) beneath the preview window let you zoom in on or
     away from your subject to more clearly see the change in shape, but this does not
▲   affect the final effect.

FIGURE 11.4

*Spherize offers two
options to create the
appearance of a bas-
ketball pressed against
your clip.*

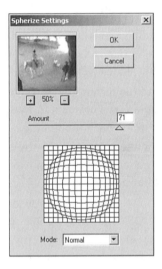

Many times a video effect's Settings dialog box offers no more options than
those listed in the Effect Controls palette. So why bother using the Settings
window? One advantage is that it usually has a preview window. The disad-
vantage is that this window, by default, displays only the first frame of your
clip (unless you've changed the poster frame) .

If you use the Effect Controls palette, the Program Monitor screen displays
whatever frame is beneath the edit line. As you change the Effect parameters in the Effect Controls palette, the results appear promptly in the
Program Monitor screen.

Take a look at three other effects from the Distort file folder:

Pinch—The "pull" move squeezes/pinches the center of the image. The "push" move
bulges out the image like Spherize.

Shear—This is the "fun-house mirror" effect. It distorts your clip along a line
that works much like the Path Text tool. Drag the line's two endpoints around the

perimeter of the box, create "handles" anywhere on the line, and drag and contort that line. The effect of your handiwork shows up immediately in the preview window.

Zig Zag—You can create pond ripples and other radial effects with Zig Zag. The Amount setting (-100 to 100, with 0 being no distortion) represents the magnitude of distortion and the reflection angle. Ridges is the number of ripples (direction reversals), and Style sets the general appearance (Pond, Out from Center, or Around Center) .

Using Keyframes: Changing Effects Over Time

What's really exciting about these last few video effects—as well as most others in the Video Effects palette—is that you can change the characteristics of the effects throughout the duration of your video clip.

You accomplish that by using keyframes, which work something like the volume-control red rubberband handles. You place keyframes (little diamond icons) on a line in the expanded view of the video (or audio) clip and instruct Premiere as to what to do with the selected effect at those keyframes. Most video and audio effects will make changes gradually from one keyframe to the next.

Task: Try Out Keyframes on an Audio Clip

I want you to try this effect first on an audio clip:

1. Drag an audio-only or linked audio/video clip to the timeline.

2. Select the audio clip.

3. Expand the audio track by clicking the triangle next to Audio 1.

4. As you did in Hour 5, "Adding Transitions: From Dissolves to Zooms," note the four icons in the lower-left area. I've highlighted them in Figure 11.5. Select the keyframe gray/white diamond icon, which brings up the keyframe line in the expanded view beneath the audio clip.

5. Open the Effect Controls palette. It should have your audio clip's name at the top.

6. Locate Echo in the `Audio Effects/Reverb & Delay` file folder and drag it to the Effect Controls palette (or to your clip on the timeline).

11

FIGURE 11.5

Expanding the audio track reveals four icons: Display Waveform, Keyframes, red volume rubberband, blue fade rubberband.

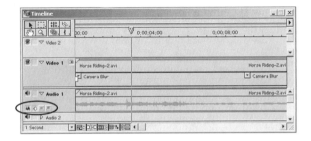

Applying an audio effect to your clip causes three things to happen on the timeline. I've highlighted them in Figure 11.6:

- The name of the audio effect (Echo) pops up in the keyframe track.
- The Keyframe Navigator appears. It's a little check box with two arrows on each side (although they sometimes don't pop up onscreen right away) to the right of the four icons.
- Square boxes appear at each end of the keyframe track.

FIGURE 11.6

Adding an audio effect displays its name in the keyframe track, pops up the Keyframe Navigator, and places two keyframe boxes in the expanded audio track.

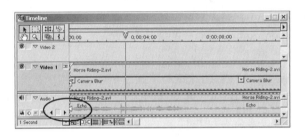

The Keyframe Navigator (the check box with two triangles) lets you move easily from one keyframe to another. The two boxes mark the beginning and end of the effect. Now, here's the next set of steps to follow:

1. In the Effect Controls palette, slide the Echo slider way to the right to make a really obvious echo.
2. Grab the left keyframe box and drag it to the right.
3. Grab the right keyframe box and drag it to the left. Your clip should look like Figure 11.7. What you've done is to tell Premiere to start the Echo audio effect somewhere in the clip (not at its very beginning) and end the effect somewhere before the clip finishes.

4. Play the clip and note when the echo kicks in and when the audio returns to normal. Note that you can click the Keyframe Navigator triangles to jump the edit line from the start to the end of the effect.

FIGURE **11.7**

Moving the keyframe start/end boxes sets new in/out locations for the Echo effect within the audio clip.

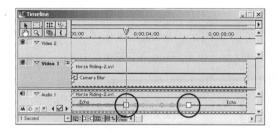

Consider how you could use this. Perhaps you want your narrator to suddenly have a booming, echoing voice. To create that, follow these steps:

1. Move the edit line to that spot in the clip.

2. Make two adjacent handles on the volume red rubberband (this lets you keep the volume at its original level right up to the booming/ echoing segment).

3. Raise the volume of the entire second half of the clip by dragging up the rubberband to the right of the second handle using the Fade Adjustment tool (the up/down-arrow tool in the Audio section of the toolbox) .

4. Add the Echo audio effect to the audio track.

5. Click the Keyframe icon next to the red rubberband icon to open the keyframe track.

6. Drag the keyframe start box to that location—meaning the volume increase will coincide with the Echo effect.

Voila—booming audio.

Task: Use Keyframes to Change an Effect Over Time

The real power of keyframing is to *change* an effect over time, not simply to switch it on and off somewhere within a clip. Here are the steps for this task:

1. Turn on keyframes by going to the Effect Controls palette and clicking that little empty gray check box next to the effect name, Echo. Take a look at the keyframe track. Those start and end boxes just changed to gray/white diamonds. Keyframing is on. I've highlighted the differences in Figure 11.8.

2. Note that the gray/white color scheme has a purpose. The white side of the diamond indicates where the effect begins or ends.

▲ TASK

▼

▼ 3. Drag those diamonds closer to the start and end of the clip to give yourself a little more room.

4. Select the "start" diamond by clicking the left triangle Keyframe Navigator icon in the expanded audio track. Note that if you drag the edit line ahead of the start diamond, the Echo effect "grays out" in the Effect Controls palette, indicating the Echo effect is nonfunctional at that location on the clip.

5. Set a low Echo value on the slider in the Effect Controls palette.

6. Move the edit line to the center of your clip. Change the Echo value slider to a much higher number. By changing the value at a new location on the keyframe line you automatically create a new keyframe.

FIGURE 11.8

After keyframes are turned on, the white boxes in the expanded timeline track change to gray/white diamonds.

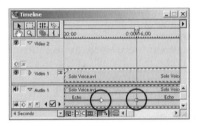

Changing the Effect value places a white diamond on the keyframe line at that point. That's the new keyframe. You can grab it and slide it to change its location.

Scrub the edit line back and forth along the audio clip and note how the Echo value on the slider gradually changes as Premiere interpolates the Echo value difference between the two points.

7. Add one other Keyframe using a different method. Simply drag the edit Line to a new location within the audio clip and click the Keyframe Navigator check box between those two triangles. This adds another keyframe with an Echo value set automatically at whatever it would have been as the value changed gradually between two other keyframes.

8. Use the slider in the Effect Controls palette to adjust that Echo value.

▲ 9. Listen to your keyframed audio clip. The echo should become more pronounced as the clip plays and then gradually fade away at the end.

> To delete a keyframe, simply select it by using the cursor (wait for it to turn to a gray hand) or by jumping to it using the triangles next to the Keyframe Navigator check box. Then click (uncheck) that check box. Alternatively, you also can delete a keyframe by dragging it off the ends of the keyframe line. This works only if that keyframe is the first or last in a sequence. If it's between two other keyframes, you can drag it only as far as a neighboring keyframe.

Using Keyframes on Video Effects

The process is almost the same for video effects, with two minor exceptions.

Remove all clips from the timeline and expand the Video 1 and Video 2 tracks. Note the differences highlighted in Figure 11.9.

FIGURE 11.9

Video 2 has only two options and Video 1 has none.

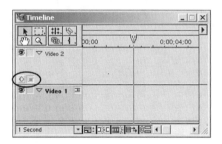

Video 2 has two option icons in the lower-left corner: keyframing and the ubiquitous red rubberband. In this case the red rubberband does not change the audio volume; instead, it alters video transparency. You can create a translucent clip and layer it over whatever is in the track(s) below it. I'll cover transparency in detail in Hour 14, "Compositing Part 1: Layering Images and Clips," and Hour 15, "Compositing Part 2: Alpha Channels and Mattes."

Video 1 has *no* options. That's because there is only one thing you can do to a video clip on track 1—add video effects to it. You cannot change the transparency of a clip on Track 1 because you can't superimpose it over a clip beneath it—it's in the lowest track. Therefore, there's no need for a red "video transparency" rubberband.

11

In all video and audio tracks are two check boxes in the upper-left corner (I've highlighted them in Figure 11.10): the eye (video) and the speaker (audio) icons indicate those tracks will be visible/heard when you play back the timeline. Clicking them removes the icons and turns off those tracks. You might do that if you want to listen to a specific audio passage on a track or see how a video clip looks without another clip superimposed over it.

The other current *unchecked* box locks/unlocks the track. Locking a track ensures you can make no changes to it, including adding or deleting clips.

To see how this works, lock a track and move your cursor over it. It changes into an ominous black arrow with a padlock on it. I highlighted this in Figure 11.10.

FIGURE 11.10

Click the eye or speaker icon to exclude or include a track in the program. Click a track's lock icon to prevent any changes. Note the highlighted locked-track cursor.

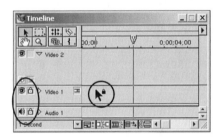

Task: Try Out Video Keyframing

To see how video keyframing works, follow these steps:

1. Drag a video-only or linked video/audio clip to the Video 1 track on the timeline.

2. Drag the Crystallize video effect (from the Stylize file folder) to the Effect Controls palette. As Figure 11.11 illustrates, the same three things that happen when adding an audio effect happen with a video effect: The name of the effect appears in the expanded video track, the Keyframe Navigator box appears, and two white squares appear at the ends of the clip in the expanded view.

3. In the Crystallize Settings window, select the smallest cell size (3) and click OK.

4. To see the Crystallize effect in action, Alt/Option-scrub through the clip or do a real-time preview by pressing Shift+Enter.

5. Click the Keyframe check box next to the clip name in the Effect Controls palette. This turns on keyframes and causes those two boxes in the expanded Video 1 track to change to diamonds (at the moment, because they're at the ends of the clip, they look only like triangles) .

▼

▼   6. Move the edit line to some point toward the middle of the clip and increase the
       Cell Size value to something such as 40. This creates a new keyframe.

▲   7. Preview/render your clip to see how this works.

Your video clip transitions from a lovely postimpressionist painting to a screen full of
animated solid-color polygons and then back to that lovely painting again.

FIGURE 11.11

*Adding a video effect
displays its name in the
keyframe track, dis-
plays the Keyframe
Navigator with its two
triangles, and puts two
keyframe boxes in the
expanded video track.*

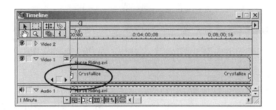

Sometimes, even with keyframes, the video effect's changes can be abrupt. Try using
keyframes with the Replicate Video effect.

You know the drill:

1. Remove the Crystallize effect from your clip.
2. Drag Replicate (from the Stylize file folder) to the Effect Controls palette.
3. Turn on keyframing.
4. Select the lowest Count value (2) .
5. Move the edit line to the center of the clip and change the Count value to its highest value (16). That creates a keyframe.

Render/preview or Alt/Option-scrub to view your handiwork. No gradual changes here.
The image jumps with each change in box number.

For now this concludes this hour's coverage of keyframing. In Hour 12, "Using Higher-
Level Video Effects," I'll cover a whole slew of exciting Premiere video effects that benefit from keyframing. Before moving on, here are the Premiere video effects that do *not*
allow keyframing:

Anti-Alias—This effect is found in the Blur file folder. Just as anti-aliasing in transitions blurs sharply defined diagonal lines, this effect softens the edges between highly
contrasting colors.

Black & White—Found in the Image Control file folder, this effect converts color
clips into grayscale.

Facet—Found in the Pixelate file folder, this effect creates the oil-painting look.

11

Field Interpolate—Found in the `Video` file folder. This is a technical fix, not a creative tool. It re-creates missing scan lines dropped during capture.

Gaussian Sharpen—Found in the `Sharpen` file folder, this effect is supposed to dramatically sharpen a clip, but it looks more like the Crystallize effect.

Ghosting—Found in the `Blur` file folder, this very nifty effect creates a "comet tail" on any moving object (including camera moves). It's great for showing the flight of a thrown/hit/kicked ball. A steady camera is a must.

Horizontal Flip—Found in the `Transform` file folder, this effect reverses a clip left to right but still plays the clip forward. Use it if you "broke the plane" while shooting a cutaway.

Resize—Found in the `Transform` file folder, this effect takes lower-resolution clips and fits them into your output frame size. I found it gives unpredictable results.

Sharpen Edges—Found in the `Sharpen` file folder, this effect looks just as odd as Gaussian Sharpen. Apparently it's only effective for very soft focus clips.

Vertical Flip—Found in the `Transform` file folder, this effect flips clips upside down.

Vertical Hold—Found in the `Transform` file folder, this effect makes your clip look like the vertical hold is out of whack.

Applying Motion to Clips and Changing Their Shape

You've seen videos that fly images in boxes over other images or fly a spinning video clip onscreen—starting as a small dot and expanding to full-screen size. You can create those effects using Premiere's motion settings.

Task: Test out Premiere's Motion Settings

Here's how it works:

1. Clear your timeline.

2. Drag a video or linked video/audio clip to the Video 1 track. Select it.

3. Open the Effect Controls palette. Click Setup (next to Motion). Up pops the Motion Settings dialog box (see Figure 11.12).

   This Motion Settings dialog box is one of Premiere's most powerful tools. The upper-left window is the preview screen. Your clip should be sliding left to right across a white screen. That's the default motion setting.

FIGURE 11.12

The Motions Settings dialog box—one of Premiere's most powerful tools.

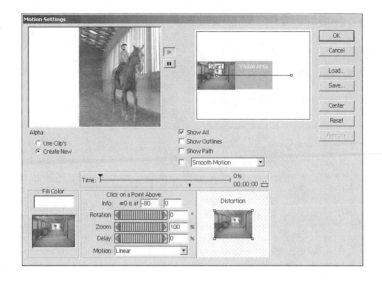

 Alternatively, you can access the Motion Settings dialog box by right/Option-clicking the Video 1 clip to access the Clip menu and then selecting Video Options, Motion or selecting Clip (on the main workspace menu bar), Video Options, Motion.

 Because this clip is on Video 1, you cannot display anything "beneath" it. So if you fly this clip onto the screen, all that your viewers will see at first is a white screen. You might want to change the color to more closely match your clip's predominant color.

To do that, either click the Fill Color box and select a background color or move the cursor over the clip window beneath the Fill Color box and use the eyedropper to select a color. The new color will show up immediately in the preview window.

4. The screen on the right shows the motion path. At the moment, your clip starts just offscreen and immediately moves horizontally from left to offscreen on the right.

   Move those start- and endpoints by grabbing their respective small white boxes and sliding them around the screen. Your cursor hand will turn gray when you are close enough to grab a box. Note how the animation in the preview screen changes.

5. Create a diagonal line, as illustrated in Figure 11.13.

FIGURE 11.13

A diagonal motion path takes the clip from the upper left to the lower right.

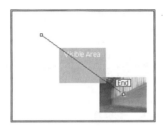

▼   6. You can create additional keyframes on the motion path. Move your cursor any-where on the path, wait until it turns into a pointing hand, and click to create a keyframe handle.

   For future reference, note that when you create a new keyframe a little triangle pops up above the motion timeline. I've highlighted that in Figure 11.14. I'll get to this timeline in a moment.

FIGURE 11.14

Placing a new keyframe handle on the motion path adds a lit-tle triangle to the motion timeline.

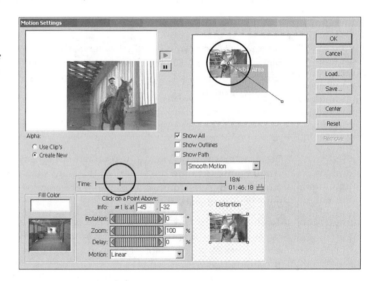

   7. Drag the keyframe to a new location and note the changed path in the preview screen.

This is where the motion settings process gets a little confusing.

Note that the original location of the keyframe handle you create—relative to the two endpoints—sets its *timing*. If you create a keyframe in the middle of the motion path, the moving clip will reach that new point on the path halfway through the clip's duration. If you drag the keyframe to a new location, even if it's right next to the start- or endpoint, the clip will adjust its speed accordingly to arrive at that point halfway through its duration and continue from there for the second half of its duration.

▼

8. To see that the new keyframe's relative timing remains unchanged, drag the new keyframe handle next to the endpoint, as I've done in Figure 11.15. Note how quickly the clip moves to that new point on the motion path and then how slowly it moves to the endpoint.

9. Drag the new keyframe handle next to the start point and note how slowly the clip moves to the new keyframe location and how quickly it jumps to the end.

FIGURE 11.15

Moving a new motion path keyframe on the motion path does not change its original timing.

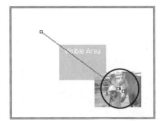

10. To change the *timing* of your new keyframe—as opposed to its location—go to the motion timeline. You might have noticed that as you moved that new motion path keyframe around, the little triangle above the timeline remained stationary. That's because it represents the *timing* of that new keyframe relative to the length of your clip.

Premiere displays that relative timing as a percentage of the clip length at the right end of the motion timeline. I've highlighted that in Figure 11.16.

11. Move your cursor over that triangle until it turns into a pointing hand; then drag it left and right. Its relative timing will change, but the keyframe's location on the motion path remains unchanged. Note how changing the relative timing changes the preview motion.

12. Just as you added a keyframe by clicking the motion *path*, you can add a keyframe by clicking the motion *timeline*. Then you adjust its physical location by moving its handle on the motion path.

▲

11

FIGURE 11.16

The motion timeline tracks keyframe actions by time, not physical location on the motion path.

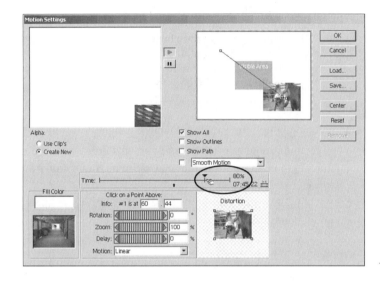

Take a look at the time display below the percentage to the right of the motion timeline. The little blue clip with the two red arrows highlighted in Figure 11.17 indicates what the time display means. If the arrows are close together, the time display is where the currently selected keyframe is located on the clip.

If you click that clip icon to separate the arrows, this will display the keyframe's location in your entire production. In this case, because you have only one clip on the timeline—your clip equals your production—the numbers should be the same. If you were to slide this video clip farther along the timeline and return to the Motions Settings dialog box, these times would be different. You use this little clip timing icon to make exactly timed moves.

Changing Values in the Motion Settings Dialog Box

Now things can get even more confusing. The Motion Settings dialog box—below the motion timeline and highlighted in Figure 11.18—needs some clarification. I'll cover each element in turn:

FIGURE 11.17

The little clip icon with its two arrows indicate whether the displayed keyframe time is its position in the clip or the entire project.

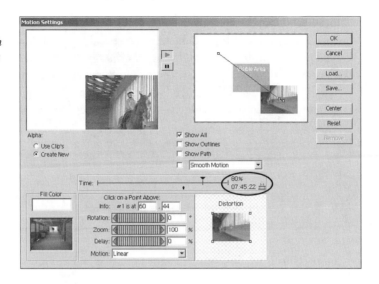

FIGURE 11.18

Some of the Motion Settings dialog box's components are nonintuitive.

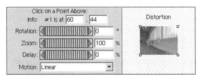

Info—This is the keyframe's location relative to the center of the "visible area" in the motion path screen. That visible area is 80×60 pixels, so a location of –40, 30 is the lower-left corner and 40, -30 is the upper-right corner. No one at Adobe knows why the Y value is positive for a point *below* the center. It just is.

You can fly multiple video clips over another video or still image—so-called "pictures in a picture." One way to add some "realism" to that process is to give your flying videos drop shadows. And one way to do that is to fly a translucent gray box "beneath" a flying clip, matching its motion but remaining slightly offset from its route. You'll use these location numbers to create those parallel routes. In Hour 17, "Tips, Tricks, and Techniques: Part 2," I'll explain this process in detail.

11

Rotation—You can input a value between -1440 degrees and 1440 degrees (that is, between four full rotations counterclockwise and four full rotations clockwise). The number represents the angle of the clip *by the time it reaches the selected keyframe.* Select 360 for the new keyframe (press Tab to record the change) and then watch. Your clip makes one full counterclockwise rotation by the time it reaches the keyframe and then spins clockwise back to zero degrees by the time it reaches the endpoint.

> If you want a clip to rotate and then hold that new position (360 degrees, for example) without rotating back to zero, you need to change all subsequent keyframe settings to 360 degrees.

Zoom—This is the clip's relative size from 0 to 500%. To see it in action, select the start point by clicking its hash mark on the motion timeline, set its Zoom to 0, select the new keyframe, and set its Zoom to 200 percent. Then select the end point and set its Zoom to zero. If you drag the start- and endpoints closer to the visible area, this change will become more apparent. Again, whatever value you select is the relative size your clip will achieve at the moment it arrives at that keyframe position.

Delay—This is the relative amount of time the moving clip will hold its position at the selected keyframe. It can't exceed the relative time remaining to the next keyframe. To see this in action, select a keyframe and give it a delay of 40% (if the value exceeds the relative time remaining in the clip, Premiere alerts you with a "beep").

That places a blue bar on the motion timeline, as I've highlighted in Figure 11.19. You'll note that your clip now pauses when it reaches the keyframe. Slide the keyframe on the motion timeline to the right. The blue bar will keep you from sliding it all the way to the end or beyond the next keyframe.

Motion—This sets the style of motion *from* the selected keyframe *to* the next keyframe. It can be Linear, Accelerated, or Decelerated. That is, the clip can move at a constant speed to the next spot, start slowly and then build speed, or start quickly and slow down at the end. Try all three using the start point and watch how your clip arrives at the keyframe.

FIGURE 11.19

Setting a delay at a keyframe places a blue bar on the motion timeline, representing its length relative the entire clip.

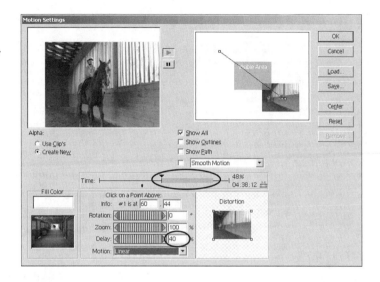

If you're flying an image onscreen and then flying it off, I think the most "comfortable" motion options are to set the start point to decelerate and the keyframe to accelerate. This means your clip flies on quickly but settles smoothly into place and then leaves gradually, zipping offscreen at the end.

11

Distortion—Drag the clip corners in the Distortion window to change your clip's shape. Again, the clip gradually will shift to that new shape as it approaches the selected keyframe, and it will shift back to normal (or to a new setting) as it moves to the next keyframe.

Alt/Option-clicking a corner lets you rotate the distorted clip on its axis (equivalent to changing the Rotation value).

If you don't like any of a keyframe's settings, click Reset. That changes all the options for that selected Keyframe back to their default values.

If you want to have a clip move to the center of the screen, select a keyframe and click Center.

Layering Clips in Motion

I will cover this topic in more detail in Hour 17. Here is a barebones overview of how to have more than one "picture in a picture" flying over a background scene. Normally when you place clips above each other on the timeline, you can see only the top clip. Being opaque, it covers all the other clips.

Using motion settings you can place several clips above one another, starting with Video 1 and climbing (to add video tracks, right/Option-click the Timeline and select Add Video Track). Give the Video 1 clip a background color and give all the clips in higher video tracks (starting from Video 2 and climbing) different motion settings. Making them cross paths shows you how clips higher on the timeline cover clips beneath—if only briefly. Preview each new clip motion by selecting Show All.

Summary

Premiere's video effects run the gamut from mundane and technical to dazzling and exciting. Adding video effects works much the same way as adding audio effects. Using keyframes to control those effects make them that much more entertaining and, well, effective. Finally, Premiere lets you easily put your clips in motion and adjust their shapes.

Workshop

Review the questions and answers in this section to try to sharpen your Premiere video and audio effects skills. Also, take a few moments to tackle my short quiz and the exercises.

Q&A

Q I shrink a clip, apply a 360-degree rotation to it, and have it stop in the middle of the screen. But when it flies off the screen it rotates counterclockwise and balloons back to full size. What's up?

A The motion control settings apply only to the selected keyframe. All other keyframes, including the start- and endpoints, retain their default settings unless you change them. So if you want to maintain the shape and orientation of your clip as it flies offscreen, you need to select the endpoint and change those settings to match those applied to the previous keyframe.

Q I try using Premiere's new real-time preview, but when I press Enter all I see is some other portion of the project. What's up?

A You need to define the *render area*. That's the yellow bar right at the top of the timeline. It's probably over another portion of your project. The easiest way to move it to your clip is to move the edit line to your clip and double-click the work area bar to set the yellow render markers to the beginning and end of the visible area in your current timeline. Drag the triangles at the end of that yellow bar to the clip you want to preview. Now press Enter to see the real-time preview.

Quiz

1. How do you make an effect start within a clip rather than at the beginning?

2. What's the difference between an audio red rubberband and a video red rubberband?

3. How do you make a clip start as a dot over a colored background in the upper-left corner of the screen and then grow to full size in the center of the screen?

Quiz Answers

1. Drag the effect's start box in the expanded track view to within the clip. If the effect has variable settings, you can set that value to its lowest number to gradually adjust the effect over the duration of the clip.

2. You use the audio red rubberband to adjust the volume within a clip. You use the video red rubberband to change opacity (more on that in Hours 14 and 15).

3. Place your clip on Video 1, open the Motion Settings dialog box, move the start point to the upper-left corner of the visible area, and then select the endpoint and select Center. Select the start point and change Zoom to zero. Select a fill color using the color box or the Eyedropper tool. As an extra task, select the endpoint and give it a delay (30 is a good amount) to hold the image at the center of the screen for a little while.

Exercises

1. Layer multiple video effects on the same clip. You might try, Crystallize, Solarize, and Replicate. Alternatively, apply Horizontal Hold and Vertical Hold to the same clip. Change the order to see whether that makes any difference.

2. Using the Black & White video effect can be abrupt. If you want a clip to gradually shift to Black & White, use the Razor tool to slice it, put the Black & White video effect on the second section, and add a cross-dissolve between the two clips.

3. Create a freeze frame and place it on Video 1. Select a number of clips that are related to that freeze frame. You could use a corporate logo as the freeze frame and clips of its products. Layer those clips over the freeze frame and give each one motion so they all end up over the logo.

11

PART III
Higher-end Effects

Hour

HOUR 12

Using Higher-Level Video Effects

Premiere's video effects run the gamut from simple to complex. They have a wide range of uses. Some you may rely on regularly, whereas others fill such narrow niches they may never see the light of day.

With 79 video effects staring up at you, it's darned hard to know when and why to use any one of them. In this hour I'll single out my favorites and try to make sense of the rest.

The highlights of this hour include the following:

- Categorizing and simplifying Premiere's video effects
- My favorite video effects and how to use them
- The hidden power of QuickTime video effects

Making Sense of the Plethora of Video Effects

It's not easy wading through Premiere's 14 video effects categories, trying to unravel what their 79 effects do and how they do it (see Figure 12.1).

FIGURE 12.1

Premiere's 14 category names for video effects do not necessarily describe their contents.

Consider that some effects have multiple functions with numerous options. The QuickTime effect alone offers 15 effects with a dozen subeffects.

The categories themselves can be confounding. The Gamma Correction video effect is in the Image Control file folder but is also a feature of the Levels effect in the Adjust file folder. Convolution Kernel is in the Adjust folder but handles 10 different functions of effects in the Blur, Stylize, and Sharpen folders. And the Transform effect is *not* in the Transform file folder.

Some effects resolve rarely encountered technical problems, such as missing fields or "interlace flicker." Still others don't seem to achieve their stated purposes.

To minimize clutter, ease access, and keep things simple, I suggest you create several new video effects file folder categories: Technical Fixes, Color Appearance, Blur/Sharpen, and Specialized After Effects. You'll continue to use Distortion and QuickTime.

To create these new categories, open the Video Effects palette, click the fly-out menu triangle, select New Folder, and create your folders. Then drag and drop effect icons to the new folders.

> Once you're done, delete the old file folder category names by selecting them and clicking the trashcan icon in the bottom-right corner. Actually, old folders never die, they "hide." If you select Show Hidden from the fly-out menu, you'll see the old, default categories at the bottom of the palette. No matter what you do, you *cannot* delete an effect from within Premiere.

There's a surprising amount of redundancy in Premiere's video effects. For instance, three effects create black-and-white video. To further eliminate clutter, I've selected the best of near-equals and placed the also-rans in one other category—Duplicates.

I'll take you through each of those categories, saving the specialized After Effects (AE) effects for Hour 13, "Wrapping Up Effects with After Effects." I'll also note my favorite effects and explain how to use them.

Technical Fix Effects

When you think of video effects, technical fixes do not come to mind. The primary reason you use video effects is to alter the appearance of your video clips—to blur, emboss, tint, or distort—or to add graphic elements, such as fire, clouds, lightning, lens flare, and film "noise."

So I'll get this mundane technical stuff out of the way first.

With one exception—Levels—you probably will not tap Premiere's technical fix video effects all that often. They typically come into play only for very specific, narrowly defined needs.

I'll introduce my top pick, list the technical fix effects with brief explanations, and then go over how to use my top pick.

My Favorite Technical Fix Effect: Levels

The Levels effect is a Jack-of-all-trades that manipulates the brightness, contrast, and colors of a clip. It has four basic functions:

Color Balance—You will use this time and time again. No matter how carefully you use white balance, some video clips will turn out too blue, or red, or green. The Levels effect lets you fix that by adjusting the individual RGB color values. (Note that the QuickTime RGB Balance effect interface is more user friendly than this Levels effect's color balance.)

12

Gamma Correction—Anyone's who's played a video game with a too-dark setting knows that bringing up the gamma levels brightens the scene without washing it out. This effect accomplishes that by bringing up the mid-tones while leaving dark and light areas unaffected.

Brightness & Contrast—This is standard TV control stuff that can significantly enhance your video.

Invert—This switches color information. The Invert effect in the Color Appearance category does a much better job. Use it instead.

Using the Levels Effect

Drag the Levels effect (in the `Adjust` file folder) to a video clip. It pops up the Levels Settings dialog box, shown in Figure 12.2.

FIGURE **12.2**

The Levels Settings dialog box is not immediately intuitive.

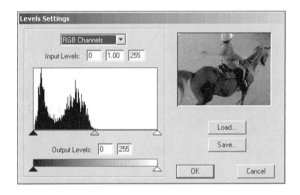

This is not your father's TV set brightness and contrast control. The interface takes some explanation. The chart is a histogram of your currently selected frame. Brightness values from dark to light run along the X-axis. The Y-axis represents the number of pixels at each brightness value.

Use the drop-down menu to choose whether you want the tonal adjustments to apply to one of the three color channels or all three at once.

The sliders right below the histogram control contrast and gamma. Drag the black triangle to the right to increase the shadows, the white triangle to the left to increase the highlights, and the gray triangle to control the gamma—the mid-tones.

The Output Levels slider reduces contrast. Dragging the black triangle to the right eliminates the darkest values in the clip, whereas sliding the white triangle to the left eliminates the brightest values.

You can save your settings and then load them later to ensure a consistent look to your altered clips.

Other Technical Fixes

Here is a list of the other technical fix effects that are available to you:

Broadcast Colors—This effect ensures color values will play back on PAL or NTSC TVs. It's a powerful tool with simple controls, but you may never need to use it.

Clip—Trims away noise from the edges of your videos, replacing the removed pixels with a user-specified frame color. It's not likely you'll want to have such a frame, so use the motion/shape settings to zoom your video to push noisy frame edges off-screen.

Field Interpolate—Rarely used. It's for instances when field loss (basically, half a video frame) occurs during capture.

Median—Median's strength is its oil painting effect (see Color Appearance). But its original purpose was to reduce video noise.

Reduce Interface Flicker—Very thin horizontal lines sometimes lead to disruptive flicker on some TVs. This seeks out those trouble spots and softens their edges to reduce flickering.

The following technical fix effects are redundant. Feel free to put them in your Duplicates folder: Brightness & Contrast, Color Balance, Crop, Gamma Correction, and Resize.

Color Appearance Effects

12

Okay, we've got the boring stuff out of the way, now for the toys.

In Hour 11, "Creating Video Effects," I demonstrated several color appearance effects, including Black & White, Crystallize, and Replicate. Some make your video look like a painting. Others shift pixels or delay their display creating embossed or ghosting effects.

The 15 QuickTime video effects handle several of the color appearance effects. Some QuickTime effects are better—more controls, better options, or improved output quality—but most are simply on par with their Premiere cousins. Because the QuickTime effect is so accessible and can replace so many Premiere effects within one consistent interface, I suggest that you "hide" duplicate Premiere video effects and use QuickTime instead. One caveat: you cannot keyframe QuickTime effects.

I've created subcategories to clarify differences within the Color Appearance category. All but the duplicates and one color appearance effect—Color Emboss—fall into my Favorites collection.

Color Appearance Painting Effects

All four of my favorite painting effects are very easy to apply. You can use keyframes for all but Facet. I covered three of them in Hour 11, so I'll simply present visual examples of those effects in Figures 12.3–12.5 and explain the fourth, Median, following those figures.

FIGURE 12.3

Crystallize creates a mosaic of colored irregular polygons.

FIGURE 12.4

Facet is a subtle effect that smoothes video into what appears to be a soft oil painting.

FIGURE 12.5

Pointillize gives your clips that Seurat look.

Median

The Median effect replaces pixels with the median value of neighboring pixels. A radius of one or two pixels reduces noise (see the discussion of technical fixes), but at about five pixels a video gets a nice soft-focus painting feel to it.

I'm guessing that of these four effects, the one you have not taken a look at yet is Median. It's tucked away in the `Image Control` file folder.

Try Median out by applying it to a clip. Note that the Radius slider, shown in Figure 12.6, goes only to 10, but you can type in higher values. The higher the number, the softer the focus. Try a value of 40. Because you can use keyframes, you can change this effect over time.

FIGURE 12.6

The Median effect's Radius slider creates a soft-focus painting look.

Color Appearance Color-Manipulation Effects

I'll explain how to use all three of these color-manipulation favorites after the following brief explanations:

Color Pass—You've seen those advertisements where one color stands out. This is how they do it. Color Pass converts a clip to grayscale (black and white), with the exception of one color.

Color Replace—This effect lets you select a color and then replace it with another. Both this, and Color Pass can be tricky and need some planning to pull off well.

Extract—This effect converts a clip to grayscale and lets you manipulate its appearance—from soft to harsh.

Color Pass is a super-slick effect that requires some careful pre-production preparation. To do it right, you need to create a setting where the object you want to highlight is a distinctly different color and evenly lit. Painting your object a color such as lime green will make it much easier to isolate with Color Pass later. Once it's converted, you can apply Color Replace to the same clip to alter that horrible lime green color into something more palatable.

Task: Use the Color Pass Effect

To use the Color Pass effect, follow these steps:

1. Drag Color Pass from the `Image Control` folder to a video clip. Select Setup to open the Color Pass Settings dialog box, shown in Figure 12.7.

2. Move the cursor into the image on the left, and it turns into an Eyedropper tool. Use it to select a color from that frame or click the color swatch to select a color from the standard Premiere color spectrum box.

3. Move the Similarity slider to adjust the "range" of the color you're going to highlight, using the right screen to find the "sweet spot." Clicking Reverse "grays out" that selected color and retains all others.

Figure 12.7

The Color Pass Settings dialog box's Eyedropper tool lets you select a color to highlight.

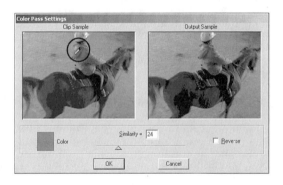

 Color Pass and a few other video effects' Settings dialog boxes display only the first frame of the selected video clip. Even if you've created a thumbnail/poster frame marker, the Color Pass Settings dialog box still displays the first frame. To see how changing the effect values impacts a particular frame, you'll need to move the edit line to that frame and then make your fixes in the Effect Controls palette, *not* the effect's Settings dialog box. The changes will show up on that frame in the Program Monitor screen.

Task: Combine the Color Pass and Color Replace Effects

To combine the Color Pass and Color Replace effects, follow these steps:

1. Keep Color Pass switched on—the *f* is in the check box—in the Effect Controls palette.

2. Drag Color Replace to the Effect Controls palette. Click Setup to open the Color Replace Settings dialog box, as shown in Figure 12.8. The image in the left window should be gray, with the exception of the color you selected in Color Pass.

3. Use the Eyedropper tool to select that color; then select a replacement color from the color spectrum window. Now you see how they do those cool TV spots.

 FIGURE 12.8
The Color Replace effect lets you select a color and replace it with any other color.

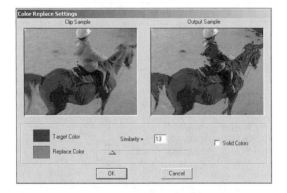

Using the Extract Effect

Clear the Effect Controls palette and drag in Extract from the Adjust folder. Its interface, shown in Figure 12.9, gives you full control over the clip's grayscale, giving your clip a textured, solarized, or standard black-and-white look.

The two triangles below the histogram set the range of pixels converted to white or black. Extract converts pixels between the triangles to white; those outside the triangle become black. Softness adds levels of gray to the white pixels. Invert swaps white with black, creating a negative, X-ray look.

Color Appearance Color Shift Effects

Slightly altering or shifting some color characteristics can create dramatic visual effects. The following five video effects fall into this catchall subcategory:

Alpha Glow—This effect provides a very slick way to give a graphic a glowing fringe or shadow by adding color around its edges. I'll explain it in detail later.

12

Color Emboss—This is the one color appearance effect that does not appeal to me. It's supposed to give elements within a clip a full-color embossed look, but it just seems to scramble colors haphazardly. I've illustrated it in Figure 12.10. The sliders set the characteristics of the embossed effect.

FIGURE 12.9

The Extract effect gives you a wide range of grayscale possibilities.

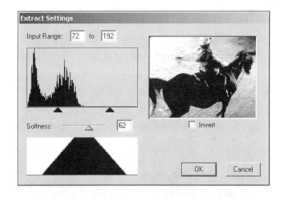

FIGURE 12.10

The Color Emboss effect.

As you can see in Figure 12.10, there is no "setup" option in the Effect Controls palette for Color Emboss. Color Emboss is an After Effects (AE) effect, and all AE effects work only from the Effect Controls palette. In Hour 13 I'll go over my favorite AE effects.

Emboss—This effect does in fact create embossed images. It offers more readily accessible controls than the Emboss element within the Convolution Kernel effect (see Blur/Sharpen, later). You'll find it in the Stylize folder. As Figure 12.11 demonstrates, Emboss has sliders similar to Color Emboss. Because the Emboss "Blend With" slider lets you add color to your image while making very distinct embossed edges, you can use it to create both black-and-white and color embossed effects.

FIGURE 12.11

The Emboss effect creates very distinct embossed effects—black and white or color.

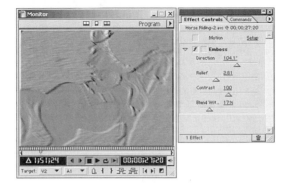

Ghosting—This is a nifty effect where pre-production planning can be a big help. It creates ghost-like "comet trails" behind anything that moves. It works great if you hold the camera really steady while something moves through the scene. You may have given it a trial run in Hour 11.

Invert—This multifunction color shifter lets you substitute inverse RGB (Red, Green, Blue) color information, HLS (Hue, Lightness, Saturation), and YIQ (NTSC luminance and chrominance values). It works much more easily than the Levels effect version. The Effect Controls palette's options are deceptively simple. Use the drop-down menu, shown in Figure 12.12, to adjust those elements by their group type or individually.

FIGURE 12.12

The Invert effect creates something like a film negative with the ability to limit those changes to specific color or luminance data.

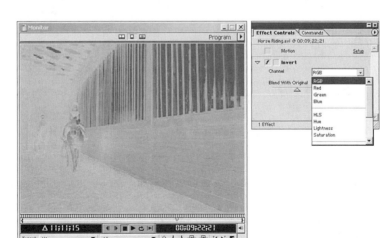

The Alpha Glow effect introduces something called an *alpha channel*. This typically is a characteristic of graphics created in programs such as Adobe Photoshop, Illustrator, and After Effects. An alpha channel is the portion of the graphic that you can make transparent or translucent. I'll go over how to use alpha channels—as well as other transparency processes—in Hour 14, "Compositing Part 1: Layering Images and Clips," and Hour 15, "Compositing Part 2: Alpha Channels and Mattes."

Task: Use the Alpha Glow Effect

To see the Alpha Glow effect work its magic, follow these steps:

1. Start by adding a graphic with an alpha channel (see the preceding note) to your project. You can find one—Veloman.eps—in Premiere's Sample folder.

2. Drag Veloman.eps (or your own graphic) to the Video 2 track directly above any other clip. You use Video 2 or a higher track because you're going to superimpose this clip over another clip.

3. In the Effect Controls palette, select Transparency Setup. That pops up the Transparency Settings dialog box, shown in Figure 12.13. I'll go over this dialog box in more detail in Hours 14 and 15.

4. In the Key type drop-down menu, select Alpha Channel.

5. Take a look at the image in the upper-right corner. Select the page peel icon—I've highlighted it in Figure 12.13—and note how that makes the white portion of the graphic become transparent, letting the video clip below your graphic in the time-line appear under the graphic.

6. Click OK.

7. Drag the Alpha Glow effect to the Effect Controls palette for your graphic and select Setup. That pops up the Alpha Glow Settings dialog box shown in Figure 12.14.

8. Give the various sliders a test drive. Try this with Fade out on and off, plus add a second color to the glow's edge using the End Color check box.

9. When you're done, click OK and check out your handiwork in the Program Monitor screen. You should see your graphic—with its Alpha Glow effect—superimposed over your video clip.

FIGURE 12.13

Use the Transparency Settings dialog box to switch on a graphic's transparent alpha channel. The page peel icon lets you see the clip below the graphic in the timeline.

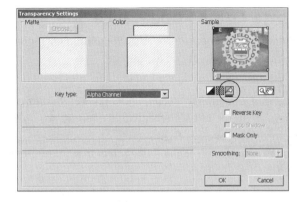

FIGURE 12.14

The Alpha Glow Settings dialog box.

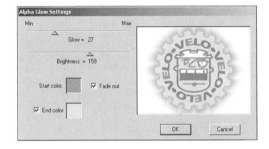

The Alpha Glow Settings dialog box displays only the graphic, not the video clip beneath it. Only after you click OK can you see in the Program Monitor screen how the colors and other elements you selected "work" with that clip. On the other hand, if you make the changes to Alpha Glow from within the Effect Controls palette, as shown in Figure 12.15, you get immediate feedback, but fewer controls are displayed. Neither approach is an elegant solution.

12

FIGURE 12.15

Alpha Glow displays fewer options in the Effect Controls palette, but you do get immediate feedback as you make changes.

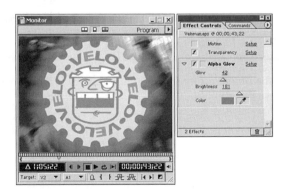

My Favorite Color Appearance Special Effects

My guess is that you will come to use each of the following three video effects, which create their own unique and nifty visual impact:

> **Lens Flare**—Most of the time you shoot your scenes trying to *avoid* lens flare. This lets you *add* that refraction to a scene. It works well for slow camera moves. If you use keyframes, you can add it gradually and adjust its location over time as your camera moves by the sun or other light source. As illustrated in Figure 12.16, clicking the scene adds crosshairs to place the flare. Select from three "lens types" and use the slider to change their brightness.

FIGURE 12.16

The Lens Flare effect coupled with keyframes lets you insert a flare, change its brightness, and alter its location.

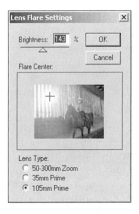

> **Replicate**—You may have tried this effect in Hour 11. Use Replicate to evenly divide the screen. The minimum setting is four rectangles—two by two. Maximum is 16 by 16. Each mini-screen displays the entire original clip.

> **Tiles**—This effect slices your clip into jittery tiles, sort of like a mosaic in motion. As illustrated in Figure 12.17, the Tiles Settings in the Effect Controls palette let you select the number of tiles per column and how much space can be between them. You fill that space with black (background color), white (foreground color), the inverse of the original image, or the image itself.

The Tiles effect works well as a transparency, letting whatever is below it on the timeline show through the spaces between the moving tiles. I explain how to do this in Hour 15.

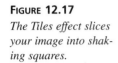

FIGURE 12.17

The Tiles effect slices your image into shaking squares.

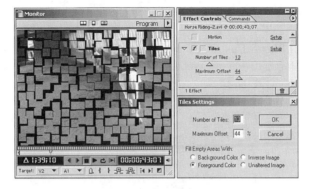

Duplicate Color Appearance Effects

QuickTime performs the following five effects as well or better (with the caveat that you cannot apply keyframes to QuickTime effects): Solarize, Posterize, Tint, Black & White, and Color Balance HLS.

Color Offset, although not technically a duplicate effect, fails to perform as designed. Its purpose is to create 3D images to use with red/blue 3D goggles, but I don't think it provides a practical means to accomplish that. Feel free to put all six of these effects in your `Duplicates` folder.

Blur/Sharpen Effects

At the core of most of the Blur/Sharpen effects is something called a *convolution kernel*. It changes the brightness values of pixels using a mathematical formula. What makes each Blur/Sharpen effect unique are the user-supplied variables—the values given to the center pixel and its surrounding pixels within a three-by-three matrix. Once calculated, the formula divides the sum of those pixel values by another user-set variable and then adds yet another user-selected value to that quotient, thus creating the desired effect.

So it's not surprising the Convolution Kernel effect can handle most of the effects in this category. But Adobe's Premiere effects creators recognize that the convolution kernel is not for the faint of heart. So you'll find that it's easier to use some specific Premiere effects rather than the convolution kernel's presets, much less attempt to deal with its variables and calculations.

My Favorite Blur/Sharpen Effects

Each of the following video effects can either soften or sharpen entire clips or elements within clips:

12

Anti-alias—You may have tried this in Hour 11. It softens edges between contrasting colors and light.

Channel Blur—This AE effect, illustrated in Figure 12.18, shifts RGB (red, green, or blue) colors individually, creating a blurring effect. It works well with alpha channels, letting you shift the colors of graphics.

FIGURE 12.18

Channel Blur lets you shift color pixels, creating unique blurring effects.

Convolution Kernel—This is the workhorse of this category. But of its 10 presets shown in Figure 12.19, only Sharpen Edges works better than its single-purpose cousins. Stick to the other recommended Blur/Sharpen effects and experiment with Convolution Kernel to create your own effects.

- **Blur**—Very subtle. Use Directional Blur or Fast Blur instead.
- **Blur More**—Directional Blur and Fast Blur work better.
- **Emboss**—Use the Color Appearance Emboss effect instead. It gives you more control.
- **Light Emboss**—Use Emboss instead.
- **Find Edges**—The After Effects Find Edges effect is a full-featured and powerful tool that identifies and emphasizes areas of an image with obvious transitions/edges. I'll go over it in Hour 13.
- **Gaussian Blur**—This is nearly the same as Fast Blur.
- **Gaussian Sharpen**—This is on par with the *non*-Convolution Kernel Gaussian Sharpen effect.
- **Sharpen**—The After Effects Sharpen effect has a slider, so it works better.
- **Sharpen Edges**—This is the only Convolution Kernel preset that outshines the specialized effect.
- **Sharpen More**—Use Sharpen instead.

FIGURE 12.19

The Convolution Kernel Settings dialog box. Changing only one or two values can dramatically alter a clip's appearance.

Directional Blur—By smearing pixels in a user-selected direction, as illustrated in Figure 12.20, this effect supposedly gives the illusion of motion. I don't think it's all that effective, but it is a good way to simply create a blurred image.

FIGURE 12.20

Directional blur is supposed to give the illusion of motion but does not fulfill that promise.

Fast Blur—This creates a much more blurred image than Directional Blur. Figure 12.21 shows how easy it is to use. Apply keyframes to create an ever-increasing blur over time. This works better than Gaussian Blur or Camera Blur.

Radial Blur—The "Psycho" look. It creates a whirlpool blur that simulates a swirling camera. Figure 12.22 shows that you can vary the location, type, and quality of the blur.

FIGURE **12.21**

Fast Blur creates the
blurriest images.

FIGURE **12.22**

Radial Blur gives a
video clip a soft
swirling look.

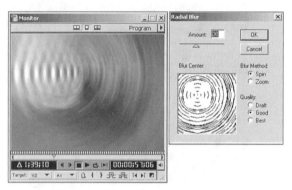

Radial Blur is a processor-intensive effect—thus the three Quality settings. At the highest quality, Premiere's Real-time Preview will likely stutter through the clip. Rendering Radial Blur at its full quality takes extra time.

Sharpen—This effect sharpens a soft-focus image by increasing contrast where color changes occur. As Figure 12.23 shows, this effect uses only a single slider. It works better than Gaussian Sharpen or the Convolution Kernel's Sharpen and Sharpen More presets.

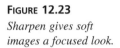

FIGURE 12.23

Sharpen gives soft images a focused look.

Duplicate Blur/Sharpen Effects

Feel free to place the following four video effects in your Duplicates folder. Other effects handle their chores as well or better than they do:

Camera Blur—Directional Blur handles this and adds a direction component.

Gaussian Blur—Same as Fast Blur.

Gaussian Sharpen—Convolution Kernel is as good.

Sharpen Edges—Convolution Kernel is as good and has more options.

Distortion Effects

With a few exceptions, these effects all do just about the same thing. They twist and contort your clip into funhouse mirror shapes. To use them well takes some experimentation on your part. Rather than explain them in detail, I'll lump similar effects together and use figure captions to identify them.

I will give brief explanations of the *non*-funhouse distortion effects at the end of this section.

Pinch, Shear, Spherize, and ZigZag

You may have checked these effects out in Hour 11. They all use a similar interface, as shown in Figures 12.24–12.27.

12

FIGURE 12.24

Pinch draws in or expands an image in the middle.

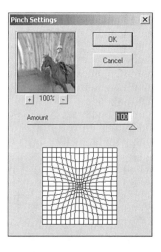

FIGURE 12.25

Shear creates a curve along a user-defined wavy line.

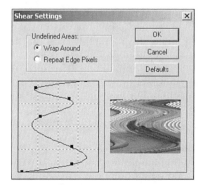

FIGURE 12.26

Spherize pushes out or pulls in the image using a ball shape.

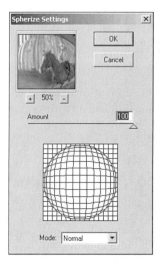

FIGURE 12.27

ZigZag creates several nice wave effects emanating from a user-selected point.

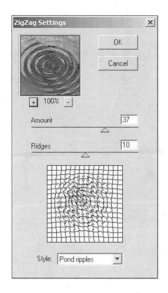

Lens Distortion, Wave, Bend, and Ripple

The four effects shown in Figures 12.28–12.31 all create undulating, twisting effects:

FIGURE 12.28

Lens Distortion lets you fill any gaps you create with a color selected from the clip or from the color spectrum window. Alternatively, you can turn that gap into a transparent alpha channel.

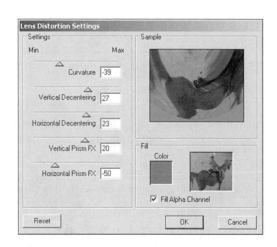

12

FIGURE **12.29**

Wave looks a lot like the following Bend effect.

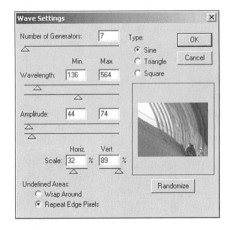

FIGURE **12.30**

Bend most closely re-creates a funhouse mirror effect. It fills the screen with the distorted image.

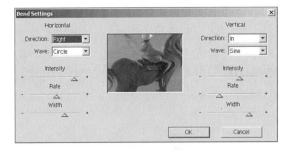

FIGURE **12.31**

Ripple is like Bend but leaves gaps around the curves that you can fill with color.

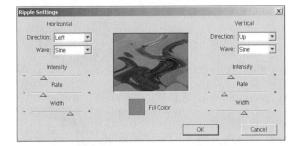

Mirror, Polar Coordinates, and Twirl

These three effects, shown in Figures 12.32–12.34, are all After Effects effects, which means they do not have separate Settings dialog boxes. Note that Mirror and Twirl have a crosshair you place onscreen to set the focal point of the effect.

FIGURE 12.32

Mirror perfectly reflects the scene at the crosshair using the angle selected, where 90 degrees creates a reflection along a horizontal line, and 0 degrees creates a reflection along a vertical line.

FIGURE 12.33

Polar Coordinates converts the clip's x/y coordinates into polar coordinates (or vice versa) to create this odd little lens distortion. The slider intensifies the effect.

FIGURE 12.34

Twirl rotates a clip around the crosshair. The greater the radius and angle, the more intense the twirl. Animate this using keyframes to create a real cool effect.

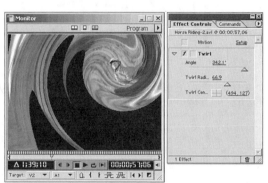

12

Horizontal Hold and Vertical Hold

The effects shown in Figures 12.35 and 12.36 give the impression that something is dreadfully wrong with the viewer's TV. You can use them both on the same clip to really make things go haywire.

FIGURE **12.35**
Horizontal Hold has a slider control to set its severity.

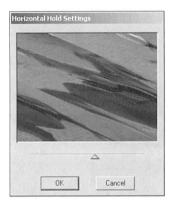

FIGURE **12.36**
Vertical Hold has no controls. Your image just rolls and rolls and rolls.

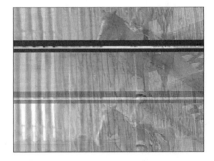

Bevel Alpha and Bevel Edges

These effects deviate from the funhouse mirror tack. They create 3D beveled frame-like edges for your clips. Bevel Alpha, illustrated in Figure 12.37, uses graphics with alpha channels. Bevel Edges, illustrated in Figure 12.38, is for regular video clips. These are great tools to use when you're using motion settings to fly clips over another image. Either effect gives those flying clips extra depth.

FIGURE **12.37**
Bevel Alpha gives graphics with alpha channels a real nice 3D look.

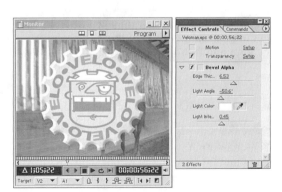

FIGURE 12.38

Bevel Edges creates a frame-like finish to video clips, but the corner lines could be more sharply defined.

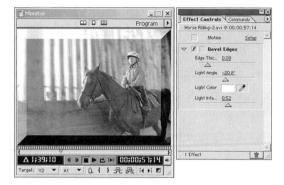

Camera View

This effect warrants special mention. As shown in Figure 12.39, Camera View gives the impression of a camera looking at your clip from different angles. In fact, it works a lot like the After Effects Basic 3D effect, which I'll cover in Hour 13, in that it rotates, flips, and zooms a clip. What makes it stand out from the Basic 3D effect is that it gives immediate feedback in its Settings dialog box.

FIGURE 12.39

Camera View lets you twist, flip, and zoom your clip, simulating a camera viewing the clip from varying angles.

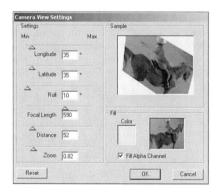

Duplicate Distortion Effects

Feel free to place the following four effects in your Duplicates folder: Horizontal Flip and Vertical Flip (Camera View is better), Image Pan (use Motion Settings instead), and Roll. Note that Roll is not a duplicate. It's simply useless. It "rolls" one edge of the screen around to the other side. This would be very cool if you could set the amount of the roll or animate it across the entire clip. Unfortunately, you can't.

QuickTime Effects

By all appearances, QuickTime video effects (and transitions) are an afterthought. Adobe provides no documentation for them. Apple says nothing about them in its QuickTime Player folder, and you have to dig deeply to find any explanation of their attributes online—an Apple QuickTime Application Programming Interface (API) reference guide written in 1999 is one source.

Don't let this apparent disregard for this lonely icon fool you. As with QuickTime transitions, there's a lot of power and utility tucked away in the QuickTime video effects file folder. As I've mentioned before, the one caveat is that you cannot use keyframes with QuickTime.

Drag the QuickTime effect to a video clip or its associated Effect Controls palette. As shown in Figure 12.40, up pops the Select Effect dialog box.

FIGURE 12.40

The QuickTime video effects interface.

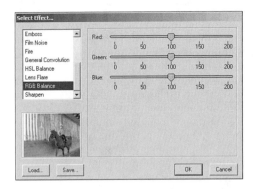

Scrolling through the drop-down list of effects, you'll note some familiar names. Several are exact or near duplicates of standard Premiere effects. In these cases, I recommend using the QuickTime versions simply because it's so easy to access this one resource and the interface is intuitive and consistent.

Several QuickTime effects are unique or much better than Premiere's, whereas others pale in comparison.

I'll take you through my eight favorite effects and their subeffects and then list the duplicates at the end of this section:

Alpha Gain—This effect works with a clip's alpha channel, varying the image's opacity and giving the alpha channel transparency. This takes some experimentation. For now, stick to the Transparency Settings (I'll discuss them in Hours 14 and 15).

Brightness & Contrast—Easier to use than the Levels effect for this narrow function (see Figure 12.41).

FIGURE **12.41**

The QuickTime Brightness & Contrast effect has two sliders for exacting control.

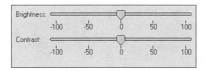

Cloud—This is a "fractal noise generator" that simulates a changing cloud formation. You can use its alpha channel to lay the cloud over an image and then give it motion to move it through a scene. It's a very cool effect. Figure 12.42 demonstrates how you control the cloud's colors and speed of rotation.

FIGURE **12.42**

The QuickTime Cloud effect.

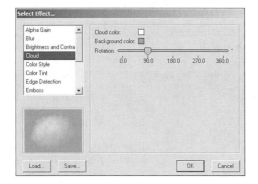

Color Style—Color Style is two effects in one: Solarize and Posterize. As shown in Figure 12.43, the two controls for Solarize give you more options than the standard Premiere effect. Posterize, on the other hand, is on par with its Premiere cousin.

FIGURE **12.43**

Color Style is two effects in one. Solarize works better than its Premiere cousin, whereas Posterize is on par.

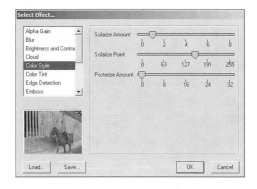

12

Color Tint—This is a very nice effect. Figure 12.44 displays its four presets and one custom tool. In each instance, the effect converts your clip to grayscale and then, in the case of the tinted effects, applies two colors to the light and dark areas. Here's an explanation of these effects:

- **Black and White**—Duplicates Premiere's effect.

- **X-Ray**—A quick-and-easy negative (inverse) grayscale image.

- **Sepia**—This gives your video a lovely, old photo style that will come in handy under numerous circumstances.

- **Cobalt**—Gives your clip a brilliant blue sheen.

- **Two Custom Colors**—Better than Premiere's Tint effect. Select your own two colors to represent dark and light areas. As shown in Figure 12.44, the custom color setting also gives you control over brightness and contrast.

FIGURE 12.44

Color Tint has four presets and one custom tool with Brightness and Contrast controls.

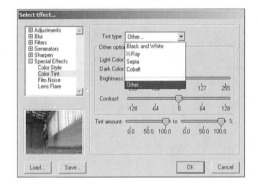

Film Noise—Offers the following two unique and excellent effects:

- **Hairs and Scratches**—This effect simulates hairs and scratches on the surface of old black-and-white film. As Figure 12.45 demonstrates, you input five values for this effect. One nifty feature is that shortly before each scratch disappears, it begins to shorten. The scratch colors are randomly chosen shades of light gray.

- **Dust and Film Fading**—This effect simulates dust particles and degradation in the color of the film stock. As Figure 12.46 shows, you choose from four different film types. Because this algorithm performs calculations on every pixel of your original clip, this is a processor-intensive effect, leading to long rendering times and stuttering previews.

FIGURE 12.45

Film Noise's Hair and Scratches effect remarkably re-creates the appearance of old, damaged black-and-white film.

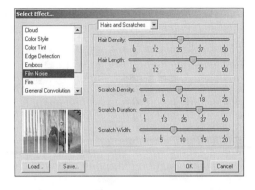

FIGURE 12.46

Film Noise's Dust and Film Fading effect is a processor-intensive effect.

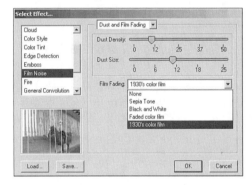

Fire—This effect simulates a wall of fire across the bottom of the screen. Like the Cloud effect, Fire has an alpha channel that lets you lay it over another clip. Figure 12.47 shows the four parameters you use to control the flames' behavior.

FIGURE 12.47

Add flames to any clip with the dazzling QuickTime Fire effect.

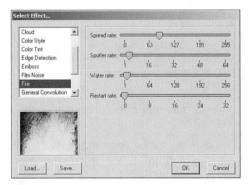

12

Lens Flare—This effect is different from Premiere's Lens Flare effect. It creates a more realistic series of flares and, as shown in Figure 12.48, has controls that let you set the flares' movement and rotation.

FIGURE **12.48**

QuickTime's Lens Flare adds a line of flares that can rotate and move, more closely mimicking real lens flares.

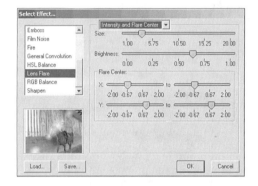

The following seven QuickTime Effects do not perform as well as their Premiere counterparts: Blur, Edge Detection (use Find Edges instead), Emboss, General Convolution, HSL Balance, RGB Balance (use Color Balance instead), and Sharpen.

Summary

Premiere's video effects vary widely in form and function. Organizing them into new, more descriptive file folders goes a long way toward easing access. Removing redundant or underperforming effects further simplifies your video production process. QuickTime offers a surprisingly full-featured and powerful set of effects.

Workshop

Review the questions and answers in this section to try to sharpen your Premiere video effects skills. Also, take a few moments to tackle my short quiz and give the best of these effects brief trial runs in the exercises to discover more ideas about how to best use them.

Q&A

Q I used keyframes to create a nice Twirl effect that gradually grew tighter and tighter, but then it suddenly jumped to the setting I applied to the first keyframe. What's the story?

A It sounds like you forgot to adjust the default last keyframe to make sure it holds the tight twirl through the end of the clip. When you set the opening "loose" Twirl setting, that numerical setting was automatically applied to both the start and end keyframes. As you added keyframes, you changed the numerical values to tighten the twirl up to your last keyframe. But you need to move to the end keyframe to make sure its setting equals the values you gave to the last keyframe you added to this clip.

Q I added an effect to a clip and used keyframes to change its behavior during the clip, but I don't like the result. How can I change this?

A Use the Keyframe Navigator—the check box with the two triangles next to the video track—to move to the frame(s) you want to fix. Use the Effect Controls palette or the Effect Settings dialog box to make your changes. If you simply want to move a keyframe, grab it and slide it to a new position. If you want to make the move frame specific, put the edit line at your new location, adjust the Effects values in the Effect Controls palette or the Effect Settings dialog box (thus creating a new keyframe at that location). Then delete the errant frame by selecting it and clicking the Keyframe Navigator check box.

Quiz

1. You shot an interview indoors but near a window. The interviewee's face is blue! How do you fix this?

2. You "broke the plane" in a cutaway. How can you get your interviewer to face the right direction?

3. You have a lovely logo created in Photoshop. How do you give it some sharp, beveled edges and fly it over a clip of your office exterior?

Quiz Answers

1. Use the QuickTime RGB Balance effect, or if you're up to the extra level of detail involved, try adjusting individual Red, Green, and Blue channels in the Levels effect.

2. Use Camera View to flip the image on its vertical axis (Vertical Flip does this as well). That way, your interviewer will face the correct direction, no longer breaking the plane.

3. Place it in a video track above your office shot. Open the Transparency Settings dialog box and select Alpha Channel from the drop-down list. Then apply the Bevel Alpha effect to it. Adjust the Edge Thickness, Light Angle, Light Color, and Light Intensity settings to suit your needs.

12

Exercises

1. Create a moving lens flare that "reacts" to a light source. Use both the QuickTime and Premiere Lens Flare effects. Apply keyframes to the Premiere effect and use the built-in x/y coordinates for the QuickTime effect.

2. Use keyframes to create a radial blur that gradually moves around an image.

3. Use Color Pass and Color Replace to isolate an object and give it a new color.

4. Use Camera View to spin and flip your clip 360 degree along both axes.

Hour 13

Wrapping Up Effects with After Effects

The cream of Premiere's crop of video effects is a 12-effect collection created with Adobe After Effects (AE). As a group they bring numerous creative possibilities to your projects.

Before presenting them I'll give you a brief overview of the powerful production tool used in their creation.

Finally, I'll take you through two projects that incorporate several elements from this and other hours.

The highlights of this hour include the following:

- What Adobe After Effects can do for you
- Premiere's premium After Effects effects
- Using techniques from what's come before

Adobe After Effects: Astounding Visual Effects

After Effects is the motion graphics and visual effects tool of choice for many topnotch video professionals (see Figure 13.1). It's the software used to create the 12 video effects featured in this hour.

After Effects is a master of many trades. In some ways it's like Premiere in that you can take graphics and video and add special effects, put images in motion, and create 3D elements. But After Effects goes well beyond Premiere in its capabilities and technology.

FIGURE 13.1

Adobe After Effects.

As shown in Figure 13.2, in After Effects most of your work takes place in one window. If you layer (also called *composite*) several graphics or video clips, you can see how they all work together as you make fixes. It's a phenomenally powerful interface.

FIGURE 13.2

The After Effects interface can display all layers of your project, showing in real time how they interact.

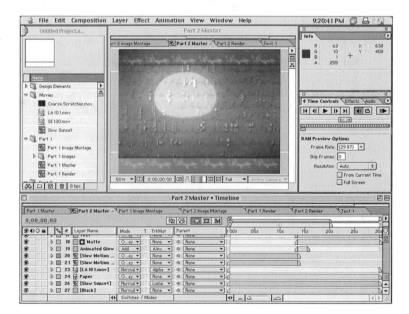

After Effects comes with a set of special effects that blow Premiere's out of the water. Its price tag reflects its utility: $650 for the standard edition.

Enjoying After Effects' Video Effects

I've saved the best video effects for last: the 12 AE effects. Nearly half of the newer Premiere video effects are AE created. Their icon—a hand with a number 4 on it—indicates that they are all products of AE 4.0. That's an older version than the latest update to AE, but these effects are still powerful and fun.

I've divided them into two categories: Color Appearance and 3D Style. To follow up on the previous hour's suggestion that you create new file folders in the Video Effects palette, you might want to add a 3D Style folder and place the Color Appearance effects in that previously created folder. I'll explain each effect in detail and offer some possible uses as well.

Color Appearance Effects

All nine color appearance effects change the "look" of your images. They can combine two images, alter certain colors, create multiple images, and break the images into moving boxes. All can add some real visual zest to your projects.

Using Blend to Combine Two Clips

As illustrated in Figure 13.3, this AE effect lets you blend two clips by letting a clip that's *lower* on the timeline show through an otherwise fully opaque clip.

You select a specific video track—from one to three—for the clip you want to blend with the selected clip. Crossfade sets a relative percentage of opacity for the top clip and the lower clip. A setting of 100% displays only the top clip. 0% shows only the lower clip, and 50% sets each at 50% opacity.

Color Only, Tint Only, Darken Only, and Lighten Only each let different values of the lower clip show through.

For an unusual effect, use a graphic for one clip and a colorful video for the other. Selecting anything but Crossfade leads to some bizarre results. If you put the graphic on the top video track, use Color Only, and move the Blend with Original slider to zero percent, which converts the graphic to grayscale and colors it using the lower video clip.

13

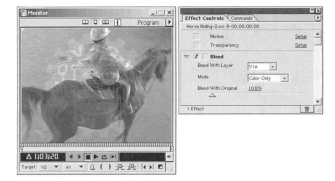

FIGURE 13.3
Blend lets a clip that's on a lower video track show through a clip above it.

Adjusting Colors with the Channel Mixer

You'll find Channel Mixer in the Adjust file folder (not the Channel folder). Once you drag it to the Effect Controls palette, as illustrated in Figure 13.4, you'll face more than the usual number of options. This is a characteristic of most of the AE effects in this hour. They tend to require plenty of user input.

Channel Mixer lets you modify each color channel. You can map one color onto another and increase or decrease a color's values to create high-quality tinted images.

The default value is 100% of each color. Dragging the sliders or inputting specific values will lead to sometimes dramatic results. Negative numbers invert the color.

Using keyframes with distinctly different values leads to some unique, gradual color changes during your clip.

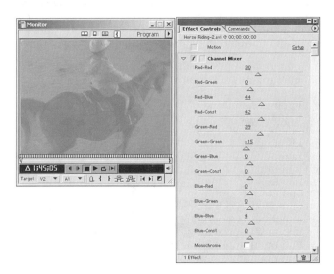

FIGURE 13.4
The Channel Mixer gives you precise control over your clip's colors.

Adding Multiple Action Images Using Echo

Echo is an exciting effect (in the Time folder) with numerous possibilities. It layers multiple sequential frames of a clip to convert simple action into streaking, smearing, or a sequence. As Figure 13.5 demonstrates, you control Echo using five parameters:

Echo Time—The time, in seconds, between echoes. Negative values create echoes from later frames, causing ghosting or streaking to follow the action. Positive values use earlier frames, laying those echoed images ahead of the action.

Number of Echoes—The number of extra frames added to the original to make this effect. Two echoes create three images—the original plus two other (subsequent or preceding) frames. The slider values go from 1 to 10, but you can type in a number up to 3,000! From what I've seen, any value greater than 10 creates only 10 echoes.

Starting Intensity—The relative brightness of the first frame in the sequence. At the highest value (1), the first frame is at normal intensity. A setting of one-half (0.5) displays the first frame at half its regular intensity.

Decay—Notes the decrease in intensity for each subsequent frame. A Decay setting of 0.5 means the first echo will be half as bright as the first, the second will be one-quarter (0.25) as bright, and the third will be one-eighth (0.125) as bright.

To create smooth streaking and trail effects, use a large number of echoes (eight or more) and a short echo time (one-tenth or so).

Echo Operator—Indicates how Echo combines frames. Here are the options:

- The Add option combines the echoes by adding their pixel values. If the Starting Intensity setting is too high, your action will turn into bright, white streaks.

To give the first frame and all echoes the same value while avoiding those bright white streaks, set Echo Operator to Add, set Starting Intensity to a value equal to 1 divided by the number of echoes, and set Decay to 1. For example, for four echoes, set Starting Intensity to .25 (1 / 4 = .25). A Decay setting of 1 means there will be no decay—all echoes will have the same value.

13

- Maximum uses the maximum pixel value from all the echoes, which emphasizes the brighter action elements.

- Minimum uses the minimum pixel value from all the echoes, displaying only the darker values.

- Screen is like Add but does not overload as easily.

- The two Composite options are for video clips with alpha channels (this will not work on most video clips). The Composite in Back option layers them back to front, whereas the Composite in Front option layers them front to back.

FIGURE 13.5

Echo converts motion into streaks, smears, and repeated actions.

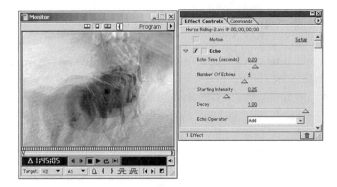

Echo is a special video effect. By default, it switches off any other effects applied before it to the clip. Those that come below it on the Effect Controls palette still work. However, there is a workaround: Create a "virtual clip." I'll explain this in detail in Hour 16, "Tips, Tricks, and Techniques: Part 1." A virtual clip is just like any other clip or set of clips with transitions, motion, and effects. You build it away from your project, usually on unused tracks. Then you select it using the Block Select tool and drag it to your project. Then you can add the Echo effect without switching off the other effects.

Building Borders Around Objects with the Find Edges Effect

Find Edges is the easiest to use of all this hour's AE effects. There are only two controls. I include it in this hour because it works so well. You'll find it in the Stylize folder. It locates elements in the image with obvious differences in contrast and color; then, as illustrated in Figure 13.6, it creates distinct dark edges on a white background. The slider lets you combine a percentage of the original image with the converted image. Invert swaps black and white, creating white lines for edges.

FIGURE 13.6

Find Edges creates what appear to be sketched outlines.

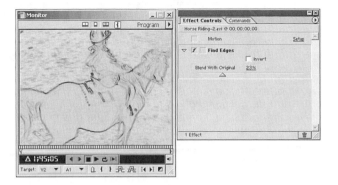

 Here's one totally bizarre application of the Find Edges effect. Use it on any clip, add the Color Replace effect, and select any of the many black borders created by Find Edges. Replace that color with something distinct—bright red for instance. Then click the Solid Colors check box to replace the black lines with the new color. Looks like you just strung everything with Christmas lights.

Adding Dazzle to Your Project with the Lightning Effect

Lightning is a wild and wacky effect (found in the Render folder). Lightning is reminiscent of QuickTime's Cloud and Fire effects in that it doesn't convert the image. Rather, it places a special effect over it—in this case, a simulated flashing electric arc like those used in old monster movies.

As you'll see when you drag it to the Effect Controls palette, its creators went overboard in the number of options—25 parameters! To avoid being equally guilty of overkill I won't go over all of them.

As I've demonstrated in Figure 13.7, you use its two crosshairs to set start and end locations for the lightning. Setting keyframes lets you alter those locations over the duration of your clip.

The many options let you set the size and intensity of the lightning. Increasing the number of segments, amount of branching, and level of detail make the flashes more jagged (kind of nastier looking). Choose any colors you like—both the core and outside colors. The default white/blue scheme works well but red/yellow provides an evil, organic touch.

13

Figure 13.7
Experimenting with Lightning is great fun. Try a red/orange color scheme.

Breaking Images into Blocks with the Mosaic Effect

Mosaic is sort of like Pointillization with rectangles. You'll find it in the Stylize folder. As Figure 13.8 shows, you select the number of horizontal blocks and vertical blocks (rows and columns)—between 1 and 200—to create a collection of rectangles. The higher the number, the smaller the rectangles and the closer the image will match the original. At 200, it's simply jittery.

The Sharp Colors check box creates a more distinct, clearly defined rectangle.

> Use Mosaic as something like a transition. Using keyframes or simply the default start- and endpoints, start the "transition" near the end of the clip by setting both Horizontal and Vertical Blocks to 200. Then drop this setting to about 20 each at the end of the clip. Start the next clip at 20 and quickly build it to 200. Uncheck the Sharp Colors box; otherwise, the transition from 200×200 blocks to standard video will be somewhat abrupt.

Giving Your Clips That Old VHS Feel with Noise

You do what you can to create clean, sharp, noise-free video. So what does Adobe do? It includes this Noise effect in Premiere to give your videos that low-light, consumer, analog camcorder look. This effect is found in the Stylize folder.

FIGURE **13.8**

You can use Mosaic to create a faux transition.

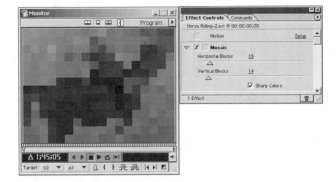

The Amount of Noise slider sets the noise level by distorting or randomly displacing pixels. As illustrated in Figure 13.9, at a setting of 75%, depending on which boxes you've checked, your clip may become unrecognizable.

Checking the Use Color Noise box randomly changes the red, green, and blue values of the image's pixels. Unchecked means all color values change equally.

Checking the Clip Result Values box creates a more realistic Noise display by letting color values that reach their maximum value "wrap around" and start over at 0% noise. Leaving it unchecked means color values that "max out" stay at that maximum level, making some portions of your scene shimmer with noise.

To completely randomize Noise, turn on Use Color Noise and turn off Clip Result Values. To reproduce "true" noise, set the slider to about 20%, turn off Use Color Noise, and turn on Clip Result Values.

FIGURE **13.9**

Setting a Noise value of 75% can obliterate a clip.

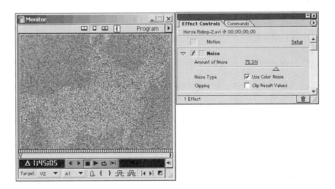

13

Giving Your Project Flash with the Strobe Light Effect

This effect, from the `Stylize` folder, opens the door to numerous creative possibilities. It works like a strobe light, flashing frames as your clip plays. Those frames can look like a super-bright strobe light or be black, transparent, or an inverse image.

The options, as illustrated in Figure 13.10, are listed here:

Blend with Original—This option blends the Strobe Light effect with the original to adjust the intensity or brightness of the effect.

Strobe Duration—Sets the length, in seconds, for each strobe flash. Less than a half second is most like a real strobe, but you may want a strobe to stay on longer to show the inverse image or another image below this clip in the timeline.

Strobe Period—Sets the time, in seconds, between the start of subsequent strobes. Setting a strobe *period* of 2 seconds, for example, and a strobe *duration* of 0.5 seconds means you would see the strobe effect for a half second. Then there would be a 1.5-second break until the next strobe effect. If the strobe period is less than or equal to the strobe duration, then the strobe stays on all the time.

Random Strobe Probability—Set at a value other than zero means the effect will have a more realistic feel. It'll cause strobing even if the strobe period is less than or equal to the strobe duration.

Strobe drop-down menu—This menu has two options: Operates on Color Only and Makes Layer Transparent. A clearer way to state these options is Opaque and Transparent. If you choose Makes Layer Transparent, you can superimpose the strobe effect clip over another, revealing the lower clip during strobes. I'll cover transparency issues in Hour 14, "Compositing Part 1—Layering Images and Clips," and Hour 15, "Compositing Part 2—Alpha Channels and Mattes."

Strobe Operator—Gives you extra control if you choose Operates on Color Only (opaque). Copy is the default setting. Subtract displays a black strobe screen, and Difference pops on an inverse image.

For a little comic relief, use the Strobe Light effect with Strobe Operator set to Difference and Duration and Period set fairly low. The resulting strobe effect is reminiscent of a cartoon character sticking his finger in a light socket.

FIGURE 13.10

The Strobe Light effect opens up numerous creative possibilities.

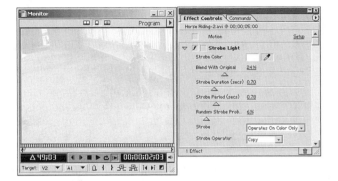

Using One Clip to Add a 3D Feel to Another Using Texturize

Here's another AE effect from the `Stylize` folder with tons of possibilities. It uses two clips. As demonstrated in Figure 13.11, Texturize embosses the lower clip on the timeline and lets that 3D feel show through on to the other clip.

Light Direction and Texture Contrast set the depth of the embossing. Texture Placement offers three options: Tile Texture, Center Texture, and Stretch Texture to Fit. I tried them all and they all created the same effect (perhaps it was a bug in my pre-beta release of Premiere). Tile Texture should apply the texture repeatedly over the clip, Center Texture is supposed to put the texture in the middle, and Stretch Texture should spread the texture to the corners of the clip.

FIGURE 13.11

Texturize embosses one clip and imparts that 3D feel to a clip above it on the timeline.

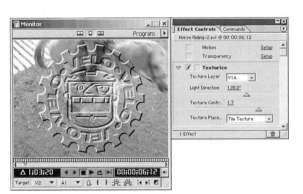

13

The name *Texturize* is too narrow. Yes, you can use a clip with obvious texture—rug, sand, or rippling water—and impart that feel to another clip above it on the timeline. But there are many other uses. You can bring up an embossed version of your logo beneath a product shot or place one distinctly different setting under another. How about embossed waving palm trees behind a frozen arctic tundra?

Adobe has not documented this, but Texturize apparently is one of those effects that will not work with motion settings. Therefore, if you want to move around your embossed logo under another clip, you'll need to create that moving logo using motion settings and turn it into a virtual clip. As mentioned earlier, I'll cover this topic in Hour 16.

3D-Style Effects

The following three effects add motion or a 3D look. Each has its strengths. As you work with them, you'll find times when you might choose to use motion settings or the Camera View effect instead. But it's good to experiment with all these effects.

Adding a Glint Using Basic 3D

Found in the `Perspective` folder, this Effect is not all that different from the Camera View effect. In fact, Camera View has more options, the most important being Zoom-in and Roll. What makes Basic 3D worth your time is its Specular Highlight option. As noted in Figure 13.12, a simulated light source can create a little moving glint on the surface of your clip as it moves around the screen.

The move takes place on only two axes:

Swivel—Controls horizontal rotation

Tilt—Controls vertical rotation

Go beyond 90 degrees in either direction and you see the back (mirror view) of your image.

Here's a list of the other options:

Distance to Image—Shrinks the image, giving the impression of moving off into the distance.

Specular Highlight—Comes from an imaginary spotlight behind, to the left and above the viewer. It appears only if the surface angle of the moving clip "allows" it. If you push the left side of your clip back (a positive Swivel value) and tilt the top back (a negative Tilt value), the highlight should appear.

Preview—The easiest way to preview the highlight's location is to check the Draw Preview Wireframe option. A green plus (+) sign indicates the highlight will be visible. A red plus sign shows its location but indicates it won't be visible.

FIGURE 13.12

Basic 3D's Specular Highlight gives it an extra level of realism.

First, Specular Highlight is a surprisingly processor-intensive effect. So much so that Real-time Preview will not show it. The only way to see the specular highlight is to render the clip. Second, there is no way to control the intensity of the highlight, and it can be very bright if the reflection is straight at you—that is, if the highlight is at the center of the screen. To avoid that, try to make your moves so the highlight travels around the edges of the screen. Alternatively, use keyframes to turn on the highlight only when it reaches an edge.

Giving Graphics Depth with the Drop Shadow Effect

Found in the `Perspective` folder, this effect works only with clips that have alpha channels (typically graphics). Premiere will give the graphic portion of the clip a drop shadow. As Figure 13.13 demonstrates, what makes this different from some drop shadow–style effects is you can extend the shadow off the edge of the clip appearing below it.

The controls work much like adding a drop shadow to text. You specify the shadow's opacity, its direction (zero degrees makes the shadow fall up; 90 degrees has it falling to the right), the distance from the edges of the graphic, and how "soft" it is.

If you want to spin your graphic and apply a drop shadow, using only motion settings won't work. The shadow will follow the rotation instead of falling realistically in a constant direction. For a realistic shadow, use the Transform effect (discussed next), Basic 3D, or Camera View to create the spinning motion and *then* apply Drop Shadow. If you use Camera View, make sure the Fill Alpha Channel check box is *unchecked*.

Drop Shadow works best when it is the last (bottom) filter on the Effect Controls palette. Therefore, apply all other effects first and then use Drop Shadow.

FIGURE 13.13

Using Drop Shadow along with a motion effect such as Camera View creates a realistic moving shadow.

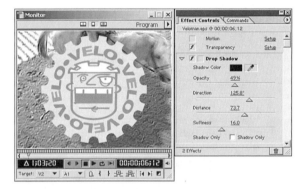

Distorting, Twisting, and Turning Clips with Transform

This effect, from the Distort folder, lets you change a clip's size, rotate it, and skew it along any axis using any point on the screen as an anchor point. Its flexibility is amazing.

Use the Anchor Point crosshair, as illustrated in Figure 13.14, to mark the point around which the image will be scaled or skewed. The other crosshair, Position, notes the center of the image. Here's a list of options:

Scale Height—Changes the clip's relative height using a percentage scale.

Scale Width—Expands/contracts the width. If you check the Uniform Scale check box, changing one scale number—Height or Width—changes the scale for both (in my pre-beta version of Premiere the other scale slider did not move to show that uniformity, but the image did maintain its proportions).

Skew—Stretches the clip in the direction of the skew axis.

Rotation—Spins the clip.

Opacity—This is a really nice feature. If you place this clip in a video track higher than Video 1 you can apply transparency, set the Alpha Channel key type, and super-impose this clip over anything below it in the timeline.

> The Use Composition's Shutter Angle check box and the Shutter Angle slider are both *nonfunctional*. I don't know why Adobe chose to display these items in the Effect Controls list.

FIGURE 13.14

Transform applies a 2D "geometric" trans-formation to a clip—moving it, spinning it, and stretching or skew-ing it.

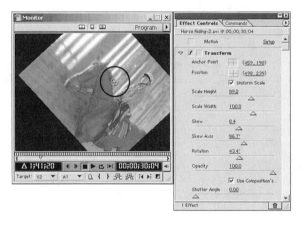

Applying Techniques Covered So Far

Here are a couple real-world applications that incorporate some of the topics covered in the past few hours.

Task: Fixing a Slanted Scene

Even the best-planned productions can go awry. One common mistake is a tripod that wasn't quite level or the perspective in a scene looks cockeyed. Fortunately, a simple fix is available. You can use motion settings to set things right. Figure 13.15 shows how my fix looks with all the new settings applied.

Here are the steps to follow for this task:

1. Open the Motion Settings dialog box either from within the Effect Controls palette for the clip in question or by right/Option-clicking the clip.

2. Select Video Options, Motion.

13

3. Select the start- and endpoints, in turn, and place both in the center of your frame by clicking Center for each.

4. Pause the preview mode.

5. Alt/Option-select a corner of the clip in the Distortion window to turn on the Rotate icon. Then turn your clip on its center.

6. Once the clip looks like it's oriented correctly, adjust its zoom to fill the frame. Make sure you set the same zoom level for both the start- and end-points. You're done.

FIGURE 13.15

Fix cockeyed clips using the Motion Settings dialog box.

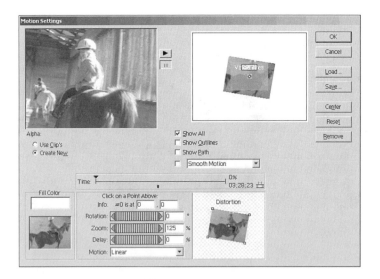

Task: Flying Beveled Clips over a Sepia Still Frame

▼ TASK

A nice way to display old family photos in a video is over a soft-focus sepia group photo. Here is a relatively simple way to do it. The one caveat is that this simplified method to create a frame around your flying images also covers their edges.

Figure 13.16 shows how your Motion Settings dialog box should look by step 8. Here are the steps to follow for this task:

1. Either create a still frame from a clip or use a scanned or videotaped photo and place it on Video 1.

2. Apply the QuickTime video effect and select Color Tint, Sepia.

3. Apply Fast Blur to the sepia-toned still. Use keyframes to create a "rack" focus a second into the clip. A Blurriness value of about 5 works well.

You may notice that when you add more than one video effect to a clip, a little drop-down menu arrow appears in the upper-left corner of the expanded view of that clip in the timeline. Its sole use is to let you access the keyframe line for each effect. If you select an effect from the Effect Controls palette list, that little drop-down menu automatically goes to the selected effect.

4. Place other clips/still frames in the video tracks above the sepia-toned clip.

5. Here's where you'll use an effect for something other than its stated purpose. Apply Clip to each clip in the upper video tracks and set each Edge value to the same number for all clips. A value of 10 works well. This will cover the edges of your clip to create a framed look. There are other ways to do this, but this method takes minimal effort.

6. Leaving the fill color black is easiest. If you choose another color, remember its value so you can re-create it for the rest of the clips.

7. Apply Bevel Edges to all the clips on the upper video tracks. Make the Edge Thickness setting equal to the value you used in Clip. A light angle of about 60 and an intensity of about 40 work well for this project. Once you select these values for the first clip, they'll show up by default when you apply Bevel Edges to each subsequent clip—a real timesaver.

8. Open the Motion Settings dialog box for each clip, starting with the lowest track and working up. Set Zoom to about 30% or so, depending on the number of clips, and make a simple path to fly on each clip. You can have them fly on from each corner to avoid clutter. Build in a small delay so they don't start flying on until after the sepia clip has blurred. Also, put a large delay on the endpoint to hold them in position for most of the clip time. As you move up the tracks, you'll see the other clips animate in the preview window so you can set paths that don't step all over the other paths.

That should do it. What you end up with is a series of flying-bevel framed clips moving over an out-of-focus sepia-toned print.

13

FIGURE **13.16**
Flying bevel-framed clips over a sepia-toned print.

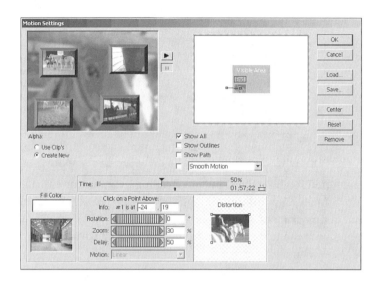

Summary

About half of Premiere's video effects were made using Adobe After Effects. Of that group, 12 warrant special mention, so I saved those for this hour. AE is a powerful graphics and animation production tool. It goes way beyond Premiere's capabilities, and it takes a dedicated and creative professional to fully tap its potential. Finally, I concluded this hour with two projects that incorporated a variety of video effects and motion settings.

Workshop

Review the questions and answers in this section to try to sharpen your Premiere video effects skills. Also, take a few moments to tackle my short quiz and the exercises.

Q&A

Q I use Echo but the clip becomes so bright it washes everything out. What's up?

A You've probably selected the Add or Screen option, which means that the brightness level of each echo adds itself to the original clip and its other echoes. If the Starting Intensity setting is high—near or at 1—then it takes only about two or three clips to obliterate your image. Set Starting Intensity to 1 divided by the number of echoes. If you use five echoes, then set Starting Intensity to 0.2 (1 / 5 = 0.2).

Q **I get that same kind of washed-out look when using Basic 3D to add a specular highlight to my clip. How do I avoid that?**

A Use the wireframe preview and the 3D move to keep the highlight (the green crosshair) near the edge of your clip. If it moves toward the center, the effect is like a mirror directly reflecting the sun.

Quiz

1. How do you create an "Electric Horseman"? If you missed this enjoyable Robert Redford/Jane Fonda flick, Redford rides out on a Las Vegas stage decked out with electric lights to promote breakfast cereal.

2. You can use the Mosaic effect to create a "transition." How do you do that?

3. How do you place a drop shadow on a moving and spinning graphic so that the shadow does not rotate with the graphic but rather continues to fall in a constant direction?

Quiz Answers

1. Use Find Edges on a clip (it doesn't have to be a horse and rider—that's just been my theme this hour) to create distinct outlines. Use Color Replace to swap a bright color for the black outline. Check the Solid Colors box to make the entire outline take on the new hue.

2. Use the Mosaic effect to give the illusion of a transition. This is not a true transition. It's simply a straight cut edit between two adjacent clips that appears to be a transition. Apply the Mosaic effect to both clips and use keyframes to have the effect start just a second or so before the end of the first clip and operate for a second or so at the beginning of the next clip. For the first clip, set the starting number of horizontal and vertical blocks to 200 and the end to something like 10; then reverse that process for the second clip.

3. I prefer using Camera View combined with Drop Shadow, but you can use Transform or Basic 3D as well. First, use Camera View to give your graphic rotation and size. The maximum rotation is 360 degrees in either direction. Then use the Motion Settings dialog box to set its path. Keep the zoom at 100%. Then apply the drop shadow.

13

Exercises

1. Use the Strobe Light effect with keyframes on a clip on Video 2 (above another clip) to flash white frames, black frames, inverse frames, and so on, through to the clip below. You'll need to set the Video 2 clip's transparency to Alpha Channel. To

make white flashes, set Strobe to Operates on Color Only and set Strobe Operator to Add or Copy (Black equals Subtract, and Inverse equals Difference). To see through to the lower video track, set Strobe to Makes Layer Transparent.

2. Use Camera View and motion settings to have one clip move back to one side like an opening door to reveal a second clip behind it. Then move that second clip back to the other side to reveal another clip behind it. You'll need to place the first and second clips on video tracks 3 and 2, respectively, and set their transparency to Alpha Channel. Put the bottom clip on video track 1. Use Camera View to make the spins—start at 0 longitude and move to 90 degrees for the first clip; then start at 360 and move to 270 for the second. Use motion settings to time the moves and to keep the outside edges of the clip flush with the side of the screen. Good luck. This is a bit of a project. And, yes, you could use a Swing In transition, but it doesn't look as realistic, plus you can use transitions only on clips residing on the Video 1 track.

3. Experiment with the Lightning effect. You'll want to have the lightning emanate from and terminate at single locations. To do that, you'll need to set the start- and endpoints and use keyframes to compensate for any camera movement (or for any motion of the source or endpoint). Change the attributes of the lightning over the duration of the clip. Increase the intensity by changing values for segments, branching, and amplitude. Also, change the color of the lightning during the clip.

HOUR 14

Compositing Part 1: Layering Images and Clips

Another great strength of Premiere is its ability to layer (or *composite*) multiple clips over one another. It can be as simple as placing a logo over a product shot or shooting actors in front of a green screen and then electronically placing them within a scene.

There are four basic composite methods:

- Reducing the opacity of an entire clip so a clip (or clips) below it on the timeline show through.
- Using "keys" to make portions of a clip transparent so clips below it on the timeline show through.
- Blocking or matting parts of one clip to let parts of other clips show through.
- Using a clip's alpha channel to create a transparency.

This hour will cover the first two topics, and I'll save the latter two for Hour 15, "Compositing Part 2: Alpha Channels and Mattes."

The highlights of this hour include the following:

- Compositing—what it is and how it can spice up your video projects
- Shooting video that you can use for compositing
- Changing a clip's opacity to let other clips show through
- Making colors transparent—using chroma-keying, blue/green screens, and the RGB Difference key
- Using Luminance-style keys to create transparencies

Making Compositing Part of Your Projects

If you've tried out Premiere's new Title Designer tool, used the Motion Settings dialog box, or worked on video effects that use alpha channels, you have already composited— that is, layered graphics or video clips over other images.

Compositing can add immeasurably to your video projects. Sometimes the impact is obvious—sliding videos in boxes onto the screen sends a clear message that you have done something out of the ordinary with your production. Other times it's subtle. We don't think twice when we see a TV weatherperson gesturing at a map or graphics. As shown in Figure 14.1, in fact that TV personality is standing in front of a green or blue wall and watching some monitors to see what he or she is pointing at.

FIGURE 14.1

Matt Zaffino, Chief Meteorologist— KGW-TV, Portland, Oregon.

Every computer game with live actors and many movies use compositing. "Green screen" studios let game developers place actors in science fiction settings created with 3D computer graphics. Such sets let actors work in relative safety while the finished product has them dangling from a skyscraper, hundreds of feet in the air.

For most budding professional video producers, such high-budget studio access may be out of the question. But you *can* add some nice composited special effects to your projects simply with a few tweaks of Premiere's tools.

Your Assignment: Grab Shots for Compositing

Most of the tasks in this hour will involve creating transparencies in clips by removing certain colors or luminance (brightness). To best see how that works in the real world, you need to grab your camcorder and tape a few quick shots.

Normally for images that you intend to key, you'd need to have your camera absolutely locked down. No camera movement at all. In this case, because it's just an experiment, don't worry too much about that. But once you see how much of a viewer disconnect there is when a keyed object bounces around over a keyed in background, you'll see why a rock-steady camera is critical.

Here's your assignment:

- Videotape an inanimate object—preferably a smooth object to minimize shadows within it—in front of a solid color. That color should be distinctly different from the color(s) of the object. Otherwise, when you later "key out" that background color, similar colors in the object will turn transparent, too, leading to some odd results.

- Tape a person talking or moving in front of a solid color background. The best is sky blue because that's complementary to skin tones. Just make sure your subject's clothes don't have colors that match or nearly match the background. Most production studios use so-called *chroma blue* (or *green*) screens. I'll highlight the advantages of each in a sidebar later in the hour.

- Tape a dark object in front of a lightly colored surface (white is best) and a lightly colored object in front of a dark backdrop. Try this with a person as well. The greater the contrast between the subject and the background, the easier it'll be to make the background transparent.

14

- Tape a distinct background with nothing moving in it—that is, no waving palm trees or soaring birds. Then, without turning off or moving the camera (this is the one exercise when you need a rock-steady shot), have someone walk into the left side of the scene, stand around for a while, and then walk back out the left side. Have that person do the same thing entering from the right side and then walking out to the right. For a bit of comic relief, have your "actor" wave toward the center of the scene before walking off camera. You'll use this in the next hour to create split screen and difference mattes, but you might as well shoot it now while you're at it.

- Finally, grab a few shots of background locations in which you'd like to place the objects/people you've videotaped. You will later key your subjects onto those locations.

Working with the Opacity Rubberband

Before keying out colors or working with luminance, I want to cover opacity.

Premiere and other nonlinear editors like it have a general operating practice. Video tracks above track 1 trump tracks below them on the timeline. In other words, whatever appears on the highest track covers up whatever is below it. However, the object *isn't* to use tracks above Video 1 to obliterate what's beneath them. It's to enhance what's down there.

Premiere offers up to 98 of those so-called "superimposing" tracks. Their purpose is for layering (compositing).

One easy way to see compositing at work is to place a video or graphic on a superimposing track. Then turn down its opacity to make it translucent, and let video(s) on lower track(s) show through.

A tool to accomplish this is the Opacity rubberband.

Task: Use the Opacity Rubberband

Here's one way to see the opacity rubberband in action. For this exercise, I'll have you place a "super" (text) in a superimposing track above a clip. Then you'll use the opacity rubberband to fade that text in, display it over your clip for a while, and then fade the text out. Your timeline will look like Figure 14.2 by step 8.

Here are the steps to follow for this task:

1. Place a video clip on Video 1. Any clip will do, but trim it to about 15 seconds to simplify things.

2. Open the Title Designer (File, New, Title) and create some simple text. Add color if you like.

3. Save your text (File, Save). It'll show up automatically in the Project window.

4. Drag the text to Video 2, drag the right edge to make it as long as the Video 1 clip, and expand the Video 2 track by clicking the triangle next to the words "Video 2." By default, the red opacity rubberband track should display (as opposed to the keyframe track).

> Even though you have not added a video effect to this clip, the expanded track reads "Alpha Key." By default, all titles have an alpha channel that is enabled when you add them to Video 2 or higher on your timeline. That means the non-text portion of the title screen automatically will be transparent, letting the lower clip show through.

5. Use the red opacity rubberband just like the red volume rubberband for audio tracks. To fade in the title, drag the start handle down to the bottom of the track.

6. A couple seconds into the clip, click the rubberband to create a handle and drag it as far up as it can go—to 100% opacity.

7. A couple seconds before the end of the clip, make a new handle. This anchors the opacity at 100% at that point.

8. Drag the end point handle down as far as it can go, fading the clip to zero.

9. Preview your clip. The title should fade up, hold for a while, and then fade down. That's compositing in its simplest form.

FIGURE 14.2

Using the opacity rubberband to fade in, hold, and fade out text over a clip.

14

Try a similar process with two video clips, but choose your clips with some care. If you select just any two clips, blending the two together can look way too busy.

Task: Superimpose Two Clips

The purpose of this task is to let the clip on the lower track show through the higher clip in a pleasing fashion. Try to use a clip on the higher track with a distinct bright or well-lit area. For my example, I used some flowers with the sky as a backdrop. Here's how this works:

1. Drag the clip you want to show through to Video 1 and the clip with the bright section to Video 2.

2. Expand Video 2.

3. Instead of fading down the start handle of the opacity rubberband, you'll use the Fade Adjustment too—I've highlighted it in Figure 14.3—to move the entire opacity rubberband line. Select the Fade Adjustment tool, hold down the Enter/Return key, and drag the opacity rubberband down to 50%.

FIGURE **14.3**

Using the Fade Adjustment tool to move the entire opacity rubberband to blend two clips.

> Just a reminder: Holding down the Enter/Return key while dragging the Fade Adjustment tool or any rubberband handle will display the exact percentage of opacity.

4. Preview this effect. The lower clip should show through the upper clip, especially in the lighter areas of the upper clip. My example is shown in Figure 14.4.

FIGURE 14.4

Two superimposed clips. Reducing the opacity in the upper clip lets the lower clip show through, particularly through light areas such as the sky.

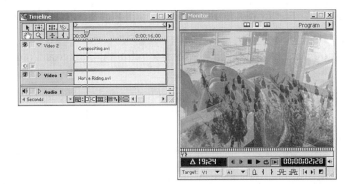

Moving on to Keying

The opacity rubberband works great with text, but when using two full-screen clips or graphics it can be an inexact science. You can get more precise compositing results using keys.

In this hour I'll go over Color and Luminance keys. In Hour 15 I'll explain Matte and Alpha Channel keys.

Using the RGB Difference Key

First up is the simplest key—the RGB Difference Key.

Use this key when you have a brightly lit scene with no shadows, a solid-color background, and a subject with a color that's distinctly different from the background. Not many scenes will qualify. Almost all have some shadows, especially when the subject has texture. But it's a good way to see how keying works—or frequently does *not* work.

Task: Use the RGB Difference Key

To use the RGB Difference key, follow these steps:

1. Place the clip from the first item in the assignment list—the inanimate object shot in front of a solid color—on Video 2.

2. Drag the location clip, the fifth item in the assignment list, to Video 1.

3. Open the Transparency Settings dialog box for the clip on Video 2.

As a reminder, to open the Transparency Settings dialog box, either right/Option-click the clip and select Video Options, Transparency or open the Effect Controls palette and click Setup next to Transparency.

14

4. In the drop-down menu, highlighted in Figure 14.5, select RGB Difference.

5. Place your cursor over the clip image in the Color window (the middle screen). It turns into an eyedropper. Use it to select the background color that you will "key out."

6. Click the Page Peel icon below the Sample window on the right. In a moment this will display how the keyed clip and the one below it will look when composited together.

7. Drag the Similarity slider to the right and watch the Sample window as your background disappears—becomes transparent—to reveal the clip on Video 1. Similarity expands or reduces the range of background color keyed out. However, the more you increase Similarity, the more likely you are to key out other colors and create transparencies in both the background and the subject itself.

FIGURE 14.5

You can access all the Color and Luminance keys from within the Transparency Settings dialog box.

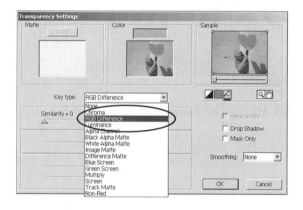

 Your subject will probably have "aliasing" or "jaggies," those stair-step edges common to diagonal lines in computer monitors and TV sets. Just as you did with Transitions, you can turn on *anti*-aliasing to fix that. It blends the pixels around the edges of your object. Use the Smoothing drop-down menu, choose Low or High, and check your results in the Sample screen.

Before moving on, check out the other controls in the Transparency Settings dialog box. Below the Sample window, as highlighted in Figure 14.6, from left to right, they are as follows:

- The Black/White icon. Clicking this replaces the keyed-out background with white. Clicking it again displays a black background.

- The Checkerboard icon. This uses a black and white pattern to replace the keyed-out background. Click it again to reverse the checkerboard pattern.

- The Page Peel icon. You've seen already that this tool reveals the clip below the keyed image.

- The magnifying glass icon is *on* by default. Move the cursor over the Sample screen and it turns into a plus sign. Click to zoom in on the image. Alt/Option-click to zoom out.

- While zoomed in you can use the hand icon to drag the image to check other portions of the clip.

FIGURE 14.6

Use the first three icons to view your "keyed" clip over a white or black background, a checkerboard, or the clip below it on the timeline. The second two icons zoom in and let you drag a zoomed image.

Using the zoom and hand icon tools, take a close look at how well the RGB Difference key worked. It probably looks mediocre. As you move the slider to make the solid color transparent, you may notice that subtle color differences within that "solid" color mean you have to move the slider so far that part of the subject becomes transparent. I've demonstrated this in Figure 14.7.

Welcome to keying. It takes some trial and error to find an approach that works.

FIGURE 14.7

Too much "similarity" can create transparent holes in the subject you want to key over another clip.

14

You may notice something unexpected when you apply even the smallest bit of transparency to a clip on a superimposing video track. You no longer see it play in the Program Monitor screen when you play your project or drag the edit line along the timeline. Normally, Premiere displays the clip on the highest track during standard project playback, as opposed to Real-time Preview or rendering. But if you reduce opacity by a mere 1% or apply any transparency, Premiere behaves as if that clip is not there.

Therefore, if you want to view that clip—to look for a logical edit point or some other purpose—you need to turn off transparency. That means either clicking the *f* check box in the Effect Controls palette to temporarily switch off transparency (while retaining the settings) or raising the opacity back to 100%.

Before using other keying types, try the RGB Difference key on the person you taped in front of a solid color. That, too, likely will be less than satisfactory. Because the person you taped probably moves around a bit that makes finding the right "similarity" around the edges of that person that much more difficult.

RGB Difference does have an option that only one other key (Difference Matte) offers: a drop shadow. This shadow falls only down and to the right. There are no options for opacity, distance, and so on. But it is a nice touch. Problems arise when your background scene has shadows going some other direction. If that's the case, you might consider using the Camera View video effect on the background to flip the image right to left to swap shadow directions.

Using the Chroma Key

Because RGB Difference works only for very limited, well-planned shots, you'll likely rely on other color or transparency keying techniques.

It's very easy to try them out. Chroma-keying is your best all-around method, but it's not as accurate as the more narrowly defined green/blue screens I'll cover later. It has more options than RGB Difference and therefore gives you a better chance to create a decent-looking key.

Within the same Transparency Settings dialog box, choose Chroma from the Key type drop-down list. As I've highlighted in Figure 14.8, in addition to Similarity, you have sliders for Blend, Threshold, and Cutoff:

FIGURE 14.8

Chroma-keying offers more options that increase the likelihood of a successful key.

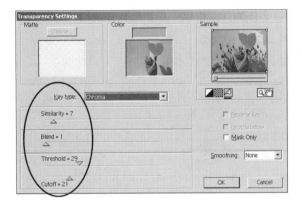

Blend—Softens the transition edges between the keyed subject and the clip below it. Zoom in on the Sample screen and gradually slide Blend to the right. Watch as the image on Video 1 begins to replace the few remaining bits of your object's single-color background. Typically those snippets of background color fall right around the subjects outline.

Threshold—Controls the extent of shadowing thrown by the subject that will show up in the keyed clip. To see this in action, zoom in on any shadow on the solid background color and see how this looks in the Sample screen.

Cutoff—Darkens or lightens shadows. Its value must be less than Threshold; otherwise, it'll invert gray and transparent pixels and your screen will become black.

A good way to use Threshold and Cutoff to your best advantage is to click the check box next to Mask Only, which displays only the silhouette of your subject and the keyed-out color/background. What you want is a black background and a white subject. What you'll probably start with is a dark gray background and a light gray subject. As you slide Threshold to the left, the background darkens. Try to turn it black. Then slide Cutoff to the right and try to get the subject as white as possible. Once you've found the right combination, uncheck Mask Only and use the magnifying glass to check your results.

Despite your best efforts, even the Chroma key may not make the entire background color transparent without punching a few transparent holes in your subject.

Try the Chroma key on the person you taped. As with the RGB Difference key, you probably will find it difficult to make a clean key, especially in and around the subject's hair.

14

Using the Luminance Key

To test this key, use the images from the third item in the assignment list—the dark object/light background and vice versa.

Use the Luminance key on those shots. The default Threshold setting is 100%, meaning the widest range of dark values will become transparent. Reduce it and you tighten that range. Cutoff sets just how transparent those dark areas will become. Higher values increase transparency.

As my subjects demonstrate in Figure 14.9 and 14.10, if you taped very contrasting scenes, the Luminance key should work smoothly. It's similar to the Image Mask transition. Whatever is dark gets keyed out (that is, it becomes transparent, letting images below it show through), and light areas remain opaque, displaying whatever is on the upper clip.

FIGURE **14.9**

The Luminance key works well if you have a highly contrasting subject and background and little texture to your subject.

FIGURE **14.10**

Use the Luminance key on a dark object like this clock shot against a light background to create this unique visual combination.

To add a realistic feel to any keyed shot, make the background blurry. Typically, you want to make the subject, which you've shot with a key in mind, the focal point of your composited clip. By using a background that's a bit out of focus, the subject stands out even more. To create that illusion, simply use the Fast Blur video effect on the background clip. I used that effect with the sand dollar clip in Figure 14.11.

FIGURE 14.11

Using the Fast Blur video effect on the background clip makes the keyed image stand out.

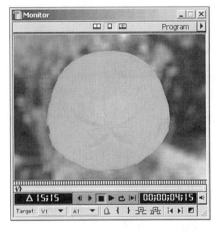

Again, this key takes some planning. When you're shooting, it's best to illuminate the light object or background and work to make the dark area as dark as possible. Objects with fine edge detail such as hair are very hard to key under any circumstances, including when you use luminance.

You can add motion to Luminance and other keys. Simply open the Motion Settings dialog box from the Effect Controls palette. As shown in Figure 14.12, when you open the Motion Settings dialog box, the entire clip—as opposed to only the keyed subject—moves through the frame, leaving large white gaps on the sides. You can fix this by using the Fill Color eyedropper on the dark background or subject. As I've highlighted in Figure 14.13, this will fill the background with the color you've told Transparency to make transparent. So now only the keyed object will move through the scene. You can create any path you'd like plus add distortion and rotation.

14

FIGURE **14.12**

A Luminance-keyed image in the Motion Settings dialog box without a color fill applied.

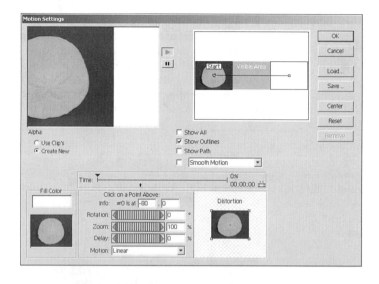

FIGURE **14.13**

The same Luminance-keyed image in the Motion Settings dialog box with a color fill applied.

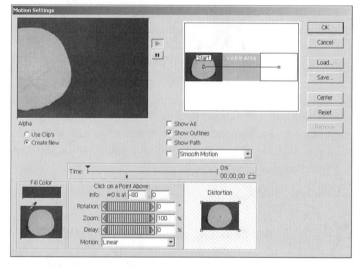

Using the Multiply and Screen Keys

The Multiply and Screen keys are like the Luminance key, but they create more subtle superimpositions. They both examine the clip below the superimposed clip on the timeline for dark and light areas. Then they make portions of the superimposed clip transparent to match those areas. The explanation for this in the Adobe manual is counterintuitive. I'll try to clarify it.

As I've illustrated in Figure 14.14, the Multiply key looks for dark areas in the lower clip and then creates transparencies above them, letting those dark areas on the lower clip play through. The superimposed clip displays its image only above the lower clip's light areas. It does so with some opacity, giving the combination of the two images that subtlety I referred to.

FIGURE **14.14**

The Multiply key creates transparencies in the superimposed track over dark areas in the Video 1 clip.

The Screen key, shown in Figure 14.15, looks for light areas in the lower clip and makes transparencies above them, letting those lighter areas of the lower clip play through the superimposed clip. The superimposed clip displays its image generally only above the dark areas of the lower clip. It is less effective than Multiply and looks more like simply reduced opacity.

FIGURE **14.15**

The Screen key reverses the Multiply key's process and looks for light areas in the lower clip.

14

Using the Blue Screen and Green Screen Keys

The Blue Screen and Green Screen keys are your best bets for accurate, relatively low-budget keying. To use them well, you'll not only need what's called "chroma blue" and "chroma green" backdrops but you'll need to follow a few procedures as well. Because this is sort of an involved process, I've included a sidebar on the subject.

The Blue and Green Screen keys' options work like other Premiere keys, only they're simpler because Premiere is looking for very specific chroma blue and green background colors.

There are only two principle slider controls—Threshold and Cutoff. Again, drag Threshold to the left to make the entire blue/green screen transparent. Drag Cutoff to the right to ensure the opaque areas look satisfactory. I asked Matt Zaffino, my favorite weatherman, to demonstrate in Figures 14.16 and 14.17 how things look before and after applying keying effects.

FIGURE **14.16**
KGW-TV's Matt Zaffino in front of a green screen before the key controls are applied.

> If at first your key does not succeed, try again. Sometimes try as you might, you cannot remove all the jaggies from the edges of your green- or blue-screened actors. This is endemic to consumer/prosumer DV (technically, DV25) camcorders. To possibly remedy that, key them twice.
>
> However, that won't work for the original clip on the timeline. If you go back to Transparency Settings to tweak the existing blue/green screen settings, that only changes them. It doesn't apply the settings twice.
>
> To do that requires creating a virtual clip. I'll explain virtual clips in Hour 16, "Tips, Tricks, and Techniques: Part 1."

FIGURE **14.17**

*How things look after
keying* out *chroma
green and keying* in *the
weather graphic.*

FIGURE **14.17**

*How things look after
keying* out *chroma
green and keying* in *the
weather graphic.*

Making Blue and Green Screens Work

Setting up chroma green or blue backdrops can be a royal pain—especially on location. About 10 years ago I hired one of Portland's top production companies to do a fairly involved blue screen shoot at a local college. They lit the heck out of that blue screen, got the dolly rails and the trucking move down perfectly, and rolled and recorded.

When we got back to the studio, try as we might, we could not completely key out the blue screen without creating some transparency in the actor. We ended up building an elaborate moving matte (it had to fit the actor's shifting silhouette). What a time-consuming hassle!

As someone once said, "It's not easy being green" (or blue). Here are some tips:

- Blue and green screens require "flat" lighting—no hot spots. If you can set up your screen outdoors, sunlight or cloudy days work best. No need to overdo the lighting. Simply make it even.

- The actor's lighting does *not* have to be flat. Controlled spot lights or lights with "barn doors" work well. Using soft lighting with umbrellas and reflectors is less dramatic but also is effective. A so-called "key" backlight aimed at the actor's head helps more clearly illuminate hair to eliminate or at least minimize blue or green screen "halos."

- If you plan to key in an outdoor background, try to re-create outdoor lighting on your subject. If you're working with live actors, further enhance the illusion by using a fan to blow their hair around a bit.

- Avoid the dreaded blue or green spill. Actors' skin will pick up the reflected color of the backdrop if they're too close to it. Move them at least a few feet away. One other way to minimize this is to use a backlight.

- Tight shots work better than full-body shots. The closer you are to your subject, the more realistic the finished product.

14

- If there is fast-paced action in your shot, you may have trouble keying right to the edges of your subjects.

- Set your camcorder to Manual and open the iris (you'll probably need to increase shutter speed to avoid overexposure). A wide-open iris—1.8 or so—limits the focal plane to your subject and throws the green screen a bit out of focus, making it easier to key out.

- To build a backdrop on a budget, consider using unofficial chroma blue or green paint (the real stuff retails for about $40 a gallon). Grab a paint sample collection, videotape it, and then use Premiere's blue screen or green screen transparency on it. Find a color that keys well and buy a gallon. Paint that on a large piece of plywood and you have a portable studio.

  Alternatively, you can buy Chroma key fabric or wide rolls of Chroma key paper. Both run about $10 a square yard. One source is www.Filmtools.com.

- Which color to use? With chroma green you have reasonable assurance no one will have clothing that matches and therefore will key out. Chroma blue works well because it's complementary to skin tones. The kind of scene you key in may be the determining factor. If you will have your actors keyed in to a scene with a blue sky, use a blue screen. In this case, the dreaded blue spill could be a nice feature.

- Consumer and prosumer camcorders do not key as well as professional camcorders. The 4:1:1 color sampling compression leads to some quality loss. Because the green portion of an RGB signal receives extra weight to correspond to the sensitivity of human eyes to different colors, green screens key more cleanly than blue. A mathematical analysis done a few years ago showed that using a green screen with a DV camcorder keys only 15% less cleanly than a broadcast-quality Betacam SP camcorder.

Using the Non-Red Key

The Non-Red key is your blue/green screen fall back. Both Blue and Green Screen keys look for very specific colors. They offer no "similarity" controls to select a color range. If you just can't quite dial in a Blue/Green Screen key because somehow the color is slightly off or there is too much fringing around the edges of nontransparent subjects, try the Non-Red key. It's a little more forgiving. As you move the Threshold slider, this key looks for non-red colors (blue/green) to key out.

As I've demonstrated in two additional "before and after" images with Matt Zaffino (Figures 14.18 and 14.19), the Non-Red key offers one other control: Blend. This ostensibly lets you smoothly blend two scenes together. I've found that it doesn't make much difference if you already have a reasonably good blue/green screen shot.

Figure 14.18

Sometimes the Chroma or Green/Blue Screen keys fail to fulfill their promise.

Figure 14.19

The Non-Red key tends to clear up the "jaggies" along the edges of your opaque subjects.

Summary

Compositing tools let you greatly enhance your projects by adding multiple layers of video and images. The principle compositing tools are opacity, the Color and Luminance Keys, mattes, and alpha channels. I covered the first two in this hour, and will go over mattes and alpha channels in Hour 15.

Making keys work well takes some extra effort. Proper backdrop colors, lighting, and keying techniques all come into play. Green/blue screens work best but invariably take some trial and error.

14

Workshop

Review the questions and answers in this section to try to sharpen your Premiere transparency techniques. Also, take a few moments to tackle my short quiz and the exercises.

Q&A

Q **No matter how many different key types I try, I get a "halo" effect along the edges of my keyed objects, especially in their hair. What should I do?**

A This is endemic to this technology. Using DV camcorders and Premiere's less-than-pixel-specific keying controls means you may never get rid of those halos. Some video capture cards, such as the Canopus Storm, have a much higher quality Chroma key tool. You may notice that your local weather forecaster does not have such halos (unless you live in a tiny TV market that's behind the technology curve). Many of those stations use a keying technology from Ultimatte (www.ultimatte.com). It offers incredible flexibility and creates very clean keying in difficult situations, such as through smoke, hair, water, and glass. Ultimatte offers a Premiere plug-in for $1,495. The hardware prices start in the neighborhood of $28,000.

Q **Why can't I see the video clip on the highest track? Isn't that how it's supposed to work?**

A If you make any kind of transparency adjustment to a track, Premiere turns off its display. Even if you use the little eye icons to turn off a video track, a clip with any transparency, even if it's only a 1% drop in opacity, becomes invisible. You can see the clip if you do a real-time preview or an Alt/Option-scrub preview, or if you render the clip.

Quiz

1. How do you blend two full-screen clips?

2. What's the difference between the two sets of Chroma Key sliders—Similarity/Blend and Threshold/Cutoff? What's a more descriptive name for the Smoothing drop-down menu?

3. When do you use the Non-Red key?

Quiz Answers

1. Either of two ways: Use the opacity rubberband to reduce the opacity of the superimposed clip or use the Screen (or Multiply) transparency for a subtle blend that lets light (or dark) areas of the bottom track show through the superimposed clip. Screen more closely approximates the opacity rubberband effect. Multiply acts more like a real key.

2. Similarity and Blend work together to set a "width" for the color range to key out of a superimposed clip and to blend the two clips smoothly together. Threshold and Cutoff deal with shadows. Threshold controls the amount of shadows from the superimposed clip that will display on the lower track's clip. Cutoff controls how dark or light those shadows are. "Smoothing" is the same as "anti-aliasing."

3. Non-Red lets you key out, well, non-red backgrounds (that is, green and blue). It's a helpful backup if the Green Screen key doesn't work as well as you'd like, which may happen if the green is not true chroma green.

Exercises

1. Use the Luminance key to isolate a ball by keying out a highly contrasting background. Then use motion settings to bounce it around a scene. Use acceleration and deceleration with the bounces and apexes to more realistically mimic a bouncing ball.

2. Create several titles. Place them in various superimposing tracks and fade them in and out of your Video 1 clip at various times, sometimes displaying more than one title at a time. Remember, you drag the edges of a title clip to make it any length you want. Finally, give a couple titles motion using the Motion Settings dialog box.

3. Experiment with the Chroma and Green/Blue Screen keys. Find a color and lighting that work well.

4. Ask to visit a local TV station or production studio to watch how they set up green/blue screens.

5. Start watching TV commercials more critically, looking for examples of compositing. It's a rare spot that doesn't use layering. This is a great source of ideas.

14

HOUR 15

Compositing Part 2: Alpha Channels and Mattes

Another way to layer is to create holes in clips—digital holes, that is—using alpha channels and mattes. Alpha channels are common elements of graphics created in programs such as Adobe Photoshop and Illustrator. Premiere turns them transparent. Mattes appear to be simple black and white, opaque images, but again Premiere uses them to create transparencies. Both are effective, useful means to composite clips in Premiere.

The highlights of this hour include the following:

- Alpha channel transparencies—straight and premultiplied
- A dozen premiere video effects that use alpha channels
- How mattes work
- Using mattes, including image mattes, track mattes, split screens, difference mattes, and garbage mattes

Working with Alpha Channel Transparencies

Most video clips and many graphics have alpha channels. Coupled with an image's red/green/blue (RGB) color information, an alpha channel defines how clips or graphics will be displayed over a background image.

The alpha channel uses 8 bits of information to describe 256 shades of gray. In typical computer graphics, white *regions* of the alpha channel are opaque—that is, they cover any clips beneath them on the timeline. Black is transparent and lets any lower clips show through. Finally, gray lets some background come through, depending on the level of gray.

On the other hand, a typical video's alpha channel describes gray values on a *pixel-by-pixel basis* instead of by a larger region, making it impractical to use the Alpha Channel Transparency setting on a video clip.

An alpha channel is either straight or premultiplied. A straight alpha channel stores its transparency information only in the alpha channel. You'll use Premiere's alpha channel transparency on straight alpha channels. I'll explain how in a moment.

A graphics with a premultiplied alpha channel includes transparency information in both the alpha channel and the edges of the graphic. If you apply an alpha channel transparency to such graphics, they'll probably look blurry or have stray pixels of variable color along their edges. To avoid that, you can use a black alpha matte or white alpha matte on them. I explain more in the "Creating Transparencies with Premultiplied Alpha Channel Graphics" sidebar, later in this hour.

Task: Make an Alpha Channel Visible

To see an alpha channel, follow these steps:

1. Place any video clip on Video 1 in the timeline.

2. Import a graphic with an alpha channel to your project and drag it to a superimposing track—Video 2 or higher—directly above the clip on Video 1. If you don't have such a graphic, use the Veloman.eps file from Premiere's Sample folder.

3. Open the graphic's Transparency Settings dialog box by clicking Setup in the Effect Controls palette. Select Alpha Channel. You'll note in Figure 15.1 that with Alpha Channel selected, there are no sliders. This transparency is either on or off. Even if the alpha channel has some gray in it, you cannot adjust that level from within the Transparency Settings dialog box.

FIGURE 15.1

The Alpha Channel Transparency Settings dialog box offers no sliders to adjust values, such as Similarity or Threshold.

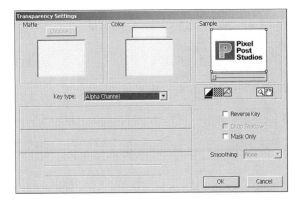

> The graphic I used for Figure 15.1 is a Photoshop document (PSD) file type. If you use the Veloman graphic from the Premiere Sample folder, you may note that it's an Encapsulated PostScript (EPS) file type. The latter, Adobe-created format contains vector and bitmap information. You can use both Adobe Illustrator and Photoshop to create EPS files. Desktop publishers frequently use EPS files because they are highly compatible and reliable.

4. Check the Mask Only box. As Figure 15.2 shows, the white area matches the edges of the logo and is opaque. The black area is, digitally speaking, as transparent as glass.

FIGURE 15.2

A logo's alpha channel mask. White is opaque, and black is transparent.

5. Uncheck the Mask Only box and preview how the graphic appears over the clip below it on the timeline by clicking the page peel icon. It'll look like Figure 15.3.

FIGURE 15.3

The logo with a trans-
parent alpha channel
over the background
image in the lower
video track.

This "white equals opacity and black equals transparency" issue may seem a bit confusing, especially because the lettering on the logo graphic I used is black but is opaque. What's more, the rectangle around the logo is white but is transparent.

What determines the opacity/transparency is not the color of the graphic but rather the grayscale level of the alpha channel. In this case, after applying the alpha channel transparency and selecting Mask Only, you'll see that the alpha channel associated with the black logo text is white. The graphic text is black, but the alpha channel beneath it is white, and white is opaque. You will not be able to see through the black text to the clip below because its associated white alpha channel is opaque.

Task: Add Motion Using the Motion Settings Dialog Box

▼ TASK

You can apply motion to a graphic using the Motion Settings dialog box. Follow these steps:

1. Select the graphic with the alpha channel.

2. Open the Motion Settings dialog box. Either right/Option-click and select Video Options, Motion or open the Effect Controls palette and select Setup next to Motion.

3. Locate the Alpha radio buttons, highlighted in Figure 15.4, below the preview screen and select Use Clip's. This will ensure that you don't see the graphic's rectangular bounding box moving across the screen. You'll see only the graphic.

▲

FIGURE 15.4

Selecting the Use Clip's radio button in the Motion Settings dialog box means only the graphic will move around the screen, not its bounding box.

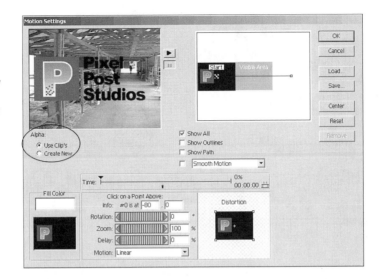

Creating Transparencies with Premultiplied Alpha Channel Graphics

Think of straight alpha channels as cookie cutters. Graphic artists "bleed" some of their graphics slightly beyond the edges of the white portion of the alpha channel, knowing that when they apply an alpha channel transparency, it will act like a cookie cutter, slicing a sharply defined edge along the graphic and ensuring there will be no gaps along the border.

In a graphic with a premultiplied alpha channel, the white portion of the alpha channel exactly matches the edge of the pixels in the RGB graphic. In most cases, premultiplied graphics have either black or white backgrounds. Because of anti-aliasing, the background color darkens or lightens these pixels along the edge of the graphics.

If you use graphics with premultiplied alpha channels, do *not* use an alpha channel transparency. If you do, you will experience some unpredictable fringing around the edges. Instead, use an alpha matte that matches the background color.

Figures 15.5 through 15.7 demonstrate how that works and what can happen if you apply the wrong transparency.

The solution is simple: To key out the white background of a graphic with a premultiplied alpha channel, use a white alpha matte transparency.

To key out a black background, use a black alpha matte transparency.

FIGURE 15.5

Applying an alpha channel transparency to a premultiplied graphic with a white background creates stair-step, aliased edges.

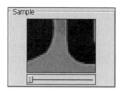

FIGURE 15.6

The same graphic with a black alpha matte applied creates a pixelated mess.

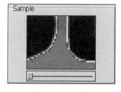

FIGURE 15.7

The same white background graphic with the white alpha matte applied looks sharp and clear.

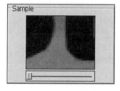

Using Alpha Channel Transparency with 12 Premiere Video Effects

Of Premiere's 79 video effects, 14 either have an alpha channel or have special adjustments for clips with alpha channels. I'll go over 12 of them. The two others have limited value.

In previous hours I've touched on all of these and noted some of their Alpha Channel characteristics so I'll try to avoid too much repetition.

I've placed them in two groups: Video Effects with Alpha Channels and Effects that work well with Graphics that have Alpha Channels.

Video Effects with Alpha Channels

Six Premiere video effects have built-in alpha channels:

- Basic 3D
- Camera View

- Lens Distortion
- Strobe Light
- Tiles
- Transform

Typically these effects move clips around the screen, revealing a background. You generally can choose a background color or opt to use the alpha channel to make the background transparent, revealing a clip beneath it on the timeline.

Revealing a Clip with Basic 3D

When you use this effect to manipulate a clip in 3D space, the default setting is to show a black matte behind it.

Instead, use it to reveal another clip as I've illustrated in Figure 15.8. Here's how:

1. Place two clips, one above the other, on Video 1 and Video 2.

2. Apply Basic 3D to the clip on Video 2 and move that clip off to one side. You'll see only black behind it.

3. To reveal the clip below it, open the Video 2 clip's Transparency Settings dialog box and select Alpha Channel. Click OK.

This reveals the clip on Video 1. You can layer and reveal multiple clips using Basic 3D.

FIGURE 15.8
Use Basic 3D's alpha channel to reveal a clip below it on the timeline.

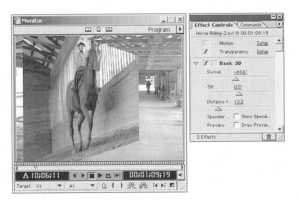

Opting to Reveal a Clip Using Camera View

This effect works a lot like Basic 3D with a few additional controls thrown in. It's not an After Effects (AE) effect, so you have the option to open its Settings dialog box. Follow these steps to try out Camera View:

1. Replace Basic 3D in the Effect Controls palette with Camera View.

2. Click Setup.

3. As I've highlighted in Figure 15.9, uncheck the Fill Alpha Channel box. If this is left checked, you can create a background color other than the default white. You'll note that despite unchecking the Fill Alpha Channel box, the Camera View Settings dialog box's preview screen does not display the clip on Video 1 behind the Video 2 clip. To remedy that, click OK.

4. Make your slider adjustments in the Effect Controls palette and watch your handi-work in real time in the Program Monitor screen.

In each of the following alpha channel examples, make sure you do two things:

- Delete the previous video effect from the Effect Controls palette.
- Keep the Video 2 clip's Transparency setting at Alpha Channel.

FIGURE 15.9

Uncheck the Camera View effect's Fill Alpha Channel box to display the clip below it on the timeline.

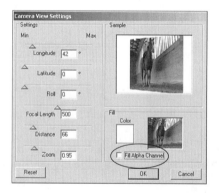

Twisting Away an Image with Lens Distortion

This effect works much like Camera View in that it's a non-AE video effect and its Settings dialog box has a Fill Alpha Channel check box (see Figure 15.10). Try this out on the Video 2 clip.

FIGURE 15.10

Lens Distortion has the same Fill Alpha Channel check box as Camera View.

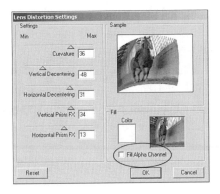

Flashing a Second Image with Strobe Light

Here you face a number of options about the characteristics of the strobe-like effect. To try this effect, follow these steps:

1. Apply Strobe Light to your clip on Video 2.

2. Using the drop-down menu highlighted in Figure 15.11, select Makes Layer Transparent. This means that each strobe flash will reveal the layer below it.

FIGURE 15.11

Strobe Light flashes can reveal the layer beneath it on the time-line.

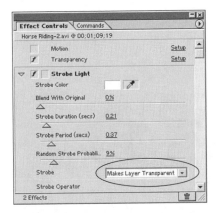

For an interesting effect, do the following:

1. Add another video track to the timeline (unless you already have a Video 3 track) by right/Option-clicking the timeline and selecting Add Video Track. Move the clip on Video 2 to Video 3. Open its Transparency Settings dialog box and select Alpha Channel.

2. Drag Strobe Light to that clip. Set a short Duration (0.2 or so). Set a strobe period about twice as long (0.4 or so). Put some randomness in (5% works well). Also, under Strobe, set Make Layer Transparent.

3. Add a graphic with an alpha channel to Video 2, drag its ends to match the length of the other two clips, and set Transparency to Alpha Channel.

4. Give the graphic on Video 2 some motion, keeping it within the screen. The faster it moves the better, so feel free to give it a convoluted and long motion path, forcing it to zip around the screen.

5. Turn the clip on Video 1 into a freeze frame by right/Option-clicking it, selecting Video Options, Frame Hold, Hold On (select In Point, Marker 0, or Out Point). Then Click OK.

6. Now preview that section. The top clip should do the strobe thing, and if the graphic moves fast enough it should bounce all over the freeze frame.

Breaking Up a Clip Using Tiles

This video effect, too, can reveal the clip below it on the timeline.

Keeping the three clips layered on the timeline, apply Tiles to the clip on Video 3.

As I've demonstrated in Figure 15.12, to display more of the two lower clips, increase Maximum Offset to something more than 50%. This widens the gaps between the jittering tiles.

FIGURE 15.12

When using Tiles on a clip in a superimposed video track, increasing the Maximum Offset setting displays more of the clip(s) beneath it.

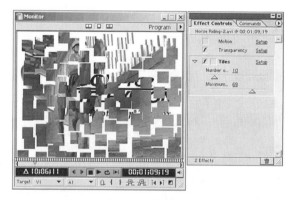

Trying Two Transparencies at Once with Transform

As with Basic 3D and Camera View, Transform moves your clip in an apparent 3D space. Once displaced from a normal full-screen aspect, it leaves black gaps around the edges of the clip. With that clip's Transparency set to Alpha Channel, you can see what's below it on the timeline.

One strength of this effect is its built-in Opacity slider, highlighted in Figure 15.13. You could use the opacity rubberband on the expanded video track to accomplish the same thing, but this is much more convenient.

FIGURE 15.13

Transform skews a clip to reveal either black or the clip(s) beneath it.

Effects That Work Well with Graphics That Have Alpha Channels

The following six video effects work best with a graphic:

- Alpha Glow
- Bevel Alpha
- Channel Blur
- Drop Shadow
- QuickTime Cloud
- QuickTime Fire

You can use Veloman.eps or any other graphic with an alpha channel.

I'll ask you to take a different tack in this section. Instead of trying each effect separately, I'll have you apply these effects to the same clip, eventually running all six at once. Admittedly, by that time, the graphic will be a hodgepodge.

Adding a Soft Edge Using Alpha Glow

This effect adds a nice, soft edge to a graphic. Follow these steps:

1. Delete or move the clip on Video 3 off to one side so it's no longer above the clips on Video 1 and 2.
2. Turn off the motion for the graphic on Video 2 (its Transparency setting still should be Alpha Channel).

3. Drag Alpha Glow to the graphic on Video 2 and open its Settings dialog box by clicking Setup in the Effect Controls palette.

> This is one of those Premiere video effect control anomalies. When in the Effect Controls palette, Alpha Glow is missing two user-selected items—Fade Out and End Color. So you need to use the Alpha Glow Settings dialog box to access them. However, that means you don't get a real-time view of how the graphic with the effect applied looks over the lower clip. You can get around this by clicking Setup, selecting an end color, making your Fade Out selection, and returning to the Effect Controls palette. Then you can make the other settings there and use the Program Monitor screen to watch the effect change in real time over the clip on Video 1.

As shown in Figure 15.14, Alpha Glow changes the width of the effect. Increasing the Brightness setting actually increases the *opacity* of the effect. Checking the Fade Out box lets the effect gradually disappear around the outside edges. Leaving it unchecked creates a hard edge. Finally, the end color creates a second, outer color.

FIGURE 15.14

Alpha Glow creates a halo around a graphic.

Giving a Graphic a 3D Feel with Bevel Alpha

Applying this effect gives the graphic a nice 3D feel. I've applied it with the Alpha Glow effect in Figure 15.15.

Drag it to the Effect Controls palette for the graphic clip on Video 2.

The greater the Edge Thickness and Light Intensity values, the more obvious the effect. In Figure 15.15, I set these items to approximately 9 and 0.9, respectively. Plus, I selected a light color to increase contrast.

FIGURE 15.15
Bevel Alpha adds a 3D edge to the graphic.

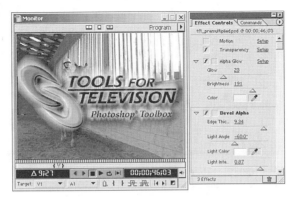

Adjusting Colors by Applying Channel Blur

This shifts individual color values—red/green/blue—as well as blurs the graphic. Feel free to make adjustments using all the sliders.

As illustrated in Figure 15.16, as you make changes using the Channel Blur effect sliders, the Bevel Alpha and Alpha Glow effects change. You may want to experiment as you add even more effects to the same clip.

Turn individual effects off and on by clicking the *f* in the check box. The order of the effects also alters the overall appearance of a clip. Drag effects to new positions in the Effect Controls palette to see what happens. For instance, as I've demonstrated in Figure 15.17, if you place Channel Blur at the top (below Transparency and Motion), any changes made when it's in that position will have a much more dramatic impact than if you place Channel Blur toward the bottom of the palette. Premiere applies video effects from bottom to top, saving Transparency and Motion (by default) for the final two compositing steps.

Giving a Graphic Depth with Drop Shadow

Drop Shadow works real well with graphics, giving them the appearance of floating above the background clip. This is the effect you use if you rotate a graphic—using Basic 3D, Camera View, or Transform—and you want to make sure the shadow falls in the same direction rather than rotates with the graphic.

When you apply it along with these three other effects, it won't have all that dramatic an impact. Alpha Glow and Channel Blur soften the graphic so much that there isn't much substance left in it to throw a shadow.

FIGURE 15.16

Because Channel Blur is, for the moment, the lowest effect in the Effect Controls palette, it blurs all effects above it.

FIGURE 15.17

Placing Channel Blur at the top of the Effect Controls palette amplifies any adjustments you make to it.

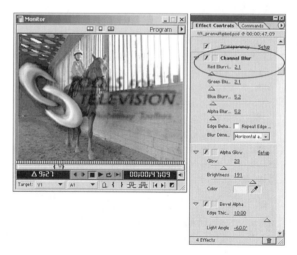

As I've shown in Figure 15.18, you can fix that a bit by increasing Opacity to 80 or greater and dropping Softness to 0.

If you drag this effect to the top of the effect chain in the Effect Controls palette, it will create a very distinct drop shadow. Toward the bottom of the palette, it acts much more in character with the other effects.

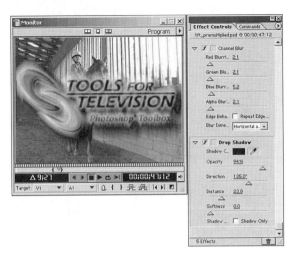

FIGURE 15.18

Drop Shadow has a subtle feel when applied to effects that have already blurred the image.

Changing the Weather Using QuickTime Cloud

Both QuickTime Cloud and Fire do two things to a clip: they switch off all other effects applied to that clip and replace the clip with the effect. Try it and see.

Drag QuickTime to the Effect Controls palette, select Cloud, and click OK. Now preview that graphic clip. All you'll see is a cloud floating over the background clip on Video 1. The original clip is gone, as are the effects.

In this case, you want to incorporate Cloud into your ever-expanding collection of effects. Here's how:

1. Make a color matte by right/Option-clicking in the white space in the Project window and selecting New, Color Matte.

2. Select a color, name the matte, and drag it to Video 3 above the graphic on Video 2. Drag its ends to make it the same length as the graphic and background clips. Your timeline should look something like Figure 15.19.

3. Set the color matte's Transparency to Alpha Channel.

4. Apply QuickTime Cloud to that color matte.

5. Preview this three-clip sandwich. As illustrated in Figure 15.20, the cloud should float in the middle of the effect.

If you want to have even more fun, add motion and rotation to the cloud. Go to the Motion Settings dialog box and create a path, rotation, and zoom to move the cloud all over the screen.

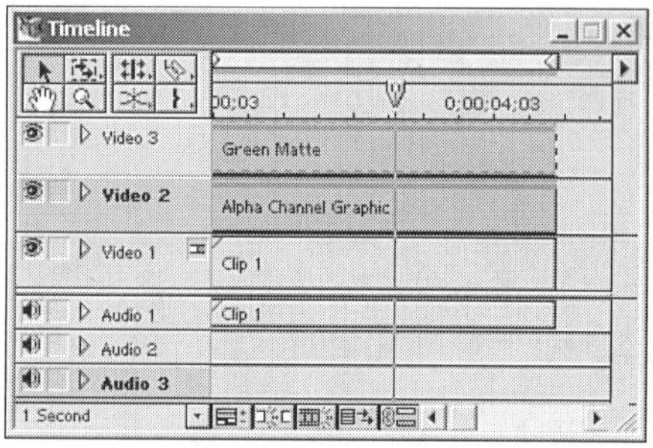

FIGURE 15.19

Use a color matte as a means to superimpose the QuickTime Cloud (or Fire) effect to clips below it on the timeline.

FIGURE 15.20

How this evolving clip looks with QuickTime Cloud applied to it.

Flame-broiling Your Clip Using QuickTime Fire

This operates the same way as Cloud. To flame-broil your entire collection of effects, follow these steps:

1. Add another video track to the timeline (unless you already have a Video 4 track) by right/Option-clicking the timeline and selecting Add Video Track.

2. Drag the color matte from the Project window to Video 4 above the three other clips (directly above the other color matte). Lengthen it to equal the three other clips.

3. Apply Alpha Channel in the Transparency Settings dialog box.

4. Apply QuickTime Fire to that matte. As shown in Figure 15.21, you can use the preview window to watch as you adjust the four controls to your liking.

FIGURE 15.21

The QuickTime Fire effect has four parameters that set the intensity of the flames.

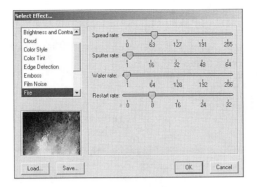

Preview this combination of six video effects that all use transparent alpha channels. It should look something like Figure 15.22.

FIGURE 15.22

Six video effects that all use an alpha channel, juxtaposed into one colossal collection.

If you're in a particularly ambitious mood, feel free to apply keyframes to each individual video effect, except for the QuickTime effects. They do not work with keyframes. I waited until the end to suggest this because now all the effects are accessible in the drop-down menu in the upper-left corner of the keyframe track below the video track in the Video 2 expanded view. Use that drop-down menu to access each effect.

Creating and Working with Mattes

On the surface, the matte is a straightforward concept. But confusing terms and applications can make using one counterintuitive.

By definition, mattes are color or grayscale images used to create transparent, opaque, and translucent areas in clips.

But that definition doesn't intuitively apply to the two mattes you've already encountered: the black alpha and white alpha mattes. They fall into the alpha channel transparency side of the compositing equation.

Then there's the difference matte, which I'll get to in a few minutes. It acts more like a Chroma key.

When is a matte really a matte? It can be bewildering.

Understanding Matte Basics

Mattes follow standard transparency rules: Black areas are transparent, white areas are opaque, and gray areas create varying levels of opacity.

If the matte is a color image, then Premiere *removes* the same level of color from the clip you are keying, thus creating an inverse image. So if you use a matte with green in it, the displayed image will look purple (red and blue).

You can create basic mattes using simple paint programs or you can use clips or images as mattes. You can use a Premiere video effect to convert a color image to a grayscale matte to avoid dealing with color inversions.

Most of the time mattes are simply black and white graphics. They work like scissors used on white paper. Any (black) holes cut into the paper lets that portion of the clip on Video 1 show through and combine with the clip above it on the timeline.

Task: Combine Clips with an Image Matte

Here's an easy way to see how mattes work:

1. Either open a simple art program such as MS Paint or use Premiere's Title Designer.

2. As I've demonstrated in Figure 15.23, create a simple shape and fill it in with solid black. Create another shape and fill it with gray.

FIGURE 15.23

Use a basic paint program or Premiere's Title Designer to create simple shapes filled with black and gray.

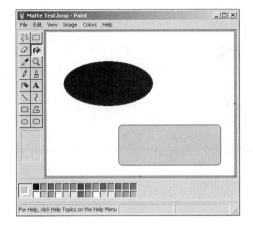

3. Save your matte or Title Designer file to the `Scratch Disk` file folder where you keep all your original video clips and give it a name such as `Matte Test`.

4. Return to the timeline and place two different video clips or still images on Video 1 and Video 2.

5. Open the Transparency Settings dialog box for the clip on Video 2 (remember, you can't apply transparency to a clip on Video 1).

6. Select Image Matte in the Key Type drop-down list.

7. Note the new button that appears with Image Matte selected—Choose. In Figure 15.24, I've highlighted it in the Transparency Settings dialog box's upper-left corner. That button becomes available for only Image Matte and Difference Matte.

8. Click Choose. Then locate and select the graphic you just created. This combines that matte with the clip on Video 2, thus "carving" those holes, I mentioned earlier, into it.

9. Preview the transparency by clicking the page peel icon. The black areas of your graphic should show the corresponding portion of the clip on Video 1. The white areas should show those portions of the clip on Video 2. The gray area should mix both clips.

You can electronically swap black with white by selecting Reverse Key. That will swap transparent and opaque areas of the clip on Video 2, letting different portions of the clip on Video 1 show through.

FIGURE 15.24

Combine your newly created matte with your superimposed image by selecting Image Matte in the Transparency Settings dialog box.

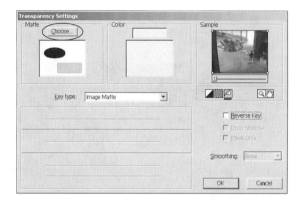

 You can use image mattes to isolate portions of a clip as a means to highlight that section or to change its characteristics for special purposes. I'll explain that technique in Hour 16, "Tips, Tricks, and Techniques: Part 1."

Putting a Matte in Motion Using the Track Matte

This works much like an image matte but at first seems counterintuitive. It's called a track matte because you place the matte on a video track rather than apply it directly to a clip. It's counterintuitive because you place that matte *above* a clip on the timeline, so you'd think white areas in the matte would be opaque and block all lower tracks. But they don't because you tell the clip right *below* it that there's a matte on the next higher track and to treat that track matte as an image matte.

You place the matte on a separate video track to apply motion to it—that is, to move the matte (and its associated transparency regions) around the screen. You use a track matte to make a moving or traveling matte. It's a very cool way to follow action in a clip.

Just about any movie involving "impossible" motion—spaceships, Superman in flight, or giant spiders (such as the 1955 cult classic *Tarantula*, with Clint Eastwood in a minor supporting role as a pilot)—use traveling mattes.

Task: Work with a Track Matte

▼ TASK

Try this:

1. Create text using Title Designer or some other graphic tool. Make the text very large—80 points or so. You will use it to display part of a clip, so you want it large enough to make sure viewers see what you're up to.

15

2. Save it and call it something like `Track Matte Text`.

3. Use the same two clips from the previous task. Place the `Track Matte Text` file on Video 3 and drag its edges to fit the other two clips.

4. Change Transparency Settings on the clip on Video 2 to Track Matte. As shown in Figure 15.25, you should see the text from Video 3 show up in the Sample window.

5. Apply motion settings to the `Track Matte Text` file on Video 3. Keep it simple.

FIGURE **15.25**
Track Matte uses a matte (in this case the matte is text) on a higher video track and applies it to the clip below it.

Preview your work. You should see the clip from Video 2 with text floating across it. Images from Video 1 should show through the text. You can reverse this process—that is, have Video 1 play with portions of Video 2 showing through the text—by going back to Transparency Settings for the clip on Video 2 and selecting Reverse Key.

You can use a track/moving/traveling matte to highlight something moving within an image. For instance, you can single out a racecar from group of cars by placing a moving matte over it and changing its color. I'll show you how to do this in Hour 16.

Using a Split-Screen Matte

You've seen movies with the same actor playing multiple characters in the same scene. There are several ways to accomplish this. Using a split-screen matte is one. This is where assignment number five from Hour 14, "Compositing Part 1: Layering Images and Clips," comes into play.

As a reminder, for this assignment you were to tape a distinct background with nothing moving in it—that is, no waving palm trees or soaring birds. Then, without turning off or moving the camera (this is one exercise where you need a rock-steady shot), have someone walk into the left side of the scene without crossing the center line, stand around for a while, then walk back out the left side. Have that person do the same thing entering from the right side and walking out to the right. For a bit of comic relief, have your "actor" wave toward the center of the scene before walking off camera.

Task: Create a Split-Screen Effect

To create a split-screen effect using your video track from Hour 14, follow these steps:

1. Go back to your paint program. Build a black rectangle that covers the left or right half the screen. It doesn't have to be exactly half and half. Save it and call it something like Split Screen Matte.

2. Place the assignment clip on Video 1.

3. Trim the left side of the clip to a point just before your actor enters the scene. Drag the trimmed clip to the start of the timeline.

4. Place the assignment clip on Video 2 and trim it to a point just before your actor enters the right side. Drag it to the start of the timeline.

5. Open Transparency for the clip on Video 2 and select Image Matte.

6. Click Choose and locate and select Split Screen Matte.

7. Preview your split screen by clicking the page peel icon and dragging the slider. As shown in Figure 15.26, your actor should enter the scene from both sides, hang around, wave to his/her other self, and then walk off.

There's a 50% chance that when you preview your split screen you will not see your actor on *either* side of the screen. That's because the black and white halves of your split screen are on the wrong sides. No worries. Either fix it the hard way by swapping clips (move the clip on Video 1 to Video 2 and vice versa) and then reapply the image matte or take the easy way out and click the Reverse Key check box.

FIGURE 15.26

Using a split-screen image matte lets you use the same actor playing two parts at once.

15

Obviously this takes some planning. The actor can't cross the centerline, for instance. The lighting can't change from one shot to the next, and there can't be any movement in the middle of the scene that might fall on the centerline.

Using a Difference Matte

This "matte" behaves more like a key. As with a split-screen matte, the difference matte lets you tape an actor working in one spot in the scene and then tape the same or another actor working in another section at a different time. It doesn't have to be distinctly left and right sides. Also, you can have multiple actors.

Here's how it works: Using a locked-down camera to avoid any movement, you tape a scene with a static background and later create a still image—the difference matte—from a segment when no actors are in the scene. Then you apply that difference matte to video clips *with* action and use it to look for matching areas in order to remove the background. When completed, you'll have a collection of clips of just actors over black (transparent) backgrounds. Then you place the static background image on Video 1 and composite all the actors onto it.

If you've seen the Eddy Murphy film *Dr. Doolittle 2* (hey, I'm the father of a seven year old), you've seen technology like this in action. In one scene they had a couple dozen animals all paying rapt attention to another animal. Those animals weren't all there at the same time. The production crew filmed them in several takes at different times and then combined them using technology like the difference matte.

Task: Work with a Difference Matte

Try it out by following these steps:

1. You could use the clips already on the timeline, but it's easier to start fresh. Therefore, clear the timeline and place the assignment clip on Video 2 (*not* Video 1).

2. Move the edit line to a section of the clip on Video 2 where there is no action taking place. You'll use that scene for your still image.

3. To create a still image, go to the main menu and select File, Export Timeline, Frame. Navigate to the Scratch Disk file folder, name the image something such as Difference Matte, and click Save. The default settings should work fine.

4. This should pop up a clip view window in your workspace. You don't want to place that image on your timeline just yet, so just close that window.

5. Open the Transparency Settings dialog box for the clip on Video 2 and select Difference Matte.

6. Click Choose and find and select your difference matte still image.

7. You're going to use that still image to key *out* the static background. Check the Reverse Key box. Use the slider below the Sample screen to move into the clip far enough to see your actor enter the scene; then use the Similarity slider to fine-tune the removal of the background. In a perfect world the background would disappear, leaving only the actor. As you can see in Figure 15.27, glitches are common.

8. Place your assignment clip on Video 3 and trim it to the point where your actor enters from the other side of the scene.

9. Apply the difference matte to it, use the slider beneath the Sample screen to show both actors at once, and use the Similarity slider to fine-tune the keying.

10. Place the difference matte still image on Video 1 and drag its edges to make it long enough to match the action on the two clips above it.

FIGURE 15.27
Using a difference matte on two clips frequently creates jagged edges in the actor(s).

Preview your project. You should see something akin to the split screen you worked on earlier. But you'll probably notice that this is far from a flawless process. Working with two clips means experimenting to find a compromise Similarity setting that allows the actors in both clips to look reasonably sharp.

You can use a difference matte to place an actor or object over a different background. But that's really the wrong technology for that effect. If you tape actors in front of a static setting, you probably want to use that setting in the final cut. If you want to place your actors into a *different* background, you might as well tape your actors in front of a blue or green screen.

Difference mattes take a very controlled and simple background to pull off. In most cases you might want to stick to split screens or blue/green screens.

> One way to see a more accurate preview of any matte or key is to create a brightly colored matte (yes, the terms can be confusing) and temporarily place it on Video 1 instead of on your planned background clip. As a reminder, to create a solid-color matte, right/Option-click inside the Project window and select New, Color Matte. Select a color, name it, and save it. It'll appear in the Project window.

Using a Garbage Matte

The garbage matte is so named because you use it to get rid of garbage in your image. This is a very simple matte. You won't find it in the Transparency Settings drop-down menu. You create it by moving the four corners in the Transparency Settings dialog box's Sample screen.

I'll just show you an example. In one of my Chroma key shots there is some video noise around the edges of the frame. You can see it in Figure 15.28.

FIGURE 15.28

Use the garbage matte to remove noise or other unwanted items from the edges of your keyed clips.

To replace that noise with a transparency, I simply drag those four screen corners to cover it up—or to cover up at least part of it. This is an inexact process because you can work only with four straight lines. You can't fine-tune it by grabbing a line midway between two points and adding a new "handle."

You also can't use keyframes to adjust the size and shape of this box over time. It works well with a blue/green screen shot where you have a boom microphone off to one side and you want to remove it from the scene.

Summary

Alpha channels and mattes round out Premiere's compositing tools. Graphics frequently have alpha channels built in. Premiere "switches on" those alpha channels, creating distinct, easy-to-use transparencies. Mattes come in several styles. The most common is a simple black-and-white graphic. When applied to a clip it makes portions transparent and other areas opaque.

Workshop

Review the questions and answers in this section to try to sharpen your Premiere alpha channel and matte compositing skills. Also, take a few moments to tackle my short quiz and the exercises.

Q&A

Q I want to use the QuickTime Cloud and Fire effects on a clip, but when I apply them to the clip all I see is the effect. My clip disappears. What's up?

A The QuickTime Cloud and Fire video effects create their own animated clip. Basically whatever clip you apply them to merely tells these effects how long to run. To use them with a clip, you need to apply them to a separate clip. It can be any clip, but to simplify things, create a color matte and apply the effects to it. That clip needs to be on a superimposing video track above the background clip on the timeline.

Q I tried using the difference matte but when I move the Similarity slider, my actor disappears, not the background scene. Why?

A The difference matte is an odd duck. It looks for *differences* between two images and removes them. But that's not what you want to do. You want to remove *similarities*. Therefore, check the Reverse Key box to do just that.

Quiz

1. When would you use a black or white alpha matte instead of an alpha channel transparency?

2. If black areas of an alpha channel are transparent, why is black text on a graphic with an alpha channel opaque?

3. What's the difference between an image matte and a track matte?

Quiz Answers

1. Most graphic images with alpha channels have *straight* alpha channels. When you use Alpha Channel Transparency on them, the edges of the graphics will be sharply detailed. Use black or white alpha mattes for graphics with *premultiplied* alpha channels—black for graphics with black backgrounds; white for white backgrounds.

15

2. The color of the graphic does not set opacity. The color of the alpha channel does. Typically artists create graphics and build an alpha channel stencil to match the graphic's borders. In that alpha channel layer, areas beneath the graphic are white to ensure the graphic remains opaque no matter what color it is.

3. You apply an image matte directly to a clip by opening that clip's Transparency Settings dialog box, selecting Image Matte, and choosing a matte. Using a track matte is sort of an indirect process. You place it on a video track directly above the clip to which you want to apply it. Then you open that clip's Transparency Settings dialog box and select Track Matte. You don't need to choose the matte because Premiere knows you're referring to whatever image is on the next higher track. You use track mattes to create traveling or moving mattes.

Exercises

1. Create a four-segment split screen. That means making three mattes with black covering three-quarters of each one. Then place the same person/object in each quadrant of the same scene.

2. Create a track/traveling matte that actually follows action. You'll need to make a matte with a simple shape—a black rectangle for instance. Put a clip with something moving through it on Video 1 and a color matte on Video 2. Place the matte on Video 3. Apply a track matte transparency to the Video 2 clip. Apply motion to the matte on Video 3. You'll need to view the clip in the Motion Settings preview window and add keyframes using the Motion Settings timeline. I'll go over this in detail in Hour 16. Good luck.

3. Tape a clear blue sky and then use the QuickTime Cloud video effect several times to add multiple clouds to it. Give each cloud motion to have them all move through the scene with the semblance of coordinated behavior.

HOUR 16

Tips, Tricks, and Techniques: Part 1

In this hour and the next I'm going to take things beyond the scope of most Premiere how-to books. In this hour I'll present four special editing concepts along with five expert tips from an Adobe corporate evangelist. In the next hour I'll offer up a bunch of nifty Premiere usability tips, my favorite keyboard shortcuts, and some fast and fun editing tricks.

These are the kinds of tools that experienced editors frequently use. But if you've never seen them in action you probably wouldn't come up with them on your own. Once you do try them out, you'll find myriad ways to apply them to your projects.

The topics this hour include the following:

- Highlighting a portion of a clip
- Following action using track mattes and clipped clips
- Multiple uses for virtual clips: two transitions at once, two special effects, and fine-tuning keys

- Using split screens for mirrored, animated effects
- Expert tips from an Adobe evangelist

Highlighting a Portion of Your Clip

Frequently you'll want to draw attention to something within your clip. You may want to apply a graphic or super there or highlight an object or person. You do that by putting the same clip on Video 1 and Video 2, using an image matte on the clip on Video 2 to highlight a portion of the clip, and applying a video effect to the clip on Video 2 to make the matted section of your clip stand out.

Task: Highlight a Portion of Your Clip

How you choose to highlight your clip is up to you. You'll see what I mean as I take you through this task. The fundamental process works for a variety of situations. In this case I'll go over how to change the color of a portion of your clip so you when you add text it stands out from the image. Here are the steps:

1. Find a brief scene—15 seconds or so—that does not have much action in it and drag that clip to Video 1 and to Video 2. To work well for this effect both clips must be lined up perfectly. Figure 16.1 demonstrates what I mean. With Snap to Edges switched on, that's a simple feat.

FIGURE 16.1

To highlight a location on a clip, start the process by placing that clip on both Video 1 and Video 2.

2. Use the Title Designer or a graphics program to create a matte. Because you will put text within a portion of your clip, a rounded rectangle will define that area nicely. Something along the lines of the one shown in Figure 16.2. Adding a gray border is a nice touch.

Figure 16.2

A rounded rectangle matte works well to frame text.

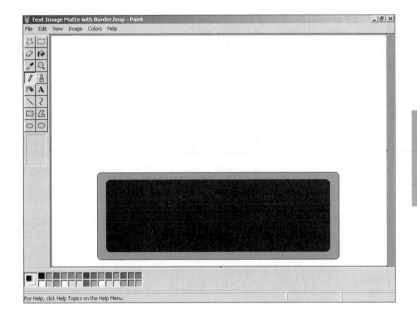

If you use a graphics program to create your matte, set its screen size to match your Project Settings. This way you avoid having Premiere distort the shape when it automatically makes your matte graphic fit the aspect ratio of your project.

If you're using NTSC DV, you probably set a frame size of 720×480. To confirm that, select Project, Project Setting, General for the main menu and note the Frame Size setting in the Current Settings dialog box.

3. Apply the QuickTime video effect to the clip on Video 2. Select Color Tint and Other in the drop-down menu.

4. As shown in Figure 16.3, you have two tinting options: You can select a color to apply to light pixels in your clip and a color to apply to dark pixels. Once these are selected, adjust the Brightness and Contrast settings. The object is to keep things bright enough so you still can see the images on the video clip through the tinting. Click OK.

FIGURE 16.3

Use QuickTime Color Tint to change the appearance of the clip on Video 2.

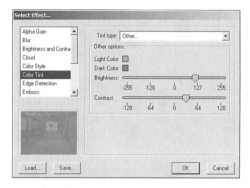

5. Open the Transparency Settings for the clip on Video 2. Select Image Matte from the Key Type drop-down menu and choose the matte you created for this task.

6. Preview it in the Sample screen. What you'll see is probably not what you expected. As illustrated in Figure 16.4, most of the image shows the QuickTime Color Tint effect. Only the area inside the matte remains unchanged. That's because the black oval in the matte is transparent and lets that portion of the clip on Video 1 show through. The rest of the matte is white (opaque) and displays the clip on Video 2, the one you altered with the QuickTime Color Tint effect.

FIGURE 16.4

The rounded rectangle transparency in the image matte is the only region not displaying the QuickTime Color Tint effect.

7. Remedy that by checking the Reverse Key box.

You can avoid this minor Reverse Key inconvenience by creating a matte with a white (opaque) oval and a black (transparent) background.

Alternatively, you can put the video effects on the clip on Track 1. Generally, though, Video 1 is where you perform the fewest effects. It serves as the base for your project, so the rule of thumb is to put effects on clips in the superimposing tracks.

8. Create text to fit within the box. Using Premiere's Title Designer is your best bet because you can see the composited effect within the Title Designer window and position your text accordingly. An example is shown in Figure 16.5. You do all this by moving the edit line to the scene, opening the Title Designer, and selecting Show Video. Create your graphic using the clip as a reference. If you want to select a different scene, you can type in a program time next to the Show Video check box.

FIGURE 16.5

Using Show Video within Premiere's Title Designer lets you accurately position your text over the rounded rectangle matte.

9. Save your text file (File, Save). It'll appear in your Project window. Drag the text to Video 3. As a reminder, if you need to create an additional video track, right/Option-click the timeline and select Add Video Track. Extend the end(s) of the text clip to make it the same length as the two clips.

10. Preview your project. It should look something like Figure 16.6.

FIGURE 16.6

Your project should end up looking something like this.

▼ 11. Now for a nice finishing touch. Fade up both the Rounded Rectangle effect and the text. As I've illustrated in Figure 16.7, you want the Rectangle effect to fade up slightly ahead of the text then have the text fade out slightly before the Rectangle effect.

12. Expand both Video 2 and Video 3.

13. Select the opacity rubberband for each in turn. Add handles a second or so after the start and before the end. Note their relative positions in Figure 16.7. The text fades up just after the Rectangle effect.

▲ 14. Drag the start and end handles to the bottom—0% opacity.

That's it. Preview this effect. This is a great way to place supers in a clip.

FIGURE 16.7

Use the opacity rub-
berbands to fade in the
Rectangle effect and
the text and then to
fade them out.

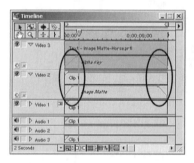

Experiment with other video effects to highlight the portion of the clip in the rectangle. A soft focus works well. Black & White and Sepia are both effective.

Following Action with Traveling Mattes

This method is an exciting way to focus attention on action. It takes the same basic approach as the previous task, only this time you'll use a track matte. The reason: You want to put that matte in motion.

Task: Follow Action with Traveling Mattes

To accomplish this effect, follow these steps:

▼ 1. Keep your previous project in the timeline. You'll need it in a moment.

2. Select a clip that has something moving around in it—for instance, a racecar coming out of a turn and down the straightaway, someone walking down a street, or an aerobatic plane doing loops. As with the previous task, place the clip on both Video 1 and Video 2, either ahead of your previous project (automatically sliding it to the right) or after it.

▼ 3. Give the clip on Video 2 a distinctive look, like the effect you created in the first task. You can choose to apply one or more video effects or you can borrow what you came up with earlier (see tip).

To reuse an effect applied to a different clip:

1. Right/Option-click the clip with the effect.

2. Select Copy.

3. Right/Option-click the clip you want to apply the effect to and select Paste Attributes. To apply the effects globally to all the clips on a track, use the Track Select tool to select a track and then select Edit, Paste Attributes. As illustrated in Figure 16.8, this opens a dialog box. You can select Content or Settings. Content deals with in- and out-points.

4. Choose Settings and, in this case, select only Filters and Fade Control. You're going to use a different transparency setting—Track Matte instead of Image Matte—and there are no motion settings to transfer.

5. Click Paste. Check how it worked by opening the Transparency Settings dialog box for your action clip and expanding the video track to see the opacity rubberband.

   You may note that the fade control (the opacity rubberband) doesn't exactly duplicate what you created in the first task. Unless the two clip lengths match exactly, the handles will fall in different locations. That's OK. You'll just slide them to the correct spots later.

16

FIGURE 16.8

The Paste Attributes dialog box lets you duplicate effects applied to other clips.

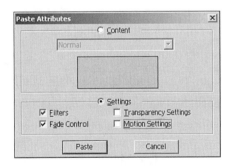

▼ 4. Create a matte with a square black box (if you want to skip that Reverse Key thing, create a white box on a black background). The box should take up about the size of the object you want to highlight. No need to be precise. You'll use the Motion Settings dialog box to fine-tune it.

▼

Just for a change of pace, in this exercise you may not want to use the Reverse Key box. Leaving it off means most of the screen will take on the video effect you applied to the clip on Track 2. Only the track matte box, which is going to follow the onscreen action, will have normal color. This, too, can be an excellent, eye-catching effect.

5. Import your matte to your project and drag it to Video 3. Extend it to match the length of your action clip.

6. Open the Transparency Settings dialog box for the clip on Video 2 and select Track Matte. If needed, click Reverse Key and preview your effect. As shown in Figure 16.9, there should be a box displaying your effect in the Sample screen.

FIGURE 16.9

With Track Matte selected, your video effect should show up in the matte box on the Sample screen.

7. The purpose here is to have the box follow the onscreen action. Open the Motion Settings dialog box for the track matte on Video 3. Make sure Show All and Alpha: Use Clip's are checked.

8. This is where things get a little tricky. You need to play and pause the clip in the preview window. With each pause, click the timeline to create a new handle. That puts a little highlight on the new handle in the Motion Path window to help you locate it.

9. Drag that new handle to center the track matte box over the object in motion. Do that until you have enough points to create a smooth path. As shown in Figure 16.10, I needed six handles in addition to the start- and endpoints to define a smooth path.

10. As the object moves through the frame, it probably changes size relative to the track matte box. You may need to gradually increase or decrease that box's area. Do that by clicking each handle within the timeline and changing the zoom percentage to adjust the box size. I've highlighted this in Figure 16.10. I changed mine from 50% to 130% over the duration of the clip.

FIGURE 16.10

Applying motion settings to the track matte lets you follow the action.

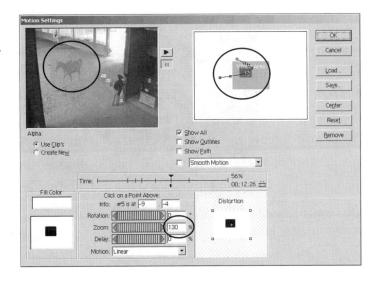

16

That should do it. Preview your project. The square track matte should follow the action in your clip.

As with all things Premiere, there is another way to use a moving box to follow action: by using the Clip video effect. I'll give you a barebones explanation and leave the details for you to wrestle with.

Just as you did with a track matte, place identical clips on Video 1 and Video 2. Apply Clip to the clip on Video 2. Leave the default fill color black (you'll key it out later). As shown in Figure 16.11, turn on keyframes by clicking the empty box to the right of the *f*.

Slide the edges of the screen in to form a box around the moving subject. Move the edit line forward a bit and adjust the box location. Do that enough times to create a smooth path for your moving box.

Open the Transparency Settings dialog box for the clip on Video 2, select Chroma Key, and use the Eyedropper tool to select the black border outside the clipped portion of your video clip.

As I've shown in Figure 16.12, there's no need to adjust the various sliders. Black keys out easily, and because you've applied a Tint effect to your clip, there should be no black in it that would become transparent.

FIGURE 16.11

Using the Clip video effect with keyframes is another way to highlight an object—in motion or static.

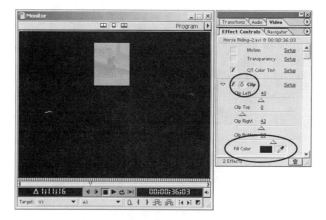

FIGURE 16.12

There's no need to move the sliders because black keys out easily.

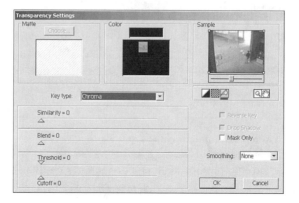

Obscuring Someone's Identity

This in another use for a traveling/track matte. Take a look at Figure 16.13. I used a simple round track matte and applied both the Crystallize and Mosaic video effects. Other options are simply a black oval and a Blur effect.

FIGURE 16.13

Obscure someone's identity by using a track/traveling matte and a combination of Crystallize and Mosaic.

16

Using Virtual Clips

Virtual clips can be a difficult concept to grasp—and knowing when to use them can be even more confusing.

A virtual clip is a segment of your project stored away on the timeline for future use. It can consist of all the usual editing tools and media you use elsewhere in your project: clips, audio, images, effects, transitions, and mattes.

You'll create a virtual clip for one of a variety of reasons:

- To use the same segment several times
- To apply different settings to the same clip in various locations in your project
- To create two or more transitions between the same two clips.

The following task provides an example of the latter.

Task: Create Multiple Transitions Between the Same Two Clips

To create two or more transitions between the same two clips, follow these steps:

1. Place two clips consecutively on Video 1. If you need to make adjustments to create tail and head room to make a smooth transition, do that.

2. Apply an obvious transition to them, such as Cube Spin. It's in the Transitions 3D Motion file folder. As a reminder, all you need to do is drag Cube Spin to the junction of the two clips and drop it there. No need in this case to adjust any settings.

▼   3. Preview the transition. One scene should appear to push the other away from left to right.

If you were to apply another transition to those clips, it would replace Cube Spin, not work in conjunction with it. To make two transitions work together, you need to create two virtual clips.

4. Click the Block Select tool. I've highlighted it in Figure 16.14. Use it to draw a box around the clip on the left, making sure the right side of the Block Select border falls right between the two clips. Snap to Edges should make that easy. I've highlighted this in Figure 16.15.

FIGURE 16.14
Use the Block Select tool to make virtual clips.

FIGURE 16.15
Carefully set the border of your virtual clip right on the junction between the two clips.

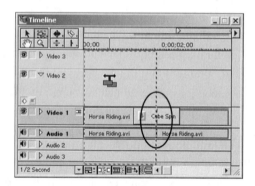

5. Release the mouse button and note that the cursor turns into a double arrow. Click and drag that double arrow and its highlighted clip to another track. Premiere will rename it "Virtual Clip." Note the times for the in- and out-points of the original clip.

6. Do the same thing for the second clip, making sure you set the left side of the Block Select border right on the junction between the two clips. Drag it to the right of the other virtual clip.

7. If you lined up the two virtual clips side by side, as they are in Figure 16.16, you can use the spacebar to play the timeline. The Cube Spin transition will play.

This ability to view a transition without previewing or rendering is a feature of virtual clips. The virtual clip plays as if it has been rendered or is in a preview mode. If you use the spacebar to play the original two clips with the Cube Spin transition in place, you will not see the transition.

FIGURE 16.16

Use the spacebar to play the two virtual clips—transition and all.

16

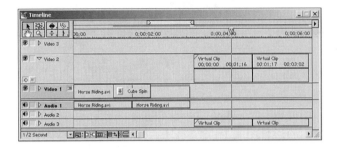

One of the confusing aspects of virtual clips is that they always remain connected to their original clips. If you change something about those original clips—add an effect, trim them, alter the transition—that will show up in the virtual clip(s). If you place a virtual clip in several locations within your project, the changes will show up in all instances.

To see that in action, go back to the original two clips and lengthen the transition from the default 30 frames (one second) to something longer. Do that by right/Option-clicking the transition, selecting Duration, and typing in a new time. Now go to the virtual clips and play them, and the transition time will equal what you just typed in.

8. Drag the two virtual clips to Video 1. I want you to add another transition to them, and Premiere allows transitions only on Video 1.

9. Drag Page Peel (from the `Page Peel Transitions` folder) to the junction between the two virtual clips and then preview your double transition. It should look something like Figure 16.17.

Using the spacebar will not play a new transition placed between two virtual clips. You need to make another virtual clip to do that. That's a so-called "nested virtual clip" (a virtual clip within a virtual clip).

FIGURE **16.17**

Using virtual clips makes it possible to apply two transitions to the same two clips.

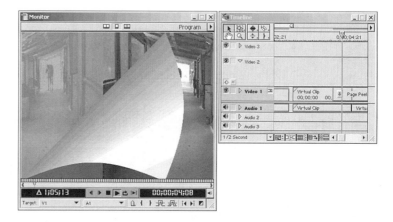

Using Virtual Clips to Enhance Two Special Effects

The Echo video effect disables all effects applied above it (before it) in the Effect Controls palette. Frequently you want to apply some other effects before using Echo. An excellent workaround is to use a virtual clip.

First, apply the effects that you want to precede Echo, create a virtual clip, and then apply Echo—and any other effects after it—to that virtual clip.

Task: Use Virtual Clips with the Echo Video Effect

▼ TASK

Try this:

1. Clear the timeline and place a clip with some action in it on Video 1.

2. Apply just about any video effect to that clip. I chose Invert. It reverses color or luminance information, creating a color negative (inverse) effect. In Figure 16.18 I selected HLS (Hue, Lightness, and Saturation). I like setting the Blend With value percentage to something greater than 60% for a nice color mix.

3. Drag Echo to the Effect Controls palette. It will immediately switch off whatever video effect you already applied. Echo causes Premiere to ignore all effects applied before it.

4. A virtual clip will remedy that. Before creating one, remove Echo by selecting its name in the Effect Controls palette and clicking the garbage can icon at the bottom right of the palette.

5. Click the Block Select tool, drag it around the clip with an effect applied to it, and drag the double-headed arrow to another location. In my case, as you can see in Figure 16.19, I dragged it just a bit farther to the right on Video 1.

▼

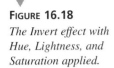

FIGURE 16.18

The Invert effect with Hue, Lightness, and Saturation applied.

FIGURE 16.19

Drag the virtual clip to another location on the timeline.

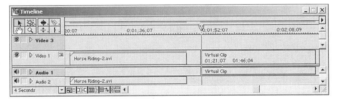

6. Apply Echo to the virtual clip. To make sure that Echo is actually working, set Number of Echoes to about 4 and reduce Starting Intensity to about 0.25. It should have a look and feel that approximates what you see in Figure 16.20.

> As a reminder, to avoid creating an overly bright Echo effect, the starting intensity should be about equal to one divided by the number of echoes (1 / 4 = 0.25).

7. Preview your work. Echo no longer trumps effects applied before it. And now you can add even more effects.

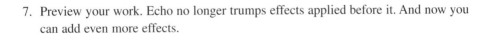

FIGURE 16.20

Using a virtual clip lets you apply Echo to a clip with another effect already on it.

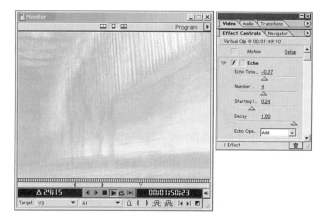

Task: Use Virtual Clips with the Texturize Video Effect

The Texturize video effect will not work with motion settings. But there are many times when you might want to add motion to a texturized effect. Once again, a virtual clip can fix that. Here's how:

1. Place a graphic on Video 1. Apply motion settings to the graphic. As I've done in Figure 16.21, have it move across the screen and spin around a couple times.

FIGURE 16.21

Apply motion settings to a graphic to prepare to demonstrate another use for a virtual clip.

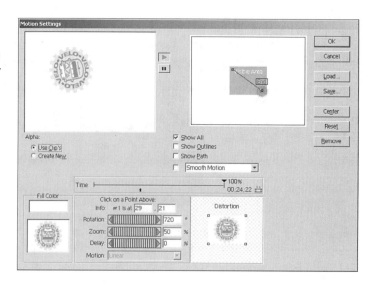

2. Place a video clip on Video 2. Because the clip is opaque, you will not see the graphic on Video 1.

3. Extend the graphic clip on Video 1 to match the length of the clip on Video 2.

4. Apply Texturize to the clip on Video 2. As I've demonstrated in Figure 16.22, select V1A as the location of the clip you're applying texture to and increase the Texture Contrast setting to enhance the effect.

16

V1A stands for the Video 1A track. However, you are not using A/B editing, so Premiere recognizes that V1A is the same as the Video 1 track.

FIGURE 16.22
Give Texturize higher contrast to further emphasize a graphic.

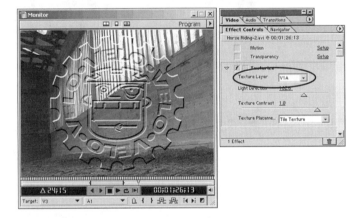

5. Preview this effect. The graphic remains stationary. Texturize turns off the motion settings in the clip it applies texture to.

6. Fix that by creating a virtual clip. Slide the clip on Video 2 out of the way. You need to do this because the Block Select tool surrounds all clips on all tracks above and below the selected clip. Then, as I've illustrated in Figure 16.23, drag the Block Select tool around the graphic on Video 1 (it should still have motion settings applied to it) and drag this virtual clip to some open space on the timeline.

7. Switch back to the Selection tool (use the V hotkey or click the Arrow icon in the toolbox) and then drag that virtual clip back to Video 1. Line up the clip on Video 2 above the virtual clip. It should still have Texturize applied to it.

8. Preview your effect. Now the logo should follow the spinning motion path and have a look and feel similar to that in Figure 16.24.

FIGURE **16.23**

*Create a virtual clip to
preserve motion set-
tings.*

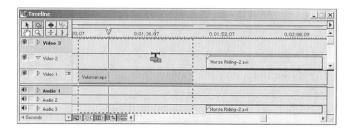

FIGURE **16.24**

*Use a virtual clip to
create a texturized
graphic with motion
settings.*

Fine-tuning Keys with a Virtual Clip

Keying can be hit or miss. Frequently you'll be hard pressed to remove pixels near the
edges of the subject you want to key over a background. Other times "hotspots"—
unevenly lit areas of your green/blue screen—will not key out. Creating a virtual clip to
apply a key twice can help. It's not a guarantee, but it frequently makes the difference
between unusable and acceptable.

Task: Fine-tune Keys with a Virtual Clip

To fine-tune keys with a virtual clip, follow these steps:

1. Use a clip from the assignment number one back in Hour 14, "Compositing Part 1:
   Layering Images and Clips." That called for you to tape a subject in front of a
   solid—and differently colored—backdrop. Drag that clip to Video 2.

2. Drag a background to Video 1.

▲ TASK

Instead of a video clip background, consider using a color matte. This gives you a more accurate representation of how well your key is working. As a reminder, to make a color matte, right/Option-click a white area in the Project window, select New, Color Matte, select a color, give your matte a descriptive name, and click OK. The matte will appear in your Project window.

16

3. Open the Transparency Settings dialog box for the clip on Video 2 and apply a color-based key: Chroma, RGB Difference, Blue/Green Screen, or Non-Red.

4. Adjust the slider(s) as well as you can without impacting the subject. My example in Figure 16.25 has a hotspot that does not key out without creating a transparency in the subject. Click OK.

FIGURE **16.25**

A first-time application of an RGB key shows a hotspot on the green screen.

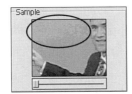

You might try different keys. RGB Difference might work better than Green Screen, depending on how closely your green screen matches true chroma green.

5. Drag the background clip away from under the keyed clip on Video 2. As I've shown in Figure 16.26, don't take it too far. You'll use it again in a moment.

6. Use the Block Select tool to drag a border around the keyed clip and drag that newly created virtual clip right above the background clip. Figure 16.26 shows how your timeline should look now.

FIGURE **16.26**

Slide the background color matte a little to one side so you can place the virtual clip over it to apply another key.

7. Apply transparency to the virtual clip. Note that when you open the Effect Controls palette, the Transparency box is not checked. This is a virtual clip, so you can apply transparency to it as if you hadn't done it in the original clip.

8. Use the same key you used in the original clip and attempt to key out the remaining unkeyed region. In Figure 16.27, I managed to key out most of the hotspot left unkeyed in the original clip.

FIGURE 16.27

Applying the RGB key a second time to a virtual clip cleans up most of poorly keyed portion of the original key.

If you carefully adjusted Similarity or other values in the original clip so there was almost no unkeyed area left, you might not be able to use the Eyedropper tool in the virtual clip to select a color to key out. Therefore, go easy on the first attempt.

Because you're working on a virtual clip, you may extend the background under both clips and readjust the keying in the original clip to give your Eyedropper tool a larger area to find a color to key out. Those changes will show up in the virtual clip. Once you've selected a color in the virtual clip to key out, you can go back to the original clip and tighten up the key there.

Using Split Screens for Animated Mirror Effects

Premiere has a Mirror video effect, so why use a split screen to create an animated mirrored effect? Because they're not the same. The Mirror effect divides a clip along a user-defined line and mirrors that portion of the screen.

The split-screen mirror you're about to try out will take an entire animated graphic (not just half of it) and create a mirrored version plus throw in some different image characteristics on the mirrored version. The Mirror video effect pales in comparison.

Before having you tackle a somewhat involved, hands-on animated split-screen mirrored effect, here are a couple quick examples.

Garbage Matte Split-Screen Mirrored Effect

Figure 16.28 shows a split screen I created using a garbage matte. Here's how I did it:

FIGURE 16.28

A split-screen mirror created with a garbage matte.

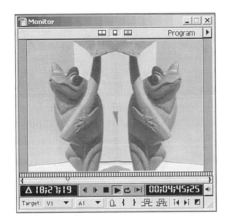

16

1. I placed the same clip on Video 1 and Video 2.

2. I used Camera View to flip the clip on Video 2 180 degrees along the vertical axis so it faced the other direction.

3. I used the Motion Settings dialog box to slide each clip to one side of the screen: the Video 1 clip to the left side, the Video 2 clip to the right. The Mirror effect cannot do this. It slices your image in two. As shown in Figure 16.29, I selected equal start- and end-points for each clip: -20,0 for Video 1 and 20,0 for Video 2.

FIGURE 16.29

Motion settings let you slide a clip to one side.

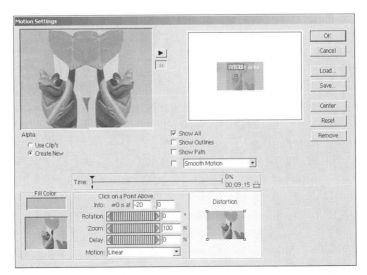

4. I opened the Transparency Settings dialog box for the clip on Video 2 and created a garbage matte by sliding the corners in the Sample screen, shown in Figure 16.30. That's it. No need to select a key type.

Unfortunately, the motion settings I applied to the clip on Video 1—sliding the clip off to one side—don't show up in the Sample screen. This is a Premiere anomaly. But in this case I know I simply want to divide the screen in half vertically.

FIGURE 16.30

The garbage matte's Sample screen does not display the Video 1 clip's motion settings.

Split-Screen Mirrored Effect Using an Image Matte

This example utilizes the exact same setup I used for the garbage matte split-screen mirrored effect.

Figure 16.31 shows the only differences. I applied the Image Matte key type, clicked Choose to select the split-screen matte used in Hour 15, "Compositing Part 2: Alpha Channels and Mattes," and dragged the garbage matte points in the Sample screen back to their respective corners. Done.

FIGURE 16.31

An image matte coupled with motion settings also can create a mirrored effect.

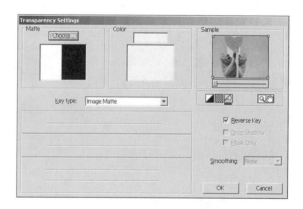

Split-Screen Mirrored Effect with Motion

Now for the trickier mirrored animation effect. This time I'd like you to try this out. You'll take a graphic, set it spinning, place another graphic above it spinning in the opposite direction, add video effects to each graphic and finally put them over a background.

Again, as with all things Premiere, there are several ways to accomplish this. This is just one I came up with.

16

Task: Create a Split-Screen Mirrored Effect with Motion

To create a split-screen mirrored effect with motion, follow these steps:

1. Your timeline should have at least three video tracks. If not, add a video track.

2. Place the `Veloman.eps` graphic from the Premiere `Sample` folder on Video 2 and Video 3. Place a clip to use for a background on Video 1. Adjust the lengths of all of them to about 10 seconds.

3. Input motion settings for the graphic on Video 2. You want to shrink it to half its size, spin it clockwise four times (set 1440 degrees on the endpoint), have it enter the left side of the screen and move off the right, and do that on the bottom half of the screen. As Figure 16.32 shows in part, I started the motion for the graphic running across the bottom of the screen at -55,15 and ended it at 55,15.

FIGURE 16.32

Use motion settings to roll the graphic across the screen.

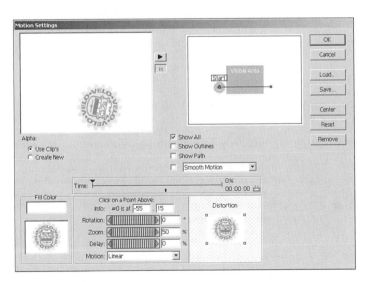

If you know you are going to use the same or very similar motion settings more than once, you can save these motion settings and apply them to another clip later. After completing the motions settings for the clip on Video 2, click Save, select your Scratch Disk project file folder as this file's location, and give your file a descriptive name. Click Save and then close the Motion Settings dialog box by clicking OK.

Open the Motion Settings dialog box for the graphic on Video 3, click Load, and select the motion settings file you just saved. Now simply change a few numbers—the y-axis number should now be -15, and the Rotation should be -1440 degrees. In Figure 16.33 I have already applied transparency to show you where I'm going with this exercise.

FIGURE 16.33

Changing only two numbers from positive to negative changes the location of the graphic and rotates it counter-clockwise.

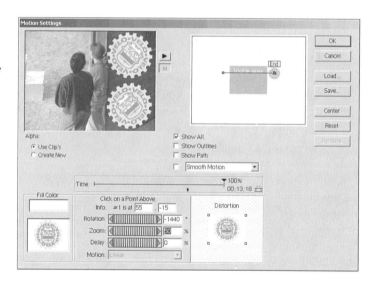

4. Apply transparency to both clips. By applying motion to these clips and accepting the default—Use Clip's Alpha (Channel)—you'll discover that when you open Transparency, the white alpha matte should already have been applied. Click OK.

5. Now apply a different video effect to each clip. Something to give them some unusual color or appearance. I chose Tiles and Wave.

6. Preview your effect. It should look something like Figure 16.34.

FIGURE 16.34

Two graphics with mirrored motion and different video effects playing over a background. You cannot do this with the Mirror video effect.

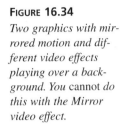

Tips from an Adobe Expert

From database integration for AT&T to digital image retouching and graphic design for advertisements in *Newsweek* and *Time*, Daniel Brown has balanced a passion for right- and left-brain abilities. Daniel formed the Web development team at Metagraphics in Palo Alto, California, (now Artmachine.com) with clients such as Apple, Netscape, Sun, Silicon Graphics, and Hewlett Packard. In 1998, Daniel joined Adobe systems in the role of "evangelist," lending a hand in product development, marketing, interface design, and customer education. He is a frequent speaker at industry events worldwide and has taught classes at Santa Fe Digital Workshops, Anderson Ranch in Aspen, Colorado, and the Pacific Imaging Center in Makawao, Hawaii. Daniel currently handles Adobe After Effects, Adobe Premiere, and Adobe LiveMotion.

Daniel Brown, Sr. Evangelist, DV/Motion Graphics, **Adobe Systems, Inc.**

Here are five of Brown's favorite Premiere tips:

Using the `Project-Archive` folder—If you accidentally erase or completely mess up a project file, don't panic. Every time you save a project, Premiere saves over the file you're currently working on, but it will also save a copy of the previous version in its `Project-Archive` folder. Depending on the installation, it may be in your `Documents` folder (see Figure 16.35) or the folder that holds the actual application. Project files are tiny compared to video files, and they're worth any extra disk space they occupy. In Edit, Preferences, AutoSave and Undo, you can specify how many versions of a single project Premiere will keep an archive of (up to 100) as well as the total number of archives Premiere will keep (up to 1,000). To restore an archived project, select File, Open and then navigate to the `Project-Archive` folder and select a project.

Docking palettes—Few people know about this trick, but it's making its way through most of the Adobe applications. If you drag a palette's folder tabs—Transitions, Effect Controls, Navigator, and so on—to the bottom edge of another palette, they will "dock" vertically (that is, they will all be visible but will move as one piece). This is great for managing screen real estate because moving one palette moves the others with it. In Figure 16.36, I've docked all eight palette folders. If you minimize the palette, it looks like Figure 16.37. Then, double-clicking a file folder opens only that folder. Double-clicking it again closes it. If you don't want a file folder in your docked group, drag its tab out of the palette. It'll form its own palette. Click the little × in the upper-right corner to send it on its way.

Selecting multiple clips in the source window—You can select multiple clips in the Project window, drag them to the Source window, and, as illustrated in Figure 16.38, choose from among them in the drop-down menu. To clear a clip from that Source window drop-down menu, use Crtl+Backspace (Windows) or Command+Delete (Mac). This will delete the currently visible clip and move the others up the list (so subsequent deletes will remove the later clips) .

Using an export bin—If you would like to use the same collection of clips in another project, Premiere allows you to export the contents of a bin to a text file. It won't look like a text file, but it is. As shown in Figure 16.39, with the bin selected, go to the Project menu and choose Export Bin from Project. For those with power shortcut tendencies, you can right/Option-click on a particular bin and use the contextual menu to export the contents. To open the bin, open it within Premiere using the File, Open command. When opened, the bin will exist in its own window. You can drag and drop the bin or its contents to your current Project window.

Using a master clip—Double-clicking a trimmed clip in the timeline will open that edited clip in the Source Monitor screen. But the cooler trick is to use Shift+Ctrl-double-click (Windows) or Shift+Command-double-click (Mac) to open the *master* clip in the Source Monitor screen with the current clip's in- and out-points displayed. I've highlighted those elements in Figure 16.40. Using the Source Monitor you can shift those edit markers to create new in- and out-points and drag that trimmed segment from the Source Monitor screen to a different spot in the timeline. This is a very easy way to pull more than one segment from a master clip.

FIGURE 16.35

Navigate to this folder to open a previous version of a current project.

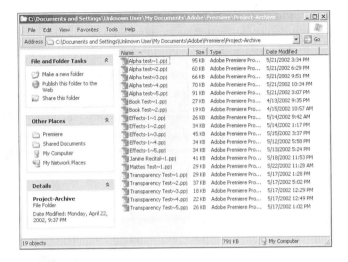

FIGURE 16.36

Docked palettes put all of Premiere's effects in one handy spot.

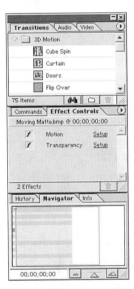

FIGURE 16.37

Double-clicking an open folder minimizes the palette.

16

FIGURE **16.38**

Drag several clips to the Source window and then access them using this drop-down list.

FIGURE **16.39**

If you plan to use the same media files in another project, save the project bin holding those files using the Export Bin from Project command.

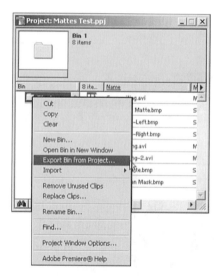

FIGURE **16.40**

Using a keyboard/mouse short-cut you can open the master clip in the Source Monitor screen, change the trim points, and add it to the time-line.

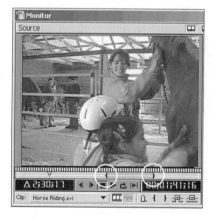

Summary

Experienced Premiere users typically have a few editing tricks up their sleeves. Unless you see them at work, you may not come up with them yourself. In this hour I've explained a few of them: highlighting an area of your clip using a matte and a video effect, following action with a track matte or a clipped clip, using virtual clips to circumvent editing roadblocks, and creating mirrored clips with animations and video effects thrown in. And it never hurts to have an Adobe evangelist toss in a few tricks. My favorite is the docking palettes tip. It's a standard part of my workspace setup.

16

Workshop

Review the questions and answers in this section to try to sharpen your Premiere editing tricks. Also, take a few moments to tackle my short quiz and the exercises.

Q&A

Q I used an image matte to highlight a portion of a clip. I wanted the highlighted portion to be in a soft focus, but it's in sharp focus and the rest of the clip is blurred. Why?

A You need to use the Reverse Key option in the Transparency Settings dialog box. The black portion of your matte is transparent and is letting the clip on Video 1 show through. Selecting Reverse Key makes the black area opaque and the white regions transparent, thus creating the desired effect.

Q I made a virtual clip, changed its settings, and then moved the original clip to a new location. Now the virtual clip looks different. What's up?

A Virtual clips reflect the current status of their original clip. If you change that original clip in any way, it will show up in all instances of that clip's virtual clips. That's why it's a good idea to create and keep the original clip in some unused portion of your timeline to keep it out of mischief.

Quiz

1. You know you're going to set the same general motion to a series of clips. What's the most efficient way to do that?

2. You plan to use the same effect(s) on a series of clips. Same issue. What's an efficient way to go about doing this?

3. Why don't you want to use the Mirror video effect to create a split screen with mirrored animated action?

Quiz Answers

1. Create your motion settings and then save them. Load them for each additional clip.

2. Here are two ways: Copy the clip (right/Option-click and select Copy) with the desired effect(s) and then paste the attributes to another clip (right/Option-click, Paste Attributes). Select Settings and then choose from among the four options. Once you've set which attributes to paste, you can use Paste Attributes Again without checking the various boxes.

3. Mirror is a wonderful video effect. It's easy to use and creates a perfect reflection, but it slices your clip into two equal halves. Unless your graphic is entirely on one side of the screen, Mirror will chop it down the middle. By creating a split screen and using motion settings to slide your clips off center, you can put an *entire* object on *both* sides of the screen. If it's a graphic, so much the better. You can use the Motion Settings dialog box to rotate it or use video effects to spin it in 3D space, all the while mirroring (or matching) the action of the same graphic on the other half of the screen. In addition, you can impart separate video effects on the individual graphics, adding more visual excitement.

Exercises

1. Highlight an area of a clip using an image or track matte. Then try out a number of different video effects—Blur, Tint, and inverted colors—on the clip on Video 2 as a means to alter it and make it stand out. Conversely, try to make it less prominent to allow something else—a graphic, logo, or text—to stand out on it.

2. Use nested virtual clips to create a "quad transition." Apply one transition to a clip. Make two virtual clips and then add another transition to it. Turn that into two more virtual clips, and so on, until you have four transitions playing at once. With each additional transition, increase the duration by two seconds. As a means to get a clearer picture of what's going on, choose Transitions with Borders and make the borders thick to further emphasize each transition. When you're done, go back and change the attributes of a couple transitions and see how that affects the final quad transition.

3. Create a split-screen mirrored animation on a diagonal. Use a graphic with an alpha channel (good-old Veloman.eps will do fine) and select Motion Settings to move the graphic following the diagonal line from the upper-left corner to the lower-right corner. You'll need to think through the start- and endpoints a bit more than when the graphic moved horizontally, but otherwise this should be fairly routine.

HOUR 17

Tips, Tricks, and Techniques: Part 2

Premiere's depth lends itself to discovery. Experienced editors frequently stumble across undocumented editing tricks that fall outside those described in the printed manual and online help file that accompany your copy of Premiere.

As many editors have before, you may stumble across some, heretofore unknown, alternate means to accomplish a routine task. You also might realize that a shortcut, intended for one use, may serve a more valuable, unexpected use.

For this hour's lesson I've assembled several tips, tricks, and techniques that fall outside most how-to guides. They should help you become a faster, more efficient and creative editor.

The highlights of this hour include the following:

- Handy keyboard shortcuts that you will come to rely on
- Productivity tips that will save you time and resolve minor annoyances
- Fun and fast editing tricks

Using Keyboard Shortcuts to Simplify Your Editing

I'm guessing that your copy of the Adobe Premiere Quick Reference Card is close at hand. In it are dozens of keyboard shortcuts, most of which you may never use.

Some take far too much effort. Consider that the Windows keyboard "shortcut" to clear a marker involves going to that marker on the timeline (that alone takes some time) and then pressing Ctrl+up arrow+C. It's easier to simply right-click the time display, select Clear Timeline Marker, and select a marker number. Your hands never need touch the keyboard.

That said, there are about a dozen shortcuts I use all the time.

Timeline Toolbox

The toolbox has eight containers. Some of those containers hold only one function—the Selection tool, for instance. Others have as many as five tools tucked away for your use. Each container has a single-letter keyboard shortcut. Nothing could be simpler.

Take a look at Figure 17.1, which shows the toolbox shortcut keys. For instance, you can press the V key to change the cursor to the Selection tool.

Take a close look and you'll notice five containers have tiny, nearly indistinguishable arrows in their lower-right corners. These are the containers that hold more than one tool. I've highlighted two of these arrows in Figure 17.1 and listed them in Table 17.1. Each time you press the keyboard shortcut for one of these containers, you cycle through its tools.

This is a huge timesaver. Instead of clicking and holding your selection cursor over a container, waiting for the fly-out icon menu, and then selecting a tool, the keyboard shortcut allows you simply to press a letter to rapidly select the tool you need.

The timeline has to be "active" for these shortcuts to work. To make it active, click somewhere inside it.

FIGURE 17.1

The timeline's toolbox with its eight single-letter shortcut keys. The five containers with tiny triangles in the lower-right corners hold multiple tools.

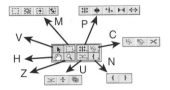

TABLE 17.1   Timeline Toolbox Keyboard Shortcuts

Shortcut	Tool(s)
V	Selection
M	Select tools, including Range, Block, Track, and Multitrack
P	Edit tools, including Rolling, Ripple, Rate Stretch, Slip, and Slide
C	Razor, Multiple Razor, and Fade Scissors
H	Hand
Z	Zoom (see the following tip)
U	Cross Fade, Fade Adjustment, and Link/Unlink
N	In-Point and Out-Point (see "Work Area Bar Shortcuts" for additional uses for the N key.)

Using the Zoom icon is the same as pressing "+" to zoom in on the timeline. Pressing Z brings up a plus sign (+) cursor, just like the one in the Sample screen in the Transparency Settings dialog box. What's more, Alt/Option-click switches the cursor to a minus sign (-) and zooms out with each click.

Work Area Bar Shortcuts

The work area bar resides at the top of the timeline. You use it to mark the portion of your project to render or export. Here are two useful shortcuts:

- You can double-click the work area bar to place "work area bar" endpoints at the edges of the visible timeline area (see Figure 17.2).

- You can press the N hotkey, as noted in Table 17.1, to cycle between the in- and out-point cursors. This action also performs an undocumented function: It lets you set the work area boundaries. Press N and then move the cursor to the work area bar. As highlighted in Figure 17.3, the cursor changes from an in- or out-point to a small triangle. Pressing N again cycles between the work area's in- and out-points. Pressing V switches the cursor back to the Selection tool.

FIGURE 17.2

Double-click the work area bar to place end-points within the visible timeline area.

FIGURE 17.3

The N hotkey switches on the work area in- and out-point cursors.

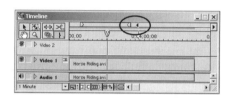

 Premiere turns on its tooltips by default, and I recommend you retain this feature. As you roll your cursor over a tool or button, a tooltip displays its name and keyboard shortcut. If tooltips do not appear, select Edit, Preferences, General and Still Image and then click the Show Tool Tips check box, highlighted in Figure 17.4.

FIGURE 17.4

Turn on tooltips by clicking the check box in the General and Still Image Preferences dialog box.

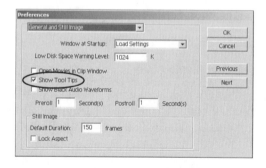

More Timeline Keyboard Shortcuts

Most of your work takes place in the timeline. In no time at all, the following shortcuts will become second nature to you:

The backslash (\) key—This is my most frequently used keyboard shortcut. Pressing the backslash key resizes the timeline to display your entire project. It's a great way to get a handle on where you are in the workflow.

Don't confuse the backslash (\) with the forward slash (/). Pressing the forward slash key deletes all frames between the in- and out-points on the Program Monitor. As shown in Figure 17.5, the timeline highlights that region with a gray area band on the time ruler under the work area bar.

That gray band sometimes appears for no obvious reason. One possible explanation is that you pressed the I and O keys —shortcuts that add in- and out-points, respectively, to the Program Monitor's timeline.

To get rid of those in- and out-points, press "G." Alternatively, you can press D to move the in-point to the beginning of the Program Monitor's timeline and F to move the out-point to the end. Doing both also will make the gray band disappear.

FIGURE 17.5

The gray band on the timeline notes the in- and out-points in the Program Monitor window.

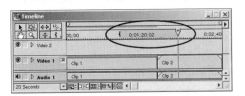

The J, K, and L keys—These, too, are great shortcuts. Normally, when working in the timeline, you play your project by pressing the spacebar. That's fine, but J, K, and L give you much more control.

The J key plays your project in reverse, the K key stops playback (as does pressing the spacebar), and the L key plays your project forward. What makes these shortcuts truly great is that pressing J or L two or three times incrementally speeds up playback.

The Home (or A) and End (or S) keys—When you're in the timeline, pressing the Home (or A) key places the edit line at the first frame of your project. Pressing End (or S) instantly moves the cursor to the last frame. Alternately, if you have a clip selected, Home/A and End/S move to the beginning and end of that clip, respectively.

The asterisk (*) key—While you're playing the timeline, pressing the asterisk (*) key on the numeric keypad (*not* Shift+8) adds a marker to the timeline. If you created a music video in Hour 9, "Advanced Editing Techniques and Workspace Tools," then you used the asterisk key. It marks in-points on the timeline for each clip from a storyboard. I'll cover markers in more detail when going over exporting your project to a DVD or for use on the Internet.

> The only non-timeline hotkey I use is Tab. Pressing Tab makes all the palettes disappear/reappear. Keeping those palettes open all the time takes processor power. Press Tab to temporarily remove them and free up some CPU cycles.

Applying Productivity Tips to Speed Up Editing and Resolve Minor Annoyances

First up, two editing tips.

Using the Overlay Button for Cutaways

In Hour 7, "Adding Audio," I explained how to add cutaways to your projects—for instance, reverse-angle shots of a reporter listening to an interviewee, crowd shots at a game, and tight shots. The process involves slicing out a chunk of video, replacing it with a cutaway of the same length, and making sure your audio track remains untouched.

Task: Use the Overlay Button for Cutaways

Using the Overlay button in the Source Monitor screen makes this process much easier. Here's how:

1. Put a video clip on Video 1.

2. Drag another clip from the Project window to the Source Monitor window (not to the timeline). You'll create in- and out-points within the window and use that shortened clip for the cutaway. In my case, I'm going to overlay a close-up, shown in Figure 17.6, to add some visual interest to this piano recital video.

> Frequently you get only one opportunity to videotape an event, and you have only one camcorder to do it. Take your daughter's first piano recital, for instance. The last thing you want to do is grab cutaways or tight shots in the middle of her performance.
>
> If possible, what you *can* do is get those shots later or, in the case of audience shots, during other performances. In this case, I just asked my daughter to play her tunes again (after the recital room had cleared) and I grabbed some close-ups.

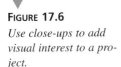

FIGURE 17.6

Use close-ups to add visual interest to a project.

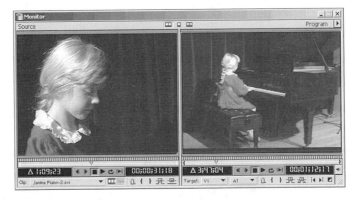

3. Set the in- and out-points for the cutaway either using the in- and out-point tools on the bottom-right side of the Source Monitor screen or by dragging the in- and out-points within the screen's scroll line.

4. Lock the Audio 1 track by clicking the empty box next to the speaker icon. I've highlighted it in Figure 17.7. This ensures that you will overlay only video and will not change the audio.

5. Use the timeline's edit line or the Program Monitor screen's controls to find the point to make the overlay.

FIGURE 17.7

Lock the audio track to avoid overlaying audio.

One way to match music with a performer's actions is to use markers. As you play the Video 1 clip, listen for the moment(s) you want to lay in tight shot(s) and press the asterisk (*) key on the numeric keypad. As explained in the "More Timeline Keyboard Shortcuts" section, that action places a marker on the timeline. Later, you can have the edit line go to that marker by right/Ctrl-clicking the time ruler at the top of the timeline and selecting Go To Timeline Marker.

6. Click the Overlay button. I've highlighted it in Figure 17.8. It's the little down-arrow icon in the bottom-right corner of the Source Monitor screen. The other

17

▼   down-arrow icon, to the Overlay button's left, inserts a clip by slicing the Video 1
        clip at the edit point, pushing everything after the slice to the right, and laying in
        the new clip. You don't want to do that in this case.

    7. Unlock the audio track by clicking the padlock icon. Otherwise, you won't be able
▲   to make any changes, additions, or deletions to that track.

    Preview your work. The cutaway should play over the original audio.

FIGURE 17.8

*Use the Overlay icon
to place a cutaway in
your project.*

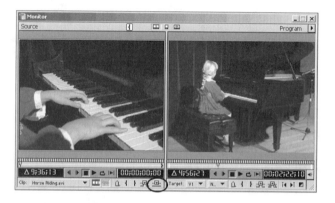

> If the tight shot/cutaway does not exactly match the action that precedes or
> follows it, use the Slip tool to change the in- and out-points of the overlaid
> clip and look for a match in the four-screen monitor window.
>
> Failing that, try the Slide tool to keep the overlaid clip intact while changing
> the in- and out-points of the adjacent clips.

Setting Start and End Keyframes First

When you want to use keyframes with effects, you tell Premiere of your intentions by
turning on the little watch icon in the Effect Controls palette. That action, by default,
places start and end keyframes at the beginning and end of the selected clip. Those
keyframes have the default values of the selected effect. Usually that means all values are
"off" or set to zero.

Before you start moving the edit line to locations within the frame to set keyframes, set
the start and end keyframe values. This saves time and minimizes the possibility of
unpredictable results later. Here's how:

    1. Place the edit line somewhere within the clip and then click the left keyframe navi-
        gator arrow, highlighted in Figure 17.9. Set a starting value for your effect.

2. Click the right keyframe navigator arrow and set a value for the endpoint keyframe.

FIGURE 17.9

Set your keyframe start- and endpoint values first.

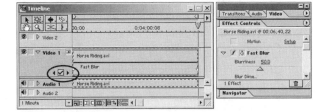

Three Performance-Enhancing Tips

As your projects grow in size and complexity, Premiere's performance may start lagging. You can restore some of that lost performance with the following three tips.

Rendering Virtual Clips and Saving Them

You create virtual clips for two basic reasons: to circumvent an editing roadblock and to reuse an involved collection of edits and effects. Each time you preview a portion of your timeline with a copy of a virtual clip in it, Premiere must redo whatever calculations it took to play back that clip in its original state. You can save some CPU cycles by rendering the clip, saving it as a file, and then importing it back to your project. This way, it will play smoothly as a straight video clip with no extra effects grabbing processor power.

Task: Render a Virtual Clip and Save It

Here's how this works:

1. Create a virtual clip. For this task, you can use any clip. No need to use any effects with it, but tossing in a couple does give you a feel later for rendering times. As a reminder, to create a virtual clip, click the Block Select tool (hotkey M), drag a border around the clip, and drag the now double-arrow icon to some other location in the timeline.

2. As I've demonstrated in Figure 17.10, set the work bar area directly above the clip.

> Try using the keyboard shortcuts I discussed earlier to set the work area bar above the virtual clip: Press N, move the cursor into the work area bar, note the direction in which the triangle is pointing, click to set the in- or out-point, press N again to swap the triangle's direction, and set that in- or out-point.

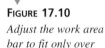
FIGURE 17.10

Adjust the work area bar to fit only over your virtual clip.

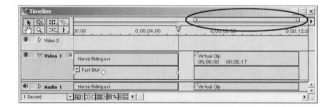

3. Export the virtual clip. Select File, Export Timeline, Movie. Then navigate to an appropriate file folder, give the clip a name, and click OK. You probably should not change the output settings because they'll match whatever settings you have in place for when you export your completed project.

> You'd think you could select File, Export *Clip* instead of Export *Timeline*. But the Export Clip command exports only the video or audio portion of a clip. Not both. I'll explain the whys and wherefores about this curiosity in Hour 19, "Exporting Premiere Frames, Clips, and Projects: Part 1," and Hour 20, "Exporting Premiere Frames, Clips and Projects: Part 2."

4. You will have to wait while Premiere renders your clip. Depending on its length and the complexity of the effects/transitions, this could be time consuming.

5. Import the clip to your Project window and drag it to the timeline. It should play back smoothly. You may now delete the original virtual clip.

Saving Bins for Future Use

You may want to reuse a set of media files in future projects, or you may have a standard project starter set that you supplement with new material. In either case, saving project bins is a great timesaver.

As shown in Figure 17.11, right/Ctrl-click the bin you want to save. Then choose Export Bin from Project, give it a descriptive name, and save it in your Scratch Disk Premiere project's file folder.

> Retrieving that archived bin is not entirely straightforward. Select File, Open and navigate to the saved bin location. Double-click it or select it and click Open. That creates a new, second Project window named "External Bin:{*your bin name*}.plb." You can drag its bin to the bin area in the default Project window and close the External Bin window, or you can close the default Project window and use this one.

FIGURE 17.11

Use the export bin from the Project window to save and later reuse a bin full of media.

17

Using Low-Resolution Clips

Even with the latest computer technology, as your project grows, Premiere slows. It takes a lot of horsepower to slog through an hour or so of high-resolution digital video.

If you're going to work on projects of that scope, you can speed up editing and previewing by using low-resolution source video clips. Once you complete your project, you can replace the low-res clips with the originals and then render the finished work. There are two ways to do this:

- Capture video at smaller frame sizes and then recapture full-screen-sized clips later
- Capture full-size clips, have Premiere convert those clips to a smaller format, use them for editing, and then replace them with the full-screen-sized clips for final video project rendering and output.

The former works only if you have camcorder equipment with Device Control, as do virtually all DV camcorders. That way, when you recapture the video, Premiere will track down the exact same, frame-specific clips.

The latter also is a good option for producers working with Device Control camcorders, and it's the *only* way you can use this approach if you don't have Device Control camcorders.

Each takes some extra effort and can be tedious because you must export and replace each clip separately. Basically, the larger the project, the more you may be inclined to use low-res clips.

Here's a quick run-through. If you capture full-size clips, place them on the timeline, one after the other.

Task: Convert Clips to Lower Resolution Files

Follow these steps:

1. Set the work area to appear over an individual clip, matching its in- and out-points.

2. Select Export Timeline, Movie. This opens the Export Movie dialog box.

3. Click the Settings button. I've highlighted it in Figure 17.12. This opens the Export Movie Settings dialog box.

FIGURE 17.12

Select the Settings button before exporting the timeline segment.

4. Select a file type. Microsoft AVI and QuickTime are your best bets for straight video export.

5. Select Video from the drop-down menu, as I did in Figure 17.13, which opens the video export settings. Select a compressor. This can be a bit overwhelming. QuickTime offers 20 codecs. Planar, Intel, or Sorensen all should work well.

6. Set the frame size, frame rate, and quality. This is your call. Keep in mind that cutting frame dimensions in half cuts the data by a factor of four.

7. You may also go to the Audio section and select a lower rate and format.

8. Once you click OK in any of these windows, these settings become your default settings for future timeline exports.

FIGURE 17.13

Change the video export settings to reduce clip file sizes and increase Premiere performance.

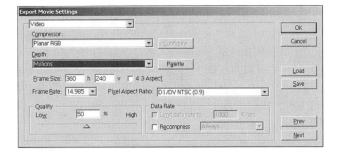

Task: Replace the Low-Res Clips with the Originals

▼TASK

When you complete your project, replace the low-res clips with the real things. Here's how:

1. Right/Ctrl-click the bin side of the Project window and select Replace Clips. This will pop up a warning stating in effect that what you are about to do is a *big deal*—and it is.

2. As illustrated in Figure 17.14, the Locate File dialog box will display the clip at the top of the Project window and ask you to find its replacement. Once this is found and selected (it can have the same name as the low-res clip but must be in a different folder), click OK.

▲   3. That swaps clips and takes you back to the Project window.

It would be better if Premiere let you stay in the Locate File dialog box so you could take care of all the replacements in one place, but that's not how it works. So you need to perform the right/Ctrl-click, Replace Clips process for each clip.

17

FIGURE 17.14

Use the Locate File dialog box to replace low-res clips with the high-res originals.

More Color Codes

As you've worked with effects and motion settings, you may have noticed a few more colors popping up in the timeline. Here's a rundown:

- A green line at the top of the Audio or Video portion of a clip indicates an audio or video effect has been applied to it.

- A red line at the bottom of a clip indicates motion settings have been applied to it.

- A red line directly below the work area bar indicates clips with video effects, motion, or transitions that need rendering before export.

What to Do If Premiere Misbehaves

This is one of those things that's hard to put your finger on. Sometimes Premiere may start behaving oddly. Unexplained sluggishness is the most likely symptom. A possible fix is to create a new Preferences file. The quick keyboard shortcut to do that is to press Ctrl+Shift (Windows or Mac) before double-clicking the Premiere program startup icon on the desktop.

That will bring up the initial Premiere 6.5 opening screen, asking you whether you want to switch to A/B or single-track editing.

One caveat and one surprise:
- This restart means the Open Recent Project and Open Recent File options will be empty. To return to an old project, simply select File, Open and navigate to the Project-Archive file folder.
- Your saved workspace(s) still will show up under Window, Workspace.

You can also rename or remove the Preferences file. In Windows you should find it at C:\Documents and Settings\[*username*]\Application Data\Adobe\Premiere. This is a hidden file folder, so you may not see it. If you search for it, make sure your search parameters include Search Hidden Files and Folders. On Macs it's normally in the Preferences folder. System Folder, Preferences for System 9.0 and User, UserName, Library, Preferences under Mac OS X.

17

Enjoying Some Fun and Fast Editing Tricks

Once you learn the fundamentals, trying out some variations on various themes should come easily. Here is a collection of eight editing tricks that should liven up your projects. Most require only brief explanations.

Using the Razor Tool to Make a Sequence of Effects on the Same Clip

Keyframes allow smooth changes to an effect. If you want to create sudden shifts, slice a clip into smaller chunks and apply different effects to each segment.

As shown in Figure 17.15, I used the Razor tool (keyboard shortcut C) to slice a clip. Then I placed dramatically different video effects on each segment.

Such slices do not leave any gaps in the clip, nor are they visible to viewers. With no effects applied it appears the sliced clip is actually intact.

You also can apply the same effect to each clip chunk and give each instance drastically different characteristics. Use this method to make quick shifts in color or quick changes from inverted images back to positive.

FIGURE **17.15**

Use the Razor tool to create mini-clips within a clip to apply dramatically different effects to one apparently continuous clip.

Using the Razor Tool to Shift from Full Motion to Fast or Slow Motion

The same razor-sliced clip approach works to make abrupt *or* smooth transitions from a full-motion clip to fast or slow motion.

Abrupt changes work well when you want to draw attention to movement. Consider a gymnast's floor exercise. Just before a twisting flip, slice the clip and place slow motion on the flip.

As another example, you could gradually slow down a horserace photo finish. As the thoroughbreds pound down the straightaway, make two or three razor slices, gradually slowing the motion in each segment.

As I've shown in Figure 17.16, you can apply different speeds to a clip by right/Ctrl-clicking the clip, selecting Speed, and typing in a new rate or duration. A negative number will make your clip play backwards.

FIGURE **17.16**

Slow down or speed up a clip using the Clip Speed dialog box.

Using Title Designer for Tinting

The QuickTime Color Tint video effect does a fine job of creating a two-tone tint. But consider using Premiere's new Title Designer to take a different, single or massively multihued, approach.

Task: Create a Unique Tint with the Title Designer

Follow these steps:

1. As I've illustrated in Figure 17.17, open the Title Designer and create a rectangle that goes well outside the boundaries in the Title window to ensure it entirely covers a clip.

2. Create a color matte. Open Fill under Object Style and select a fill type. Solid will give you a single color tint, whereas 4 Color Gradient creates a rainbow effect. Couple the latter with a twisting, contorted video effect and it's the 60's all over again.

3. Use the Opacity settings and the Show Video check box to preview your matte. You can save this color rectangle at full 100% opacity and use the opacity rubber-band to fine-tune its translucency later.

▲

17

FIGURE 17.17

Use Premiere's Title Designer to create color mattes to tint your clips.

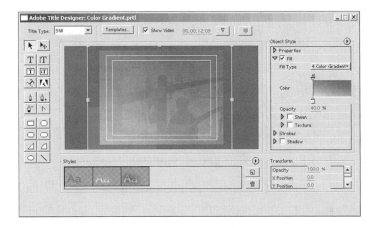

Adding Drop Shadows to Clips in Motion

This is a great way to add a sense of depth and realism to images or clips you float over another image. It works by placing a translucent black matte "beneath" each floating image (picture-in-picture) and just off to one side to give the impression of a shadow moving across the lower image. It's a little involved, but once you create the first floating clip with a drop shadow, adding more shadows is straightforward.

You may ask, Why not use the Drop Shadow Video Effect to do this? You can, but it's more tedious and less user friendly. To use Drop Shadow you first must use Transform to change the size of the clips you'll put in motion. Then you need to use keyframes to create a motion path. But as you move the edit line to a new position to set a new keyframe, the floating image disappears from the monitor window. It becomes a hit-or-miss proposition. The Motion Settings dialog box gives you immediate visual feedback.

Figure 17.18 shows how your timeline might look after completing this task.

FIGURE 17.18

How your timeline might look if you put several clips with drop shadows in motion over a clip on Video 1.

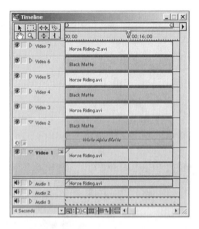

Task: Add Drop Shadows to Moving Clips Using Mattes

Here's how you do this:

1. Place a clip on Video 1. For this task, trim it to about 15 seconds or so.

> Using a still image or freeze frame as the background clip on Video 1 simplifies this process. Plus it looks better and lets you place each floating clip in locations that work well with the background.

2. Create several extra video and audio tracks. You'll need two video tracks for every clip you want to float above the clip on Video 1. Even though you'll delete the audio portions of the extra clips, you need available extra audio tracks; otherwise, Premiere will not allow you to place linked video/audio clips on the timeline.

3. Add a clip to Video 3 (*not* Video 2—you'll use that track for a black matte) and trim it to the same length as the clip on Video 1. Open the Motion Settings dialog

box and give your clip some motion. You can make it as convoluted as you want—you can even distort the clip. In any event, reduce the clip to about 30% so it doesn't crowd the rest of the clips.

> As you add video clips, unlink their audio tracks and delete those audio segments; otherwise, you will have a cacophony.

4. Save your motion settings. I've highlighted that button in Figure 17.19. This is a critical step because you'll use these saved motion settings on the black matte shadow. Give your file a descriptive name (for example, Motion-1) because you're going to do this for each clip you place above Video 1.

5. Create a black matte. Right/Ctrl-click within the Project window and select New, Color Matte. The Color Picker pops up, and the default color is black—all zero values for Red, Green, and Blue. Click OK and name it Black Matte.

6. Place this black matte on Video 2 and extend it to equal the other clips.

7. Expand the video track and use the opacity rubberband to reduce its opacity to 50%. That'll give the black matte shadow a realistic transparency. Use the Fade Adjustment tool (keyboard shortcut U) and hold down Shift to get an exact percentage.

9. Open the Motion Settings dialog box for the black matte and load the file you just saved. The matte's motion will duplicate the clip on Video 3. If you preview it, you won't see the matte because the clip on Video 3 will cover it up.

10. Here's where you create the drop shadow. Change the location for each point along the motion path. They're in the Info area highlighted in Figure 17.19. I recommend placing the matte two units down and two units to the right of the clip above it.

11. Repeat this process for as many clips as you want. Four clips work well.

> You can get a real-time view as you apply your location information. Click the endpoint in the motion path window and the clip will show up in that position in the preview screen. As I've illustrated in Figure 17.19, when you apply new location info to the black matte, the drop shadow will show up around the edges of the clip in the preview screen.

FIGURE **17.19**

Change the location for each point on the matte's path to match the clip above it but to fall just a bit down and to the right. Check your results in the preview screen.

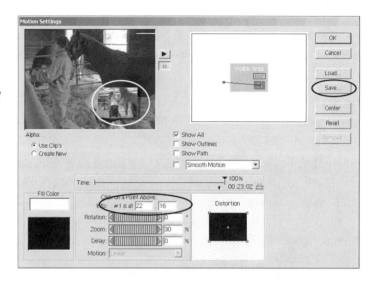

The motion settings' "visible area" is an 80×60 grid. So if your project has a 640×480 resolution, each unit in the Motion Settings dialog box translates to eight pixels. As a reminder, the motion settings' X/Y coordinates don't follow standard Cartesian methodology. The center point *is* 0, but the Y axis is reversed. The top is –30, and the bottom is +30. The X axis works as you'd expect—left is negative and right is positive.

For example, to move the black matte two units down and to the right from –21, -8 would mean shifting it to –19, -6.

Creating Animated Text

Another use for motion settings is to give text some zest. As I've demonstrated in Figure 17.20, you can use the Title Designer to create some text. For this exercise, large text works well because you'll zoom in on it in the Motion Settings dialog box. I included a rounded rectangle backdrop as well.

Whether you make the background graphic first or last is not critical. To place it "behind" the text, select Title, Arrange, Send to Back (from the main menu bar).

FIGURE **17.20**

Large text works well when using motion settings to zoom in on it.

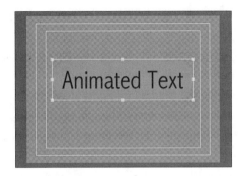

17

Place your text on Video 2 and place a background on Video 1. I chose the color gradient I made for the tinting task earlier.

Apply motion settings to the title. As shown in Figure 17.21, I chose to duplicate that old newsreel effect of a spinning title appearing from a great distance, zooming to full screen (or beyond), and then zooming off the page. What also works well is applying distortion to the clip.

FIGURE **17.21**

Apply motion settings to your text for a dramatic effect.

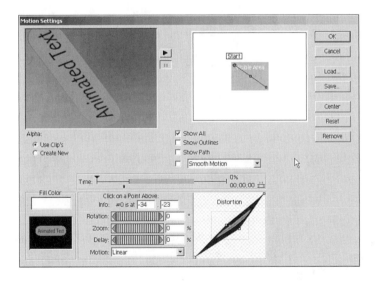

I like using motion settings in part because the process is intuitive and offers real-time feedback. You can achieve similar results using the Basic 3D or Transform video effect.

Panning Across and Zooming In on Stills

This is a really effective way to make a static shot more interesting. I use it a lot when making family history videos. If you've watched a Ken Burns documentary, you've seen it exploited to its maximum value.

Use the Motion Settings dialog box as your tool to create the pans and zooms. Zoom in on areas of interest, or start tight on an image and create the appearance you're panning across it (actually you're moving it across the screen). Here are some basic tips:

- As illustrated in Figure 17.22, I started my image at full screen and zoomed to 150%. I set the start at the center by clicking the start hash mark on the Motion Settings timeline and clicking the Center button. The endpoint is a bit off center because I wanted to zoom in on an area of interest away from the middle of the photo.

FIGURE 17.22

Use motion settings to pan across and zoom in on an image.

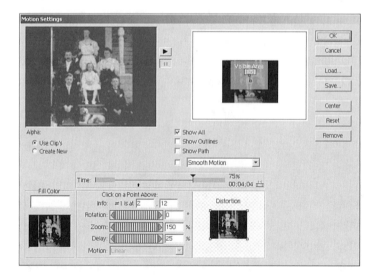

- If you plan to zoom or pan, then scan your image in more than the standard 72 dpi (dots per inch) TV screen display. That way, when you zoom in, the image will remain crisp.
- As is the case with most images, they probably don't exactly match your project's aspect ratio. When you view them in the Program Monitor screen, they may look squashed or elongated. To resolve that, right/Ctrl-click the clip and select Video Options, Maintain Aspect Ratio.

- Scan some images twice. One as a wide shot and another tight. Then place them side by side on the timeline and do a cross-dissolve between them. Use motion settings to zoom in on each but add a pause at the beginning on the tight shot to let the dissolve finish before starting the zoom.

- To further emphasize the zoom, later dissolve in a track matte (see the following tip).

- Consider putting a frame around your image. Do that either by using the Clip video effect and dragging in the edges a bit or by shrinking the clip slightly in the Motion Settings dialog box, placing a black matte beneath it, and applying the same motion settings to the matte.

> In the previous hour I explained how to use a matte created in a graphics program to highlight an area of your image. As shown in Figure 17.23, you also can use Premiere's Title Designer to create that matte.
>
> When creating that matte, use Show Video to line it up with the subject.
>
> Place it on the timeline above the clip, setting Transparency Settings to Alpha Channel and Reverse Key.
>
> To add some visual interest to your still image, use the opacity rubberband to fade it up to about 60% after you've zoomed in on the clip.
>
> As illustrated in Figure 17.24, this process will dissolve in the rounded rectangle without completely blocking out the rest of the image.

17

FIGURE 17.23

Use a graphic created in Premiere's Title Designer to highlight a portion of your image.

FIGURE **17.24**
Here's how this effect turned out.

The preceding tip brings up the "alpha channel, black equals transparent and white equals opaque" issue again. When you're using the Title Designer, all *non*-text regions (or, in this case, *non*-graphics regions) make up the alpha channel. The text, no matter what color it is, is not in the alpha channel and has an adjustable opacity. In this case, the rounded rectangle should be at 100% opacity.

When you use this rectangle, it acts as text and covers up whatever is below it on the timeline, while the alpha channel portion remains transparent. If you use Reverse Key, the alpha channel becomes opaque and the text or graphic portion becomes transparent.

One little quirk: If you apply opacity to the graphic within the Title Designer, using Reverse Key displays the inverse of that opacity. That is, a 20% opacity setting will display, when using Reverse Key, as 80% opaque. Therefore keep your black rounded rectangle at 100% to ensure it becomes completely transparent.

For an odd little effect, give the rectangle a color besides black and set 100% opacity. With Reverse Key on, this will create a color rim around the edge of the oval. If you want to give your oval a little tint with a color border, give it a color and set opacity to 80% or so.

Reducing Noise in Low-Light Clips

Video shot in low-light conditions typically looks "noisy." There are a few tricks you can use to try and fix that:

- Adjust the contrast and brightness.
- Use the slider controls below the histogram in the Levels video effect to increase shadows and highlights.
- Try using the Color Balance video effect to boost Red values a bit.

Using the Storyboard to Create a Slideshow

This is a great way to display a bunch of still images. It uses the same basic storyboard methods covered in Hour 4, "Using the Storyboard and Timeline for Cuts-only Editing."

There are a couple fundamental differences in this case:

- If you want your clips to play for anything other than the default five seconds, set a new default duration for still images. Do that by selecting Edit, Preferences, General and Still Image and changing the default duration to whatever works for you (30 frames equals one second).

- A transition between each "slide" works nicely. Select a "default" transition by opening the Transitions palette, selecting a transition (I recommend something really obvious, such as Center Peel), opening the fly-out menu (as illustrated in Figure 17.25), and selecting Set Selected as Default. That opens the Default Effect dialog box. Set the duration and the alignment (Center at Cut works best with still images).

FIGURE 17.25

Set a default transition using the fly-out menu.

- Instead of Automate to Timeline, you could choose Print to Video. This is one of several means to export a video. I'll go over exporting projects to video and other media in Hours 19 and 20, but you can try this feature now. Just make sure your camcorder is ready to record (if it's analog, start recording before clicking OK).

Accept the defaults and click OK. It should put your DV camcorder into record mode and record your slideshow to tape. It'll also display the slideshow on your computer monitor.

Summary

There's a lot more to Premiere than you might expect. Software this deep is bound to foster plenty of undocumented or thinly referenced functionality. Rather than have you wade through the dozens of keyboard shortcuts in the Quick Reference Card, in this hour I listed my favorites. In Premiere there is almost always more than one way to perform an action. I gave you a few shortcuts for routine tasks, and I tossed in eight fun editing tricks you can apply to many projects.

Workshop

Review the questions and answers in this section to sharpen your tips, tricks, and techniques when using Premiere. Also, take a few moments to tackle my short quiz and the exercises.

Q&A

Q I tried using the overlay method to place a cutaway in a piece. But each time I click the Overlay button, it places the cutaway in a completely different location or I get the message "The Source and Destination Durations Don't Match." What's going on?

A I have not found any documentation about this issue, but here's what I think is happening: Take a look at your timeline. Is there a gray band in the time ruler? That's the culprit. It shows the location of in- and out-points placed in your Program Monitor window. Sometimes those in- and out-points seem to appear for no apparent reason. Because all it takes is single-key shortcuts to put those in- and out-points in the Program Monitor window (I for In and O for Out), that could be how they showed up. In any event, they trump the edit line when it comes to telling the timeline where to place an overlay. So get rid of those in- and out-points. Press D and F to do that.

Q I want to apply a video effect gradually over the duration of a clip so the effect reaches its maximum values at the end of the clip. But it always returns to the default settings as it approaches the end. What's up?

A This is why I suggested setting the start and end keyframe values before working on any others. The end keyframe does not reflect any values you've placed in the middle of the clip. Unless you change it, it will retain the original, default value of the effect.

Quiz

1. The N key is versatile. What are its two shortcut functions?

2. When floating clips over another clip, how do you make sure the drop shadow matte follows the same path?

3. You want to reuse a matte you created in the Title Designer to highlight a different clip. But that means you need to adjust its position and change its size. How do you do that?

Quiz Answers

1. With the Timeline "active," pressing N selects the In- or Out-Point tool. Pressing it again changes from In to Out, or vice versa. With that tool selected, moving the cursor to the work area bar lets you select the right or left end of the work area.

2. After you create a path and select other motion settings for a clip, save those settings. Then when you open the Motion Settings dialog box for the black matte below the clip on the timeline, load those saved settings. Offset the matte from your floating clip by changing the location for each point along the motion path.

3. Use motion settings. Place the title on a superimposing video track and select Motion in the Effect Controls palette. Adjust that matte's location and size using the Motion Settings dialog box.

Exercises

1. Convert a collection of clips to smaller-sized clips by exporting them and giving them smaller frame sizes and using a compression codec. Edit a piece with them and when completed, swap the compacted clips with the real thing. This way, you'll see whether it's worth the conversion inconvenience. The slower your system, the more likely you'll want to do this more often.

2. Place several clips in motion over a still image adding black matte drop shadows, a Title Designer–created tint with slight blurring to the background, and an alternative tinting to the floating images.

3. Scan some old family photos. If you don't have a scanner, videotape them using a tripod. Do the Ken Burns thing and (using motion settings—not your camcorder) zoom in on them, pan across them, and dissolve between wide and tight shots. Give your project a consistent look by creating a sepia tone for one clip, copying that clip, and using Paste Attributes to give that look to all the clips.

PART IV

Working with Other Adobe Products and Exporting Your Videos

Hour

Hour **18**

Using Other Adobe Products for Video Production

I would be remiss if I did not take a brief detour from hands-on, how-to material and venture into some other Adobe graphics-creation products used in video production.

Photoshop is the de facto image-editing industry standard bearer. If you aspire to professional video production status, Photoshop is a must.

An inexpensive means to ease into the Photoshop graphics-creation and photo-retouching world is with its "lite" sibling, Photoshop Elements.

Finally, Adobe Illustrator has a narrower, more print- and Web-oriented vector graphics approach, but it too is a useful tool for a video production professional.

The highlights of this hour include the following:

- A quick tour of Photoshop Elements
- An overview of Photoshop
- Expert tips for first-time Photoshop users focusing on its video applications
- An overview of Illustrator
- Expert tips for first-time Illustrator users

Taking a Tour of Photoshop Elements

There's a lot to like about Photoshop Elements. It has most of its more-robust sibling's power and features at a fraction of the price: $99 versus $600. It's an able replacement to Photoshop LE (Limited Edition), which had a hard time striking a balance between user friendliness and power.

FIGURE **18.1**

Photoshop Elements replaces Photoshop LE (Limited Edition).

Photoshop Elements' obvious forte is image editing. But its subtle strength is its support for Photoshop-style, standard, layered alpha channel graphics.

In a departure from most Adobe products, Photoshop Elements features some handholding. Not too much but enough to help you get your feet wet. As Figure 18.2 shows, the opening screen has a link to a brief tutorial.

FIGURE 18.2

Photoshop Elements' opening interface eases budding photo editors and graphic artists into its powerful workspace.

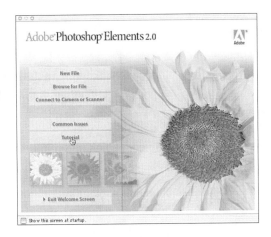

You've seen Premiere's pop-up tooltips. Photoshop Elements takes them one step further, making its tips more narrative and calling them *hints*. Recipes is another helpful feature. As illustrated in Figure 18.3, recipes offer step-by-step instructions on several dozen functions, such as color correction, image cleanup, and text enhancement. Instead of working like a standard online help file, a recipe step can be used to locate, open, and handle a particular function.

18

FIGURE 18.3

Recipes offer step-by-step instruction—with an option to automate the process—on common Photoshop techniques.

The photo-editing elements include the *de rigueur* red-eye remover, crop/rotation, and lighting-correction tools. It's three darkroom tools emulate two age-old techniques—dodging and burning—while adding a "sponge" tool that subtly alters the color saturation of an area.

Elements offers 98 filters, many of which will be familiar to Premiere users. The helpful palette display, illustrated in Figure 18.4, offers nice thumbnail views of how each works.

FIGURE 18.4

The thumbnail images make it much easier to find a filter that matches a specific need.

In a confusing move, Elements offers another category of filters called *Effects*. I show a few in Figure 18.5. Some are a combination of several filters, others you apply to text, and still others create a background. The help file adds to the nomenclature confusion: "*Filters* let you apply special *effects* to your images."

FIGURE 18.5

Most effects appear to be filter combinations. The nomenclature can be confusing.

Elements offers a Photomerge tool, used to stitch together photos to create sweeping panoramas and other multi-image photos. As I've illustrated in Figure 18.6, it works like similar products that ship with some digital still cameras. As I move an image near its neighbor, Elements real-time image analyzer marries the two without a hitch.

In a small nod to the Internet, Elements offers a means to move images to the Web. It's adequate but barebones at best. The GIF animation tool (part of the Save For Web dialog box), shown in Figure 18.7, is a nice touch. Elements also offers tools and links to some "share your photos" sites.

FIGURE 18.6
Photomerge stitches together several photos to create a panorama.

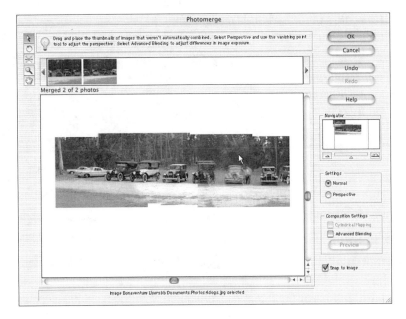

FIGURE 18.7
The GIF animation option in the Save For Web dialog box ports simple graphics to the Web.

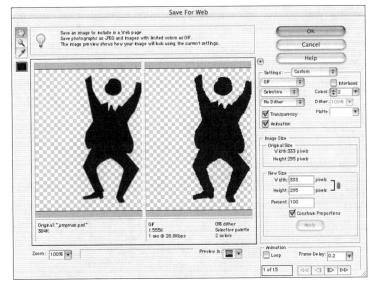

Behind all these features is the principal driving force of Photoshop Elements: Photoshop-style layering. Elements automatically places every object you make for a graphic into a separate layer. The interface, shown in Figure 18.8, lets you turn those layers off or on, edit or apply effects to them separately, or connect elements between layers so moving one object proportionately moves another.

FIGURE **18.8**

Photoshop Elements emulates its elder sibling by offering Photoshop-style layering and alpha channel transparencies.

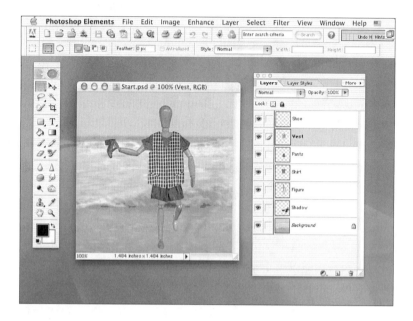

To create layered artwork takes not much more than a simple drag and drop. Move an object—text, artwork, or scanned image—to an existing layered graphic and Elements automatically creates a new layer for it. There you can apply numerous filters, effects and opacity values to individual layers, noting the changes immediately in the window. It doesn't take long to turn the little stick figure in Figure 18.8 into the psychedelic picnicker in Figure 18.9.

FIGURE **18.9**

Applying filters, gradients, and effects quickly transforms a layered image.

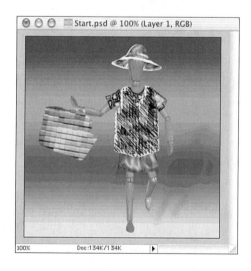

Photoshop Elements faces stiff competition from Ulead PhotoImpact, Jasc Paint Shop Pro, and Microsoft PhotoDraw. What sets Elements apart from this crowded field is its direct link to Photoshop, the undisputed image-editing king. If your goal is to graduate to that level of professionalism, then Photoshop Elements is the logical first step.

Moving Up to Photoshop

Making the move to Photoshop means joining forces with just about every image-editing professional on the planet. It's that ubiquitous.

FIGURE 18.10

Adobe Photoshop is the undisputed Mac/Windows image-editing tool of choice.

Adobe has ensured that making the move from Elements to Photoshop will be easy. With the exception of some palette tab locations, the Photoshop workspace, shown in Figure 18.11, has a look and feel that's very similar to Elements.

Although you get some real power in Elements, Photoshop offers much more flexibility and additional tools.

Elements simplifies some processes with presets, but that limits creativity. Photoshop offers deep customizability. The Layer Style dialog box in Figure 18.12—very reminiscent of Premiere's Title Designer—is a case in point. Everything you need is at your fingertips.

FIGURE **18.11**

The Photoshop work-space nearly dupli-cates Elements.

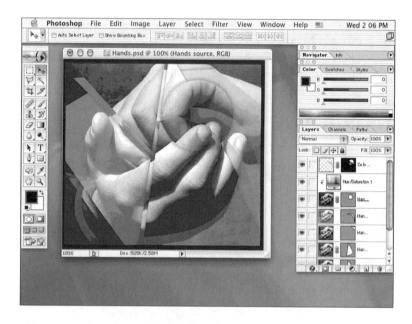

FIGURE **18.12**

Photoshop's Layer Style dialog box puts major functionality within one intuitive interface.

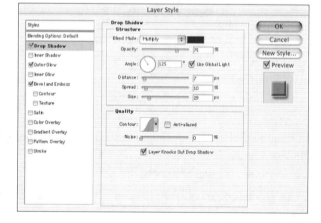

The drawing tools and Artwork palette in Photoshop virtually duplicate those in Elements. Using them, it takes only a few minutes to create a graphic like the one in Figure 18.13.

Photoshop adds some professional paintbrush tools—Charcoal, Pastel, Oil Paint—to that palette. Using them with a graphics tablet, such as the pressure-sensitive Wacom Intuos, means you can apply more or less texture as you draw.

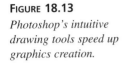

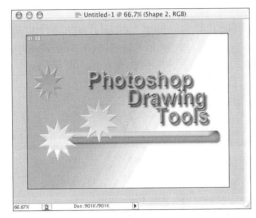

Other Photoshop features include the following:

- A "healing" brush that does amazingly accurate and automatic dust, scratch, and blemish removal while compensating for differences in lighting, shading, and texture.
- Auto color correction, which analyzes an image and balances color with a single click. This works well on photos shot under fluorescent lights.
- More powerful Web integration.
- A spell checker. This may not seem like a standard image-editing tool, but graphic artists have clamored for it.

Of primary importance to the scope of this book is just how strongly Photoshop is connected to Premiere and to video production.

An obvious example is Premiere's Edit Original command. Place any Photoshop graphic on the timeline, right/Ctrl-click it, and select Edit Original. This opens Photoshop and lets you immediately edit the graphic. Once saved within Photoshop, the new version of the graphic shows up in Premiere.

Here are three of my favorite Premiere/Photoshop connections:

- Premiere offers a "filmstrip" feature specifically designed to work with Photoshop. Convert video clips into filmstrips—collections of individual frames—using File, Export Timeline (or Export Clip), Movie. Click Settings. For File Type choose Filmstrip and then choose the frames to export from the Range menu. Open the frames in Photoshop and paint directly on the clips using a process called *rotoscoping*.

- Export a frame of a video to Photoshop to create a matte to mask or highlight certain areas of that clip. Here's how: Create a shape using the Marquee or one of the Lasso tools. In the Tool Options bar, set Feather to about 15 px to give it that soft border. Fill the interior with black to make it transparent. Fill the rest with white to make that part opaque. Within Premiere you can use this mask as a track matte to adjust its location and size and to follow action. Plus, you can line up the original clip on both Video 1 and Video 2, apply some blur to Video 2, and use the soft-edged matte to highlight an element in your clip while throwing everything else out of focus.

- You can use Photoshop to cut objects out of a scene and fill in the gap using the Clone tool or the new healing brush. Then place the removed object in a separate layer so you can animate it using Premiere's Motion Settings dialog box. Monty Python-esque comical situations come to mind. Consider a photo of a statue in a park. Move it off the pedestal and slide it next to an unsuspecting park patron seated on a bench.

Before you can start using these features, you'll need to learn the fundamentals. If you choose to add Photoshop to your digital video production repertoire, peruse the tips for first-time users provided by a Photoshop expert in the following sidebar.

Using Photoshop in Video Production—Expert Tips

To find experts in various Adobe Digital Media products I contacted Adobe. Two corporate evangelists concurred that Glen Stephens fit the bill. He enthusiastically agreed to provide tips for first-time users of Photoshop and Illustrator.

Glen Stephens,
Pixel Post Studios.

Stephens' company, Pixel Post Studios (http://www.pixelpoststudios.com), provides training and design services for the broadcast video industry.

Stephens is an expert Photoshop user and designer for desktop and broadcast video with extensive experience with Illustrator and After Effects. He has more than 10 years experience as a graphic designer, editor, and director in broadcast video.

He runs a broadcast cable station for the City of Mesa in Arizona and teaches television production at Arizona State University for the Walter Cronkite School of Journalism and Mass Communications. Stephens is a contributing writer for *Photoshop User Magazine* and a member of the Adobe Solutions Developer Network.

Stephens is the developer of the Tools for Television – Photoshop Toolbox (http://www.toolsfortelevision.com), a valuable resource of tips, techniques, tutorials, and automation tools for anyone using Photoshop for video production.

Adobe's director of product management for Photoshop notes that, "as a powerful, general-purpose image editor, Photoshop has become an indispensable tool for video designers. Tools for Television extends these capabilities to address specific photo-editing needs in video production. This enables a more efficient video production environment while ensuring professional-quality, broadcast-ready graphics."

Here are Stephens' tips for using Photoshop in your video productions (note that * indicates that actions are available on the Tools for Television – Photoshop Toolbox CD to automate the task):

- **Place each element of your image onto a new and separate layer.** This allows you to keep your designs editable in case you decide to make changes later. It's tempting to flatten your images when you are done to reduce their file size, but this prevents you from later making text or color changes.

- **Use the built-in features of Photoshop, such as layer styles, to create effects such as drop shadows, glows, and bevels.** Layer styles and adjustment layers are very valuable and allow you to create powerful image effects that are always adjustable later in the process, as long as you do not render or rasterize them. Experiment with these and get into the habit of using them.

- **Use safe areas.** * Overscan on television sets covers about 10% of each side of your image. Therefore, when creating graphics for video, make sure you place all your content inside the "title-safe" portion of your image (see Figure 18.14). It's okay to let background images and elements extend to the edges so that they appear to fill the screen, but overscan will cover any text that extends outside of the title-safe area. A Web site where you can download a grid can be found at www.toolsfortelevision.com/downloads/.

18

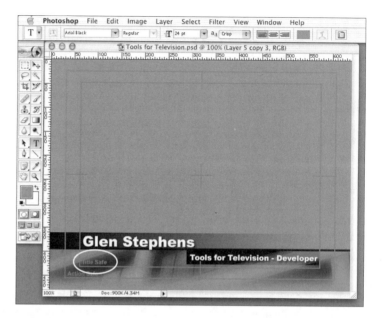

- **Add alpha channels to your graphics.** * Once you are done creating graphics or any elements that need to be keyed over video, you must manually create an alpha channel so that Premiere knows what portion of your image to keep and what portion of your image to replace with background video. Photoshop will not automatically do this for you. It's a multistep process. By step 5 your graphic should look something like Figure 18.15. Here's how you do it:

   1. Create a new, empty layer at the top of your image.

   2. Hide the Background layer and the layer that your safe grid is on, assuming you have one in your image, by clicking the eyeball icon in the Layers palette. At this point you should see a checkerboard in the background of your image, representing the alpha channel that Premiere will later key out.

   3. Make sure you turn on all the layers that you want visible in the final graphic.

   4. With your new, empty layer selected, hold down Option (Mac) or Alt (Windows) and select Layer, Merge Visible. This creates a composite of your image while keeping the other layers separate for designing.

   5. Convert the transparency of this layer to a selection by Command-clicking (Mac) or Ctrl-clicking (Windows) it.

   6. Convert this selection into an alpha channel. In the Selection menu, choose Save Selection. This saves the merged layer as an alpha channel in the Channels palette of your image.

7. You may now delete the merged layer from the layer's palette that you previously created. This layer is used *only* to identify the transparent areas of your overall image. Your alpha channel should now look like Figure 18.16—a white cutout of the shape of your image on a black background.

FIGURE 18.15
You must add an alpha channel manually to your Photoshop graphics to enable Premiere to create a transparency.

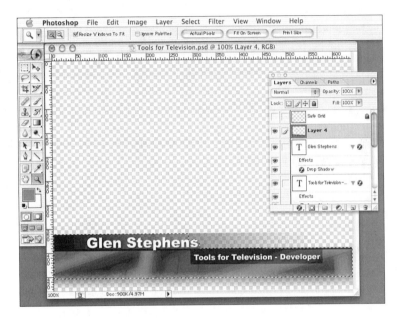

FIGURE 18.16
The white areas in the alpha channel delineate opacity. Gray areas are translucent, and black areas are transparent.

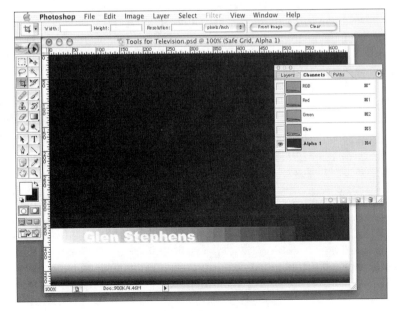

Your image can have only one alpha channel when it is saved. If you make changes to your images and need to create a new alpha channel, delete the old one first.

- **Watch your font sizes.** Font sizes of 24 points or larger work best. Anything smaller may look like dust specks on a TV screen. For a header or primary text, 32 to 48 points work well, depending on how much text you use. (Note that typeface sizes vary. A 24-point font for one typeface may be smaller/larger than a 24-point font for a different typeface.)

  Also, space your text evenly. Don't crowd the screen with too much large text, and avoid thin fonts that may become illegible in an interlaced video signal.

- **Adjust image dimensions to compensate for non-square pixels.** * Photoshop works only with square pixels. But some TV systems use so-called *non-square* (slightly rectangular) pixels. To ensure your Photoshop graphics translate well to the final video output format, you may need to make some resolution adjustments.

  Computer monitors, Regular NTSC (non-D1 or DV), and HDTV (High-Definition TV) use square pixels. Photoshop graphics will display just fine on them. Simply create your Photoshop graphics in the same screen resolution at the planned output format (for example, 640×480 for regular NTSC).

  NTSC D1, NTSC DV, and PAL use non-square pixels. When you plan to have Premiere output to those formats, you *do* need to create Photoshop graphics in different resolutions to ensure your images look as you intended. If not, they'll look like the graphics in Figure 18.17—stretched or squashed, depending on the video system.

FIGURE 18.17

Failing to use the correct resolution in a Photoshop graphic may lead to squashed or elongated images, depending on the output video format.

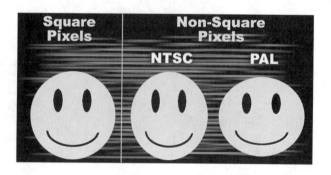

Table 18.1 runs down video systems and their associated Photoshop image resolutions.

TABLE 18.1   Video Formats and Their Associated Photoshop Graphics Screen Resolutions

Video Format	Screen Resolution	Pixel Type	Recommended Resolution
NTSC (non D1 or DV)	640×480	Square	Same as screen resolution
NTSC D1 (CCIR 601)	720×486	Non-square	720×540
NTSC DV	720×480	Non-square	720×534
HDTV	1280×720 or 1920×1080	Square	Same as screen resolution
PAL	720×576	Non-square	768×576

Unless you plan to zoom in on a graphic within Premiere, it's best to create all Photoshop images as RGB images at 72 dpi resolution (see the section, "Scanning tips for photographs" later in this chapter for more info).

18

- **Using bitmap versus vector graphics.** Computer graphics fall into two main categories: bitmap and vector. You can import both types into Premiere, but Premiere converts vector graphics to bitmap images before editing them. Here's a basic overview of both types:

  - Bitmap images—technically called *raster images*—use a grid of colors known as *pixels*. Some pixels have been magnified in Figure 18.18 to illustrate this. Each pixel is assigned a specific location and color value. When working with bitmap images, you edit pixels rather than objects or shapes.

    Bitmap images are the most common electronic medium for continuous-tone images, such as photographs, because they can represent subtle gradations of shades and color. Bitmap images are resolution dependent—that is, they contain a fixed number of pixels. As a result, they can lose detail and appear jagged if they are scaled larger.

    All images created in Photoshop are bitmap.

  - Vector graphics are made up of lines and curves defined by mathematical objects called *vectors*. Figure 18.19 demonstrates how vectors describe an image according to its geometric characteristics. For example, a circle in a vector graphic is made up of a mathematical definition of a circle drawn with a certain radius, set at a specific location, and filled with a specific color. You can move, resize, or change the color of the circle without losing the quality of the graphic.

FIGURE **18.18**
Magnified bitmap pixels.

Vector graphics are resolution independent—that is, they can be scaled to any size and printed at any resolution without losing detail or clarity. As a result, vector graphics are the best choice for representing bold graphics that must retain crisp lines when scaled to various sizes (for example, logos).

All images created with Adobe Illustrator are vector based.

FIGURE **18.19**
Vector graphics are made up of mathematical objects—lines and curves—to ensure sharp, crisp images, no matter how much they're scaled up.

- **Fixing interlacing and "shaky" graphics.** * If your Photoshop graphics vibrate when displayed on a TV set, this is likely due to interlacing.

  This happens when thin horizontal lines, especially bright lines, in your graphic or image fall between the interlaced scan lines of your video signal. It's a common occurrence with scanned photographs. You want to avoid this.

  You fix it by either making horizontal lines thicker or applying a motion blur. Figure 18.20 demonstrates the latter.

  Select Filter, Blur, Motion Blur. This opens the Motion Blur dialog box. Apply one pixel at 90 degrees to the problem area in the image. This stretches the width of the horizontal lines into the next scan line in the video signal and corrects the problem. In some cases one pixel will not be enough. Try two or three if the problem is really bad.

FIGURE 18.20

Use Photoshop's Motion Blur effect to resolve jitters on inter-laced TV sets caused by thin lines in the graphic.

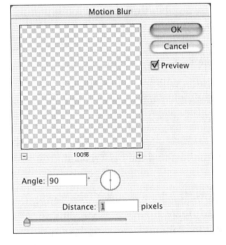

18

For still images you also can apply Premiere's Flicker Removal function.

Apply the blur only to the problem areas in the image. If you apply the blur to the overall image, it may lose sharpness. In the case of a scanned photo, you may need to apply it to the entire image.

You can use Premiere's Edit Original command on the suspect graphic to automatically open Photoshop to do your graphic touchup work. When you save the altered graphic, it will show up in its new form within Premiere.

- **File-management tips:** When you're working in Photoshop, I suggest using a file folder system that keeps two sets of image files for a project: design and production.

  Design files are the original Photoshop (PSD) images that contain text data, layers, adjustment layers, layer masks, and the safe grid and background.

  Production files are the flattened files you can export to other software applications. These files do not have any layered information and cannot be edited later. You can save these files in any format your editing software will take. It is a good idea that these files be flattened because many applications cannot read layer styles or adjustment layers from Photoshop, and items such as drop shadows may be lost in the editing software. Simply select Save As in Photoshop and uncheck the Layers button in the Save dialog box to flatten the image.

- **Color-selection tips:** Certain colors work better than others when working with video. Any color that is highly saturated and too bright will cause problems when transferred to video. Muted, less bright colors will yield better results. Typically red is *not* a good color to use. However, if you keep the saturation and brightness down, you may be able to get away with it. Blues, yellows, and greens work well.

  Photoshop has a filter that will help shift "illegal" colors into an NTSC safe-color space. Select Filter, Video, NTSC Colors to use it. However, just because a color is NTSC safe does not mean it will not bleed or look bad!

  When working with text, make sure there is a significant amount of contrast between the color of the text and the background. You want the text to jump off the screen at your viewers.

  I rarely use color in text. If I do, it is just a faint shade. Your viewers' eyes will be drawn naturally to the brightest portion of your image. Try to "guide" your viewers to what you are trying to communicate with them.

The book *Color Harmony* by Hideaki Chijiiwa is an excellent resource if you want to learn color theory and how to use colors to help communicate your message.

- **Scanning tips for photographs:** When scanning photographs for use in a video project, it is not necessary to scan images at a high resolution. Because all video graphics end up at 72 dpi, anything more than that is overkill.

  There are exceptions, though. If you plan to pan, move around, or zoom in on the image in Premiere, you will want to scan at a higher resolution than 72 dpi.

Because Photoshop works with pixels, if you scan a small image and try to scale it larger in Photoshop, you will end up with a blurry version of your image. Scaling down does not make an image look worse, but scaling up does.

In general, scan all images at a slightly larger size than the expected output video resolution so that you can scale the image down to the size you want it on your video screen.

Table 18.2 lists image sizes that will fill a screen at 72 dpi for each video format. If your original image is smaller than the sizes listed here, scale it up in the scanner to ensure sharper detail in the final edited video.

TABLE 18.2   Video Frame Size Versus Optimum Size of Original Document to Ensure Sharp Onscreen Display

Video Frame Size	Minimum Image Size to Ensure Sharp Onscreen Display
640×480	8 7/8 × 6 5/8 inches
720×480	10 × 6 5/8 inches
720×486	10 × 6 3/4 inches
720×576	10 × 8 inches
1280×720	17 2/3 × 10 inches
1920×1080	26 2/3 × 15 inches

18

Filling a Narrow Video Production Niche with Adobe Illustrator

Adobe Illustrator is the standard bearer in the world of drawing programs. Illustrator's vector-based graphic-creation tools lend themselves to print and Web media. Mathematical formulas are used to describe vector graphics. Whether scaling an image way up to poster size or down to an icon, vector graphics retain their clarity and definition.

Its connection to digital video is less direct. Frequently digital media designers use Illustrator to create original images, port them to Photoshop for further editing, then finally pass them on to Premiere for inclusion in a video project (see Figure 18.22).

FIGURE **18.21**
Adobe Illustrator.

FIGURE **18.22**
*Adobe Illustrator
offers creative artists a
deep collection of
drawing tools.*

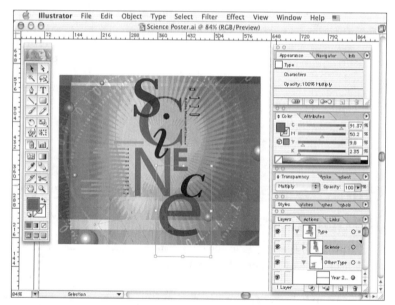

The latest update to Illustrator includes some exciting new features:

Symbols—Artists can use Illustrator's new Symbols tool to create repeating instances of a single graphic, giving it slightly different characteristics. It's an excellent way to create randomized effects such as nature scenes.

Dynamic data-driven graphics for the Web—Provide a means to create many graphics while using minimal data. You can create templates that link to a database and then create one Web banner in a unique style and simply update the database to change the displayed information without changing the overall appearance of the graphic.

Specialized drawing tools—The biggest winner here is Live Distortion. Apply this to any object (text or graphic) and you can twist, contort, and bend it as much as you like. New curve-creation tools work as easily as drawing a straight line, and the Liquefy Brushes let you apply filter effects using brushstrokes rather than converting an entire object.

Illustrator gives artists a reliable and powerful resource.

Expert Tips for First-time Illustrator Users

Glen Stephens, who provided the Photoshop tips earlier in this hour, offers the following advice for first-time Illustrator users.

Illustrator is a very valuable tool when preparing graphics for Premiere. You can directly import Illustrator vector-based graphics into Premiere, which promptly *rasterizes* them—converts them to bitmap graphics—for further editing.

However, I take a less direct but more commonly used approach. I create vector artwork in Illustrator and then pass that on for further editing, primarily in Photoshop but in After Effects as well. Only then do I use that artwork in Premiere.

No matter which route you take, I think the following tips will help ensure your Illustrator graphics look their best:

- **Use a resolution for your Illustrator graphics that will guarantee the proper video output aspect ratio.** When starting a new document in Illustrator, set the color mode to RGB. Then refer to Table 18.1 in the Photoshop sidebar and set the resolution to match the video output format—for example, 720×534 points for NTSC-DV. This will make sure you are working with square pixels.

- **Make Premiere think your graphic fills the entire frame.** The artboard in Illustrator does not set the size for your overall image, as does the canvas in Photoshop. If you place a small square inside the Illustrator artboard, that square will not expand to fill the screen in Premiere. You need to trick Premiere into thinking that the entire 720×540 artboard is being used. Do that by making and then releasing crop marks to define the outside edges of your image. Here's how:

  1. Create a blank layer in your new file.

  2. Select Object, Crop Marks, Make. Illustrator automatically will place the crop marks on the edges of the artboard. This box is on the active layer in your image, so be sure not to delete this layer later.

18

3. Select Object, Crop Marks, Release.

- **Stay within the title-safe boundaries.** The same "title safe" rules described in the Photoshop sidebar apply to Illustrator graphics as well. Make sure you keep important elements within the title-safe area. You may download the Illustrator title-safe grid shown in Figure 18.23 at `http://www.toolsfortelevision.com/downloads`.

FIGURE 18.23

Use title-safe boundaries to ensure your important elements are visible on standard TV screens.

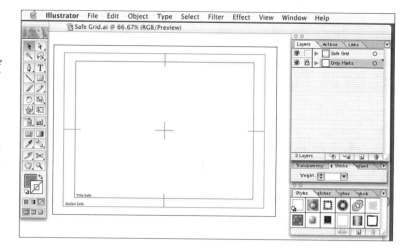

- **Use compound paths to create "stencils."** The one question I get asked more often than any other about Illustrator is, How do I cut a shape out of another object, leaving a hole in it? For instance, Figure 18.24 illustrates cutting a star out of a square, leaving a hole behind.

  Because Illustrator is a vector-based application, this is a very simple process. Simply use its Compound Path tool.

  Select the two shapes simultaneously with the Selection tool. Do that by first selecting one object, pressing Shift, and then clicking to select the second. From the main menu, select Object, Compound Path, Make. That's all it takes.

If you want to use text as a stencil shape for your compound path, first convert the text to outlines (see the next tip) .

FIGURE 18.24
Creating a stencil is only a two-step process.

- **Convert text to outlines.** Text in almost all software applications works something like vector art. You can increase font size and not see any loss in sharpness. But if you want to use *outlined* text in Illustrator—as a stencil for instance—you need to convert it to true vector-based artwork.

  Once converted, text is no longer editable, and you can't change the font style. So, before converting text to outlines, make a copy of your original text layer and save it.

  Figure 18.25 shows how this process looks. Use the Selection tool to highlight the text. Then in the main menu select Type, Create Outlines.

FIGURE 18.25
Converting text to a vector graphics lets you use it as a stencil or a 3D object in other programs.

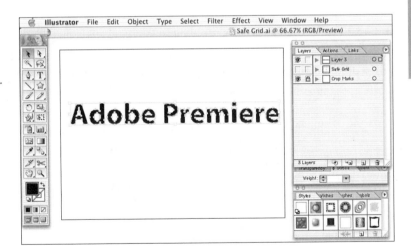

18

People working with 3D applications frequently import text as vector artwork and convert it into 3D objects.

- **Use Illustrator for logos and cross-media applications.** The biggest strength of Illustrator is that its vector-based artwork is resolution independent. You can scale the artwork large or small and print at a high or low resolution without losing image quality. As you resize the artwork, mathematical calculations ensure consistent, sharply defined edges at all resolutions.

  This is a very important feature when working with logos or artwork that will be used in varying sizes on the Web, in video, and in print.

> Illustrator *can* rasterize its vector artwork. However, once it's converted to a bitmap image, you cannot get that vector information back.

- **Import Illustrator files into Photoshop.** There are three ways to import Illustrator vector-based artwork into Photoshop:

  - **Use Photoshop's Place command.** First, open an existing Photoshop document or a new document. Then select File, Place. This will place the Illustrator image onto the selected layer in your Photoshop document.

    If your currently selected layer has image information on it, Photoshop will create a new layer for the new image. Once the image is in Photoshop, handles appear around the image so that you can select the size you would like the object to be. The object can be scaled as large or as small as you want it, without jeopardizing the integrity of the image.

    You may drag your image borders beyond the edges of the Photoshop image borders and retain all the original Illustrator image information. Simply select that layer and drag the Illustrator graphic around inside the Photoshop window.

    Press Enter/Return or double click the image to rasterize it into a bitmapped image.

  - **Use the Open command in Photoshop (File, Open) and open the Illustrator image as its own document.** Photoshop will give you a dialog box that asks you what color mode you wish to work in and what size and resolution to open the file in. The file is then rasterized into a bitmapped image. The size of your image will be whatever size you selected for the canvas. Keep the Constrain Proportions and Anti-Aliased buttons checked.

  - **Copy and paste from Illustrator to Photoshop.** Within Illustrator, select Edit, Select All and then select Edit, Copy. As with the Place command, switch to Photoshop, open a new document or an existing document, and then select Edit, Paste. Your options are Pixels, Path, and Shape Layer. If there are multiple colors in your image, choose Pixels. If there is one color only, use Shape Layer. This latter option keeps the image in a vector format in Photoshop.

Summary

As you move deeper into video production, you may want to expand your artistic horizons by branching out to one or two graphic art–creation programs. Adobe Photoshop is the image editing tool of choice for just about any artist with a computer. Photoshop Elements, a much less expensive subset of Photoshop, is an excellent means to test the waters. It has most of Photoshop's features for a small fraction of its price.

Adobe Illustrator offers excellent resources for artists looking to create scalable graphics geared for print and Web pages. In addition, video producers frequently rely on it to create original art destined for a video project.

As mentioned in Hour 13, "Wrapping Up Effects with After Effects," the other Adobe product that rounds out the video production process is the powerful special effects and layering tool, After Effects.

18

Hour 19

Exporting Premiere Frames, Clips, and Projects: Part 1

Premiere offers a dizzying array of so-called *export options*. More than you will ever use. Making sense of them is the goal of this and the next hour.

The simplest task is to use Premiere as a VCR—to record your completed project to videotape. But even there, the plethora of possibilities can make your head swim.

Moving on, you can export a still frame or frame sequence to your hard drive for use in other programs, create an Edit Decision List for further editing on separate production equipment, or simply convert a video segment from one format to another.

You may want to post your clips on a Web site, put them on a multimedia CD-ROM, or create a DVD movie.

I'll save the Internet options and DVD output issues for the next hour. I'll go over the rest now.

The highlights of this hour include the following:

- Deciphering Premiere's confusing export nomenclature
- Choosing an export format—AVI, QuickTime, Still, Sequence, or Filmstrip
- Wading through export options
- Finally, exporting your project

Print to Video or Export to Tape—What Does It All Mean?

When you purchased Premiere you may have had only one basic concept in mind: Create a video project to put on a VHS tape and play it on the home VCR. Turns out that's only one of many possibilities.

As technology has changed, Adobe has responded by adding new output features to Premiere. A few years ago the idea of creating a video for playback on the Internet was unheard of. And DVDs weren't even on the radar. Now they are both major elements of Premiere.

Perhaps because Adobe adds these technologies on a piecemeal basis, Premiere's export (or output) terminology and menus have become kind of confusing. Simply deciphering what it all means will go a long way to easing the export/output process.

I'll start that deciphering process by taking a tour of the various Export methodologies:

1. By now you've saved a few projects. Load one of them by selecting File, Open Recent Project or File, Open and then navigating to a project in the file folder `{your}` `Documents/Adobe/Premiere/Project-Archive`.

2. Place the edit line somewhere in the project and click the video portion of a clip under the edit line. This identifies that particular clip to Premiere.

Take a close look at the clip you just selected. As shown in Figure 19.1, you'll notice "marching ants" running around both the video and audio portions of the clip. This indicates that if you trim or move any part of the clip, that action will affect both the video and audio portions.

Note also that two horizontal gray bars now run along the top and bottom of the video portion, which indicates you specifically selected that element of this audio/video-linked clip.

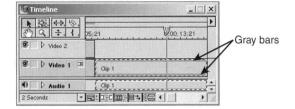

3. Select the File menu. As shown in Figure 19.2, you'll note two export options: Export Clip and Export Timeline.

FIGURE 19.2

The File menu has two export options.

4. Select File, Export Timeline. As highlighted in Figure 19.3, you have 10 options.

FIGURE 19.3

Export Timeline offers 10 options and is your main starting point for most export functions.

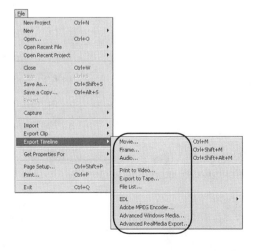

19

Clarification #1: What does Adobe mean by "Export"? When you "export" something from Premiere, it doesn't go all that far—either to your hard drive or your camcorder/VCR. Basically export means *create a file* or *record to videotape*.

Clarification #2: Export Timeline versus Export Clip (or a frame, a sequence, or the entire project). Export Timeline is Premiere's way of saying, "Export *anything from* the timeline." You will select this menu to take a clip, frame, sequence, or the entire project and convert it to a file on your hard drive. You also can take some section of the project or the entire project and record it to videotape.

Here are the different export processes:

Movie—Converts anything on the timeline, *other than* a single frame or an audio-only clip, to a file. You'll use it to create (export) QuickTime or Windows AVI videos as well as image sequences and animations. More on all that in a few minutes.

Frame—Creates a still image file of the frame identified by the edit line.

Audio—Creates an audio file. You can select the entire project, an audio-only clip, or the audio portion of a linked video/audio clip.

Print to Video—See Clarification #3.

Export to Tape—See Clarification #3.

File List—Creates a text file of all the clip names in the Project window bins. You may never use this menu item.

EDL (Edit Decision List)—See the following note.

Adobe MPEG Encoder—This is a *big deal*. Really. This option allows you to create DVDs, "super" and regular video CDs, and cDVDs (specialized CDs that play videos on PC CD or DVD drives). Adobe has tightly integrated it with the DVDit! DVD-authoring module bundled with Premiere. I'll cover this export process in detail in Hour 20, "Exporting Premiere Frames, Clips, and Projects: Part 2," and cover the entire DVD-authoring process in Hours 21–24.

Advanced Windows Media (PC only), Advanced RealMedia Export, and QuickTime File Exporter (Mac only)—The first two options are the means to create video for use in Web pages (and for other uses). I'll cover them in detail in Hour 20. The QuickTime File Exporter is a Mac-only product geared toward creating MPEG-2 videos for users with DVD Studio Pro or iDVD installed or MPEG-4 for those with QuickTime 6 Pro.

Clarification #3: Print to Video versus Export to Tape. These are the only two Export Timeline options for recording something to videotape. What's the difference?

You use Print to Video if your video recording machine—camcorder or VCR—does *not* have what's called *Device Control*. Most analog consumer recorders don't have that technology.

Use Export to Tape if your recording device *does* have Device Control. Most DV camcorders do. We'll try out both output methods a bit later.

Edit Decision Lists (EDLs) are a vestige of the old days.

They allow you to work "offline" (that is, use low data-rate clips to edit a rough cut of your project and produce an EDL—a text file). You then take that file and the original higher data-rate video clips to an expensive post-production facility for final editing.

In theory the process is supposed to save money and create a better-looking product.

The reality these days is that you don't need to work offline. Your computer should have all the data storage and throughput you need. EDLs can handle only a few transitions and no motion settings or special video effects. Premiere is chockablock with transitions, layering, and special effects that blow anything you can store on an EDL right out of the studio.

Clarification #4: Export Clip versus Export Timeline. As I completed the chapter, this was an unresolved issue. An Adobe official told me they were going to change Premiere to fix this but had not done so by the time I finished the book.

Here's the deal: Export Clip should mean that you can select a clip from the timeline and export only that clip. But it doesn't work that way. If you select a clip from the timeline and then select Export Clip (as Premiere was configured during my testing), you could export only the audio or video portion of that clip. Not both.

After swapping several emails with Adobe about this, they told me they would fix it. The way it's supposed to work is that if you select a clip on the timeline, the Export Clip menu option should be grayed out (that is, it should not be an option) .

If you still see it as an option, *ignore it*.

Instead, if you want to export only a clip (with audio and video intact), double-click that clip name within the Project window to open it in a Clip window. From the main menu select File, Export Clip. Then you'll have all the options available in the Export Timeline process.

19

The principal reason to export an unedited clip is to convert it to a different, lower data-rate format and then use it in the timeline to speed up editing. It's a labor-intensive process that involves placing clips, one at a time, on the timeline, marking the work area bar, and using the Export Timeline process.

Choosing an Export Format

Most Premiere how-to books go through just about every type of export process, one at a time. That means repeating a lot of information. I think that's counterproductive and fails to paint the big picture.

Instead I want to give you a basic idea of the export formats and options at your disposal. Then I'll take you through only a few export processes, referring tangentially to the many options.

Your export format choices fall into two main categories: videotape and files. Exporting to videotape is remarkably easy, and I'll go over that process in a few minutes.

The file side of things has many more possibilities. You'll use this export process if you plan to use your project in any medium other than videotape. Here's how to see all the output formats under Export Timeline, Movie:

1. Select Export Timeline, Movie. That opens the Export Movie dialog box.

2. In the Export Movie dialog box, click the Settings button at the bottom of the screen. That opens the Export Movie Settings dialog box.

3. As highlighted in Figure 19.4, click the File Type drop-down menu. Here are your basic File Type options:

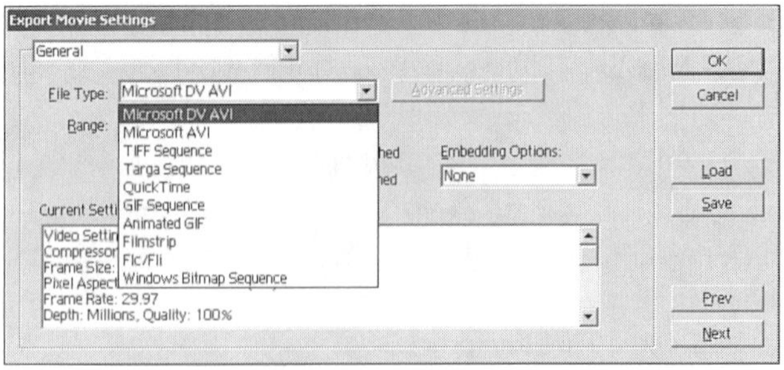

FIGURE 19.4

The Export Movie Settings dialog box's File Type drop-down list displays all the video output formats.

Microsoft AVI—Audio/Video Interleave is the long-standing Microsoft video format. It's still in heavy use but is being superseded by Advanced Windows Media.

QuickTime MOV—This is the long-time Apple video format, released before AVI. It now plays on both Macs and PCs.

Still Frame Sequences—Includes TIFF, Targa, GIF, BMP (Windows only), and PICT (Mac only). If you choose any of these you will create a collection of sequentially numbered still frames (one for each video frame). Choose your image format based on your needs.

Animations—Includes Animated GIF, Filmstrip, and Flic. Each of these formats fit very narrow niches:

- Animated GIFs generally are little graphic animations that play on the Web. The Animated GIF Artists Guild offers a slew of them at www.agag.com.

- Filmstrip provides a means to send a sequence of video frames to Photoshop for *rotoscoping* (that is, adding graphic elements on a frame-by-frame basis).

- Flic is an Autodesk Animator file scheme: FLI is the smaller frame size (VGA), and FLC supports higher-resolution SVGA. Both work best on graphic animations, not video frames.

MPEG, Windows Media, RealMedia, and QuickTime File Exporter—As I mentioned earlier, these all create files that can play on most computers. But MPEG and QuickTime File Exporter are geared toward DVD production, whereas Windows Media and RealMedia work well on Web pages. I'll cover these export formats in Hour 20.

Task: Export a Single Frame

This is a very simple process:

1. Select Export Timeline, Frame to open the Export Still Frame dialog box.

2. Click Settings to open the Export Still Frame Settings dialog box.

3. Click the drop-down File Type list. As Figure 19.5 shows, you have four options: TIFF, Targa, GIF, and Windows Bitmap.

4. Click Cancel to return to the Export Movie dialog box. Click Cancel again to return to the workspace.

19

▼ TASK

▲

FIGURE 19.5

The Export Still Frame Settings dialog box offers only four file types.

Task: Export Audio

The audio side of things is a little different. It follows the same basic steps as exporting a movie:

1. Select Export Timeline, Audio to open the Export Audio dialog box.

2. Click Settings to open the Export Audio Settings dialog box.

3. Click the drop-down menu. As shown in Figure 19.6, you have four choices, all of which are very similar. Windows Waveform creates WAV files and is the only audio-specific format. Microsoft AVI and QuickTime are the same as those found in the Export Video Settings window.

4. Click Cancel to return to the Export Movie dialog box. Click Cancel again to return to the workspace.

FIGURE 19.6

Like the Export Still Frame Settings dialog box, the Export Audio Settings dialog box offers only four file types.

Yesterday's standard audio file types—WAV, AVI, and MOV—are today's "been there, done that" formats. Unless you have a compelling need to create an audio file using one of these file extensions, my recommendation is to ignore the Export Timeline, Audio process.

Instead, use Advanced Windows Media or Advanced RealMedia Export to create audio files. I'll cover these two plug-ins in Hour 20.

Wading Through Export Options

This is where the export process gets bogged down. So many options are available, and it may not be immediately apparent which to use and why. I'll try to simplify and stream-line the process:

1. Select Export Timeline, Movie to open the Export Movie dialog box.

2. Click Settings to open the Export Movie Settings dialog box with General Settings selected in the drop-down list. That list opens four other Export Movie submenus: Video, Audio, Keyframe and Rendering, and Special Processing. I'll cover them in turn. First up, General.

Export Movie Settings—General

Illustrated in Figure 19.7, this is a straightforward dialog box with few options. Two have obvious uses—Open When Finished and Beep When Finished. Here are the rest:

FIGURE 19.7

The General version of the Export Movie Settings dialog box has few options.

- File Type is the export format that you've already checked out.

- Range is the part of the project you'll export: the entire project or whatever is under the work area bar.

- Export Video and Export Audio are available for A/V output file types. This is why you don't need to use Export Clip if you want to create a video-only QuickTime file, for instance.

- Embedding Options applies only to AVI and QuickTime video files. Selecting Project Link lets you import the exported file back to Premiere and other supported programs that use the Edit Original command to do additional editing on it.

Edit Original lets you select a clip in the timeline and open it in its original software to change it. Once resaved, it shows up back in Premiere in its newly edited form. You can access Edit Original in the main menu: Edit, Edit Original.

- Advanced Settings applies only to Animated GIF and GIF Sequence files. It offers options to ensure proper Web-safe colors, set a transparency color, and loop Animated GIF files.

- Current Settings displays all settings applicable to the currently selected file type. If you change these settings within the four other Export Movie Settings dialog boxes, those changes will show up here.

> Besides exporting from the timeline, you can export from the Clip or Source Monitor screen. In those cases, if you mark in- and out-points and then select Export Clip, Movie, Settings, Range, you will see two choices: In to Out and Entire Clip. But as I've mentioned before, you will not be able to export both video and audio. Therefore, stick with using the Export Timeline menu.

Export Movie Settings—Video

Video is the single most important Export Movie Settings dialog box. Here, you set the video quality, including codec, frame size, frame rate, color depth, and quality.

There is the sense that things can become a bit complicated here. Figure 19.8 only begins to show the huge number of options. I'll try to simplify things by breaking the process down by type of export file.

Some options make huge differences in the quality of your exported file, whereas others have minimal differences. Which options are available depends entirely on the file type you select in the General version of the Export Movie Settings dialog box.

FIGURE **19.8**

The Video version of the Export Movie Settings dialog box just begins to show all the many options available.

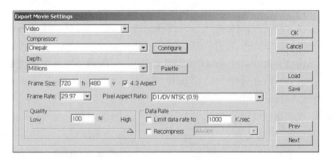

The options used for most file types are Frame Size, Frame Rate, Depth, and Quality. All are fairly self-explanatory. Some are dependent on the chosen *codec* (compression/decompression algorithm). The smaller the frame size and lower the frame rate, color depth, and quality, the smaller the exported file size. This used to be a critical issue. Many older computers could not handle higher data-rate A/V files. It's not that critical any more. Here are some of the other options:

- DV Output has virtually no options. It operates only at its highest quality. You choose between NTSC and PAL. You also set the pixel aspect ratio—basically wide-screen or regular.

- Microsoft AVI and QuickTime present the most options. The most perplexing is the codec you'll use. AVI works with 7, QuickTime with 20. Which one you choose is largely up to your needs. Adobe does not offer documentation on any of the codecs supported by Premiere. I wrote up a simplified rundown in the following sidebar.

  Some of these codecs let you set a maximum data rate. Originally this was to ensure the newly created video file did not exceed the speed ratings of lower-end CD-ROM drives. That, too, is ancient history. Checking Recompress gives you two options: Always recompresses every frame, even if it is below the stated maximum data rate, and Maintain Data Rate recompresses only those frames above the maximum rate.

- Quality, which can have a setting from 0 to 100%, is another narrow-purpose option. If you captured video using a codec and choose a lower-quality setting, you should use that same quality setting or less for export. Because you probably will work with DV source video most of the time—and therefore will not do any compression during capture—this issue rarely will be a factor.

Codec Characteristics

The number of codecs available in the Video version of the Export Movie Settings dialog box is overwhelming. You will find no documentation on any of them in your Premiere printed manual or online help file. (A caveat: The manual and help file were not completed when I wrote this book, but Adobe did not address codecs in previous Premiere manuals.) Here is a barebones rundown:

Standard video QuickTime/Windows AVI codecs—Cinepak and Indeo. Cinepak, developed in the late 1980s, is the Old Guard industry standard. Indeo 4 is better than Cinepak but requires a fast computer.

Newer video codecs (QuickTime only)—Sorenson and Motion JPEG. Both are a step up from Cinepak and Indeo. In general, Sorenson is your best bet of all standard QuickTime codecs. Motion JPEG is used mainly for storage, not playback. (Note that Photo JPEG creates high-quality images but is slow.)

Graphic animation codecs (QuickTime only)—Animation and Planar RGB.

Still image codecs (QuickTime only)—TIFF, BMP, TGA, and PNG.

Others (QuickTime only)—H.261 and H.263 are for video conferencing.

For more information on video codecs, see http://www.siggraph.org/education/materials/HyperGraph/video/codecs/Default.htm.

19

Export Movie Settings—Audio

Right off the bat, this may be a bit confusing. Here's why: Earlier you accessed the Export Audio Settings dialog box by selecting Export Timeline, Audio and clicking Settings. Do that again and then select QuickTime as the file type and use the drop-down menu at the top of the Export Audio Settings dialog box and select Audio. That opens the Export Audio Settings, Audio dialog box. Click the Compressor drop-down menu. As shown in Figure 19.9, this displays 12 audio codecs.

FIGURE **19.9**

Export Audio Settings, Audio dialog box.

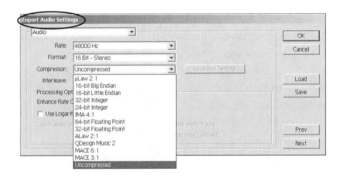

Exit out of this dialog box and select Export Timeline, Movie. Click Settings, select QuickTime from the File Type drop-down list, and use the drop-down menu at the top of the dialog box to open the Export Movie Settings, Audio dialog box. Again, open the Compressor drop-down list. This is shown in Figure 19.10.

FIGURE **19.10**

The Audio version of the Export Movie Settings dialog box. Looks the same as Figure 19.9.

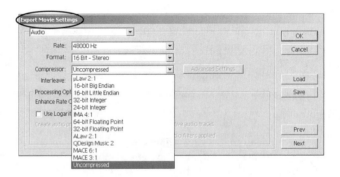

These dialog boxes are the same, with the only difference being the window names, as highlighted in the figures.

What this means is that if you want to export only the audio from your project—be it audio-only clips or only the audio portion of your project—you might as well select

Export Timeline, *Movie*, click Settings, uncheck the Export Video box, select a file type—QuickTime or Microsoft DV AVI or regular AVI—and proceed to the Export Movie Settings, Audio dialog box. The only thing you'll miss is the rarely used Microsoft WAV audio file option.

> Audio settings apply only to exported files created with Microsoft DV AVI, Microsoft AVI, and QuickTime. All other file types create images only—as single frames, sequences, or animations. If you select one of those file types and go to the Export Movie Settings, Audio dialog box, Premiere will have grayed out all the audio options.

Now that you're in the Export Movie Settings, Audio dialog box, you face only a few options. All are intended to compress your audio to make it play smoothly at a lower data rate. Again, with faster computers, this is much less critical than it used to be.

Here is a rundown of the audio options:

- Rate sets the number of samples per second. 44.1 KHz is CD music quality. It's best to capture audio at the planned export/output rate to avoid "resampling," which can lead to some quality loss.

- Format sets the bit rate for each sample. Higher is better. Your choice is 16 or 8 bit, stereo or mono.

- Compressor is the audio codec. In general, the best choice is Uncompressed. The audio portion of a video consumes much less bandwidth than the video portion. Although Adobe probably will not provide documentation on audio *or* video codecs in Premiere's printed manual or online help file, the company does offer up a few Web pages on the subject and the Audio Codec section is fairly up to date: http://www.adobe.com/support/techguides/premiere/prmr_codecs/main.html.

- Interleave sets the rate that Premiere inserts audio information among the video frames of the exported file. Smaller numbers require less RAM but may lead to audio breakup. The default value of one second should work fine.

- Enhance Rate Conversion is another means to improve audio quality while increasing export processing/rendering time. Selecting Good or Best means Premiere will take longer to analyze audio data and change its sampling rate to match your selection.

- Use Logarithmic Audio Fades smoothes audio volume changes, mimicking the logarithmic audio scale used by the human ear and standard volume controls. This, too, uses extra processing power.

19

- Create Audio Preview Files … has nothing to with exporting audio. As covered earlier in this book, you adjust this if the real-time preview of the timeline has audio pops or hissing.

Export Movie Settings—Keyframe and Rendering

With the exception of one item—Fields—you may never use the settings in this dialog box. To see how all of them work, you need to go back a couple steps:

1. Click the drop-down menu at the top of the Export Movie Settings dialog box and select General. In that dialog box's File Type drop-down list, select Microsoft AVI or QuickTime.

2. Move to the Export Movie Settings, Video dialog box by using the drop-down list at the top and selecting Video. In that dialog box's Compressor drop-down list, select Cinepak (this codec works with both Microsoft AVI and QuickTime video files). Cinepak is one of the few codecs that uses keyframes (not the keyframes you apply within Premiere to change effects over time but rather frames of video Cinepak analyzes as part of its compression process).

3. Move to the Export Movie Settings, Keyframe and Rendering dialog box by using the drop-down list at the top of the page and selecting Keyframe and Rendering (see Figure 19.11).

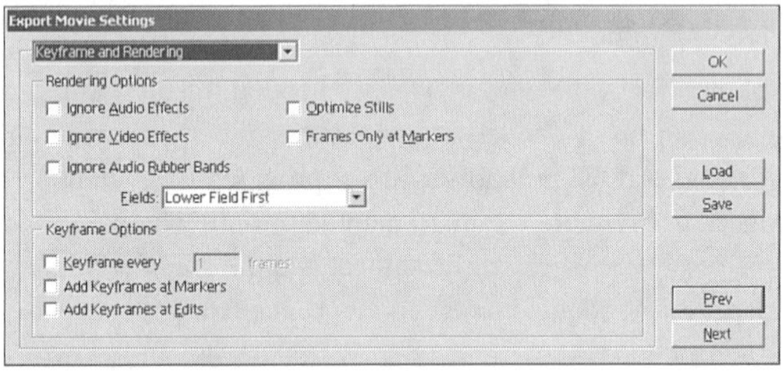

FIGURE 19.11

The Export Movie Settings, Keyframe and Rendering dialog box.

Here's a rundown on what's available in this window:

Ignore Audio Effects, Ignore Video Effects, Ignore Rubberbands—Why, you might ask, would you want to "ignore" all those special effects you spent hours applying to your project? You probably won't want to do this. But if you do want to make a "rough cut" of your video to show someone to discuss possible changes, this is one way to do it. Uncheck these boxes when you export the real thing later.

Optimize Stills and Frames Only at Markers—Why you'd use these options, I don't know. Optimize Stills saves disk space by converting still images into single, longer-playing frames instead of playing 30 frames per second. Frames Only at Markers exports only still images of the frames you've identified with markers on the timeline. In that case, you might as well make still frames one at a time.

Fields—This is one of those easily overlooked "gotchas." The default setting for all DV output should be Lower Field First. For computer monitors, it's No Fields. Premiere should automatically change this setting, depending on the file type. However, that does not appear to be the case. Therefore, do check this. Some video hardware needs to have an Upper Field setting. You'll have to check your documentation to find out.

Keyframes—Offers a level of control few video producers will ever need nor want to exploit. Some codecs—Cinepak, Intel Indeo, Sorenson, and others—offer this user-selected option. Basically, more keyframes means better-looking compressed video and more rendering time. But this is serious engineering overkill.

Export Movie Settings—Special Processing

Holy cow! Just when you thought it was safe to start rendering, even more—largely unnecessary—fine-tuning options. Most of these options, shown in Figure 19.12, let you reduce the data rate of your compressed video even more. But again, that is yesterday's news. Today's computers don't demand this level of compression. But in case you were wondering, here's a rundown:

19

FIGURE **19.12**

The Special Processing dialog box.

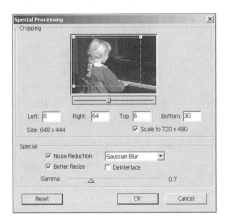

- Cropping lets you shrink the portion of the screen that will display in the entire compressed data file. The slider lets you see how that cropped image will look throughout your entire project, but you can't set keyframes to move the cropped area around or adjust its size. If you crop, you can check the Scale box to have the codec expand the cropped image to fill the final output screen size.

- Noise Reduction lets you set a degree of blurring that increases compression efficiency. Blur is subtle, Gaussian is stronger, and Median attempts to keep object edges sharp.

- Better Resize uses a Premiere compression "helper" to improve the video quality of cropped videos. If you crop, check this box.

- Deinterlace is another Premiere "helper" that produces better images when you're creating QuickTime or AVI files.

- Gamma lets you adjust the brightness of mid-tones to lighten darker videos, and vice versa. Adobe recommends a Gamma setting of 0.7 to 0.8 (a brighter overall look) for Mac/Windows cross-platform playback. My take is that this, too, is unnecessary. But if your QuickTime videos look fine on a Mac but dark on a PC, this is where you can fix it.

Finally, Exporting Your Project

Tired of all these options? Most are holdovers from the days of slower computers. With the exception of videos running on the Web over dial-up connections, you want to aim for high-quality output. We'll start with the obvious—DV. Here's the process:

1. Connect your DV camcorder to your computer, just as you did when you captured video. Set it to VTR.

   At this point you could go directly to Export Timeline, Export to Tape. If everything is in order, Premiere immediately renders your project's unrendered transitions and effects, puts your camcorder in Record mode (after a couple button clicks on your part), and exports your project to DV tape. Simple.

   But before doing that, it's a good idea to make sure everything *is* in order.

   Each time you start Premiere, you click through the Load Project Settings dialog box. You probably select the same setting each time. Although more than a dozen presets (and even more if you have a video capture card) and uncountable options are available, the bottom line is that there are only three video output formats: DV, Video for Windows, and QuickTime.

2. To check up on your output settings, select Project, Project Settings, General from the main menu. This opens the Project Settings dialog box, shown in Figure 19.13.

FIGURE 19.13

FIGURE 19.13

The Project Settings, General dialog box displays your overall capture/output values. Click the Playback Settings button to adjust the output to your camcorder.

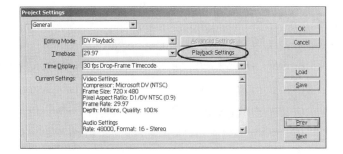

Here is another of those potentially confusing Premiere-isms. If you move through the various Project Settings dialog boxes—Video, Audio, and Keyframe and Rendering—you'll see some familiar screens. Although it's good to be able to access settings like this in various ways, the inconsistent dialog box names—Project Settings, Export Movie Settings, and Export Audio Settings—create confusion, especially because they all do the same thing.

3. Open the Editing Mode drop-down menu. It displays the preset you selected at startup: DV Playback, Video for Windows, or QuickTime. If you're using a Mac and working with DV, then QuickTime's DV mode should be visible.

4. Click the Playback Settings button highlighted in Figure 19.13. For Windows users, this displays the dialog box shown in Figure 19.14. Mac users have a QuickTime DV dialog box with similar options.

FIGURE 19.14

Use the DV Playback Options dialog box to select whether Premiere displays video on your computer and camcorder.

In either case you can choose where you'll see video playback during editing and exporting. If while recording to your camcorder frames are lost, uncheck both the Playback on Desktop box and the Play Audio on Desktop while Scrubbing box.

19

Export to Tape

Now, finally, follow these steps to export to tape:

1. Make sure your work area bar covers your entire project and does not include any virtual clips.

> To give your project a little breathing room on your DV tape, add black video to the beginning of your project. You know the drill: Right/Option-click in the Project window, select New, Black Video. Drag that to the start of your project and give it a duration of around five seconds (right/Option-click the clip in the timeline, select Duration, and give it a time) .
>
> If you're going to have a postproduction studio duplicate your tapes, add 30 seconds of "bars and tone" to the beginning so they can set up their gear. Same drill as black video: Right/Option-click the Project window, select New, Bars and Tone. Drag it to the beginning of your project and change its duration to 30 seconds.

2. Select File, Export Timeline, Export to Tape. Premiere should pop up a display like the one in Figure 19.15 to note that it's building a preview. If you have already rendered all transitions and effects, Premiere may skip this step.

FIGURE 19.15

Premiere first builds a preview before exporting to your camcorder.

Once Premiere completes rendering your project, it pops up the Export to Tape Settings dialog box, shown in Figure 19.16.

Most times you'll accept the default settings. In case you need an extra level of control for your export process, here's an explanation of each value:

FIGURE 19.16

The Export to Tape Settings dialog box lets you fine-tune the export process before starting to record your project to your DV device.

- Select Activate recording deck to let Premiere control your deck.
- Assemble at time code lets you specify where on the tape to begin recording. If you don't select this option, recording begins at the current tape location.
- Movie start delay may not apply to you. Some camcorders need a delay between the time they receive the record command and the time the movie starts playing from the computer.
- Preroll lets your deck back up to "get up to speed" before recording begins. Again, with newer camcorders you don't need to use this.

> To experiment, try recording a short clip (place the work area bar over only a few seconds of your project) and record with no preroll. Go back and see whether your camcorder captured all the frames. If so, don't sweat the Preroll option.

3. Click OK. Premiere should start your camcorder and record your project to it. Somehow, I think there should be a drum roll with a cymbal crash here.

> If you have an analog recorder with Device Control—this typically is an expensive broadcast-quality device—you follow basically the same process with one additional step. Because it's analog, you need a video capture card. Also, you need to use its analog output settings. Select them by going to Edit, Preferences, Scratch Disks and Device Control and selecting your device control plug-in from the Device list. Then go to File, Export Timeline, Export to Tape.

19

Print to Video

This is the non-Device Control recording method. Technically, you can use this for a DV device, but you might as well stick with Export to Tape for that.

Because this is intended for recording to analog devices, you need a video capture card with Analog Out plugs. Here are the steps to follow:

1. In the timeline, place the work area bar over the entire project or segment you want to record. Render it by pressing Enter or Shift+Enter, depending on whether you have Real-time Preview enabled or not. You should see the preview playing in your recorder's monitor.

2. Select File, Export Timeline, Print to Video. You should see the dialog box in Figure 19.17.

FIGURE 19.17

The Print to Video dia-
log box lets you add
color bars and black to
the beginning of your
project.

This dialog box offers a couple nifty little extras: color bars and black video. No need to create them and place them in the timeline because Print to Video takes care of that for you.

3. Start your recorder and then click OK. You should see your project playing in your recorder's monitor.

> Print to Video is a nifty way to see your project in full-screen mode *without* actually recording it. Simply go through the regular Print to Video steps, selecting Full Screen (Windows) or Zoom Screen (Mac). No need to turn on a recorder. Simply click OK and watch. Select Loop Playback to watch it over and over and over.

Task: Export a Movie

This task covers all other export modes, with the exception of Frames (a very simple process). Because you've already waded through all the file types and options, I'll just take you through one export process. Any other one would be very similar. In this case, you'll export (create a new file) your project using QuickTime.

You know the drill:

1. Select File, Export Timeline, Movie. Click Settings to open the Export Movie Settings dialog box.

2. Select QuickTime from the File Type drop-down menu.

3. Select Work Area or Entire Project, depending on your needs.

4. You can choose to export only audio or only video by unchecking the appropriate box. Check or uncheck Beep When Finished and Open When Finished.

5. Click Next or use the drop-down menu to move on to the Export Movie Settings, Video dialog box. There, select a codec—Intel Indeo, Sorenson, or Cinepak (all will work fine). Make any adjustments to Frame Size, Frame Rate, and Quality that suit you.

▼   6. Move on to Export Movie Settings, Audio and make any adjustments there.

7. Check to see that No Fields is selected in the Keyframe and Rendering window.

▲   8. Click OK. Navigate to an appropriate file folder, give your project a name, and click Save. Premiere will go into a render mode, applying the codec and other elements you selected in the Export Movie Settings dialog box. When done, it'll save the file and, if you checked Open When Finished, will open a clip window to allow you to play this newly created file.

The process is nearly the same for Frame Sequences and Animations. In those cases, just about the only adjustments you'll need to make are to the Frame Size and Frame Rate.

If you want to create still frames, use Export Timeline, Frame and then select a graphic type and frame size.

Summary

Premiere offers two basic means to export your project: recording to videotape and creating a file. Recording to videotape is straightforward. Creating a file offers many more options. You can create video files, still frames, sequences of still frames, or animation files. In each instance, you can adjust various settings to reduce file size, generally as a means to streamline playback.

Workshop

Review the questions and answers in this section to try to sharpen your Premiere export skills. Also, take a few moments to tackle my short quiz and the exercises.

19

Q&A

Q When I use Print to Video to view a full-screen version of my project and to watch it in my DV device monitor, playback on my computer is choppy. What's up?

A Your computer may not have the power to process both video data streams. Go to Project, Project Settings, General, Playback Settings. Because you probably want to view this on your computer monitor, turn off Playback on DV/Camcorder. If you want to view it on your DV/camcorder monitor, turn off Playback on Desktop.

Q I have a VHS VCR and want to export to it, but I don't have a video capture card. Is there a workaround?

A Yes. Record your project to your DV camcorder. Then connect your DV camcorder to your analog VCR/camcorder and dub your DV videotape to it. You may be able to save a step and pass the DV signal from your computer through your DV camcorder to your analog recorder and record on both machines at once.

Quiz

1. How do you export a clip without using the Export Clip process?

2. What's the difference between Project Settings, Audio; Export Audio Settings, Audio; and Export Movie Settings, Audio?

3. How do you create a sequence of still images, selecting one frame per second from your project?

Quiz Answers

1. Select the clip in the timeline by placing the work area bar over it. Select File, Export Timeline, Movie. Click Settings and make the necessary file type and option selections to suit your needs. Alternatively, you can select the clip in the timeline and then select File, Export Timeline, Export to Tape and record the clip directly to your DV device.

2. Nothing. An Audio Output Settings dialog box by any other name would work as sweetly.

3. Use the Export Timeline process. Place the work area bar over the portion of your project from which you want to create still images, select File, Export Timeline, Movie. Click Settings. Choose a sequence file type—TIFF, Targa, GIF, or Windows Bitmap—move to Video and select a frame size and change the Frame Rate setting to 1.

Exercises

1. Do a personal test on video and audio codecs. Set the work area bar over a small section of your timeline and then export it using different codecs. Use the same Frame Size, Frame Rate, and Quality settings. When completed, note the file sizes and playback quality of the saved files.

2. Contact a local postproduction studio and ask about EDLs (Edit Decision Lists). Get their take on the value of an EDL and see what compatibility issues there may be between their equipment and Premiere.

3. You can use Premiere's export process as a file-conversion program. Try a few examples by placing Windows AVI files, QuickTime MOV files, or Windows WAV audio files on the timeline and using Export Timeline to convert them to their competing platform counterparts.

HOUR 20

Exporting Premiere Frames, Clips, and Projects: Part 2

A valuable component of Premiere's suite of tools is the MPEG Encoder. This tool converts Premiere video projects into industry-standard, high-quality MPEG videos for inclusion on DVDs or specialized movie CDs. You'll give this powerful product a test drive this hour.

Mac users have other means to convert Premiere projects to MPEG-2. I'll explain how that works in a sidebar.

Posting your Premiere-created videos on the Internet has never been easier thanks to two plug-ins included with Premiere: Advanced Windows Media (Windows only) and Advanced RealMedia Export. Both create compressed files that play back on HTML pages and incorporate special URL markers to load Web pages during playback.

The highlights of this hour include the following:

- Revisiting MPEG
- Using the new Adobe MPEG Encoder for DVDs and video CDs
- Preparing your projects for use on the Web
- Using the Advanced Windows Media plug-in for Web and Desktop media file export (Windows only)
- Using the Advanced RealMedia Export plug-in for Web apps

Revisiting MPEG

Why a special "encoder" for MPEG? As I mentioned in Hour 2, "Premiere Setup," MPEG-2 is the de facto standard codec for DVD movies and videos. It presents sharp video and CD-quality audio at about one-thirtieth the data rate of regular analog video and one-fourth the data rate of DV. You've seen movies on DVD and know how good they look. And you've seen those razor-sharp digital satellite TV images. Both systems use MPEG-2-encoded videos.

If you want to create similar quality DVDs to play on your home or business DVD video system, you must use MPEG-2-encoded video files. That's been the case ever since DVD movies arrived on the scene a few years ago.

Because you probably shot your videos using prosumer DV, they will not look as good as Hollywood DVD movies. Hollywood DVD movies start their lives as 35 mm (or larger) film. DV can't touch that for quality. And those great video images you see on digital satellite systems—while running under MPEG-2 compression—probably started as broadcast-quality analog video signals—also a cut or two above prosumer DV.

Only now are professional video producers embracing this technology. It took the convergence of two technological advances to bring us to this point of putting a software-based MPEG encoder in Premiere:

- First, MPEG is asymmetrical. It takes a lot of computer horsepower to *encode* a DV or analog TV signal into MPEG-2 or other MPEG formats (I'll touch on QuickTime 6's connection to MPEG-4 in the following sidebar). On the other hand, *decoding* (playback on your DVD player) takes much less processor juice. Until relatively recently, encoding MPEG-2 required some expensive hardware, priced beyond the reach of most video producers. Now increases in processor power and improved MPEG-encoding software have eliminated the need for hardware MPEG encoders.

- Second, DVD recorders have come way, way down in price. Pioneer Electronics is driving this continuing downward price spiral. By mid 2002, its standard DVD recorder retailed for less than $500. Along with this drop in hardware pricing, DVD recordable media prices have dropped dramatically, to as low as $3 per disc when purchased in bulk.

What this means is that now you have an opportunity to create media that will play on most DVD players and is interactive and high quality. DVDs are replacing PowerPoint presentations. You know what its like to click through menus on a movie DVD. Using Premiere's MPEG Encoder and the bundled DVDit! authoring software means Windows OS users can create that same experience for their family or clients. Mac users need to pursue some other options.

MPEG-2 on a Mac? It Depends.

Some real confusion surrounds whether Macs can create true "DVD-quality" MPEG-2 videos.

In general, only new, high-end Macs can. To create MPEG-2 videos on a Mac, you need a 933 MHz or better Power Mac G4 bundled with a DVD-R (recordable) SuperDrive and iDVD.

iDVD, Apple's entry level DVD-authoring software, puts an MPEG-2 encoder in QuickTime. That means if you want to convert a Premiere project to MPEG-2 for use on a Mac, you need to have iDVD installed.

Premiere made sure it integrated its export functions tightly with QuickTime. Because it is a separate product, I won't cover its functionality here. However, using the QuickTime File Exporter in Premiere is a very straightforward process.

Here's how you Export Premiere projects to QuickTime:

1. Select Export Timeline, Movie.
2. Click Settings and select QuickTime File Exporter from the File Type drop-down menu.
3. Click Advanced Settings and specify the file type under Export. Click OK, and the encoding should begin.

QuickTime 6 Pro, which should be out of Beta by the time this book hits store shelves, features an MPEG-4 codec (if you have iDVD, it will load its MPEG-2 codec into QT 6). MPEG-4 is a relatively new video-compression scheme, created in 1998, and is strongly supported by Apple. Its developers based its file format largely on QuickTime's.

20

MPEG-4 has many strengths, but its largest use will likely be for streaming video and audio on the Internet. To really see and hear it at its best, you need a broadband connection. If that's the case, download the QuickTime 6 player from www.apple.com and then go to http://www.apple.com/quicktime/preview/instanton_gallery/ to see just how sharp these MPEG-4 videos look and sound, plus how quickly they start playing.

Despite my glowing take on MPEG-4, it still cannot match MPEG-2's picture and sound quality.

Some Beta testers grumbled that Premiere should have bundled an MPEG-2 encoder for the Mac as well as Windows. Adobe's explanation to me was that Mac owners who want to make DVDs have systems with iDVD preinstalled and don't need an MPEG encoder.

The downside is that Mac owners who want to create MPEG videos for media other than DVD have to purchase third-party MPEG-encoding software.

Using the New Adobe MPEG Encoder

Before we get into the exporting/encoding details, I want to give you a little background on this new Premiere plug-in. To begin, select File, Export Timeline, Adobe MPEG Encoder.

Figure 20.1 shows the encoder's main interface. You'll note in the upper-right corner it says, "Powered by MainConcept." This is a long-standing German firm (from the days of the Amiga) with a solid reputation as a creator of powerful multimedia tools and codecs.

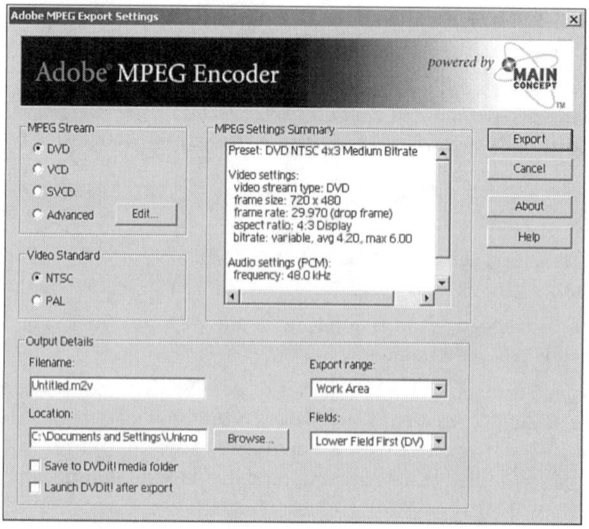

FIGURE 20.1

The new Adobe MPEG Encoder, "powered by" MainConcept.

As I mentioned in Hour 19, "Exporting Premiere Frames, Clips, and Projects: Part 1," including a software MPEG encoder in Premiere is a *big deal*. Up until now, if Premiere users wanted to create MPEG-2 videos, they had to buy a third-party plug-in, such as the $250 Ligos LSX-MPEG, or use a hardware encoder. Now Windows users get a powerful encoder for *free*. In a head-to-head competition with the Ligos encoder (conducted by MainConcept), the Adobe MPEG Encoder came out on top in speed and image quality.

Its two-layer interface—Main and Advanced—makes the most commonly used settings available in the main dialog box while giving "power users" the ability to tweak a variety of parameters in the Advanced dialog box. Another strength is its integration with Premiere and DVDit!, the DVD-authoring software I'll go over in Hours 21–24.

MainConcept has a support/resource site for the Adobe MPEG Encoder. It includes a FAQ about the encoder and MPEG in general, new settings files to download, test results, and a link to the Adobe MPEG Encoder User-to-User forum on Adobe.com. The link to the support/resource site is `http://www.mainconcept.com/adobempeg.html`. You also can get to the Web site using a hotlink accessed by clicking the Encoder's About button.

MainConcept's Web site is worth a visit at the very least because it offers free "texture loops"—four-second (1MB) motion video clips you can drop into Premiere for some dazzling background animation. Figure 20.2 illustrates how one looks. One use for them is as text backdrops.

It's a simple matter to copy/paste the same loop several times to create a smooth background animation. When placed end to end, there is a seamless transition from one copy of the clip to the next. You may also change the speed/duration of the clips to alter the character of the animations.

FIGURE 20.2

Visit www. mainconcept.com to pick up a few texture loops like this one for use within Premiere.

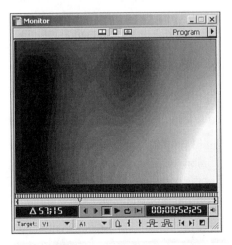

20

Task: Encode an MPEG-2 File

To export or convert a Premiere project or timeline segment to MPEG-2, follow these steps:

1. For the moment cancel out of the encoder and go back to your timeline.

2. Load a project and place the work area bar over a *small* segment—15 seconds or so. No need to encode an entire project for this task. Despite MainConcept's successful speed trials, MPEG-2 encoding still takes about as long as the duration of your project.

> As a reminder, use the N hotkey to set the work area bar boundaries. Press N once, roll it over the work area, highlighted in Figure 20.3, and see which direction the triangle is facing. Click to set one endpoint for the work area bar, press N to switch the triangle's direction, and set the other endpoint. Press V to switch the cursor back to the Selection tool.

FIGURE 20.3

Use the N hotkey to set endpoints for the work area bar.

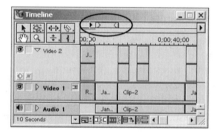

3. Select File, Export Timeline, Adobe MPEG Encoder to return to the MainConcept interface. Your first option is to choose an MPEG stream. The selections are shown in Figure 20.4.

FIGURE 20.4

Select an MPEG "stream."

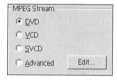

Here's what these options mean:

DVD—Selecting this option means the MPEG Encoder will create two MPEG-2 files—one for video and the other audio—for inclusion on a DVD. DVDs can hold up to 4.7GB of data (133 minutes of MPEG-2 video) per side. You also can place VHS-quality MPEG-1 video on them. They play in both standalone DVD players and in computers with DVD drives.

> DVD is not an official acronym. Most companies say DVD stands for *Digital Versatile Disc*, but that's not the case. DVDs started as "digital video discs," but industry politics killed that idea. A journalist suggested "versatile" and through repeated usage that has become the de facto, standardized name.

VCD (Video CD)—If you select this option, the Adobe MPEG Encoder will make an MPEG-1 file of your project. Later, using standalone CD-authoring and/or writing software that supports VCD, you can "burn" up to about an hour of MPEG-1 video onto a CD that will play on most consumer DVD video players and computer DVD and CD drives. A good online resource for VCD and SVCD issues is
`http://www.vcdhelp.com/svcd.htm`.

> The documentation accompanying the MPEG Encoder notes that DVDit! LE, the DVD-authoring product bundled with Premiere, does *not* support VCD creation. I tried running VCD (and SVCD) MPEG files in DVDit! and they both worked fine. The folks at Sonic Solutions, the company behind DVDit! tell me they have not run these file types through their extensive test matrix to check that everything works. It can sometimes be the case that such "untested" files will work, but Sonic Solutions cannot guarantee they'll work on every system.

SVCD (Super Video CD)—This is a step up from VCD. In this case, the Adobe MPEG Encoder will create a reduced bitstream rate, specialized MPEG-2 file. Depending on parameters you set, you can put up to about 45 minutes of video on a CD using this low-end MPEG-2 (still better than MPEG-1) video. Again, you need authoring- and/or CD-burning software that supports SVCD to create an SVCD CD-ROM.

20

> SVCD creates videos in a 480×480 resolution. If you play them back on standard video players such as the Windows Media Player or within Premiere in the Source window, they'll look "tall" (that is, squashed in at the sides). If you open these files in software that recognizes this standard MPEG format, such as DVDit!, they will play in the proper aspect ratio. If you place them

▼

on Premiere's timeline and play them in the Monitor window, they will display in the proper aspect ratio, but as noted later in the sidebar, "Why Premiere Does Not Edit Native MPEG Video," Premiere is not designed to handle any MPEG format.

What about cDVD? Although DVDit! may or may not create VCDs or SVCDs, it certainly does create cDVDs. This is a Sonic Solutions proprietary product that puts MPEG-1 or MPEG-2 files at virtually any quality level on CDs that are playable on PC CD-ROM and DVD-ROM drives. When you use DVDit! to burn a file onto a recordable CD, that authoring product adds an MPEG player on the disc. That player runs directly from the CD—nothing is installed on the user's hard drive. A cDVD should play smoothly on any Windows PC CD-ROM drive. The downside to this is that you cannot play cDVD discs in standalone DVD players.

Advanced—This option takes you to another interface that I'll cover in a few minutes.

4. Select an MPEG stream. In this case, select DVD (MPEG-2). The default settings show up in the MPEG Settings Summary, shown in Figure 20.5.

FIGURE 20.5

The MPEG Settings Summary displays the default settings for each MPEG stream.

5. Select a video standard: NTSC or PAL.

6. In Output Details, shown in Figure 20.6, you can give your file a name and a file folder location.

If you plan to use DVDit! to create DVDs, then check the Save to DVDit! Media Folder box. That automatically places the folder name in the Location window. If you want to launch DVDit! after the export, check that box as well.

▼

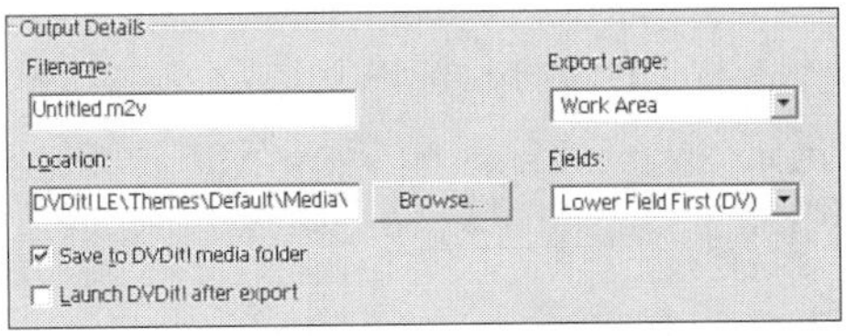

FIGURE 20.6

Output Details is used to set the filename, location, and other basic options.

7. As you did with the Export Movie Settings dialog box, choose an export range: Entire Project or Work Area.

8. Finally, select the Fields option. This is something of a hit-or-miss proposition. It sets the so-called *field order* or *interlace*. Most DV starts with Lower Field First, but analog capture cards can use Lower or Upper Field First.

> If you're unsure about the Fields setting, select No Fields to produce acceptable but not optimal video. The workaround is to experiment by creating a file with one setting and watching the clip to see whether it's jittery. If so, switch settings.

9. Click Export.

The MPEG encoding begins. Because you accepted the default settings, the Adobe MPEG Encoder compresses more or less in real time (that is, it takes as long to encode as the length of your project). In this case, it takes about 15 seconds.

To view and listen to your newly created MPEG-2 files, you may import them to your Project window or open DVDit!, start an MPEG-2 session, and view them in its window.

Just to make sure all is in order, import the video and audio files into Premiere and drag them to the timeline. Place the audio directly under the video and link them together.

> As a reminder, the Link tool hotkey is U. (You may need to cycle through the Crossfade and the Fade Adjustment tools first.) Once it's selected, click both the video and audio clips to link them.

20

Advanced Interface

Accepting default settings for any of the three MPEG stream types may be all you'll ever need to do, but the more you use this encoder the more likely you'll want to fine-tune it. Here's how:

1. Open the MPEG Encoder again by going to the main menu and selecting File, Export Timeline, Adobe MPEG Encoder.

2. Click the Edit button next to Advanced in the MPEG Stream section. That opens the Advanced MPEG Settings dialog box, shown in Figure 20.7.

FIGURE 20.7

The Advanced MPEG Settings dialog box lets you fine-tune your MPEG encoding process.

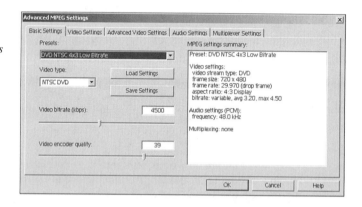

 There's no need to click the check box next to Advanced in the MPEG Stream window. Doing so keeps the current default settings in the Settings Summary window.

The depth of customizability in this interface is remarkable—too much to discuss in detail here. Of the five tabs, you may never access more than two: Basic Settings and Multiplexer Settings. Here are some highlights:

Basic Settings—This is one of the simpler of the settings pages. Select the preset drop-down list and note that half (nine) are for NTSC and the other half for PAL. Three are for 16:9 (wide-screen) aspect ratios; the rest offer higher or lower bitrate settings than the default presets:

- Video Type provides a simple way to revert to the default settings for an MPEG stream.

- Video Bitrate adjusts the maximum bitrate.

 The bitrate settings are generally safe to adjust when encoding for DVD only. VCD and SVCD High Bitrate CBR (Constant Bitrate) have very narrow allowable bitrate values. Parameters need to be within the legal limits for the format. The Adobe MPEG Encoder will present warning messages when invalid settings are chosen.

- Encoder Quality means the lower the quality the faster the encoding.

The Video Encoder Quality slider controls a few different parameters that tell the encoder how big of a search area within each video frame to examine for matching blocks of pixels. The surprising thing is that with many videos you can turn the slider down significantly (resulting in faster encoding) without any noticeable quality loss. For general use, a Video Encoder Quality setting of 28 will usually provide a very happy medium of fast encoding and great quality. See Advanced Settings, later in the list, for additional Video Encoder Quality tips.

DVDit! LE does *not* support 16:9 screen widths. The Adobe MPEG Encoder does. Adobe included this option in the encoder in case you have other authoring software that works with 16:9. DVDit! PE (Professional Edition, a $500 upgrade from DVDit! LE) does.

Selecting a high bitrate means you will experience long encoding times. Use this only to preserve high-quality video or film images.

You may load presets obtained from other sources into the MPEG Encoder. The MainConcept/Adobe support Web site will be one source. Simply download them—they're small files—and use the Load button to select them. If you want to add one to the Preset drop-down list, save it to the default `Settings` folder.

Video Settings—This page offers up some complexity, including GOP (Group of Pictures) settings, and is only for those who are steeped in MPEG arcana.

Advanced Video Settings—Even the folks at MainConcept make a point of admonishing Premiere users to forgo this collection of complex selections. Unless you're dripping with knowledge about ITU-R Rec, 624-4 System B, and G matrix coefficients, take a pass (with two exceptions—see the following tip).

20

If you adjusted the Video Encoder Quality slider, you may want to fine-tune that by tweaking two values in the Advanced Video Settings page:

Motion Search—A setting of 5 to 8 is appropriate for most material. 5 provides faster encoding but with the potential for quality loss (although at higher bitrates or in material with low movement, this potential is reduced significantly).

Noise Sensitivity—This control sets a motion search threshold, depending on the noise in the video. The noisier the video the higher this should be set, but it generally is not advisable to go over 15. The higher the setting, the faster the encoding. Here are some recommended values:

- 0–5 for material with no noise at all, such as computer animation
- 3–9 for material with nearly unnoticeable noise (such as DV)
- 7–13 (or higher) for material with high noise, such as TV capture

Audio Settings—Same story here. Unless you have a specific need to change the audio frequency, type, or bitrate, skip this page.

Multiplexer Settings—This is the other page you may want to access. As you noted when you created the MPEG-2 video (by selecting the DVD MPEG stream), you ended up with two files: video and audio. This page, shown in Figure 20.8, lets you multiplex (combine audio and video into one file). That means software such as Windows Media Player and RealOne Player will play audio while playing video. Of the three MPEG stream types, only DVD does *not* multiplex by default. To change that, simply select MPEG-2 from the Multiplexing Type drop-down menu. I've highlighted that in Figure 20.8.

FIGURE 20.8

Selecting MPEG-2 in the Multiplexing Type drop-down list combines video and audio into one MPEG-2 file.

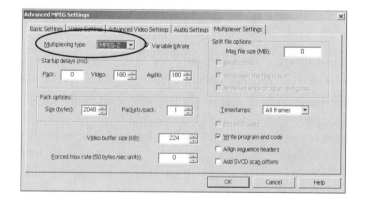

DVDit! can work with multiplexed (or *muxed*) files. But it works more efficiently with "elementary stream" (separate video and audio) MPEG files.

Why Premiere Does Not Edit Native MPEG Video

As I put together this hour on MPEG encoding, I swapped several emails with the MainConcept U.S. subsidiary Chief Operating Officer, Mark Bailey.

Bailey is the company's primary liaison with Adobe. His solid grasp of the MPEG compression universe completely impressed me. After reading several emails from several Beta testers on the Premiere forum asking why Premiere didn't offer MPEG editing, I asked Bailey for his take on this topic. The remainder of this sidebar summarizes what he had to say.

Although MPEG is an excellent way to deliver material, it has some limitations as an editing format. Because of its high compression and the way that some frames are calculated, MPEG material can be subject to significant quality degradation when rendered multiple times. Because video editing and compositing projects often involve many generations of rendering, there is the potential for noticeable loss.

Of course, it's best to start any editing or compositing project with the least-compressed source material available. Using highly compressed media from the start could present serious problems.

The workflow explained in this book—editing in DV and encoding the finished project to MPEG—works very well.

There are some cases in which people might need to edit MPEG, and some companies offer plug-ins that enable it with varying results. Of course, MainConcept could create a superb MPEG-editing plug-in, offering the best possible results given the nature of the format. Even so, editing MPEG still isn't the best way to go in many cases.

One of the most popular arguments for MPEG editing is to save the time-consuming process of MPEG encoding. However, in our tests the Adobe MPEG Encoder is running at nearly real-time on a 2.2 GHz Pentium 4 system. Therefore, MPEG encoding is not the lengthy ordeal it once was, and it will be even less painful as CPU speeds continue to increase.

20

Preparing Your Projects for Use on the Web

If you plan to use your videos within HTML pages—on the Internet or an intranet—consider tying specific Web pages to events in your project. Premiere offers a very clever feature that lets your videos pop up Web pages at opportune moments.

Consider a training video, for example. As you cover certain points, you can have them appear in a bulleted list next to your video. If you're pitching a product, you can pop up a Web site with additional info and an email link.

Advanced Windows Media, Advanced RealMedia, and QuickTime support these URL markers.

This assumes you have some basic knowledge of HTML coding and Web page creation. If not, this may be an impetus to delve into these fields.

Task: Add Web Links to Video Projects

▼ TASK

To add Web links to video projects, follow these steps:

1. Open a project.

2. Create a marker somewhere in the project. For this task, anywhere in the project is fine. Obviously, if you plan to use a video to trigger the display of new Web pages, you want to select your marker locations carefully.

> As a reminder, to create a marker, move the edit line to a location within your project and press the asterisk (*) key on the numeric keypad (not Shift+8). As highlighted in Figure 20.9, that places a little gray pointer in the time ruler.

FIGURE 20.9

Pressing the asterisk key on the numeric keypad places a marker on the time ruler.

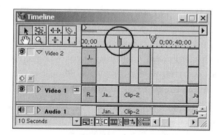

3. Open that marker's info box by double-clicking it or right/Option-clicking on it to open a context-sensitive menu and selecting Edit Timeline Marker. That opens the dialog box shown in Figure 20.10.

4. Under Web Links, as shown in Figure 20.11, type in the URL for the associated Web page. If you are using frames, enter a filename in the Frame Target field. If you're not using frames, type in **_blank**. Leaving that space empty means the newly loaded URL will stop your video.

▼

FIGURE 20.10

Use the timeline marker's info box to associate a Web page with a specific frame in your video.

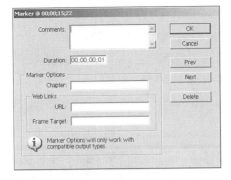

FIGURE 20.11

Type in a URL and a frame filename or "_blank."

You can use markers to create DVD "chapters" in your video. Some DVD-authoring products let you create links to specific locations or chapters within a complete project. You've seen this in action in the scene-selection menus for DVD movies that take you to scenes within the movie (not to a separate collection of scene files, as some think).

However, DVDit! LE, which comes with Premiere, has the chapters feature disabled. It's enabled in the SE and PE versions. iDVD also does not support chapters. Its $1,000 big brother, Apple's DVD Studio Pro, does.

Using the Advanced Windows Media Plug-In

This is the most versatile video format for use in Windows PCs and for playback on the Internet. It supports URL markers and creates single files with multiple bandwidth bit stream rates to compensate for varying Internet user connection speeds.

As far as the actual export process goes, there's good news, not so good news, and sort of good news:

- The good news is that using the Advanced Windows Media plug-in is very easy.
- The not so good news is that you can use it *only* on your entire project, not a selection under the timeline.
- The sort of good news is that workarounds are available if you want to export a portion of your project to a standard Windows Media WMV file.

20

Task: Export Your Project to Advanced Windows Media

To convert your entire project into a Windows Media WMV file, follow these steps:

1. Open a project. I'd suggest selecting a short project because Advanced Windows Media is an all-or-nothing proposition.

2. Select File, Export Timeline, Advanced Windows Media. That opens the dialog box shown in Figure 20.12.

FIGURE 20.12

The Windows Media 8 Export Plug-in for Adobe Premiere dialog box gives you a raft of user playback profiles.

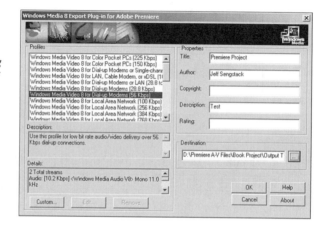

3. Scroll through the Profiles list and note there are 30 options. Most are self-explanatory.

4. Select the third profile—Dial-up Modems or Single-Channel ISDN Connections. As highlighted in Figure 20.13, that profile will create a file with *seven* bandwidth streams to accommodate dial-up connections as slow as 7Kbps to as fast as 45.3Kbps.

FIGURE 20.13

Some profiles create single files with multiple bandwidth streams. This profile creates seven such streams.

▼
5. Note the Properties section. All these fields are optional and will display in the Windows Media Player.

6. Select a destination by clicking the button highlighted in Figure 20.14.

FIGURE 20.14

Select a location for your WMV file by clicking this button.

7. You could start the export (file conversion) now, but first look at the custom settings by clicking that button below the Details window. This opens the Manage Profiles dialog box shown in Figure 20.15. Click the Details button to expand the window.

FIGURE 20.15

The Manage Profiles dialog box lets you fine-tune your export settings.

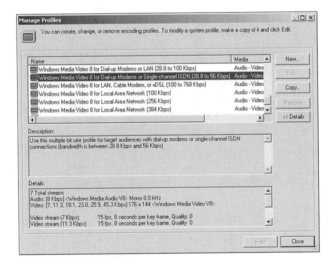

8. Locate the same profile you selected earlier: Dial-up Modems or Single-Channel ISDN. At this stage in the process you could create your own profile using this as a starting point. I'll give you a brief explanation in a later tip. For now, close the Manage Profiles dialog box.

Things may become a bit confusing here. The profiles displayed in the Manage Profiles dialog box are not in the same order as they are in the Windows Media 8 Export Plug-in for Adobe Premiere dialog box. You'll need to search around a bit.

Some profiles read "no audio" in their title but in the Media column indicate "Audio-Video."

▼

20

VBR means *variable bitrate*.

To create or edit profiles, use a default profile as a starting point. Don't worry, you cannot change the default profiles. You use them to create custom profiles.

Return to the Manage Profiles dialog box, select a profile close to what you want to accomplish, click Copy, give it a unique name, and click OK. Now it'll appear in the Name window. Select it and click Edit. That opens a series of windows that lets you select a target audience by denoting bandwidths, choose from a handful of codecs, and, as I've shown in Figure 20.16, input specific settings for each selected stream.

You cannot combine high- and low-bandwidth streams in the same profile. If you specify a bandwidth less than 80Kbps, you cannot select a bandwidth higher than 300Kbps.

FIGURE 20.16

Use the Edit Profile dialog box in this case to tweak each bandwidth stream.

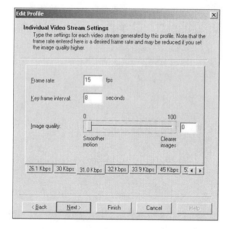

9. Go back to the Windows Media 8 Export Plug-in for Adobe Premiere dialog box. Make sure to reselect (if necessary) the original profile: Dial-up Modems or Single-Channel ISDN. Click OK. The encoding should begin.

When you're finished, check out your work by navigating to the newly created file and double-clicking it. That should open the Windows Media Player and display your video. It will likely play at the highest bandwidth because it's coming right off your hard drive.

Workaround to Create a WMV File for a Portion of Your Timeline

This workaround is relatively simple. It applies only to those with Windows Me or XP. Those versions of Windows ship with Windows Movie Maker; earlier Windows versions did not.

Task: Export the Work Area to a Windows Media File

TASK

To create a WMV file of a portion of your project, you will create an AVI file, open it in the Windows Movie Maker, and convert it to a WMV file there. Follow these steps:

1. Select Export Timeline, Movie. Select Settings and then choose Microsoft AVI for the File Type setting and Work Area for the Range setting.

2. If you want to tweak any settings, move on to the Video and Audio windows and do that.

3. Click OK. Give the file a name and file folder location; then create the AVI file.

4. Once this is completed, open Windows Movie Maker as shown in Figure 20.17.

FIGURE 20.17

Use Windows Movie Maker to convert AVI files to WMV.

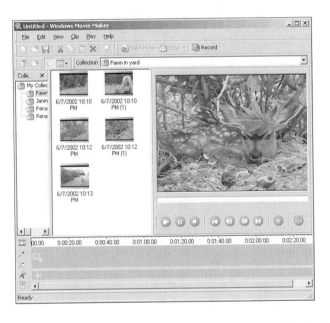

20

5. Open a new project and import your AVI file. Click Save Movie and you're done.

There is one other workaround (there's always more than one way). You can take that AVI file you just created and import it into Premiere. Place it by itself on the timeline and then export the timeline to Advanced Windows Media. However, if you do it this way, you might never take a look at the Windows Movie Maker, which has some cool features.

Using the Advanced RealMedia Export for Web Apps

This is the Premiere dual-platform (Mac/Windows) powerhouse export module, with a strong emphasis on the Internet. If there's a way to tweak video/audio compression, then the folks at RealNetworks have included it here.

First, four caveats:

- Unlike Advanced Windows Media, if you want to play back a RealMedia file with multiple bandwidth streams, you need to buy RealNetworks' RealSystem Server Plus ($2,000). The not-so-elegant workaround is to create and then offer on your Web site multiple files covering a range of bandwidths.

- When you first use RealMedia Export, it likely will prompt you to download an update and in the process ask you for a bunch of intrusive marketing information.

- If you're connected to the Internet, after completing the encoding, you'll probably see some obnoxious pop-up ads for RealNetworks' products.

- You need to register the RealMedia Export plug-in. Expect a few more intrusive questions during that process.

▲ TASK

Task: Convert Your Premiere Project into a RealMedia File

To export/convert an element from the timeline or an entire project to a RealMedia file, follow these steps:

1. Select Export Timeline, Advanced RealMedia Export to open the Advanced RealMedia Export dialog box shown in Figure 20.18. It has a friendlier look and feel than the Windows Media 8 plug-in.

2. Note how easy it is to characterize the audio and video format settings in the RealMedia Clip Settings window shown in Figure 20.19. Instead of technical parameters, RealNetworks chose to use user-selected styles of video and audio to set appropriate encoding techniques. The audio choices are self-explanatory. Here's what the video choices mean:

   Normal Motion—Used with clips with mixed high action and limited action.

▼   **Smoothest Motion**—ppUsed with limited-action clips

▼ **Sharpest Image**—For high-action clips.

Slide Show—Creates a series of still photos to ensure optimum image clarity

FIGURE 20.18

The Advanced RealMedia Export dialog box has a friendlier look and feel than its Windows Media counterpart.

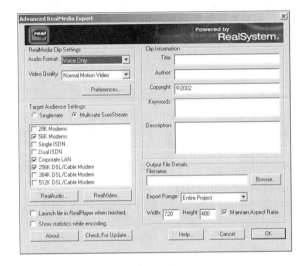

FIGURE 20.19

Simplified, real-world format settings are a nice feature of the RealMedia Export module.

Three buttons within the Advanced RealMedia Export dialog box let you access more detailed, customized settings: Preferences (in this Clip Settings window) and RealAudio and RealVideo (in the Target Audience Settings window). I'll go over these in a few minutes.

20

3. The default selection in the Target Audience Settings window, shown in Figure 20.20, is not surprisingly Multi-rate SureStream. This setting allows multiple bandwidth streams within the same file, but an expensive RealNetworks server is needed to play them.

4. At this point, take the pragmatic view and select Single-rate and accept the default 56K Modems target audience. I'll explain in a few minutes how you can fine-tune
▼ this audience setting using the RealAudio and RealVideo buttons.

FIGURE 20.20

Take the much less expensive (free is a very good price) single-rate Target Audience Setting route.

5. Just because they're both nifty features, place checks in both boxes below the Target Audience Settings window: Launch file in RealPlayer when finished and Show statistics while encoding.

6. In an unusual move, the output settings, shown in Figure 20.21, let you adjust the output frame size. With Aspect Ratio checked, changing one number immediately, and proportionately, changes the other. Give your file a name and location, plus select an export range: Entire Project or Work Area.

FIGURE 20.21

Output settings take the unusual step of offering frame size settings as well as file location.

7. The clip information is optional. One great tool is the Keywords window. This lets search engines such as Google.com scan your site for keywords you chose to identify your video content. It's a great way to direct traffic to your videos.

8. Click OK to render your RealMedia file. Because you selected Show statistics while encoding, you'll see more than you want to know about the progress of your file conversion. When the process is completed, the RealOne Player should pop up and play your clip. Then you get to see one of those intrusive pop-up ads.

Advanced RealMedia Export Properties

Access the RealMedia Export customizing properties from three separate locations. Start with Clip Settings, Preferences. That opens the Preferences dialog box shown in Figure 20.22. I clicked past the opening page to the one that is worth your while to visit: Video Codec.

20

FIGURE 20.22

Use the Preferences dialog box to access 2-Pass Encoding. It's worth the extra effort.

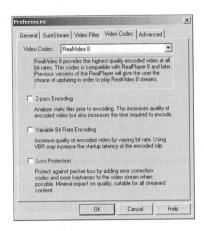

The one box really worth checking is 2-Pass Encoding. This analyzes the clip in detail and slows the encoding process. But that extra time translates to higher image quality.

The other Preference dialog box tabs are fairly routine. General lets you offer up your videos for download.

> The two buttons at the bottom of the Target Audience Settings section should have different, more descriptive names. RealAudio actually opens a window for audio-only clips or audio with multimedia clips. RealVideo opens a window where you can make video and audio adjustments for video clips.

Click the RealAudio button. It opens the settings dialog box in Figure 20.23.

This dialog box is geared primarily to audio-only clips, not video clips with linked audio. It lets you stipulate some narrow values for your audio.

Select RealVideo to open the Target Audience Settings – Video Clips dialog box shown in Figure 20.24.

Select any of the Audio page's drop-down lists and note the overwhelming number of choices. Although you can select anything, the bandwidth of your target audience really dictates how far you can stray from the default settings.

Under the Video tab, you can adjust only the number of frames per second. Target Bitrate lets you select a value, but again you need to stay close to the range to suit your target audience.

FIGURE 20.23

The Target Audience Settings – Audio Clips dialog box is geared to audio-only clips or multimedia presentations such as slideshows, not video clips with audio.

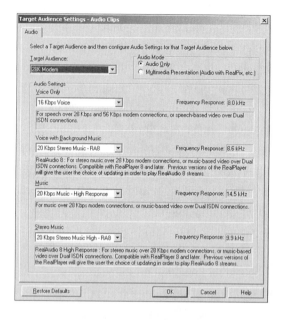

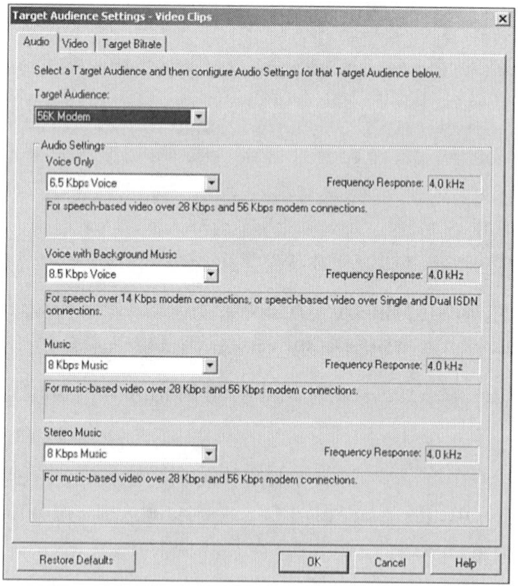

FIGURE 20.24

The RealVideo button opens this dialog box, which features both video and audio.

Summary

As more of your video projects move to DVD and the Internet, you will rely heavily on the three high-end export modules covered in this hour: Adobe MPEG Encoder, Advanced Windows Media 8 plug-in, and Advanced RealMedia Export. Creating MPEG files opens the door to DVD authoring and placing MPEG files on CDs. Windows Media has the power of Microsoft behind it and the assurance that Windows Media files will play on most up-to-date PCs. Finally, RealMedia has the strongest feature set for creating cross-platform video for the Internet.

Workshop

Review the questions and answers in this section to try to sharpen your Premiere advanced exporting skills. Also, take a few moments to tackle my short quiz and the exercises.

Q&A

Q I encoded an MPEG-2 file, but it stutters on playback. Any idea why?

A Did you select Lower Field First in the Fields drop-down menu in the MPEG Encoder? If you selected Upper, that may be the cause (a slow PC could be another reason). No Fields is the safest choice if you don't know which to choose, but its output quality is not as good as finding the correct setting—Upper or Lower.

Q I encoded an MPEG-2 file, played it back in the Windows Media Player, and there was no audio. What's up?

A By default, the Adobe MPEG Encoder creates "elementary streams" (separate audio and video files) when encoding MPEG-2 files. To create a multiplexed (or *muxed*) file, select DVD for the MPEG Stream setting, click Edit (next to Advanced), click the Multiplexer Settings tab, and select MPEG-2 from the Multiplexer Type list.

Quiz

1. What's the difference between MPEG-1, MPEG-2, and MPEG-4?
2. How do you place a URL marker in a video and then later edit it?
3. How do you convert a section of your timeline into a Windows Media file?

20

Quiz Answers

1. MPEG-1 is VHS-quality compression geared primarily to CD-ROM playback. MPEG-2 is broadcast-quality compression geared to movies and videos on DVD and digital satellite systems. MPEG-4 is the newest of the three codecs (released in late 1998) with a focus on streaming video on the Internet.

2. Set your edit line where you want a Web page to pop up or change during playback of your video. Press the asterisk (*) key on the numeric keypad or right/Option-click and select Set Timeline Marker. Double-click the marker and type in a URL. To edit it later, either double-click it or access it by right/Option-clicking anywhere on the time ruler and using the Go To Marker menu.

3. Place the work area bar over the portion to export and export the timeline to an AVI file. Then open Windows Movie Maker, create a new project, import the newly created AVI file, and save it as a WMV file.

Exercises

1. Create both Windows Media and RealMedia files using similar settings and see how long the encoding processes take, how large the files are, and how the encoded clips look and sound.

2. Take a small step into the highly technical world of customized MPEG settings by opening the Advanced window in the MPEG Encoder and changing the Video Encoder Quality slider value. Then tweak Motion Search and Noise Sensitivity in the Advanced Video Settings tab following the recommendations in the tips I provided in the MPEG Encoder section.

3. Experiment with RealMedia's 2-pass encoding to see whether you think it's worth the extra compression time. Access this feature by selecting Preferences in the RealMedia Clip Settings dialog box and then clicking 2-Pass Encoding under the Video Codec tab.

PART V
DVD Authoring

Hour

HOUR 21

Designing Your DVD Project and Creating Menus

With Premiere, its bundled DVDit! LE, and a DVD recorder you now can make DVDs. DVDs can store massive amounts of video, images, music, and data. They offer amazing versatility and interactivity and have near universal compatibility.

Creating projects that exploit these characteristics takes planning. I'll suggest ways to organize your ideas and turn them into coherent and cohesive DVDs.

Well-organized menus are critical to taking advantage of DVD interactivity. I'll show you how to use menu backgrounds, make buttons, and keep things simple.

The highlights of this hour include the following:

- How DVDs are driving the next technology wave
- Deciding what you want to accomplish—menu structure

- A first-time DVD authoring experience
- Creating menus—image backgrounds and buttons

DVDs Are Driving the Next Technological Wave

A decade ago CD-ROMs ushered in a new era in computer entertainment and ultimately fostered many technological innovations. Their massive storage capacity gave savvy game developers opportunities to enhance their offerings with video, deep graphics, and CD-quality sound. After enough gaming pioneers demonstrated the viability of this formerly unproven technology, there was no turning back. When's the last time you bought computer software on floppy disks?

Until now, games have driven the PC technology boom. CD-ROM drives, 3D graphic cards, and high-end sound cards are standard equipment because of PC games.

That a nonlinear video editor such as Premiere can even function on a consumer-level PC or Mac is due largely to this rapid, game-driven growth. Now, however, something else is driving personal computer technology: DVDs.

Like in the early days of CD-ROM drives, computer buyers have had the opportunity to include DVD-ROM drives in their new boxes but until now have had no compelling reason to do so. The massive storage offered by DVDs has not been enough of a selling point—nor has watching DVD movies on a PC been much of a thrill.

But *making* DVD movies on a computer is.

Unlike VHS tape, DVDs use higher-quality digital media and allow you to create an interactive experience. DVDs are more compact and more durable than videotapes. Once you make your first DVD you'll never want to use videocassettes again. Consider the following:

DVD is the fastest-growing consumer electronics product in history. There are more than 30 million DVD set-top players and more than 25 million DVD-equipped PCs in the U.S. market today. One in four U.S. homes has a DVD machine. DVD movie and video sales and rentals are skyrocketing—up 75%, year over year, in the latest quarterly report. At least one major retailer has stopped carrying VHS versions of motion picture films. From now on, it's DVDs only.

DVD will soon replace videotape as the video-publishing format of choice for video professionals and video enthusiasts. The production possibilities are endless:

- Home video makers now easily can create full multimedia productions, combining videos, photos, text, narration, and music—from interactive family vacation videos to family history projects.

- Businesses can develop compelling product demos, point-of-sale video displays, corporate backgrounders, and interactive training materials with no concerns about platform-compatibility issues or a need for high-priced playback devices.

- For commercial filmmakers, putting movies on DVDs offers consumers a convincing reason to *buy* movies rather than simply *rent* them. The extra offerings—director's comments, outtakes, multiple languages, subtitles, and scripts—create a rich viewing experience.

Deciding What You Want to Accomplish— Menu Structure

DVDs feature menu-based interactivity. If you think in terms of a simple outline, you can visualize a DVD project. It may be best to start with the basics (video-only projects):

- Family vacation highlights
- A corporate backgrounder
- Real estate promotion
- Watching your child grow
- Weddings and special events

The beauty of DVD is that these don't have to be single programs that viewers watch from beginning to end. You can split them up into digestible chunks:

- Put four vacation videos on one DVD.
- Create a collection of corporate product videos.
- Promote a housing development with separate videos of interiors, exteriors, views, schools, and local amenities.
- Use a DVD for a half-dozen birthday parties.
- Divide the wedding into preliminaries, the ceremony, and the reception.

Figure 21.1 shows a basic, video-only DVD menu. Four buttons on the opening splash screen of your DVD project give viewers instant access to four different videos. While watching any of the four videos they can press the Menu button on their remote control and return immediately to the opening menu.

21

FIGURE 21.1

A basic, video-only DVD menu interface.

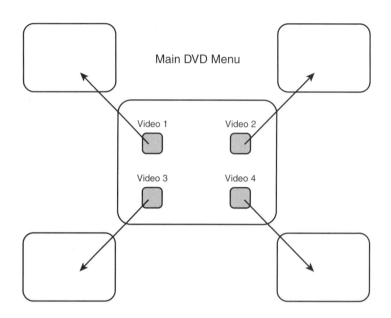

Consider displaying more than simply a collection of videos. You can add photos and music. So-called "nested" menus—one menu accessing another—allow much greater interactivity.

Take a look at Figure 21.2 for a simplified family history DVD example.

FIGURE 21.2

Using "nested" menus adds extra layers of interactivity.

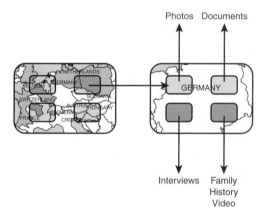

In this case—using a map for a menu background—viewers of your family tree DVD access the opening menu, select a country of origin, and in a nested menu select from Photos, Documents, Interviews, and Family History Video.

That nested menu concept may continue on past Family History Video. You may want to divide it into separate eras: Old Country, Immigrants, and Present Day.

Consider your child's baseball season. An opening menu could have buttons for Game Videos, Stats, Interviews, and Funny Moments. Accessing each of those would reveal additional menus. For instance, Game Videos could have menu buttons for each game—or Regular Season and Championship Series. Stats could be graphic displays created in Photoshop Elements.

Remember, this is video. Text displays need to be simple, clear, and minimal. That said, the beauty of DVDs is that with some authoring software you can add DVD-ROM material to them for users who may view DVDs on their PCs. That DVD-ROM data can be any kind of file that will run on a PC, including word processing documents and spreadsheets.

However, DVDit! LE does not let users add DVD-ROM files to their projects. Its more expensive older siblings—SE and PE—do.

Once you start playing with DVD creation and seeing the smiling faces of those viewing your masterpieces, you'll start thinking in terms of putting just about anything on DVD—for instance, holiday greetings, music compilations, and archived videos.

A First-Time DVD Authoring Experience

"Exciting" is how Leonard Broz describes burning his first DVD. "I waited my whole life for this moment," he adds with a smile.

Now, when he shows family video albums and "mini-travelogues" to relations and friends, there's no more time wasted waiting to swap tapes and fast forwarding or rewinding looking for clips. "Plus the video quality is higher than dubbing it off to VHS," he says.

A former technology and industrial arts teacher from suburban Chicago, Broz now winters in Arizona, where he teaches computer-based video-and photo-editing techniques to other seniors in his community. DVD, he tells his students, is the ideal medium both for storing their collections of memorable moments and for sharing them with family and friends.

21

To show them how easy it can be to make DVDs—and also to create his own personal DVD albums—Broz uses Sonic Solutions' entry-level DVD authoring program, MyDVD. Using MyDVD's built-in wizards, Broz explains, even his students who are just getting started with computers find it very straightforward to record video "direct to DVD" or to create menus with preset styles and then burn their own DVDs (see Figure 21.3).

Broz creates the raw materials for his projects using both a still camera and a video camcorder. "For instance, when I travel to places like Mesa Verde," he says, "I take a whole bunch of flower photos with my digital camera and shoot some scenery with my Mini-DV camcorder."

He edits 90 minutes of raw video down to 10 minutes or so, converts his digital images into a slide show with transitions, and then adds a narration and music. After converting it to MPEG-2 he imports it to MyDVD, chooses a "style," (see Figure 21.4) and records it all to DVD.

MyDVD's custom styles allow him to quickly personalize attributes such as the font, text size, and background image of his menus as well as to save his preferences as new styles.

Broz is so enthusiastic about the DVDs he's made with MyDVD that he's turning his attention to the 300 or so videotapes he has of family footage shot over the years, starting with his wedding day.

He plans to transfer those tapes to the computer, scan in family photos, edit them down to manageable size, and create "the story our life on DVD."

Broz knows his family will be receptive to the idea of a video album on DVD because he's already created discs in a similar vein. "My son was married last year," he explains, "and we had video from the reception, shots from showers that were thrown for them, and their photos from the honeymoon. I used MyDVD to put it all onto one DVD (see Figure 21.5), and I sent it to him about a week ago. He's just elated with it."

FIGURE 21.3

Broz said it was a breeze to use the consumer-level MyDVD to convert vacation photos and videos into interactive DVDs.

FIGURE 21.4

MyDVD's Style menu makes it easy to create menus.

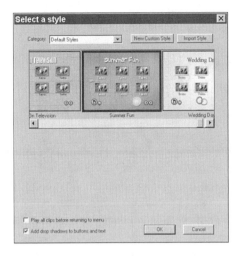

FIGURE 21.5

Broz's son's wedding DVD was a big hit.

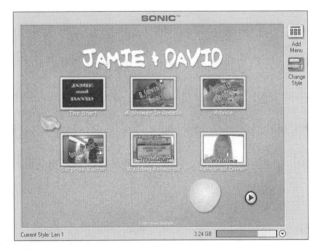

DVD Authoring—Initial Phase

Now it's time for some hands-on work.

Task: Take a Tour of DVDit!

Before building a menu I want you to venture around the DVDit! interface. Follow these steps:

1. Open Sonic DVDit! LE. After the small splash screen disappears, select Start a New Project from the opening menu shown in Figure 21.6.

21

FIGURE **21.6**
The DVDit! opening menu.

2. The opening menu changes appearance and offers up two drop-down lists. Choose NTSC or PAL—depending on your country's TV standard—and MPEG-2 (DVD Compliant). Click Finish. That opens the DVDit! interface shown in Figure 21.7. In a few moments you'll use its TV screen to create menus.

FIGURE **21.7**
The DVDit! interface streamlines the production process.

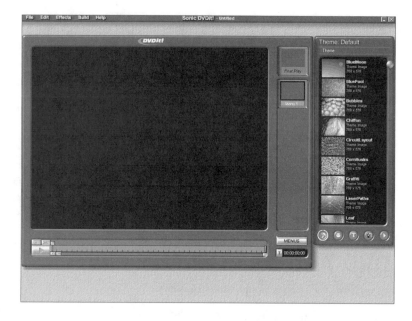

3. For now check out the Theme window, shown in Figure 21.8. Here you will find all the elements to create your DVD project. DVDit! comes with a nice variety of graphics to ease you into DVD authoring. Note the five buttons I've highlighted in Figure 21.8. Click each in turn to open its respective palette:

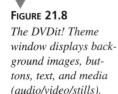

FIGURE 21.8

The DVDit! Theme window displays background images, buttons, text, and media (audio/video/stills).

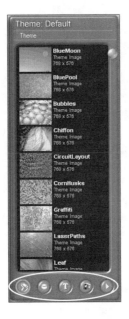

Background—You may use any of the images in this palette as menu backdrops.

Buttons—Use the buttons in this palette to create links from menus to media or other menus.

Text—Use this palette to access any font installed on your system and to apply text to any menu.

Media—Any video clips, audio cuts, and images you've stored in the Sonic Solutions media folder show up in this palette, including MPEG files created using the Adobe MPEG Encoder with the Sonic Solutions file folder option checked.

> To test your media, right-click a file icon and select Play. If you selected a video clip, it should play in the TV screen portion of the DVDit! interface. To stop playing, right-click again and select Stop. Still images display for five seconds.

Plays—Clicking this button opens a pushbutton remote control–like interface, shown in Figure 21.9, that you'll use to test drive your DVD project before burning a DVD or CD. Click the × in the upper-right corner to close this interface.

21

FIGURE 21.9

Use this remote control–like interface to test the functionality of your DVD project before burning a DVD or CD.

Task: Combine DVDit!'s Graphics into One File Folder

▼TASK

Sonic provides two sets of backgrounds and buttons—Default and Corporate—with this LE version of DVDit! There really is no reason to keep these groups of items in separate folders. Follow these steps to combine them all into one personalized location:

1. Open "My Computer" or the Windows Explorer to navigate to the Sonic Solutions Themes directory—C:\Program Files\Sonic Solutions\DVDit! LE\Themes—and create a new folder in the Themes folder. As I've illustrated in Figure 21.10, call it something like My Graphics.

2. Open the Themes/Default file folder and copy/paste its three folders into your newly created folder.

3. Go to the Themes/Corporate/Backgrounds folder and copy/paste its one file—Corporate_Backgrounds.SonicTheme—to your Backgrounds file folder.

4. Do the same with the Themes/Corporate/Buttons folder and copy/paste its one file—Corporate_Buttons.SonicTheme—to your Buttons file folder.

5. Test to make sure that everything fell into place by opening DVDit!, clicking the small-print "Theme" in the Theme window, and selecting your newly created file folder. I've highlighted that in Figure 21.11.

▲

You should end up with 30 backgrounds and 40 buttons—all readily accessible. No need to open a new theme to search for a graphic.

FIGURE 21.10

Create a new file folder to store all your graphics and media for use in DVDit!

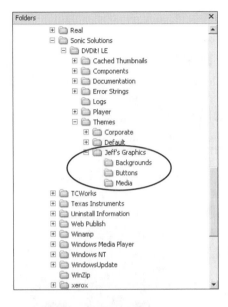

FIGURE 21.11

Click the small-print "Theme" to open your newly created Theme folder.

Make sure you do not change the DVDit! "Themes" file folders naming convention: Backgrounds, Buttons, and Media. These names "cue" DVDit! to handle files from those folders in specific ways.

Creating Menus—Image Backgrounds and Buttons

Your first choice is whether to start your DVD with a video clip or a menu. This is called your "first play." For this example you'll start with a menu. We'll deal with how you include video clips in your project in the next hour.

21

Task: Create a Menu

The opening menu is the foundation of your DVD project and sets its tone. To create that first impression, follow these steps:

1. Open DVDit! The Theme window opens by default to the Backgrounds palette. Select a background and drag it to the First Play placeholder screen. I've high-lighted it in Figure 21.12. This does three things:

   - It places the chosen background into both the First Play and Menu 1 place-holder screens.

   - It displays the background in the main screen.

   - It adds a new Menu 2 placeholder screen next to the main screen.

FIGURE 21.12

Dragging a back-ground to First Play placeholder adds it to the Menu 1 place-holder and the main screen as well.

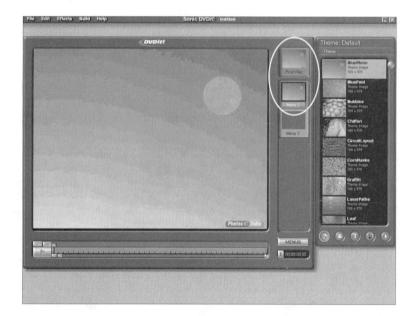

 It's best to give your menu a descriptive name. To do that, simply click "Menu 1" in the small screen to the right of the main screen. This will high-light the Menu 1 name. Type in something descriptive and press Enter.

 You may notice an icon in the lower-right corner of your selected back-ground. The bad news? You're stuck with this bit of advertising. Yes, Sonic

Solutions was kind enough to provide several dozen graphics, but not without a plug for the company that distributes them.

The good news? The logo falls outside the Safe Area. People watching DVDs created with these backgrounds won't see the logos.

You are not stuck to using only the backgrounds that ship with DVDit! LE. You may use your own graphics. DVDit! supports the following graphic file types: BMP, RLE, JPG, PIC, PCT, PSD, PNG, TIF, TGA, VDA, ICB, and VST.

To import your background graphics to DVDit!, open the Background palette and select Theme, Add Files to Theme. Navigate to your graphics file(s), select one or more, and click Open.

A caveat: For best results your image should have a 4:3 aspect ratio such as 640×480. If it's a smaller resolution than 640×480, DVDit! will expand it and some sharpness will be lost.

I present more information about creating and importing graphics in the next hour.

2. If you want to change the background for the First Play screen, simply drag a new background to that window.

DVDit! LE has a little idiosyncrasy. If you change the name of Menu 1, that also changes "First Play" to the name you give Menu 1. If later you drag a different menu to the First Play window, it does not display the name of this new menu; instead, it retains whatever you typed in originally for Menu 1.

This can become confusing. Just keep in mind that whatever menu is in the top "First Play" screen (no matter what name this screen has on it) is the menu that plays right after the DVD is inserted into the drive.

3. To create an additional menu that you may link to the First Play menu or to other menus, simply drag a background to the newly created Menu 2 placeholder screen. That automatically creates a new Menu 3 placeholder for your next menu, if you choose to add more.

4. Open the Buttons palette. Select the top button, Glass Green, and drag and drop it on the main screen. As shown in Figure 21.13, the proportions of the button on the main screen don't match the icon in the palette.

21

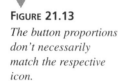

FIGURE 21.13

The button proportions don't necessarily match the respective icon.

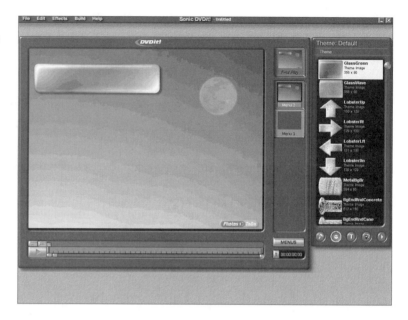

5. Highlight the button to put a frame with red handles around it. Now you can resize and change its proportions by dragging the corners or edges. Holding down Shift while resizing maintains the current aspect ratio.

> In a slightly different twist to graphic resizing, Sonic Solutions added a center handle. Click and drag it around to see how this changes the shape of the button while holding its position over the menu using that center point.

6. Delete this button and then drag three Glass Green buttons to the main screen.

7. To change the shape of all three buttons uniformly, select all of them by Ctrl-clicking one at a time. While holding down the Ctrl key, drag the edge or center handle of one, and all three act in unison, as illustrated in Figure 21.14.

FIGURE 21.14

Uniformly change the shape of selected buttons by Ctrl-clicking them one at a time and then dragging an edge or handle of one button.

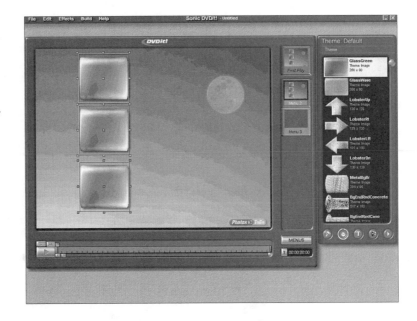

As with most graphics programs, you can copy and paste these buttons. Here's how:

1. Create one button to your satisfaction and select it by clicking it.

2. Select Edit, Copy from the main menu.

3. Select Edit, Paste. That places a duplicate button on top of the original. Drag this duplicate to a new location.

Although you can uniformly resize several buttons at once, there are no tools such as a grid to help you line them up perfectly.

Here's a workaround: Create a "dummy" button first. Place it on the screen and expand its size to fit where you want to line up your buttons. Then add your buttons on top of the dummy button using it to line up their edges. Once this is completed, select the dummy button and delete it.

One other point: Dragging your buttons with the mouse does not lead to pixel-specific placement. However, you can nudge them to get them reasonably well lined up by using the keyboard arrow keys.

21

TASK

Task: Creating Buttons from Other Sources

You have other means to add buttons to a menu. Follow these steps:

1. To create text buttons, click the Text icon in the Theme window, select a font, and drag the button to the main screen.

2. Click "Text" to display its red-handled frame. Click again to highlight the word "Text." Now type in something else. You'll note that the box won't change size. Instead, the text scrolls. I've displayed all three types of text displays in Figure 21.15.

FIGURE 21.15

The three types of text displays, depending on the number of times you click the text in the menu.

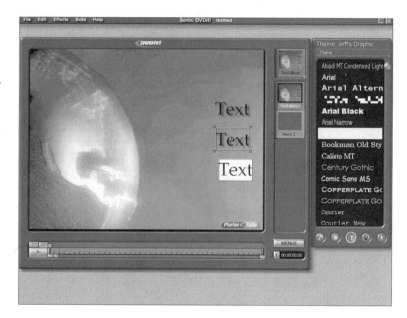

> The order in which you add buttons to a menu is the order in which they will play if your DVD viewers press Next or Previous on their remotes. In general this order may be a nonissue, but you may have a sequence in mind, so create your buttons accordingly. If you want to keep the buttons but change the sequence, you can drag and drop the buttons on the interface to change the appearance of the sequence or change whatever movie, still image, or menu you link to particular buttons. I'll cover how you link buttons to media and menus in the next hour.

3. When you're done typing, click outside the text area to accept what you've typed.

> By default, your text has a drop shadow. I'll show you how to adjust this in the next hour.

4. Click your text to bring up the red-handled frame again. You now can drag the frame to reposition the text or change its shape.

5. To edit your text, click inside to highlight the text, click again to place the cursor within the text, and then type your new text.

> You may apply this text *over* a button, use it to *identify* a button, or use it *as* a button. I'll explain how you "link" media and menus to buttons in the next hour.

6. To create a button from a frame in a video clip, open the Media palette by clicking the filmstrip icon at the bottom of the Theme window.

7. Select a still image or a video and drag it to the menu in the main screen. In Figure 21.16 I dragged three still images to the menu. DVDit! automatically gives them beveled edges and a drop shadow. You can't change the beveling, but can adjust the shadow. I'll cover that in the next hour.

FIGURE 21.16
Creating nice beveled-edge buttons from media files is a simple drag-and-drop process.

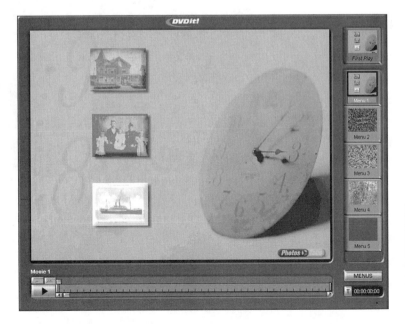

21

There is one other way to drag and drop a movie button onto the main screen. To use that method, you first must add videos to the project. I'll explain both processes in the next hour.

8. As with text and graphic buttons, you can select these "media" buttons and change their shape and size.

9. To create a button to link from one menu to a second, open the menu you are going *from* in the main screen.

10. Click and drag the second menu from the menu screens onto the first menu on the main screen. As shown in Figure 21.17, a small version of the second menu appears as a button, which you can resize and move to any location in the main menu.

FIGURE 21.17

Dragging one menu onto another creates a button with a link between menus.

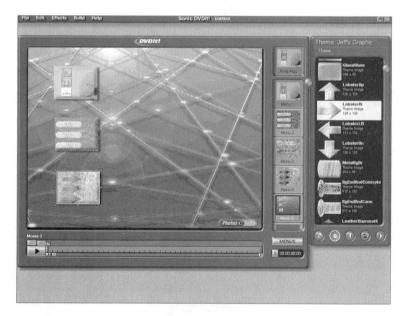

When creating a link from one menu to another, it's a good idea to make a link going *back* from the second menu back to the first.

> When you drag a menu to another menu to create a linked button, the button looks like a mini version of the menu it came from. If you update that second menu in any way, the button will *not* change to reflect that update. By the time you finish laying out your project, menu buttons may bear little resemblance to their original menus.
>
> You can fix that by selecting and deleting the nonupdated button and replacing it by selecting and dragging the updated menu from the menu's placeholder screen to the deleted button's position.

Summary

DVDs are the next "big thing." And Premiere is right there at the leading edge, offering DVD authoring along with video/audio editing and MPEG encoding.

Creating DVD projects is a lot like creating a basic text outline. Each main outline point can serve as an opening menu button that links viewers to submenus, which can link even deeper in the project via "nested" menus.

It may take more time to plan your project than to create its menus. The process is straightforward and consists primarily of dragging menu backgrounds to menu placeholder screens and then adding buttons. Establishing links from one menu to another is a mere drag-and-drop process.

Workshop

Review the questions and answers in this section to try to sharpen your DVDit! menu-creation skills. Also, take a few moments to tackle my short quiz and the exercises.

Q&A

Q I'm having trouble working with text in DVDit! I drag a font to a menu but when I type nothing happens. I click the word "Text" and start typing, and again nothing. What should I do?

A Click one more time. Changing the DVDit! text is a three-click process: one to select and place the text on the menu, another to put a frame around the text to change its shape and move it, and another to highlight the text for editing. When you're done typing, click outside the box to complete your work. Later, if you want to edit the text, it's another three-click process: one to create the frame, a second to highlight all the text, and a third to put a cursor within the text.

21

Q **I create buttons and select all of them by Ctrl-clicking to change their shapes all at once, but when I click a center handle only that button changes shape. What's going on?**

A You probably clicked a white center handle as opposed to a red handle. Even though all the buttons are highlighted with frames, only one will have a red center handle. This is a conscious design decision by Sonic that I think is counterintuitive. I think you should be able to click any handle on any button to change all their shapes at once. Nevertheless, if you want to use a center handle to change the buttons' shapes, select the button with the red center handle. One other possibility is that you did not click directly on the red center handle. Even if you missed it by a pixel, DVDit! thinks you're selecting the button, not grabbing its handle.

Quiz

1. How do you change the menu background for the First Play menu?

2. How do you change the First Play menu?

3. How do you make menus using your own background graphics?

Quiz Answers

1. Drag a new background to the menu placeholder screen for the menu that is currently the First Play menu. Don't drag that new background to the First Play screen (even if it's no longer named "First Play"). That will turn that background into a new menu and put it in the First Play screen, kicking out the former First Play menu.

2. Drag any menu from the stack of menu screens to the First Play placeholder screen (always the top menu screen). The new menu will show up in the First Play screen, and the former First Play menu will remain in its place among the menu screens.

3. First, import your background(s). Open the Background palette and select Theme, Add Files to Theme. Navigate to your graphics file(s), select one or more, and click Open. Check the bottom of the Background palette. Your backgrounds should be there. Select and drag one or more to separate menu placeholder screens.

Exercises

1. Create four blank menus by dragging different backgrounds to the menu placeholders. For each menu, drag the three other menus to it in turn, linking one menu to the other three. Open the Remote Control interface. The First Play menu should be in its display. Start clicking the menu icons to see how easily DVDit! lets you jump from one menu to another.

2. Use a text outline—or better still, flowcharting software—to create a menu layout for a family video project—be it vacations, outings, family history, or sports. Think in terms of nested menus two or three levels behind the main menu. This is purely for planning purposes. There is no way to import such an outline into DVDit!

3. Create still images from your Premiere video project to use as menu backgrounds or buttons. As a reminder, in Premiere's workspace, place the edit line over the desired frame, select Export Timeline, Frame, and then save it. You can import these images into DVDit!'s Background and/or Button palettes by selecting Theme, Add Files to Theme. If you use a full-screen image as a button, it will fill the screen. Simply grab a handle and shrink it to fit. One drawback: It won't have that nice beveled look you get if you drag a menu or video's first frame to a menu.

21

Hour **22**

DVD Authoring

Adjusting the look and feel of your menus, bringing in your videos and images, and laying down audio tracks comprise the second step in the authoring process. I'll show you how to create "timed" images, add audio to still images, link videos to simulate "chapters," and link all your media to your menus.

The highlights of this hour include the following:

- Adjusting image, text, and menu characteristics
- Adding videos and stills and changing their properties
- Using audio to enhance your DVD
- Sidebar: The Peoria Hockey Mites on DVD
- Linking media to your menu buttons to make your project flow

Adjusting Image, Text, and Menu Characteristics

DVDit! lets you do much more to text and button elements than moving them around the menu and changing their size and shape. You can adjust the color, saturation, and brightness for individual menu elements or the menu as a whole. Also, you can give text and buttons drop shadows using an intuitive and customizable tool.

Task: Change the Characteristics of Menus, Backgrounds, Buttons, and Text

The button at the top of the Button palette is called "GlassGreen." Don't let that stop you from turning it into "GlassRed." Follow these steps to change the characteristics of anything that appears in a menu:

1. Select a menu and place some text and two buttons on it. Select all three items by Ctrl-clicking them in turn.

2. Select Effects, Adjust Color from the main menu. This opens the Color Adjustment dialog box, shown in Figure 22.1.

FIGURE 22.1

The Color Adjustment dialog box lets you change color characteristics of any object, menu, or combination of items you select.

3. Open the Color Adjustment dialog box's drop-down menu. You have three selections: Current Menu Background, Selected Menu Items, and Current Menu. Select each one in turn and note how the display in the Color Adjustment screen changes. This is a very nifty tool. You can adjust any selected menu item(s), only the background, or the entire menu—background, text, buttons, and all.

4. Make a selection and move the sliders. Turns out the GlassGreen button can be any color you want. If you check the Save Settings box, you can apply the same settings on other menus or menu items.

5. Cancel out of the Color Adjustment dialog box. Select only the text by clicking it and then select Effects, Text Properties. This opens the Text Properties dialog box, shown in Figure 22.2.

FIGURE 22.2

The Text Properties dialog box lets you fine-tune text, including color and brightness.

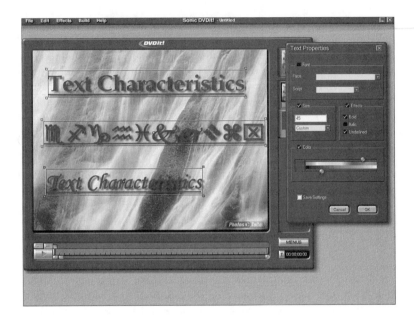

6. The Text Properties dialog box lets you make the usual text changes, including font typeface, size, and bold/italic/underlined. It does have two interesting functions:

- The Script drop-down menu lets you change the lettering from Western to five other alphabets.

- The Color area actually controls the color and brightness. The top slider changes the text color, and the bottom slider changes the brightness.

7. You can change the drop shadow characteristics for menu items by selecting buttons and/or text and then selecting Effects, Drop Shadow to open the Drop Shadow dialog box, shown in Figure 22.3.

8. The Drop Shadow dialog box is an intuitive and fun toy. Using simple sliders you can adjust the shadow's characteristics down to its color, blur, direction from the object, and opacity. Selecting Apply To: Items in Current Menu means any changes will affect all items equally, giving your menu buttons a more consistent and realistic look.

FIGURE 22.3

This interface makes adjusting drop shadow characteristics intuitive and, well, fun.

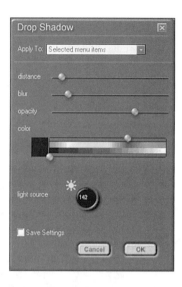

Creating Graphics for Use in DVDit!

DVDit! offers a nice variety of backgrounds and buttons, but its developers assume most users will opt to create their own graphics in Photoshop. If you do, here are three tips:

- DVDit! resizes any graphic or still to a 4:3 aspect ratio. To avoid distorted images—flattened or elongated—here are two points to keep in mind:

  - Images for menu backgrounds should have a 640×480 resolution or a 4:3 aspect ratio. If you use less than 640×480, DVDit! will expand your image to fit, and it may not look as sharp as you'd like.

  - Images that you'll use as stills should have a 720×540 resolution or a 4:3 aspect ratio. For images that don't match that resolution or aspect ratio, add borders to properly size them. Again, lower resolutions will lead to less crisp-looking images.

- When using Photoshop, to compensate for its square pixels and NTSC-DV and PAL's non-square pixels, create full-screen images (typically backgrounds) with Photoshop's opening palette set to 720×540, with Mode set to RGB color, and Contents set to Transparent. When completed, resize your graphics to 720×480. They'll look squashed in Photoshop, but when you import them to DVDit! they will look as they did when you created them.

- DVDit! supports Photoshop alpha channel transparencies, even holes in graphics. Create a button with a transparency in Photoshop and then add slightly altered versions of that button in several layers within the same graphic. After you import this button to DVDit! (Theme, Add Files to Theme), DVDit! will display each layer as a separate button in the Theme window.

Adding Videos and Stills and Changing Their Properties

This is the exciting part of DVD production. You have various types of media in hand and are ready to pull them all together to draw your videos, photos, narration, and music into a cohesive whole.

Task: Take a Dry Run

Before you start adding videos and other media to your project, give one of your videos a dry run. This will give you a feel for how to manipulate videos within the authoring software. Follow these steps:

1. Open DVDit! to a new project.

2. Click the media button at the bottom of the Theme column. I've highlighted it in Figure 22.4. You should see thumbnails of all your media files.

FIGURE 22.4

Clicking the filmstrip icon opens the folder holding your media files.

3. Right-click a thumbnail image and select Play. As I've illustrated in Figure 22.5, if you've selected a video, it'll play in the large playback window. A still image will display for five seconds, and an audio file will run with no animation.

4. To stop any playback, right-click the thumbnail again and select Stop.

You also can use the large playback window controls to manipulate media. However, these controls are rudimentary at best.

DVDit! does not have controls that "fast forward," "rewind," or automatically return the cursor to the beginning.

Also, you can't "scrub" or search through a video—watching the images flash by as you slide the cursor. Instead, if you're looking for a particular scene, you need to move the cursor to an approximate location in the clip and release the mouse button. Then take a look at what pops on the screen and adjust your location accordingly.

FIGURE 22.5

Videos and stills display on the main playback screen. Two other interface sections— Placeholder windows and Files—make it easy to access media, menus, buttons, and text.

5. You can use your video's timecode as a means to move to a specific scene. The timecode window, shown in Figure 22.6, is below the silver Movie/Menu button at the lower-right corner of the video playback window. Clicking the Play button will start the video at that point.

FIGURE 22.6

Type in a timecode to jump directly to a scene in your video.

Notice that the timecode window has a small silver button with the letter *T*. If this were a full retail DVDit! product, you could click that button to bring up the letter *C* for "chapters." However, the Chapters function is disabled in this LE version of DVDit!

One final item about the video playback window—you can adjust the timeline interval display. The default is to display the timeline for the entire length of the selected video. The longer the video, the more time interval hash marks displayed and the closer they are together. You can expand or contract those hash mark spacings by clicking the small or large "mountains" above the Play button shown in Figure 22.7.

This will "stretch" your timeline, changing its scale by increasing the spacing between the hash marks. This works much the same as clicking the plus or minus sign in Premiere's Timeline window.

In DVDit!, this is an inexact process because DVDit! does not indicate how much time each hash mark represents. Nevertheless, spreading out the hash marks makes it easier to find the frame you're looking for.

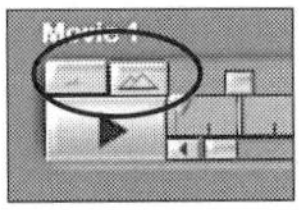

FIGURE 22.7

Clicking the small or large "mountain" icon changes the time interval hash marks on the timeline.

Adding Videos—First Play

As part of your project planning you decide what you want viewers to see the moment after they pop your DVD in their drive—the so-called "first play." In Hour 21, "Designing Your DVD Project and Creating Menus," you used a menu. But a brief introductory video can be much more effective.

Your "first play" can be a video, an image, or a menu. If it's a video (or an image), you can design your project to play through it to its conclusion and then display the opening menu. Some producers creating copyrighted material open with one of those ubiquitous and oft-ignored standard FBI warnings before jumping to a video or menu.

Task: Add a Video (or Still Image) to First Play

Because a bit of action off the top is almost always a good thing, using a video in First Play window is something you'll do often. To do that, follow these steps:

1. Open DVDit! to a new project. In the main interface, click the silver button I've highlighted in Figure 22.8 at the bottom-right corner of the viewing screen, and then select Movies. In the column to the right of the viewing screen you'll see a small window at the top labeled First Play, as well as one below it labeled Movie 1.

▼

FIGURE 22.8

Select Movie from this drop-down menu to display movie place-holder screens.

2. Click the media button (that little filmstrip icon) below the Theme window to display your media clips.

3. Select the video file you want for your first play and drag it to the First Play window. You'll notice that your video thumbnail image will show up not only in the First Play window but in the Movie 1 window as well. This simplifies matters if later you want to link a menu button to that movie.

4. If you need to add audio—for instance, music or narration—select and drag an audio file to the First Play window.

5. If instead you want to start your DVD with a still image, open the media file folder by clicking the filmstrip icon under the Theme column; then drag and drop your image file to the First Play window (it displays there, plus DVDit! automatically assigns it to its own movie placeholder window) .

6. DVDit! automatically sets the duration of that image display to five seconds. To change that length, right-click the placeholder window and select Properties. That brings up the Movie Properties dialog box shown in Figure 22.9. Change the Duration setting to suit your needs.

FIGURE 22.9

Use the Duration field in the Movie Properties dialog box to change the default five-second still image display length.

▼

7. You also may add audio to this image by dragging an audio clip to the First Play window or its movie placeholder screen. Adding audio changes the duration that image will display from its default value of five seconds to the length of the audio clip.

8. You can "loop" the audio clip—that is, make it play over and over until the viewer takes some action such as clicking the "next" button on the remote control. Here's how:

   - Right-click its movie window placeholder and select Properties.

   - Click the arrow on the End Action scroll-down menu at the bottom of the Movie Properties dialog box, shown in Figure 22.10, and select Loop.

22

FIGURE 22.10

Selecting Loop in the Movie Properties dialog box means your audio will keep playing until the viewer clicks the Menu or Next button on the remote.

 If you have a still image that you want to use, both as part of your DVD program and as a menu background, there is no need for you to copy/paste it into both the Background and Media file folder directories. Simply store it in the Media folder and drag it to a menu or movie placeholder screen.

 DVDit! LE works with only two audio file types: WAV and MPEG-1 Layer II. When you create MPEG-2 files using the Adobe MPEG Encoder and stick with the default elementary streams, the Encoder creates separate MPEG-2 video and WAV audio files. When you finally tell DVDit! to burn a DVD, no matter what frequency the WAV files are set to, DVDit! converts all audio to 48 KHz PCM audio.

Sonic's retail DVDit! products let you add audio to menus. The LE version does not. This points out the multitiered approach to DVD authoring used by Sonic and other DVD-authoring software companies. As you step up to higher priced products, you'll gain options such as animated menus that incorporate moving graphics or videos, plus sound, multiple audio tracks, a wide-screen format, subtitles, and more. I'll go over what higher-priced authoring products can do for you in Hour 23, "Enhanced DVD Authoring."

Adding More Videos and Still Images

Once you've created a first play, you'll find it's fairly easy to bring in the rest of the videos and stills you plan to include in your DVD project.

Simply open the Movie column (clicking the silver button at the lower-right corner of the display window and switching to Movies), open the Media palette, and then drag and drop your videos one by one into individual movie windows. You'll note that after you drag a video clip to a movie window placeholder, DVDit! automatically creates a new, empty movie screen placeholder for your next video or still.

DVDit! uses a default movie/image placeholder naming convention, simply referring to each added media file as Movie 1, Movie 2, Movie 3, and so on. This can be a bit confusing because your original media file names probably will be different.

If your project includes a couple dozen image, video, and audio files, using distinctive and logical placeholder naming conventions will help you keep things straight. Here's how to do that:

1. Click the movie name beneath the placeholder window (for example, Movie 1).

2. Note that the name becomes highlighted in yellow.

3. Type in the name you prefer and press the Enter.

You'll note several other options in the Movie Properties dialog box. I'll explain them later in Changing Movie, Image, and Menu Properties.

The Peoria Hockey Mites on DVD

When the members of the Peoria, Arizona, Junior Polar Bears hockey team gathered for their season-ending party, there was something unexpected awaiting them. The group of eight-to-ten year olds and their families had gathered at the one home with the largest TV screen and viewing area. What they saw "surprised and amazed them," says team historian Ed Loeffler.

Loeffler popped in a DVD and for the next two hours the gathered families clicked back and forth through menus and videos, reliving the highlights of their travels all around the Southwest (see Figure 22.11). "They loved it," Loeffler says.

When completed, Loeffler handed out 25 copies of that DVD, giving each family "a lifetime of memories," he says. "I saw joy on each person's face."

Those DVDs, made with Sonic DVDit!, are the perfect vehicle for preserving experiences and sharing them with everyone who cares about the team. "More than just hockey, the DVD was about the whole experience we had together: the parents, the kids, and what we did all season."

The project is a distillation of DV and 3000 (!) digital photos Loeffler took of the team. Loeffler used DVDit! to define menus for quick access to the individual clips and to burn the actual DVDs on his DVD drive (see Figure 22.12). "Authoring with DVDit! was all very straightforward and easy," he says.

Loeffler's already making plans for next year. He wants to step up to a full-featured authoring product such as Sonic DVD Producer that lets him create animated menus and buttons, work in Dolby audio, and use wide-screen features. "It's addictive," he says. "I want to do it even better next time."

Ed Loeffler and his eight-year old hockey-playing son, Taylor.

22

FIGURE 22.11
Loeffler's opening menu organizes the season by each road trip.

FIGURE 22.12
Loeffler used photos to create menus.

Linking Media to Your Menu Buttons to Make Your Project Flow

With your menus and media in place, it's time to connect the dots—create the links between your menus and media to ensure everything works together.

This can be a bit tricky. The object is to avoid creating a situation where your DVD viewers get "stuck" deep into your DVD project with no escape. You need to see to it that all buttons are, in fact, actual links that will take viewers somewhere. When viewers press Menu or Next on their remotes, your project actually should take them to a menu or to the next item on the DVD.

This is where you'll see why I suggested giving your movie placeholders descriptive names. In DVDit!, the means to link movies to your menu buttons is a bit counterintuitive. Instead of using the placeholder windows as you'd expect, you create links by dragging the movie names from the drop-down list below the playback window.

22

Task: Link Media to Buttons

▲ TASK

Your first task is to link all your media—videos, stills, and any associated audio—to their respective menu buttons. Follow these steps:

1. Open a menu by clicking its placeholder image in the Menu column.

2. Click the Movie drop-down list, highlighted in Figure 22.13 and located at the bottom-left corner of the playback window, above the timeline's start button. Select the movie you want to link to a menu button.

FIGURE 22.13

To link a movie to a menu button, first select a movie from this highlighted drop-down list.

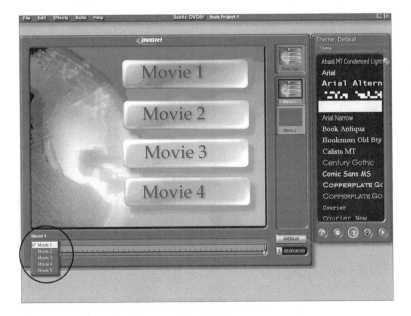

3. Roll your cursor over the tiny "chapter" triangle, highlighted in Figure 22.14. The word *Chapter* will appear (by default, the first frame is always Chapter 1, even though DVDit! LE does not support chapters). Click that triangle and drag your mouse to the button link.

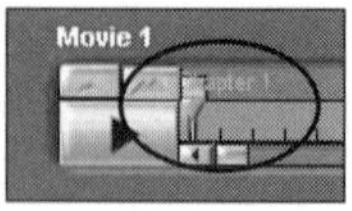

▼
FIGURE 22.14
Create the link by dragging the high-lighted "chapter" triangle to the appropriate menu button.

4. Do the same for every movie on every menu.

> If you create a button and place text on it, when you later drag a movie (or menu) to that button, you may make a link only with the text portion of the button, not the entire button. To ensure you've created a link with the entire button, drag the movie (or menu) to the edge of the button, away from the text portion. Alternatively, you can drag the movie to both the text portion *and* the button.

5. If you want to use a clip from the video as a button, simply drag that tiny triangle to an empty space on the menu. DVDit! is supposed to select the first frame as the button image but instead uses a frame a few seconds into the clip.

▲

> To see all links, right-click any button and select Show Button Links. As shown in Figure 22.15, the graphics disappear and text info about the links appears in their place. You'll notice that DVDit! automatically numbers each button. If you create four buttons and then apply text to each, the buttons will be numbered 1 to 4 and the text will run from 5 to 8.

> By design, the quick-and-easy buttons, created by dragging menus and movies onto a menu, are 3D beveled-edge rectangles. Although you *can* resize them, change their shape somewhat, alter the drop shadow, and adjust the colors, you're stuck with that beveled button look. If you want something else, the best option is to go back to Premiere, grab stills from your videos, open them in Photoshop, and create buttons there.

FIGURE 22.15
*Right-click a button
and select Show
Button Links to get text
info on each button's
link.*

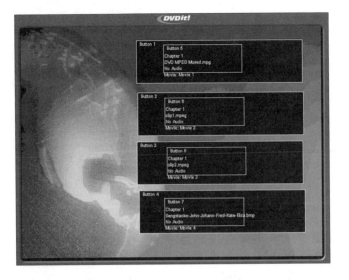

Changing Movie, Image, and Menu Properties

Finally, you may need to make some small but critical adjustments to one, some, or all your movies and menus. At issue is, what happens when the movie ends or if a viewer presses Next or Menu on the remote control?

You'll use the Movie Properties and Menu Properties dialog boxes to tell the DVD what to do. It's a tedious and time-consuming but necessary process.

Unfortunately, DVDit! LE has limited this feature to only the First Play object: Movie or Menu. I have included instructions for versions of DVDit! that allow you to make changes to all movies (videos and still images) and menus just in case you do upgrade to one of the retail versions of DVDit!

Changing Movie and Image Properties

If you are using the version of DVDit! LE bundled with Premiere and your First Play item is a menu, then go to the "Changing Menu Properties" section later in this hour. If your First Play item is a movie (video clip or still image), then continue reading here.

Select your First Play movie by right-clicking it in its placeholder window (not the First Play placeholder but rather the placeholder of the movie itself). That opens the Movie Properties dialog box, shown in Figure 22.16. Here are some points to keep in mind:

FIGURE 22.16
*Tie up loose ends in
the Movie Properties
dialog box.*

- If your "movie" is a still image, you can change the default duration from five seconds to whatever time you want, or you can select Infinite to display that image until the viewer presses a remote control button.

- If your movie is a video, selecting Infinite means the video will play to its conclusion and display the last frame until the viewer presses a remote control button.

Because many videos end with a black frame, this could be disconcerting for your viewers—they'll end up staring at a blank screen, wondering what went wrong. Therefore, I'd suggest using Infinite only when you know your video's last frame is something other than black.

For both still images and videos, you need to decide what action will occur when the viewer presses the Menu or Next button on the remote control or what happens when the image or video finishes playing.

Usually you have a default menu in mind for all or most movies—typically the opening menu—but because you're probably going to use nested menus you'll likely want to return to whatever menu brought your viewer to the current video.

In any event, this is a three-step process using the three drop-down menus shown in Figure 22.17. When you're working with the Movie Properties dialog box, those menus are as follows:

Menu Button—This tells the DVD player which menu to display when the viewer presses the remote control's Menu button. The options are Do Nothing, Select One of Your Menus, and Last Menu. Choosing the Last Menu option moves the viewer back one menu to whatever menu he or she used to arrive at the current position. Choosing the Do Nothing selection does just that. The viewer will need to press the Next button to go to another movie menu.

Next Button—This tells the DVD player which menu or movie to display when the viewer presses the remote control's Next button. The options are Do Nothing, Select One of Your Menus or Movies, and Default Next (this applies to chapters, which are not supported in DVDit! LE).

End Action—This tells the DVD player which menu or movie to display when this movie finishes playing. The options are Same as "Next," Select One of Your Menus or Movies, Last Menu, and Loop.

FIGURE 22.17

The final step in the authoring process is telling your DVD what to do when the viewer presses certain buttons on the remote control.

Changing Menu Properties

If your First Play item is a menu, you'll use this process to set its properties. If you have only the DVDit! LE bundled with Premiere, you can change only the menu selected for First Play. If you're working with a retail version of DVDit!, you can apply settings to all your menus.

When working within the Menu Properties dialog box, shown in Figure 22.18, you'll choose from three drop-down menus with some minor differences from the menus in the Movie Properties dialog box:

Default Button—Select the menu button that is automatically highlighted when this menu displays (as your viewers roll the cursor over different buttons, they get brighter).

Return Button—Select the action that happens when the viewer presses the Return button on the remote.

End Action—If you set a Duration value (other than Infinite), use this menu to tell the DVD what to do when time is up. Typically you'll select a button that starts a clip or opens a submenu.

FIGURE 22.18

The Menu Properties dialog box has some slight differences from the Movie Properties dialog box.

Making all these selections is labor-intensive work. But failing to tie up all these loose ends could leave your viewers stranded in the middle of your DVD. That's why, when it's completed, you'll want to give your project a thorough road test. I'll cover that in Hour 24, "Burning Your DVD."

Summary

DVD authoring involves designing the project's menu structure, creating the menus and buttons, adding media, and linking all the elements. In this hour we covered how to give buttons and menus some pleasing visual characteristics, such as color and drop shadows. We added all the media files—video, audio, and stills. Then we tied all the menus, buttons, and media into a neat bundle. That final step is tedious but necessary. You'll give it all a dry run before burning your DVD in Hour 24.

Workshop

Review the questions and answers in this section to try to sharpen your DVDit! authoring skills. Also, take a few moments to tackle my short quiz and the exercises.

Q&A

Q I imported some old family photos to use as stills, menu backgrounds, and buttons, but they look squashed or elongated when I bring them into DVDit!. What's going on?

A DVDit! alters images to match a standard TV 4:3 aspect ratio. If your images do not exactly fit that ratio, DVDit! will stretch or squash them to fit. Images for menu backgrounds should be at least 640×480, and stills should be 720×540. If your images are less than those resolutions, DVDit! will expand them, causing them to lose some sharpness. When you scan your photos, do it at 72 dots per inch. TVs can't display at a higher resolution.

Q **I created a set of layered buttons in Photoshop and saved them directly into the DVDit! Buttons folder. But all I see is a white frame with one button in it. When I drag that to a menu, there is no way to remove that white frame or use the other buttons. Why is that?**

A You need to let DVDit! actually import that graphic. It's not enough to put it in the proper file folder. Open DVDit!, select Theme, and then select your theme from the list or select Open Theme to find and open your theme. Go to the Button palette, click Theme, select Add Files to Theme, select your Photoshop PSD file, and then click Open. DVDit! will now note that this is a layered Photoshop file with an alpha channel transparency and split up the file into its constituent buttons.

Quiz

1. You can change a still image's duration in two ways. What are they?

2. You've created the First Play menu with some great buttons and links, but now you want to use a video clip for the First Play item. How do you do this?

3. You've set a specific play duration for a still image in First Play. Upon completion, how do you have it jump automatically to a menu?

4. Drop shadows look more realistic when the shadow colors seem to pick up the color of the background. If you have a multihued menu background, it's nice to adjust the shadow colors to match. How do you give your text and buttons different drop shadow colors that fit with different background colors in the same menu?

Quiz Answers

1. Right-click that image's placeholder screen, select Properties, and change the Duration setting. Alternatively, you can drag an audio file to that image placeholder screen. The image will display for the length of the audio clip.

2. Open the movie placeholder screen's window and drag the movie that you want to open your DVD with to the First Play placeholder screen. It will replace the menu but does not delete the menu. It remains in its placeholder screen.

3. Right-click the still image's movie placeholder screen and select Properties. In the End Action drop-down menu, select the action to follow when the still image reaches the end of its duration. Usually this is the opening menu. While you're at it, check the other options. In the Menu Button drop-down list, select the menu that viewers will go to if they press Menu on their remotes during playback of this still. Also, in the Next Button menu, select where you want viewers to go when they press Next.

4. I admit, this is going the extra mile. Open the Drop Shadow menu (Effects, Drop Shadow) and select Items in current menu from the drop-down list. Give all the items the same drop shadow characteristics: Distance, Blur, Opacity, and Light Source. Click OK. Now select each item in turn, open the Drop Shadow interface, select Selected Menu Items, and adjust only the color for that graphic. Do that for each item, attempting to match the background color within the shadow.

Exercises

1. Create a menu with five buttons using the same shape for each but giving each different color and saturation characteristics. Then apply text to each button. Now give the buttons one set of drop shadow characteristics, making them look as if they are floating far above the menu. Then give the text different drop shadow characteristics, making it look close to the buttons. If you're really motivated, adjust the color of each drop shadow to approximate its background.

2. If you're proficient in Photoshop, create some buttons. Then import them to DVDit! using the Theme menu and selecting Add Files to Theme. You may create those buttons in layers. You do need to create a transparency layer; otherwise, the buttons will appear as full-screen boxes, with the buttons' graphics within the boxes.

3. Yes, family history fascinates me. So humor me and create a family tree DVD using still images as menu backgrounds and buttons. Add sound effects or period music to enhance still images. Use text to create banners titles for menus. Oh, and when you have a few minutes, use Premiere to create an entire family history video.

Hour **23**

Enhanced DVD Authoring

DVDs open myriad new possibilities to businesses, such as interactive sales presentations, multimedia product catalogs, point-of-sale kiosks, employee training, and software and data distribution. Businesses can enhance DVDs with links to Web sites and data files.

To fully exploit those production areas frequently means going beyond the capabilities of DVDit! LE. Knowing what higher-end DVD-authoring tools can do will help you if you choose to upgrade to professional-level DVD-authoring software.

I spoke with two companies that fully exploit those high-end tools. I'll explain what they do in two sidebars.

I also will fill you in on the latest consumer DVD recording technology as well as some industrial DVD playback machines that do darn near anything.

The highlights of this hour include the following:

- Higher-end DVD authoring enhancements
- Stepping up to DVDit! PE or other mid-range DVD authoring products
- Top-flight DVD Authoring tools
- Sidebar: Creating Interactive DVD Fun for Children
- Professional DVD playback
- Sidebar: MGM Mirage Has DVD Vision

Higher-End DVD-Authoring Enhancements

You may be itching to "burn" your first DVD, but I want to pause a moment to consider what your DVDs someday may be like. With DVDit! LE you have a product that is a cut above consumer-level DVD-authoring tools but a far cry from the software used to create Hollywood movies.

Nevertheless, at its center is the same core technology that drives those high-end authoring tools. Sonic Solutions, the developer of DVDit!, is virtually the only provider of DVD-authoring tools to major film studios. DVDit! LE is a subset of those very expensive and powerful tools.

Those top-flight authoring products mean most film studio DVDs offer some of the following features:

- Scene selection
- Director comments
- Wide screen
- Subtitles
- Foreign language audio track(s)
- Dolby AC-3 digital surround sound
- DVD-ROM content
- Animated menus with audio
- Animated menu buttons

Some DVDs let you view scenes from more than one angle. Others have links to Web sites. Still others offer up features such as Easter eggs, games, deleted scenes, storyboards, production notes, making-of featurettes, actor bios, and character development sketches.

DVDit! LE is designed as an entry-level bundled product that focuses on basic DVD creation. You can, however, take advantage of some of the more advanced capabilities DVDs have to offer. All it takes is a cash infusion.

Before I cover those higher-priced opportunities, I want to give you some specific examples of cutting-edge titles. I'd suggest you give these DVD movies a critical look to see what's possible:

- *The Matrix.* This is the breakthrough DVD that shook things up in Hollywood and in the PC world. Although it's now available as a two-disc set, the original single-DVD release caused technical problems for some set-tops and PCs. You could opt to have a white rabbit occasionally appear onscreen (shades of *Alice in Wonderland*), admonishing you to momentarily break away from the movie and follow it to a separate, how-we-made-this scene. Creating that rabbit and staying within the DVD specifications was a huge challenge. But it worked, and it demonstrated that many DVD players did not completely meet those DVD specs.

- *Shrek.* Pop this in your PC (it won't work in a Mac). It is loaded with games that will not show up on your TV using a standalone set-top DVD player. The 12 games and activities include coloring pages, Shrek pinball, and bowling with gnomes. Topping the technological gee-whiz list is Shrek's ReVoice Studio, which lets you record your own voice and insert it in Shrek scenes.

- *Moulin Rouge.* This engaging film features high-energy dance scenes shot from multiple angles, presented with rapid-fire edits. The DVD offers an option to watch some of those musical numbers from user-selected camera angles. It's a great way to take it all in.

- *Terminator 2: Judgment Day.* If you want to learn about the art of filmmaking, view this DVD. It includes the complete original screenplay text, 60 behind-the-scenes clips, various audio commentaries, multiple audio tracks detailing the sound design process, storyboards, and an interactive film-school-on-a-disc explanation of the making of the film. Plus, there is a complete additional cut of the film hidden as an "Easter egg." To view it, open the Special Edition menu, enter 82997 using your remote, pressing Enter after each number (August 29, 1997 is Judgment Day in the movie), and then click Play Extended Special Edition.

- *Harry Potter and the Sorcerer's Stone.* If your kids (or you) are into Harry Potter, this two-DVD set will hold their interest. With a nod to *Shrek*, it offers some rudimentary DVD-ROM games and features. But it breaks new ground by including a self-navigating virtual tour of the Hogwarts Castle (if you've seen QuickTime VR—it works like that). Also, you can attend classes to learn and then try out potions as well as bone up on Quidditch. To see the seven deleted scenes requires solving a series of mini-puzzles.

23

Until recently, *renting* movie videos was the norm. Now, DVD features like these create compelling reasons to *buy* movies. Although adding DVD elements like these to DVDs may be out of reach for most of us, they do demonstrate the power of DVDs.

Stepping Up to Mid-range DVD-Authoring Products

For a bundled add-on, DVDit! offers powerful functionality. Even going up against some competitors' products, retailing for several hundred dollars, it comes out on top. Before giving you some specifics, here's a rundown on just who those competitors are.

The universe of DVD-authoring software firms is very limited. These days, Sonic Solutions (www.sonic.com), the makers of DVDit!, absolutely dominates the industry. Until 1999, about a half-dozen companies created DVD-authoring software and charged thousands of dollars, sometimes tens of thousands of dollars, for their products. That's when Sonic, primarily an audio production software and hardware developer, introduced DVDit! for $500.

Consolidation quickly followed. Sonic purchased the rights to Daikin's Scenarist DVD-authoring tool, and Apple bought two DVD developers, Spruce and Astarte, and soon began shipping DVD Studio Pro for the Mac. The only other "name" players currently offering prosumer-level products are Ulead Systems, with its DVD Workshop, and Pinnacle Systems, which entered the DVD-authoring market by buying Minerva's Impression DVD-Pro authoring software.

Your bundled, free copy of DVDit! LE offers several more features than the $300 Ulead DVD Workshop and is nearly as feature rich as the $600 Impression DVD-Pro. In either case, DVDit! stands out from this prosumer crowd because of the following extra characteristics:

- The ability to create thumbnail image buttons using movie frames and stills
- Button and text color, shadow, and transparency adjustments
- First Play navigation properties
- The ability to link text "buttons" to clips

You may never need any more than DVDit! has to offer. But if you want to incorporate into your projects some of the elements I listed at the beginning of this hour, you'll need to spend some money.

You can take one of three routes to step up from DVDit! LE:

- Upgrade to Sonic's DVDit! SE (Standard Edition) or DVDit! PE (Professional Edition).
- Migrate to mid-range products such as Sonic's ReelDVD and Pinnacle's Impression DVD-Pro for Windows or two products for the Mac: Apple's DVD Studio Pro or Sonic's DVD Fusion.
- Move beyond mid-range to Sonic's higher-end products, including ReelDVD, DVD Producer, Scenarist, and DVD Creator.

23

Sonic offers two retail versions of DVDit! SE and PE. When we went to press, the SE upgrade from LE was $200 and the PE version was $500.

SE offers these additional features:

- AVI and QuickTime file import and encoding to MPEG
- Movie- and menu-navigation properties
- Timed menus and still images
- Chapters with frame image thumbnail buttons
- Adding DVD-ROM data to the disc
- Timed menus
- Audio menus

PE is geared more to higher-end productions. It has all the SE features plus the following:

- Dolby Digital audio import and encoding
- Wide-screen (16:9) support
- Output to DLT (Digital Linear Tape) for mass duplication

Pinnacle Impression DVD-Pro (www.pinnaclesys.com) lists for $600. It has a couple features missing in DVDit! PE but lacks quite a few more. Here are the elements it has that DVDit! PE doesn't:

- Eight audio tracks versus DVDit!'s one
- Thirty-two subtitle tracks versus DVDit!'s one
- Motion menus
- Two video angles versus DVDit!'s single-video viewpoint

On the other hand, DVDit! SE and PE's menu and button properties and DVD-ROM features outshine Impression DVD-Pro.

Mac owners with Apple's bundled, consumer-level DVD authoring product iDVD can turn to two mid-range authoring products: Apple's DVD Studio Pro (www.apple.com) and Sonic's DVD Fusion. The minimum platform that can accommodate these products is an 800 MHz iMac ($1,900) or a 933 MHz Power Mac G4 ($2,300) .

On a feature-to-feature comparison, DVD Studio Pro and DVD Fusion are in a virtual dead heat. They offer the same number of audio tracks, subtitle tracks, camera angles, and support for DVD-5 and DVD-9.

> DVD-5 is the standard DVD we're used to: single sided, single layer. DVD-10 is double sided, single layer and is usually used for DVDs with wide-screen format on one side and regular 4:3 on the other. DVD-9 is single sided, double layered. And DVD-18 is double sided, dual layered. DVD-18 discs are rare. Some DVD-18 discs were produced for the Terminator-2 DVD set.

What may give DVD Fusion an edge over DVD Studio Pro is price ($800 versus $1,000), a timeline interface that will seem very familiar to Premiere users, and full DVD interactivity options.

> The DVD specifications permit up to 16 general parameters (GPRMs) to store and manipulate values to create interactivity.
>
> DVD Studio Pro offers only eight. DVD Fusion makes all 16 GPRMs available to the user. In addition, DVD Fusion's Command Editor simplifies advanced navigation programming and allows users to readily create highly interactive titles such as those referred to in the "Creating Interactive DVD Fun for Children" sidebar later in this hour.

Top-flight DVD-Authoring Tools

There really is no competition at the higher end of the DVD-authoring scale. Sonic owns this market. Although some Hollywood movie studios use some custom-built DVD production hardware/software suites from Panasonic and others, most rely on Sonic Solutions products.

For the multimedia professional, Sonic offers DVD Producer for Windows and upgraded versions of DVD Fusion for the Mac.

For feature film production, Sonic offers DVD Scenarist for Windows and DVD Creator for the Mac. These come in numerous configurations, with or without hardware. Prices range far and wide.

To cover specific features would go beyond the scope of this book. Suffice it to say, if you've seen an exciting graphical or interactive element in a DVD movie, the developers probably used a Sonic product to create it.

One media production firm that quietly has been on the leading edge of this technological and creative wave is Chicago Recording Company. Here's a brief look at its latest work.

23

Creating Interactive DVD Fun for Children

The Chicago Recording Company is a DVD "graybeard," says Hank Neuberger, CRC's executive VP and general manager. The company purchased Sonic DVD Creator more than three years ago after a client said it wanted to create 13 music/video combo DVD titles. "We ended up working closely with Platinum Entertainment to repackage archival audio tapes, VHS footage of concerts, and videotapes of television appearances," he recalls.

One of Chicago's leading music and advertising recording studios, the 26-year old CRC has found DVD Creator's audio-friendly orientation an invaluable asset for sustaining a steady flow of music-related DVD productions, including titles by Roger Daltry, the Beach Boys, Cheap Trick, Luther Allison, George Clinton and the P-Funk All Stars, and Harry Chapin.

But those music/video compilations are yesterday's news. The company's latest DVD products are "light years" beyond those early pioneering efforts says CRC's DVD-authoring specialist Sean Sutton. "We are pushing the envelope of the DVD specs."

CRC's latest efforts have focused on creating innovative and interactive DVDs for children. Working with Big Idea Productions, developers of *Veggie Tales*, *3-2-1 Penguins!* (see Figure 23.1), and *Larryboy* videos and games, they've produced DVD movies with kid-friendly mazes, trivia quizzes, and other fun activities.

The challenge is to use "a technology designed only to play nice-looking pictures and good sound," says Sutton, "to somehow make games that are fun and accessible to children who may not yet be able to read." Navigating the maze in Figure 23.2, for instance, requires only the use of the arrow keys on a DVD remote control. Each button click seamlessly displays a new screen showing the changed location. It takes 300 such images and some horribly tedious coding of If-Then statements to create this maze.

The deceptively straightforward-looking penguin quiz in Figure 23.3 took advantage of part of the standard DVD specs that allow randomizing—sort of like hitting random play on your music CD player. Sutton exploited that function to display questions in different sequences each time children play the DVD.

Other elements create additional DVD design complexity:

- Fashioning a way to get the DVD to respond to wrong answers by returning to the original question
- Having it not repeat previously asked questions
- Getting it to keep track of a child's score.

Another fun DVD feature that took some programming magic is the *Veggie Tales* Voice Swap, illustrated in Figure 23.4. This lets kids give characters the voices of other characters in a variety of settings. Because DVDs can have multiple audio tracks, you'd think this would be a fairly routine process. Far from it. Timing issues and varying character interactions precluded the use of parallel audio tracks. Instead, Sutton calculated all the permutations and created separate video clips for each possible choice—96 clips in all.

Clearly it's no longer enough to simply slap a 30-minute video on a DVD. CRC fills each Big Idea product to the limit.

Coming up with these workarounds is just part of the joy of DVD authoring. "I love it," says Sutton. "I get to combine several creative arenas—video, audio, and programming. It's lots of fun."

Looking to the future, Sutton sees authoring becoming easier with software taking on more of the tedious tasks. For now, he enjoys sitting in on kid focus groups as they play his creations. "It's a real positive experience."

FIGURE 23.1

CRC creates Big Idea Productions' 3-2-1 Penguins! *DVDs as well as* Veggie Tales *and* Larryboy.

FIGURE 23.2

It took 300 stills to fashion this maze.

23

FIGURE 23.3

Official DVD specifications include a randomizing feature used to keep this quiz fresh.

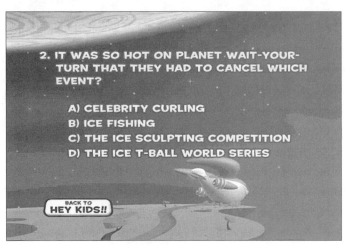

FIGURE 23.4

This mix-and-match character and voice activity required 96 different video clips.

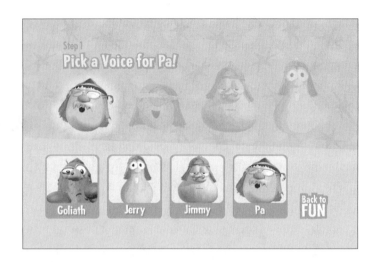

Professional DVD Playback

Professional (industrial) standalone DVD players might help you advance your video production capabilities.

Pioneer was first to market with industrial players. Both Philips and Panasonic offer competing players.

These playback machines have amazingly deep programmability. Users can have them play back selected video clips at specific times and respond to touch-screen input from customers. They are used for in-store promotions, museum displays, and point-of-sale kiosks. They are deeply versatile and reliable. Prices hover at around $700 for these feature-packed devices:

- Pioneer DVD-V7400
- Philips ProDVD 175
- Panasonic DVD-T2000

One company that relies heavily on professional, industrial DVD players is MGM Mirage.

MGM Mirage Has DVD Vision

Randy Dearborn was there at the beginning. As multimedia director for MGM Mirage's massive 10-casino empire, he has led the charge to DVD.

Four years ago, Dearborn began replacing the company's unwieldy, expensive, and unreliable laserdiscs with DVD players. Now, all the laserdiscs are gone and DVD and MPEG-2 videos are on display throughout the MGM Mirage resorts nationwide. The integrated capture, compression, and authoring capabilities of Sonic DVD Creator gives MGM Mirage Resorts the power, ease, and flexibility to make full use of DVD's advantages.

Underscoring DVD's versatility, the DVD projects at the MGM Mirage Resorts cover diverse areas, such as point-of-sale video displays, exterior signage, corporate archives, and "back of the house" communications with the company's 10,000-strong workforce. "We use DVD Creator to capture and encode the video and then either transfer the MPEG-2 stream to the hard-disk player or author and burn DVDs for standalone DVD players," says Dearborn.

The resorts use Pioneer 7200 drives (the precursor to the current 7400 drives) that have built-in software that allows playback by clips or through interaction with touch screens. Some interactive touch-screen kiosks let customers select music CDs and listen to specific cuts. Figure 23.5 shows a kiosk menu.

One application for DVD is feeding video to the giant "reader boards" on the casinos' towering marquees on Las Vegas Boulevard. The former system required playback from $15,000 Pentium workstations with specialized video cards. Now Dearborn and his four-person crew program the Pioneer drives to play back video clips in a specific order and at specific times (see Figure 23.6) .

"I bought two of these decks, one as a backup, for only $1,600, and I'll never have to worry again about whether Windows will decide to crash."

MGM Mirage corporate executives now supplement their investor road shows with DVDs—a far cry from days gone by. They used to bring a videotape and rely on the AV person at the control board to manually switch back and forth between a video deck and the laptop running the presentation. Now they simply load the DVD in their laptops and at opportune moments click a button in an HTML page to bring up the DVD menu shown in Figure 23.7. Then they jump instantly to an MPEG-2 video to further amplify a point. "I author the DVDs with several videos so the presenters can pick and choose, depending on the audience."

Dearborn's department is now transferring the entire video archives of the company to DVD, categorizing clips and creating menus that make it easy for users outside the department to access the material.

Dearborn remains on the cutting edge of this technological tidal change. His foresight means his department continues to be one of the busiest in the MGM Mirage empire.

23

FIGURE **23.5**

Shoppers can listen to
music from Cirque du
Soleil before buying
the music CD.

FIGURE **23.6**

MGM Mirage uses
professional DVD
players to display
images like this on its
huge reader boards.

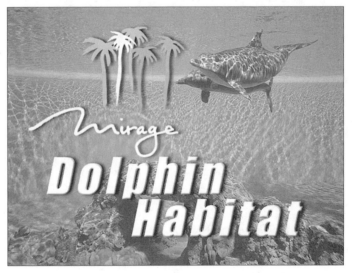

FIGURE 23.7
MGM Mirage corporate executives now rely on DVDs for presentations.

Summary

DVDit! LE opens the door to many creative possibilities in DVD production. But if your goal is to duplicate the techniques used in the creation of Hollywood movie DVDs or even those used by multimedia professionals, DVDit! LE will not suffice. Although it offers myriad possibilities, only a handful of higher-priced DVD-authoring products provide the tools to accomplish these techniques.

Simply knowing what those higher-end products can do may help trigger the creative process. As you author more and more DVDs, you'll likely find areas that could benefit from the extra features more expensive products provide. In the meantime, prices keep dropping and tools continue to become more accessible.

HOUR 24

Burning Your DVD

Recording a DVD takes more than simply clicking an onscreen button. I'll show you how to pretest your project. I'll offer tips on selecting user-friendly DVD recorders and reliable recording media.

Then it's on to burning and testing your first DVD. You may want to turn your newly acquired DVD-authoring skills into a business. I'll offer up some tips. Finally, for those looking to mass-produce their DVD projects, I'll present some advice on dealing with DVD replicators.

The highlights of this hour include the following:

- Testing, including checking all links and ensuring logical project flow
- Choosing DVD recorders and recordable media
- Burning your DVD
- Sidebar: The Business of DVD Authoring
- Tips on dealing with a mass replicator

Testing: Checking All Links and Ensuring Logical Project Flow

Before you create your first DVD, it's best to take it for a dry run. Check all the links and settings. I'll take you through that process using the LE version of DVDit! plus give you a taste of the extra features available in SE and PE.

Task: Test Your Project

▼ TASK

In this task you'll simulate what it's like for a viewer to sit down with a remote control and start clicking through your DVD. Follow these steps:

1. Open DVDit!. Select Open an Existing Project and select the project you want to test and "burn."

2. Check your Menu and Movie links, as I've highlighted in Figure 24.1, by right-clicking any button on your project's opening menu and selecting Show Button Links. Check each button and note its button number. Do this for each menu in your project.

FIGURE **24.1**

Check your button numbers and links before previewing your project.

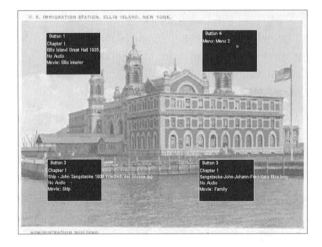

As you later click Next or Previous on the Preview Remote Control, you'll move ahead or back in sequential "button number" order.

▼   3. Click the Preview button in the lower-right corner. This opens the Remote Control interface shown in Figure 24.3.

FIGURE 24.2
Select the Preview button to access the Remote Control interface.

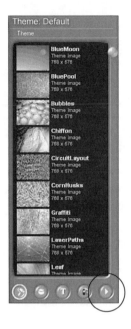

Most of the buttons are self-explanatory. I've highlighted four in Figure 24.3 that may not be. Moving clockwise from the upper-left corner they are as follows:

Title—Clicking this takes you to the menu at the top of your menu placeholder list.

Return—Performs whatever function you specified in the Movie/Menu Properties dialog box for your First Play item.

Next—Following the numerical order of your menu's buttons, pressing Next jumps to the next button's menu or movie.

Previous—Jumps back to the previous button's menu or movie.

4. Use the Remote Control's buttons to navigate through your project. Try out everything. Make sure they do what you expect. If there are any buttons with no links or buttons that take you to the wrong media or menu, return to your project's menus and fix them.

▼   5. To exit out of the Remote Control interface, click the × in the upper-right corner.

24

FIGURE 24.3

Four buttons in the Remote Control interface may not be self-explanatory: Title, Return, Next, and Previous.

If you were testing your project with DVDit! SE or PE, the procedure would be the same. The only difference would be in the number of possibilities. With this bundled version of DVDit! LE, you can set navigation properties only for your First Play menu or movie. With SE and PE, all your media and menus have Properties menus leading to many more branching opportunities.

Choosing DVD Recorders and Recordable Media

You've come this far, so it's a good guess you already have a DVD recorder in your PC. If so, you might consider replacing it with something new. If not, you definitely need to go out and buy one. In either case, in this section I'll give you an overview of the DVD recorder business and present a basic rundown of the major brand-name PC DVD recorders.

A DVD recordable format war is going on. It's unclear how this will shake out. The latest entrants—drives using write-once DVD+R and rewritable DVD+RW—seem to have the greatest potential for universal compatibility, ease of use, and performance. But being late to the party may mean they'll miss out on all the fun.

Virtually all DVD+RW drives from Philips, Sony, and HP have Ricoh DVD+RW drives at their core. Despite the different labels, they are essentially clones. Ricoh's latest, the MP5125A, is the second-generation DVD+ drive that finally supports both DVD+R and DVD+RW. Ricoh sells this drive under its own label in Europe and Japan.

For the moment, the write-once DVD-R format has the greatest overall acceptance and compatibility. All DVD-RW drives and some DVD-RAM drives write to DVD-R media.

If you plan to have a replication firm mass-produce your DVD project, you have two options for mastering media: DVD-R and DLT (Digital Linear Tape). DLT is not all that appealing because you have to buy a DLT machine and upgrade your DVD-authoring software to one with DLT as an output option (DVDit! PE has that capability).

DVD-R clearly is your best bet for making a replication master. At the moment, most mass replicators do not accept DVD-RW, DVD-RAM, DVD+R, or DVD+RW masters. Rewritable discs are not suitable because the data may not be contiguous on the disc. For an extra fee you can have a replicator copy files from any of these media types to DLT or DVD-R.

24

DVD-RAM may find itself relegated only to data backup because it can be rewritten at least 100,000 times, versus 1,000 times for DVD+RW and DVD-RW. Also, DVD-RAM drives cannot record CD-RW and CD-R discs, so they have limited appeal as general-purpose recordable drives.

All versions of DVDit! support all DVD formats: DVD-R, DVD-RW, DVD+R, DVD+RW, and DVD-RAM.

Here's a quick rundown of the heavy hitters in the PC DVD recorder game:

Pioneer—Its fourth-generation product, the DVR-A04 or DVR-104 DVD-RW drive, is a small step up from the A03/103 (a.k.a. the Apple SuperDrive). Pioneer set the recordable DVD market on fire with its earlier models and continues to drive prices down and foster further DVD-RW acceptance with this model. It writes to DVD-RW, DVD-R, CD-RW, and CD-R.

Panasonic—Its LF-D321U records to both DVD-RAM and DVD-R media. The company promotes the LF-D321U primarily as a DVD-video production drive. In some ways it may be the dual-role drive many customers seek: DVD videos plus data archiving using the very durable DVD-RAM discs.

Hewlett-Packard—Its second-generation DVD+RW drive, the DVD200i, replaces the first-generation, non-DVD+R-compatible DVD100i. The 200i outscores the Pioneer A04 in performance tests. Drawbacks include the higher-priced media and lack of consumer acceptance.

Sony—It, too, is in the DVD+RW camp. Its second-generation DRU120A (replacing the DRU110A) is on par with HP's DVD200i. If you plan to go the DVD+RW route, the choice between these two may come down to bundled software and price.

Philips—Surprisingly its latest DVD+RW drive (the DVDRW208, as of June 2002) is a *first*-generation DVD+ drive and as such does not support DVD+R. The company has indicated a DVD+R-compatible drive is in the works, which means this Philips drive, as well as the HP DVD100i and the Sony DRU110A, all are landfill candidates.

Toshiba—Its SD-W2002 has limited appeal. It writes only DVD-RAM discs, not DVD-R or any other write-once media. Few non-DVD-RAM drives can read DVD-RAM discs. Therefore, the SD-W2002 simply cannot function as a recorder for DVDs you plan to play in set-top boxes.

Selecting Recordable Media

DVD recordable media is swiftly approaching commodity status. That is, there soon may be no discernible difference between one brand and another. For the moment, though, it still appears that you get what you pay for.

Selecting "house brand" media remains a hit-or-miss proposition. One unsubstantiated test I saw showed some store-brand recordable DVDs have 40% failure rates. That is, 4 out of 10 discs became proverbial cocktail coasters.

Obviously, companies that sell branded drives along with their own branded media—HP, Pioneer, Panasonic, and Sony—want you to think that you can't have one without the other. But selecting from that top tier of the price chart may be overkill (although, their prices are coming down).

I recommend taking the middle ground: Buy name-brand, generic media from firms such as Verbatim, Memorex, Maxell, Mitsui, and TDK.

Because prices continue to drop, it makes little sense to include specific prices here. In general, though, here are some points to keep in mind:

- DVD-R is the least expensive.

- DVD-RW and DVD+RW are both about 50% more than DVD-R. Because they're rewritable, you don't need all that many of them anyway.

- DVD+R, being the latest media and in limited demand, is about twice as expensive as DVD-R.

- DVD-RAM remains the most expensive media, nearly three times as expensive as DVD-R.

As DVD recordable media approaches commodity status, there are still a few minor "gotchas" to watch out for:

DVD-R Authoring versus General—Authoring media is specifically for authoring drives such as Pioneer's DVR-S201. You probably don't own such a drive. Early DVD-R drives were able to make bit-for-bit copies of other DVDs. By early 2001, the movie industry responded by creating the Content Scrambling System (CSS) encryption scheme and getting DVD manufacturers to change their drives to make it physically impossible for them to copy CSS discs. So, if you have a DVD-R-capable drive, it probably uses DVD-R General recording media.

Matching media quality to your drive recording speed—If you want to take advantage of faster DVD recording speeds, you need to buy media rated for those speeds. For instance, look for 2× in the product name or specs if that's the speed of your drive.

Capacity—You may never need to buy anything other than 4.7GB DVD recordable media. That is, standard single-side, single-layer media at full DVD capacity. Several other capacities are available, so make sure you get ones that suit your project size and drive specifications.

24

"Burning" Your DVD

After all this effort—editing your video and authoring your DVD—recording a DVD is relatively simple. I'll explain the few steps you need to follow and will point out the extra options available in the SE and PE versions of DVDit!.

▼ TASK Task: Make a DVD Disc

If all goes smoothly, in a few minutes (or longer, depending on the extent of your project) you'll have a DVD in hand ready to play on your set-top DVD player or PC. Follow these steps:

▼ 1. Open DVDit!, select Open an Existing Project, and select the project you want to "burn."

2. Put a blank recordable disc (DVD-R, DVD-RW, DVD+R, DVD+RW, or DVD-RAM) in your recorder. You may also record to CD-R or CD-RW. For more on that, see step 6.

3. As illustrated in Figure 24.4, open File, Project Settings and set the output size to match your recordable disc. Check Current Project Size to make sure your project does not exceed your disc capacity. Give your project a name and click OK.

FIGURE 24.4

Adjust the project settings and give your DVD a name.

4. Select Build, Make DVD Disc to open the Make a DVD Disc dialog box, shown in Figure 24.5.

After selecting Build in the main menu, you also can choose to make a DVD "folder." This is a hard drive folder containing all your project media. It's kind of a superfluous option. Its purpose is to make everything accessible and let you play your MPEG files to make sure they work well before actually creating your DVD.

It's also a bit confusing, because when you later create a DVD from that folder, DVDit! calls it a DVD "volume."

▼

FIGURE 24.5

*Set a few parameters
in this interface and
then start recording
your DVD.*

5. Choose the source. In this case the default setting, Current Project, is what you
   want.

From the Make a DVD Disc Source drop-down list, you also can choose DVD
Volume ("Folder") or Disc Image.

A disc image is a file produced by higher-end authoring products such as
Sonic's Scenarist. It has no directory structure and contains all the DVD project data in the exact position it'll appear on the final DVD.

6. If you're writing to a CD-R or CD-RW, choose Include DVD Player. That will add
   Sonic's proprietary cDVD player to the CD so it can play your DVD project from a
   PC CD player. The finished CD will *not* play in a set-top, standalone DVD player,
   however.

7. Select your DVD recorder from the drop-down list.

8. If you want to make more than one copy, change that value.

9. Because this is your first DVD, select Test and Create Disc. Once you see that your
   DVD recorder can operate smoothly, you can skip the test step on subsequent projects.

10. Click the Advanced tab to switch to the interface shown in Figure 24.6.

24

FIGURE 24.6
The Advanced page lets you select filename types and whether you will use a temporary directory while burning your DVD.

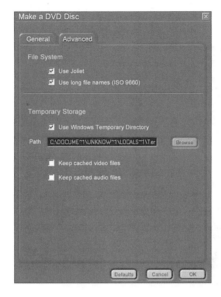

You have the following two general options:

File System—This applies more to the SE and PE versions of DVDit!, which allow for the addition of DVD-ROM files to your project. In the case of DVDit! LE, accept the default settings—Use Joliet and Use long file names—*only* if you're including the cDVD player on the disc. If you accept them despite not having a cDVD player, it won't create any problems other than adding some extra files to your DVD. I'll explain more about these two filenaming conventions in the DVDit! SE and PE overview following this section.

Temporary Storage—By default, DVDit! places your media and project files in a temporary file folder before recording them to your DVD. Only if you have limited hard drive space should you deselect this option. In that case, DVDit! writes all files directly to the DVD. You can opt to save the cached files, but there is little reason to do so.

▲ 11. Click OK. DVDit! should start recording your project to your recordable DVD.

The recording may take a while, depending on the size of your project and the recording speed of your DVD drive. When it's completed, take your DVD to a set-top standalone DVD player and check out your masterpiece.

If your DVD player is reasonably new, your DVD should work fine. If not, try your disc out on your PC. Sonic bundles Power DVD, a full-featured DVD player, and that should play your disc with no glitches.

If there are compatibility problems with your set-top DVD player, I'd suggest visiting one of several online sites that list DVD players and whether they play back DVD-Rs or other recordable DVD media. Apple has an exhaustive list at http://www.apple.com/dvd/compatibility/. At the very least, take your DVD to a local consumer electronics store and try it out in several DVD players.

Extra Features in DVDit! SE and PE

I want to give you an idea of what DVDit! LE's more full-featured siblings have to offer when getting ready to burn a DVD. Figure 24.7 shows the small differences in DVDit! SE and PE's Project Settings dialog box:

- Access to the Video tab to set encoder quality settings for AVI and QuickTime files (DVDit! LE does not work with these files).
- Access the Audio tab to choose between PCM (standard with DVDit! LE and SE) or Dolby Digital with its user-set bitrate (PE only) .
- An option is available to add DVD-ROM data files.

24

FIGURE 24.7

DVDit! PE's Project Settings dialog box has an option to add DVD-ROM data files and gives you access to the Video and Audio tabs.

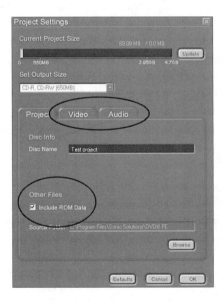

If users use DVDit! SE or PE to add DVD-ROM files to their DVDs, then choosing filenaming conventions is critical to compatibility with older PCs.

All DVD discs contain at least two file systems: the Universal Disc Format (UDF) file system and the ISO 9660 file system. Among other things, these file systems define DVD-ROM filenaming conventions.

The UDF file system allows filenames of up to 255 characters. All modern computer operating systems read the UDF file system.

Older operating systems, such as Windows 95, read only the ISO 9660 file-naming convention, which limits filenames to 8+3 characters (like MS-DOS filenames). If you want your DVD-ROM files to be usable on older systems, you must limit the filenames to that 8+3 character set.

Both the Joliet and long filename systems let you get around some limitations of ISO 9660. Joliet works only with Windows 95. The long filename system does not work with DOS.

The simplest solution may be to rename all files to comply with the 8+3 file-naming convention of old and not use the Joliet or long filename system.

DVDit! PE offers a Build Disc feature not found in SE or LE—an option to create a DLT master for mass replication. That option no longer has the kind of cachet it once had because many mass replicators now accept DVD-R discs as masters.

As your DVD-authoring skills deepen, you may consider pursuing authoring as a business. This sidebar offers up some practical advice.

The Business of DVD Authoring

Jim Benz spent 20 years as executive vice president of Mobile Fidelity Sound Lab, an internationally known firm specializing in audiophile remasterings of classic albums from the likes of Frank Sinatra, The Beatles, and Louis Armstrong.

In 1999 he saw that DVDs created a new opportunity to re-purpose other archival material—in this case, historic movie footage and older feature films. He formed Whirlwind Media, Inc., began releasing DVD products in May 2000, and within two years had released more than 40 DVD titles. The Timeline Series, illustrated in Figures 24.8 and 24.9, is one of several Whirlwind DVD series.

To jumpstart his new company he tapped the expertise of several Mobile Fidelity employees to handle sound mastering, graphics, the sourcing and cataloging of elements, and licensing. Where he lacked expertise was in DVD authoring.

For that Benz turned to commercial DVD-authoring studios.

Benz's experiences with DVD-authoring firms cover the full spectrum of quality. If you are considering turning your newly acquired DVD-authoring expertise into a business, take the following tips to the bank:

- Educate your clients about DVD authoring. What it can and cannot do. As they learn more, their expectations will become more realistic. And your working relationship will improve.

- The DVD authoring service business is highly competitive and fees are dropping rapidly. To succeed you need to make your work stand out from the crowd. One selling point is longevity. Clients will flock to you if they feel your company will be around for a while. Another is follow-through. Even if your clients handle mass replication on their own, make sure you are available to respond to last-minute issues so as not to delay a release schedule or production deadline.

- Don't sell yourself short. Smart clients don't hire the cheapest authoring company. They are willing to pay more for quality and reliability.

- Focus locally. Clients like to deal face to face with production studios.

- Don't try to wrest creative control from your clients. At Whirlwind Media we go so far as to provide a detailed flow chart and hard copies of screens to the authoring technician to allow for as little margin of error as possible. Not all clients will take that extra step. Nevertheless, make sure you know what they want. Keep the lines of communication wide open.

- Make sure you clearly state in writing what you will do for your clients. Will you charge by the hour or by the job? Will there be additional fees to correct mistakes? What about quick fixes: spelling errors or a video edit? What happens if you miss a deadline? Your clients may expect you to forfeit part of your fee.

- Always make two copies of the DLT or DVD-R master. This will let your client send one to the replicator and keep the other in a safe place. If the duplication plant damages the DLT, your client will have a backup.

- Relinquish all original elements to the client at a project's conclusion. You don't want to be responsible if something gets lost, misplaced, damaged, and so on.

- Keep it simple. The DVD format allows for lots of intricate navigation channels, full-motion screens with sound, "hidden" chapters, Web site connections, and so on. Do these things make it easier for your audience to enjoy your client's project or are they lots of extra frosting on the cake?

- If you plan to create a series using the same authoring style, then keep in mind that complex authoring with lots of bells and whistles is difficult to duplicate on later DVDs, especially when working with a *different* technician.

- It's true that DVDs are a new technology. But it's the content that counts. Make your clients' content as accessible as possible without spending too much energy focusing on technological features. The DVD format is a means to an end, not an end in itself.

24

FIGURE **24.8**
Whirlwind Media's Timeline Series is one of several DVD-only series the company produces.

FIGURE **24.9**
Whirlwind Media's Timeline DVD menu uses a very straightforward approach, giving viewers direct access to its archival material.

Dealing with Mass Replicators

Burning multiple DVDs of the same project, one at a time, is tedious. Mass replication may be an appealing alternative.

These days working with a replicator is not all that difficult. Your finished project recorded to a DVD-R and some liner and/or DVD disc artwork is about all you need.

Creating DVDs takes more steps and is more complicated than creating CDs. Here's a barebones explanation:

The process involves coating a DVD-sized glass disc with light-sensitive material and then converting the data into laser pulses that create tiny scorch marks on the disc along a spiral track. Using several chemical and electrolyte baths, those tiny pockmarks are converted to a thin layer that when viewed through a microscope appears to be a bumpy wafer. It's placed in a very high-pressure molding machine that's injected with molten polycarbonate to create the DVD layers (two such layers for each DVD). A thin layer of reflective metal, such as aluminum, is added to each molded surface, and the plastic/metal sandwich is bonded and covered with a protective lacquer finish.

To ensure a smooth DVD replication process, here are some points to keep in mind:

- Start by visiting the DVD Association Web site at http://www.dvda.org. It has a list of member replication firms. Many of these companies are *mass* replicators, meaning they deal with film studios and publishers, handling multiple orders annually for millions of copies. Few will touch an order of fewer than 1,000 discs. Don't let that discourage you. Contact a replicator from the list and ask whom they recommend for smaller orders.

- If you want to make a single-side, single-layer DVD-5 disc, all you need is a DVD-R (or a DLT) to serve as a master.

- For a double-sided, single-layer DVD-10, you'll need two DVD-R discs.

- DVD-9 (single sided, double layer) and DVDs encrypted with the CSS copy-protection scheme need DLT masters.

- Make sure you've tested your DVD-R master on a set-top DVD player. Click every menu and press all the remote buttons to make sure your DVD does what it's supposed to do before you send it off for duplication.

- Your most difficult hurdle may be artwork. Most DVD replicators will give you artwork templates to use in various graphics programs to create your liner and DVD label art.

- Make sure you proofread everything. And check your colors. Your labels may look dramatically different from one replicator to another.

- Allow enough time for your project. From delivery of your master along with label artwork, expect to wait two weeks for completion of your order.

Summary

We've reached the end of this video production journey. Its conclusion is the creation of a DVD. For such a technology-driven action, the recording process is fairly routine. Selecting the right DVD recorders and media will minimize the number of coasters you create.

24

With your newly found DVD-authoring skills, you may consider pursuing DVD creation as a business. I tapped the expertise of someone who has worked with several DVD-authoring studios for some sage advice. And you may want to use a mass replicator to create many copies of your DVD for marketing, friends, or commercial purposes. That process, too, has become fairly routine.

Workshop

Review the questions and answers in this section to try to sharpen your Premiere DVD-creation skills. Also, take a few moments to tackle my short quiz and the exercises.

Q&A

Q **My set-top DVD player's manual states that it recognizes CD-RW discs, but it won't play the CD-RW I made with DVDit! LE. Why not?**

A Set-top boxes that recognize CD-RW will play it only if it has CD music or is a video CD. DVDit! can make neither type of product. If you try to play a CD with Sonic's cDVD player in your set-top DVD player, it will either eject the disc or do nothing. On the other hand, it should play from most PC CD and DVD drives.

Q **I want to send DVDs to my clients and include some PDF and other data files on them. I don't see any way to do that.**

A With this bundled version of DVDit!, you can't. If you upgrade to DVDit! SE or PE, you can use the DVD-ROM file feature to add data files to your DVD project. Alternatively, you can use standard CD/DVD recording software, such as Prassi PrimoDVD or whatever was bundled with your DVD recorder, to create a CD-ROM or DVD-ROM disc with an MPEG-2/WMV/MOV/AVI version of your video on it, along with the data files. Your clients will be able to watch the video using readily available players, such as Windows Media Player and QuickTime, and access the data files, but that won't give them the interactivity that DVDs authored in a product such as DVDit! SE or PE offer.

Quiz

1. You want your project to display a menu for 15 seconds and if there is no viewer input simply start the movie. But when you test it, 15 seconds go by and nothing happens. How do you fix that?

2. You want to show your DVD project to someone who does not have a DVD set-top or PC player. How do you do that?

3. What's the difference between DVD-R Authoring and General? If you use DVD-R drives, which should you use?

Quiz Answers

1. Close the Preview Remote Control interface by clicking the little × in the upper-right corner. Right-click the First Play menu and select Properties. Check the Duration window. Uncheck Infinite (if that's the offending culprit) or change the duration time to 15 seconds. Also, you can check End Action and make sure you select your movie as opposed to "Loop" or some other option.

2. Make a CD-R. Under Project Settings, select CD-R, CD-RW (650MB). Make sure your project does not exceed the capacity of the CD (CDs have about one-seventh the capacity of DVDs). In the Build, Make a DVD Disc dialog box, select Include DVD Player. Click the Advanced tab and make sure the Use Joliet and Use long file names options are checked. This is required when adding the DVD player to a CD. Click OK.

3. DVD-R Authoring and General are two different recordable DVD technologies. Authoring is the name given to earlier versions of DVD-R recorders capable of exact bit-to-bit duplication of DVDs, including DVD movies with protection schemes. DVD General replaced those drives. It uses a different laser and cannot copy encrypted DVDs. If you have a DVD-R drive, it's probably a General drive.

Exercises

1. Go to www.dvda.org, select a DVD replicator, and talk to them. Check on minimum order quantities, prices, label/liner graphics templates, and whether they accept DVD-R masters. If their minimum quantities are too steep, ask whether they can recommend smaller replicators. Visit a local replicator.

2. Go online to check on the latest recordable DVD drives and other developments in this very dynamic industry. I'd suggest using http://news.com.com/ as your starting point. Navigate to the Hardware/Storage section (use the Site Map link at the top-right corner of the page as an aide) and then choose DVDs and go from there.

24

INDEX

How can we make this index more useful? Email us at indexes@samspublishing.com

X-Z